LIVING

MOCHI

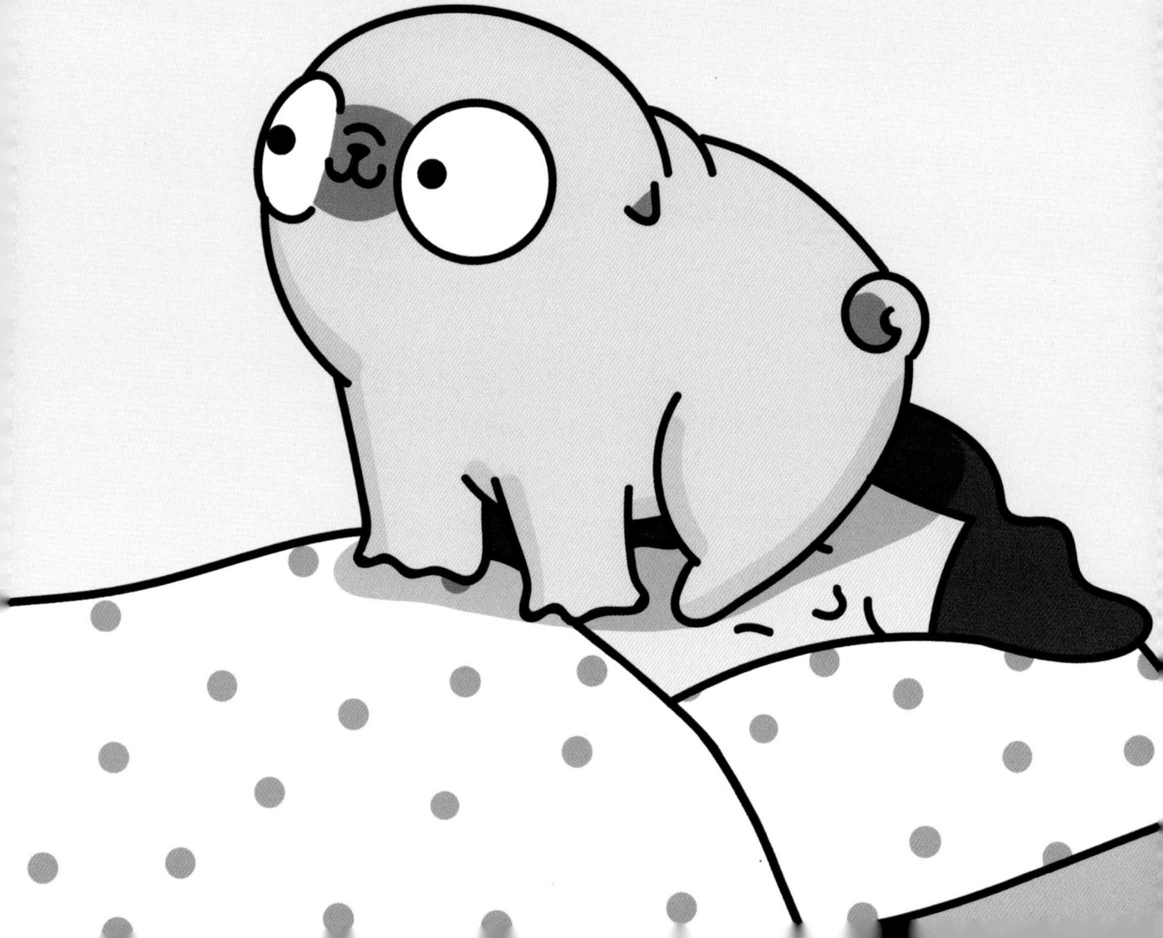

Andrews McMeel Publishing
a division of Andrews McMeel Universal
1130 Walnut Street, Kansas City, Missouri 64106

21 22 23 24 25 SDB 10 9 8 7 6 5 4 3 2 1

ISBN: 978-1-5248-6610-5

Library of Congress Control Number: 2020947665

Editor: Lucas Wetzel
Art Director: Sierra S. Stanton
Production Editor: Jasmine Lim
Production Manager: Tamara Haus

Book Design by Gemma Gené

www.andrewsmcmeel.com

ATTENTION: SCHOOLS AND BUSINESSES

Andrews McMeel books are available at quantity discounts with bulk purchase for educational, business, or sales promotional use. For information, please e-mail the Andrews McMeel Publishing Special Sales Department: specialsales@amuniversal.com.

LIVING WITH
MOCHI

GEMMA GENÉ

Andrews McMeel
PUBLISHING®

TO MY BABY AND BEST FRIEND, **MOCHI**, AND TO MY GODMOTHER, **MERI**, WHO WITHOUT LISTENING TO ANYONE, BROUGHT MOCHI INTO MY LIFE, CHANGING IT FOREVER.

CHAPTERS

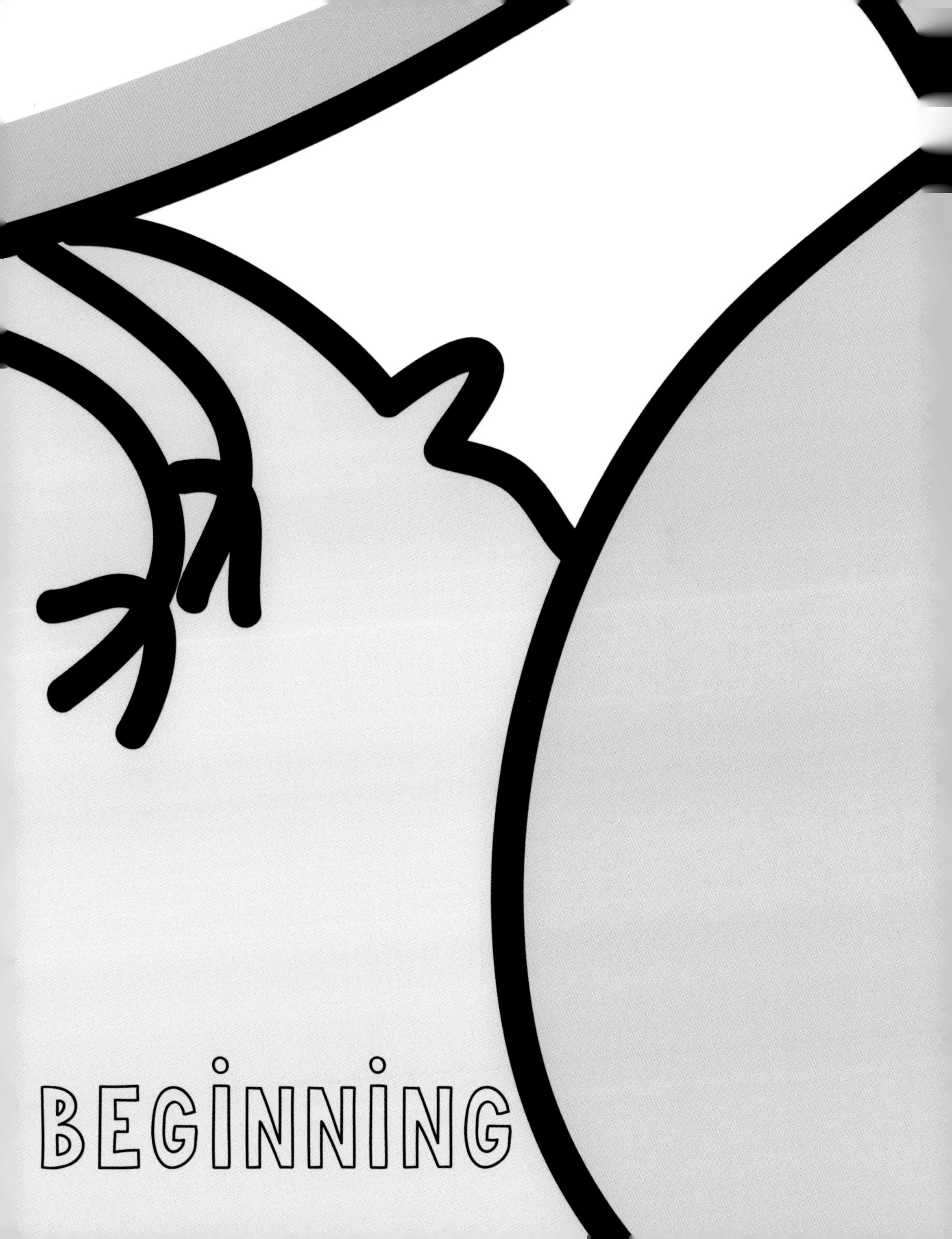

BEGINNING

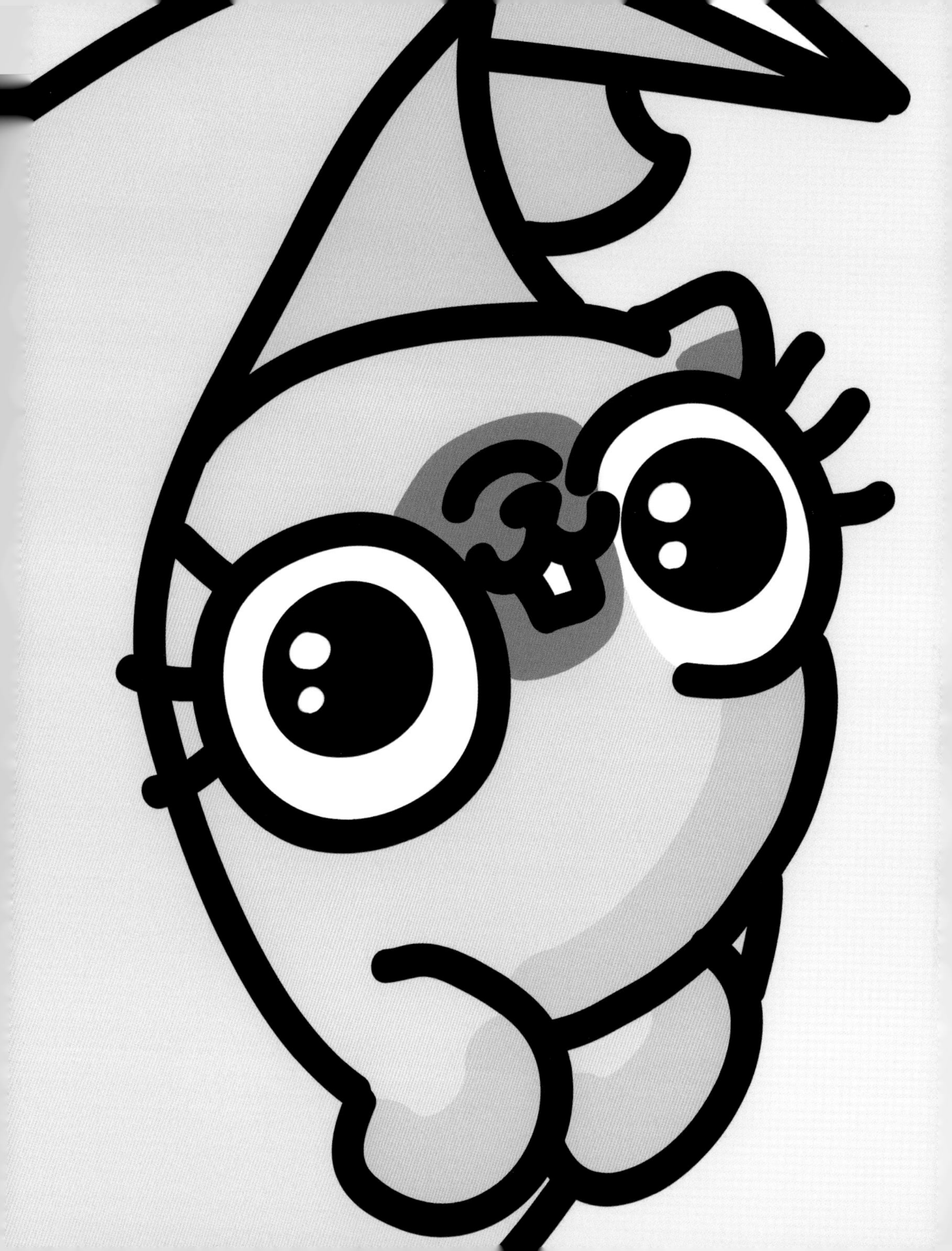

AFTER MY DOG TACA PASSED AWAY FROM OLD AGE, MY PARENTS DECIDED WE WOULDN'T HAVE ANY MORE DOGS. FOR YEARS AND YEARS AND YEARS, MY LIFE WAS LIKE:

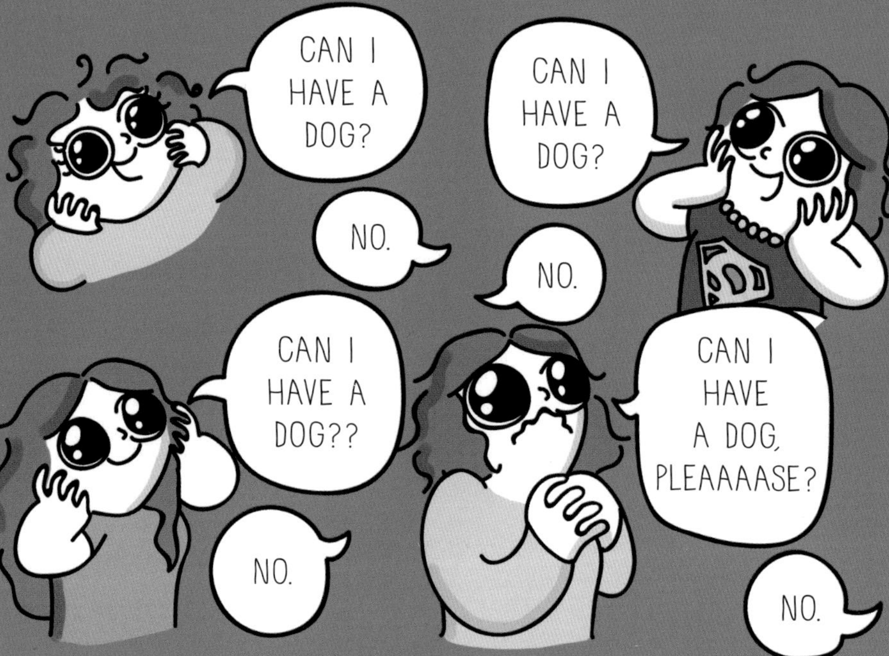
CAN I HAVE A DOG?
NO.
CAN I HAVE A DOG?
NO.
CAN I HAVE A DOG??
NO.
CAN I HAVE A DOG, PLEAAAASE?
NO.

ONE DAY, PELI AND I MOVED IN TOGETHER. FINALLY, WE COULD HAVE A DOG! THE ONLY PROBLEM WAS THAT WE MOVED TO AN APARTMENT OWNED BY PELI'S PARENTS, AND THE RULES WERE CLEAR . . .

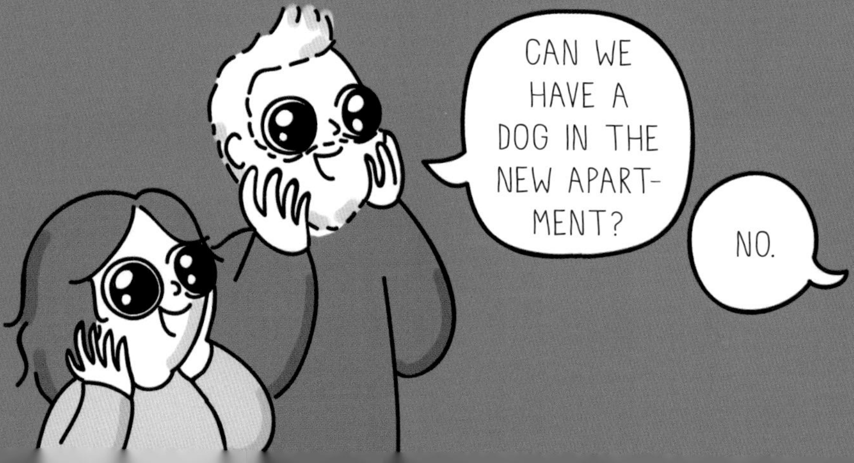
CAN WE HAVE A DOG IN THE NEW APART-MENT?
NO.

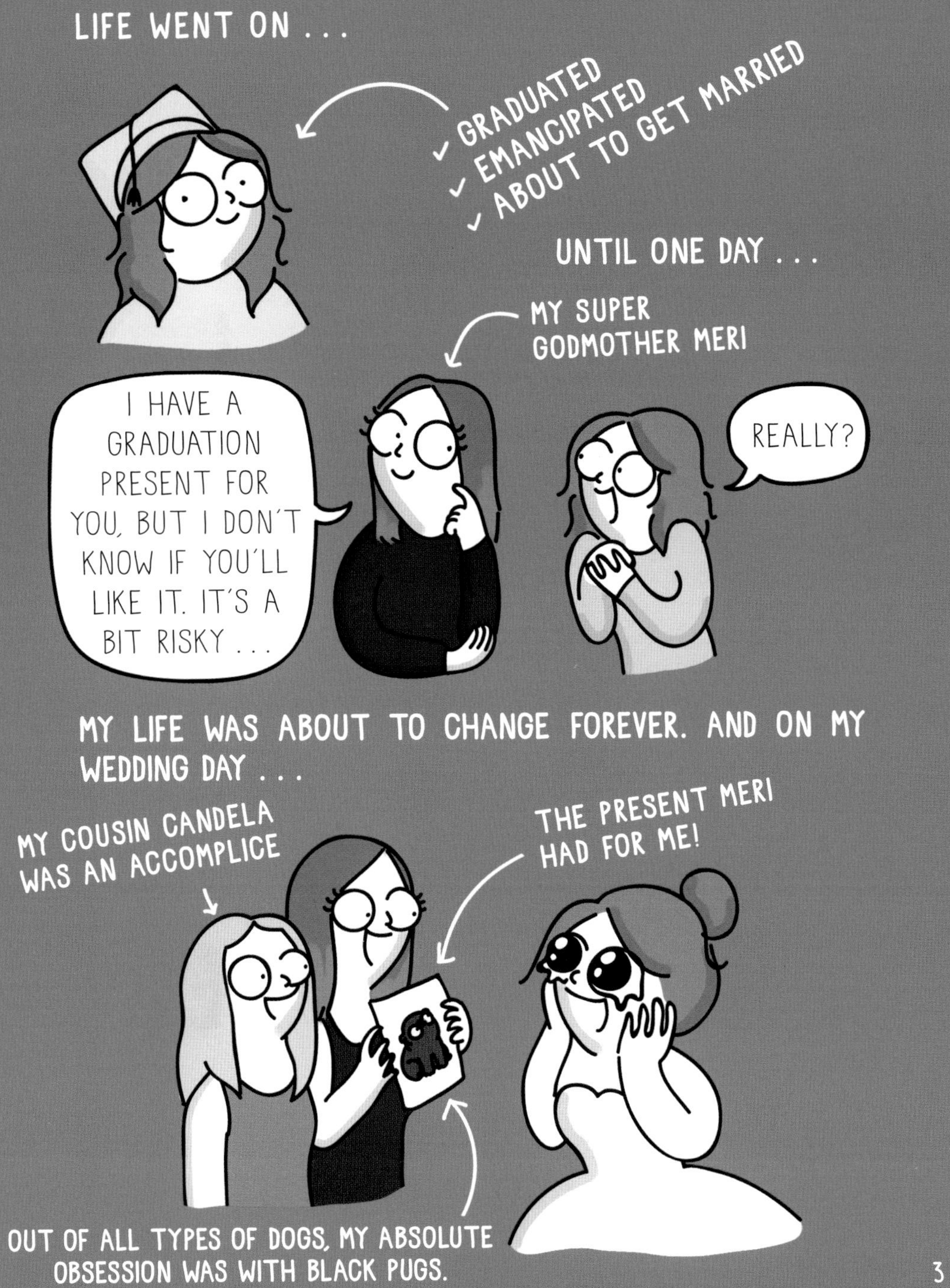
LIFE WENT ON . . .
✓ GRADUATED
✓ EMANCIPATED
✓ ABOUT TO GET MARRIED
UNTIL ONE DAY . . .
MY SUPER GODMOTHER MERI
I HAVE A GRADUATION PRESENT FOR YOU, BUT I DON'T KNOW IF YOU'LL LIKE IT. IT'S A BIT RISKY . . .
REALLY?
MY LIFE WAS ABOUT TO CHANGE FOREVER. AND ON MY WEDDING DAY . . .
MY COUSIN CANDELA WAS AN ACCOMPLICE
THE PRESENT MERI HAD FOR ME!
OUT OF ALL TYPES OF DOGS, MY ABSOLUTE OBSESSION WAS WITH BLACK PUGS.

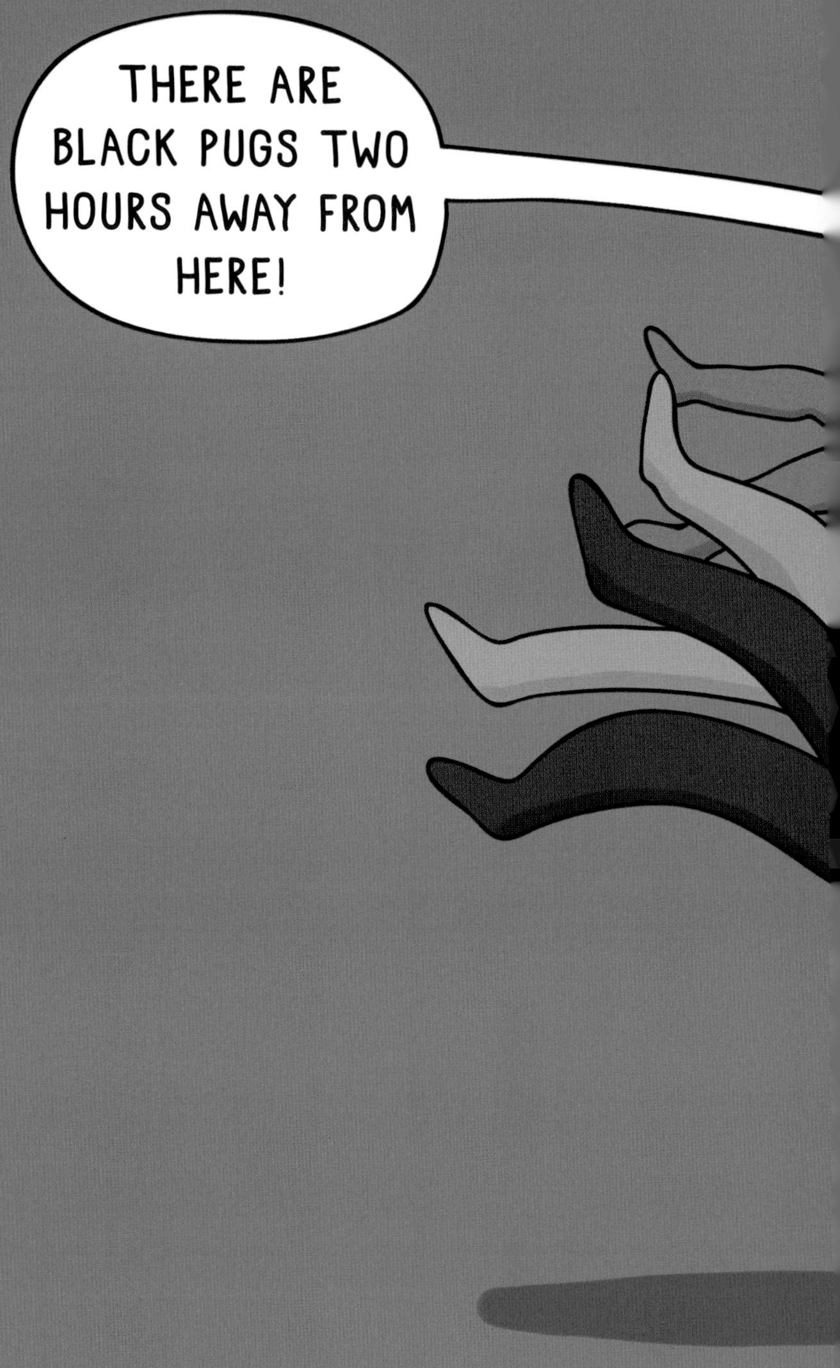
THERE ARE BLACK PUGS TWO HOURS AWAY FROM HERE!

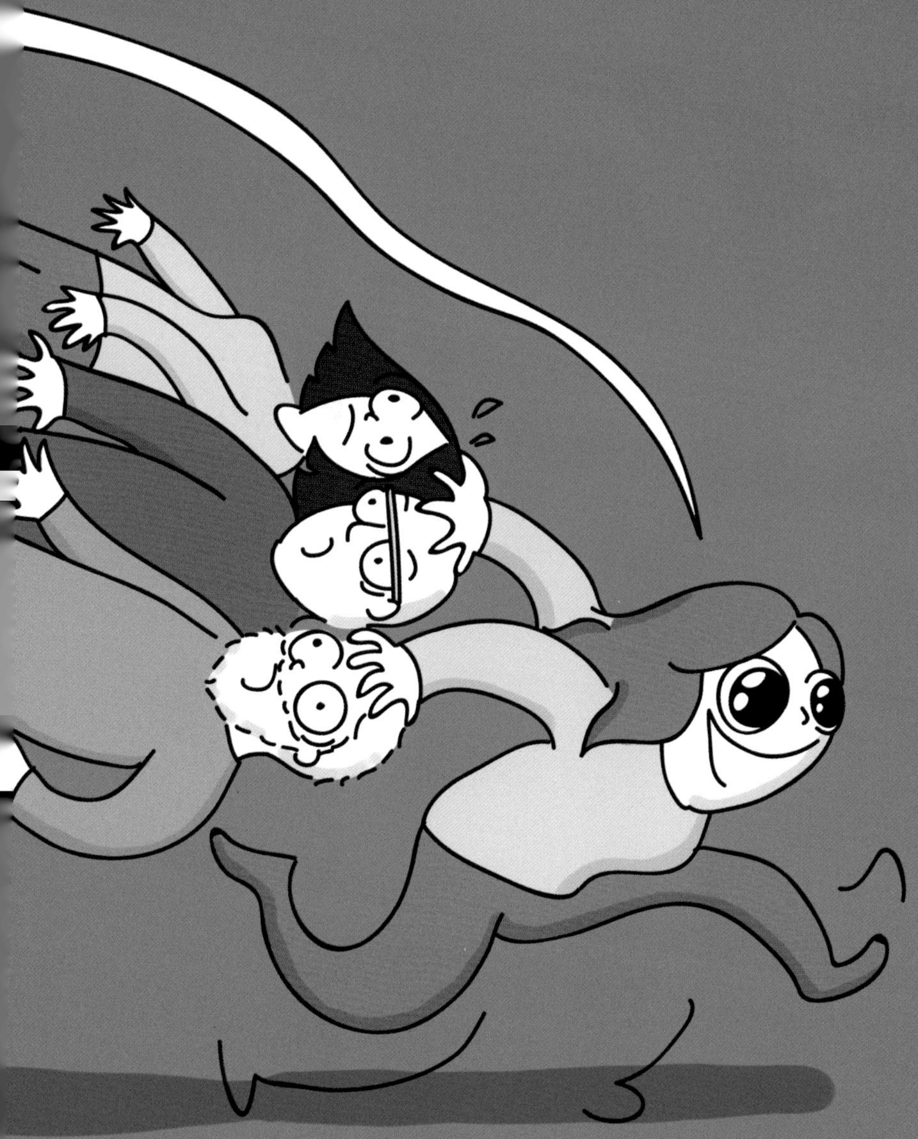

WE FINALLY ARRIVED

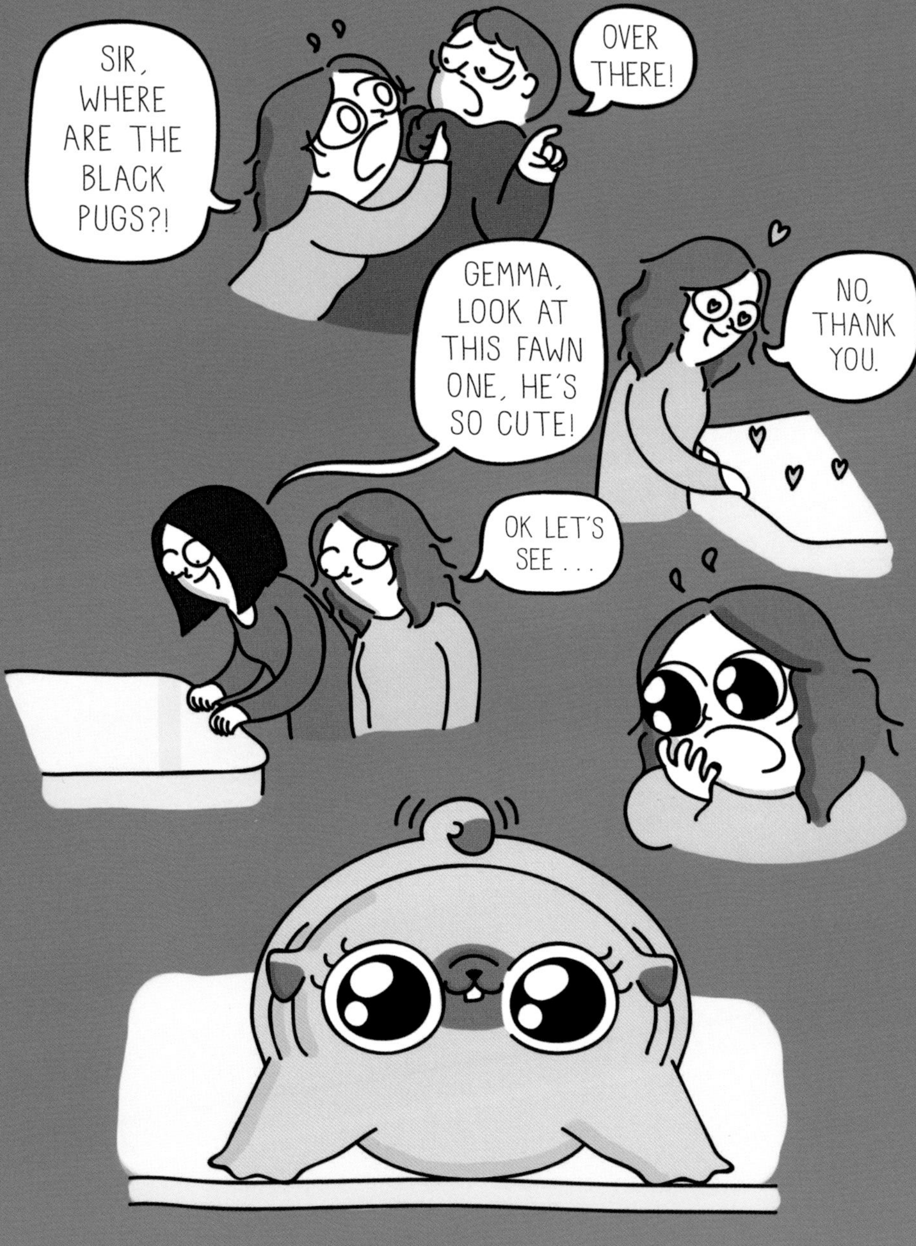
SIR, WHERE ARE THE BLACK PUGS?!
OVER THERE!
GEMMA, LOOK AT THIS FAWN ONE, HE'S SO CUTE!
NO, THANK YOU.
OK LET'S SEE . . .

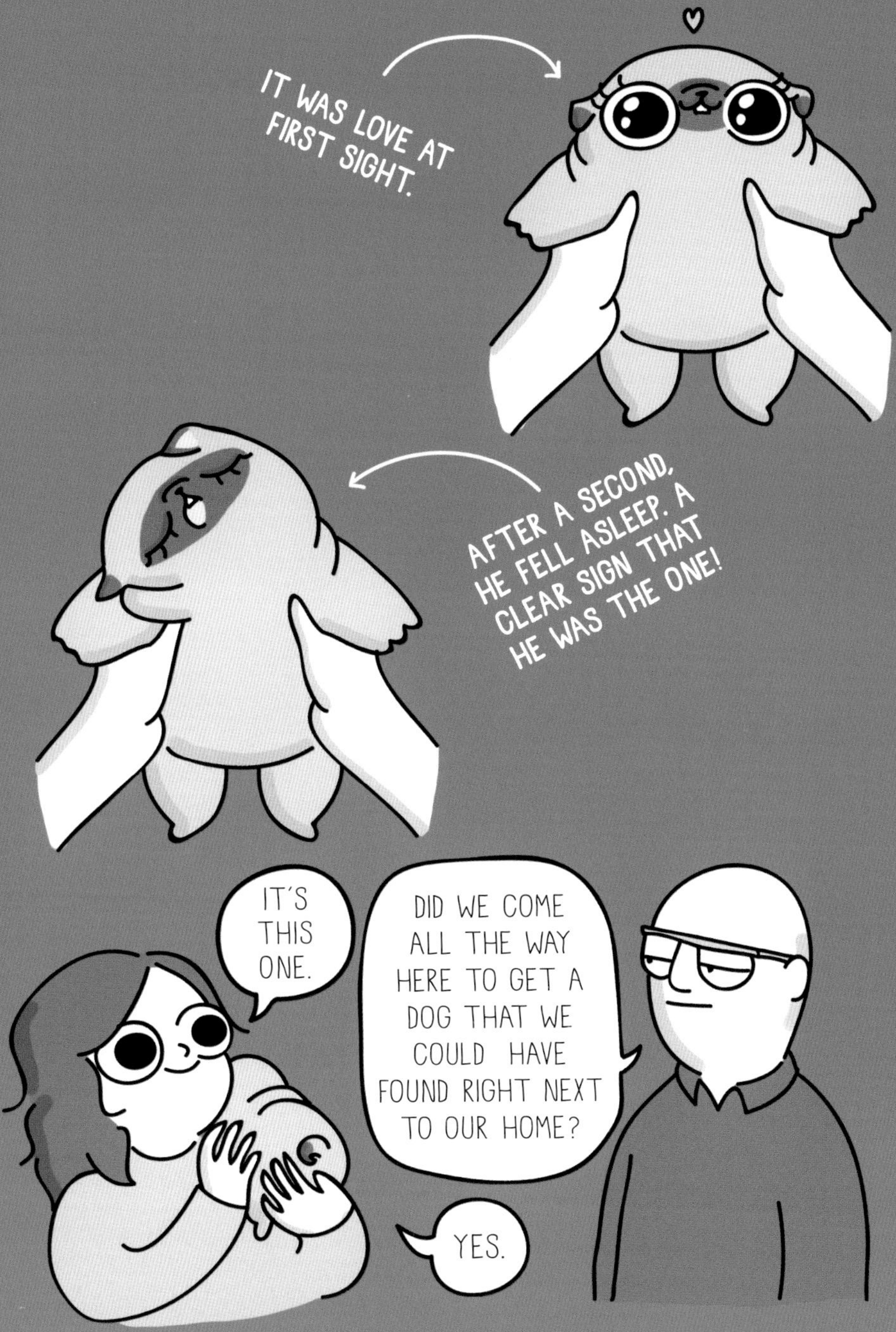
IT WAS LOVE AT FIRST SIGHT.
AFTER A SECOND, HE FELL ASLEEP. A CLEAR SIGN THAT HE WAS THE ONE!
IT'S THIS ONE.
DID WE COME ALL THE WAY HERE TO GET A DOG THAT WE COULD HAVE FOUND RIGHT NEXT TO OUR HOME?
YES.

AND ON OUR WAY HOME . . .

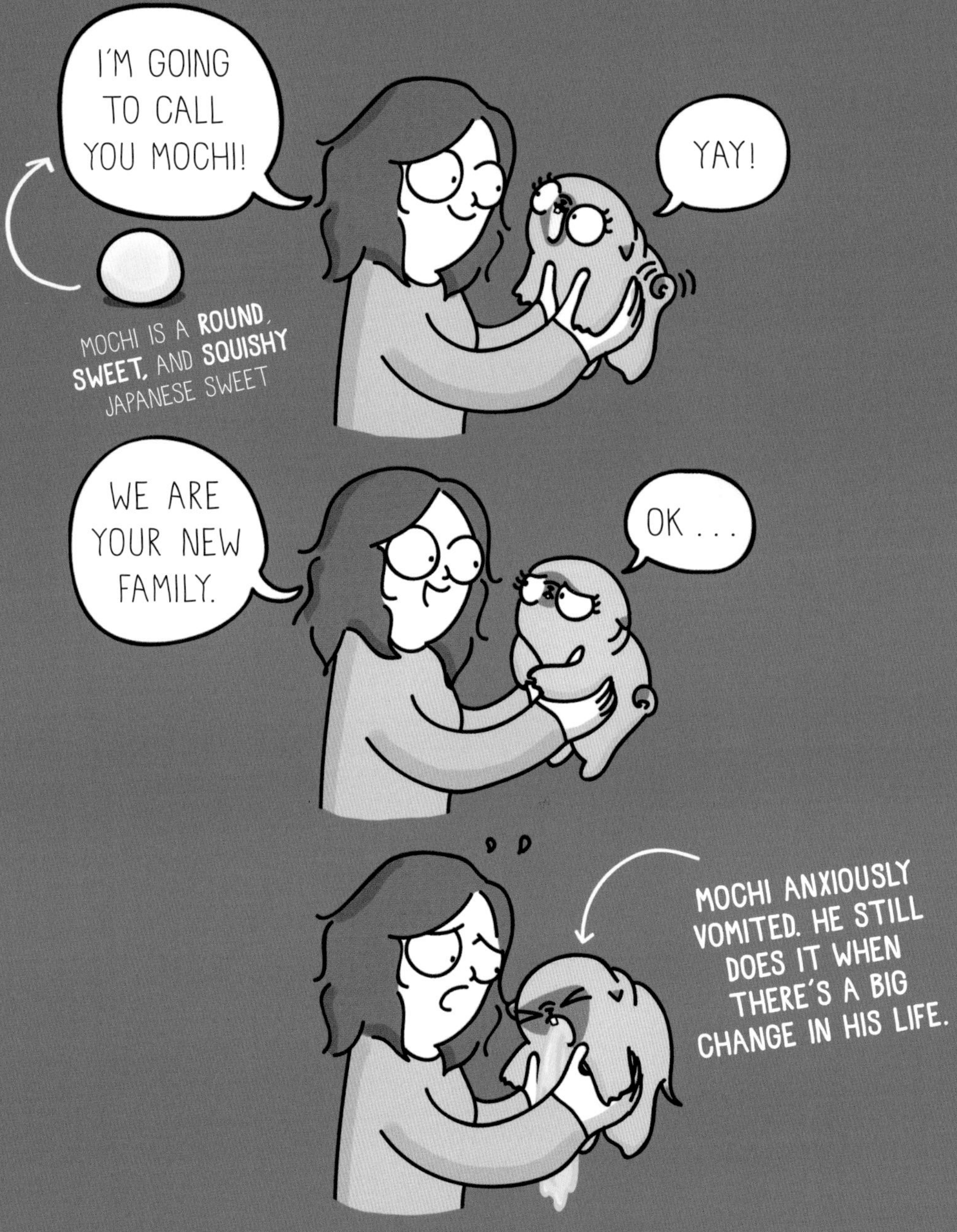

I'M GOING TO CALL YOU MOCHI!
YAY!
MOCHI IS A **ROUND**, **SWEET**, AND **SQUISHY** JAPANESE SWEET
WE ARE YOUR NEW FAMILY.
OK . . .
MOCHI ANXIOUSLY VOMITED. HE STILL DOES IT WHEN THERE'S A BIG CHANGE IN HIS LIFE.

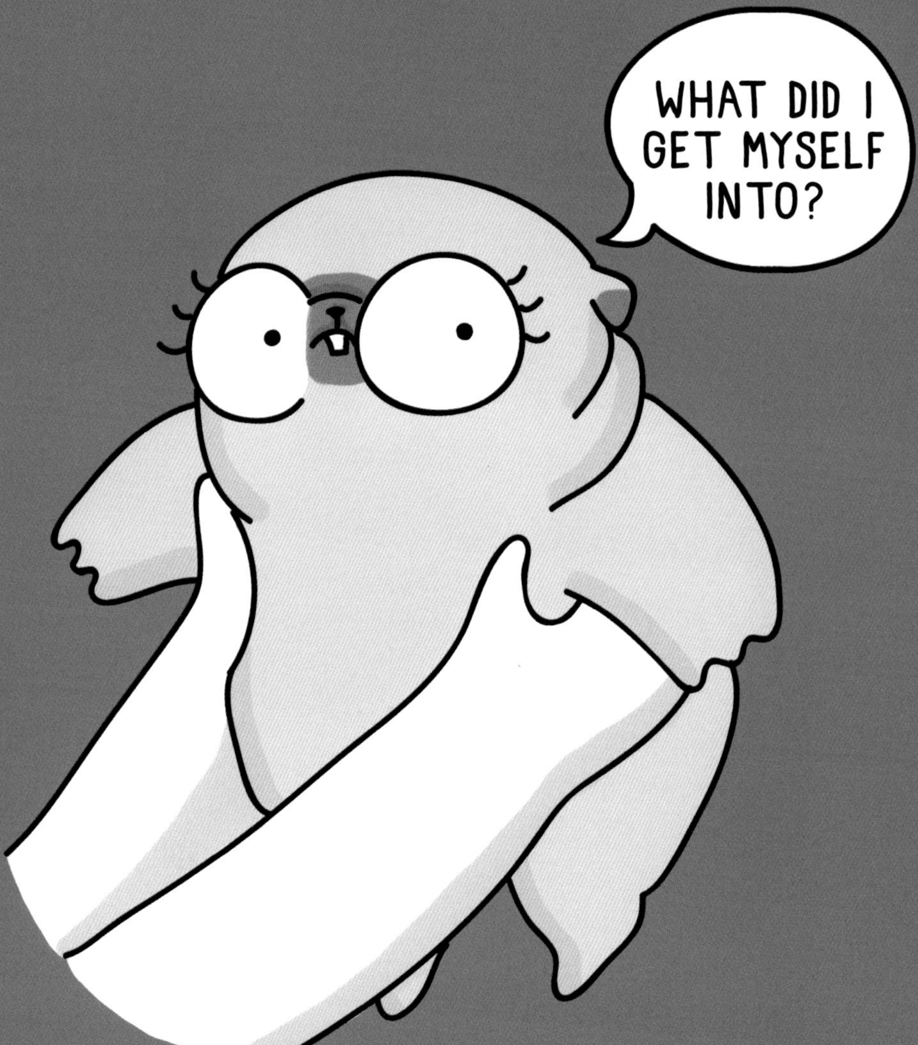
WHAT DID I GET MYSELF INTO?

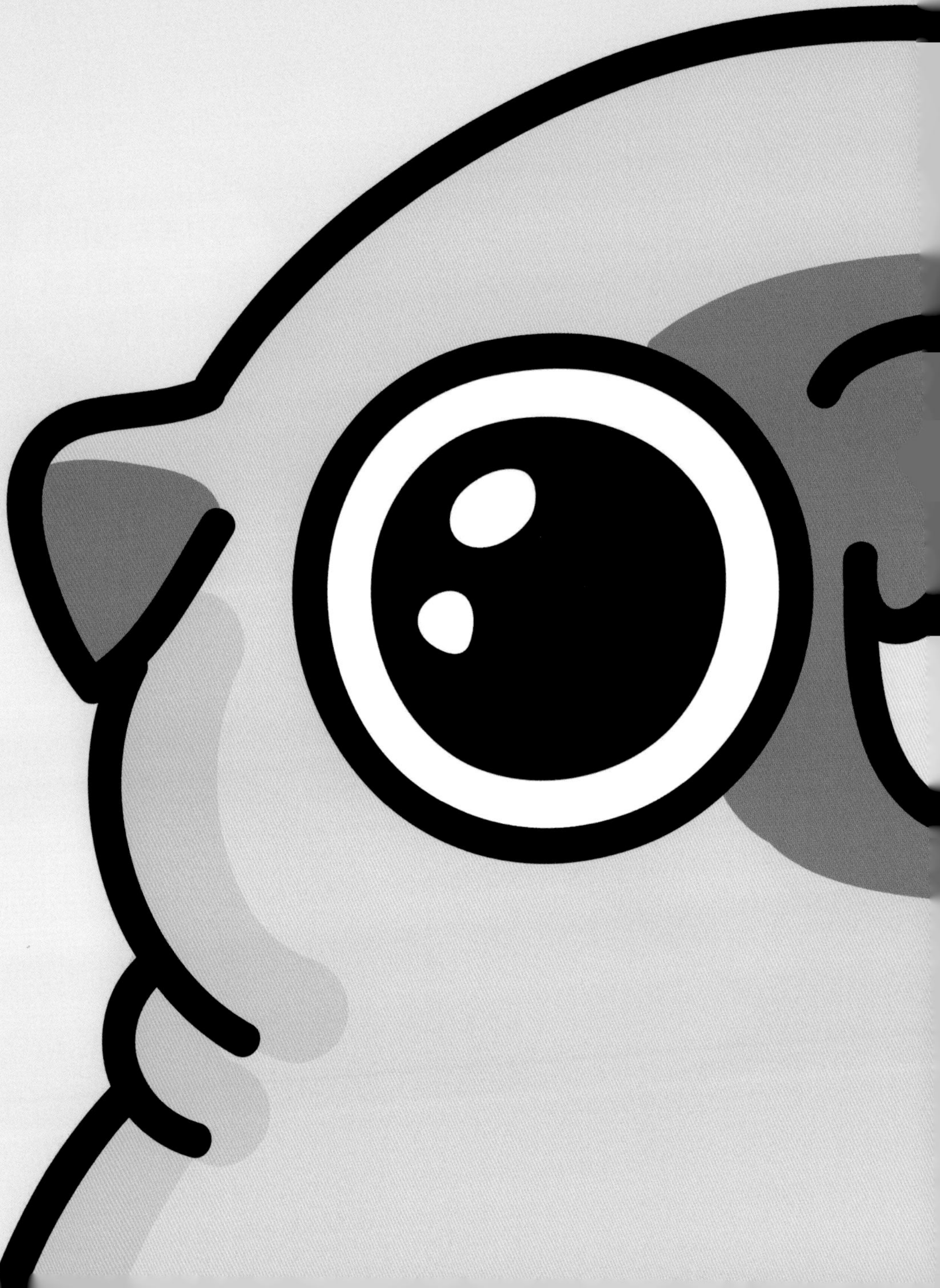

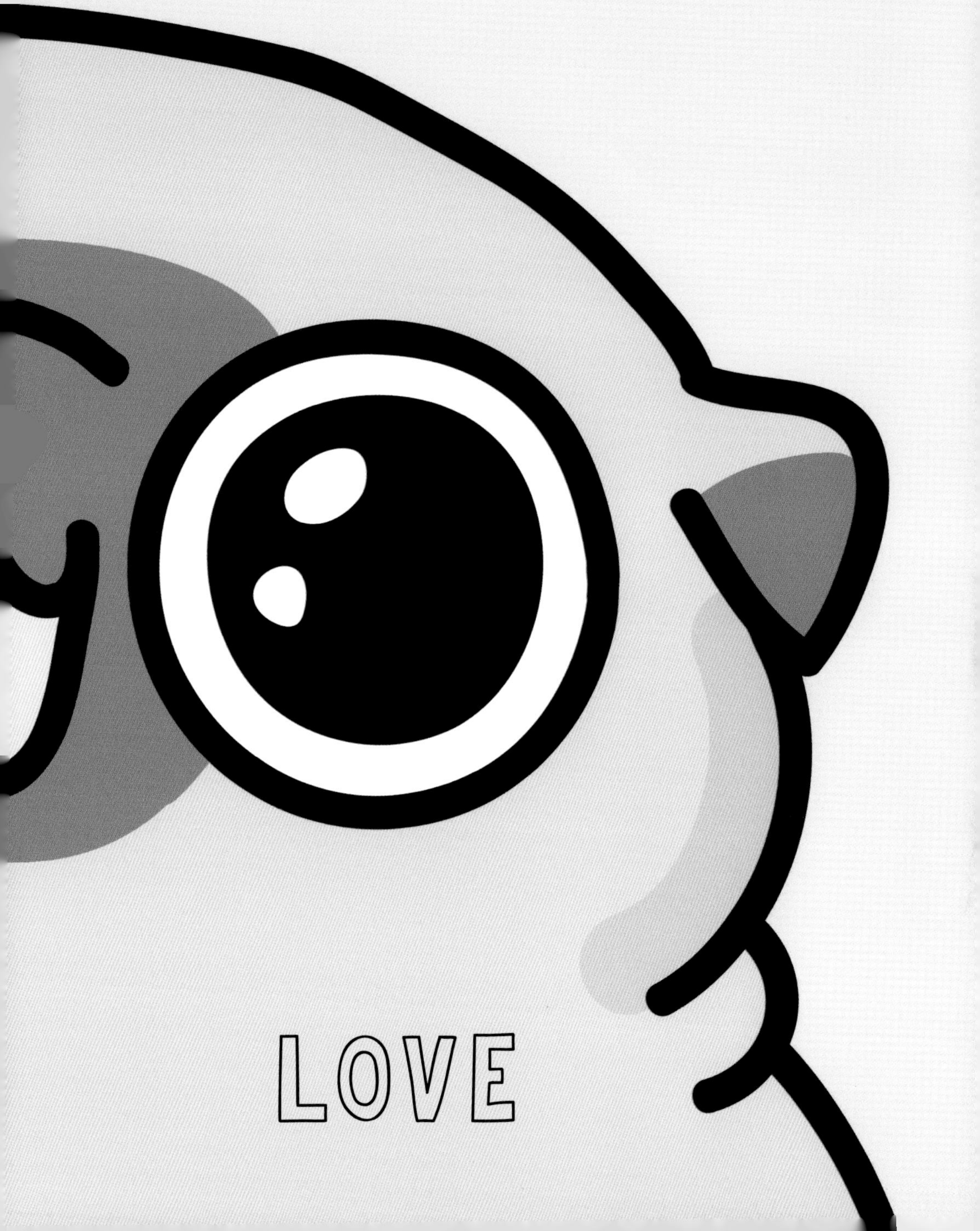
LOVE

THINGS MOCHI LOVES

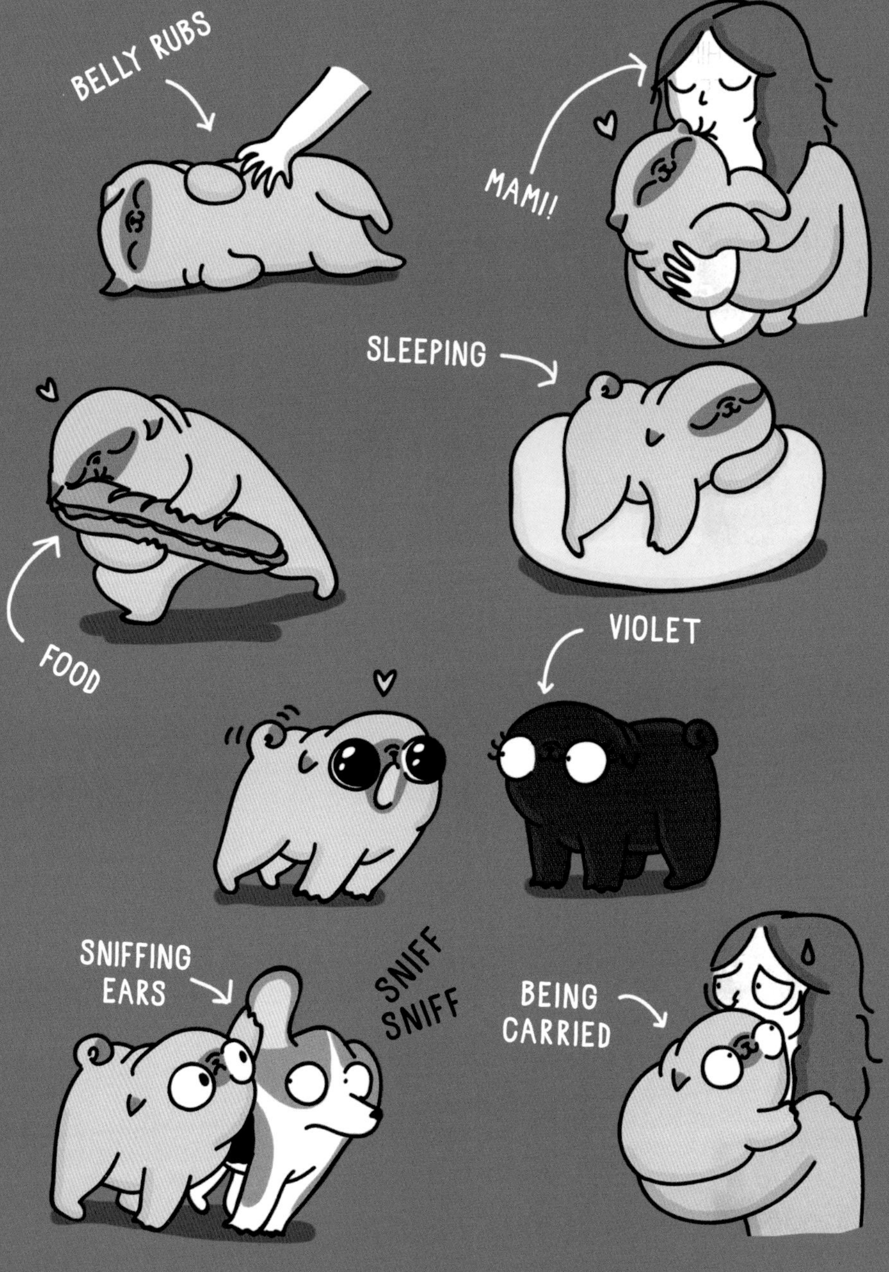
BELLY RUBS
MAMI!
SLEEPING
FOOD
VIOLET
SNIFFING EARS
SNIFF SNIFF
BEING CARRIED

THINGS MOCHI DOESN'T LOVE

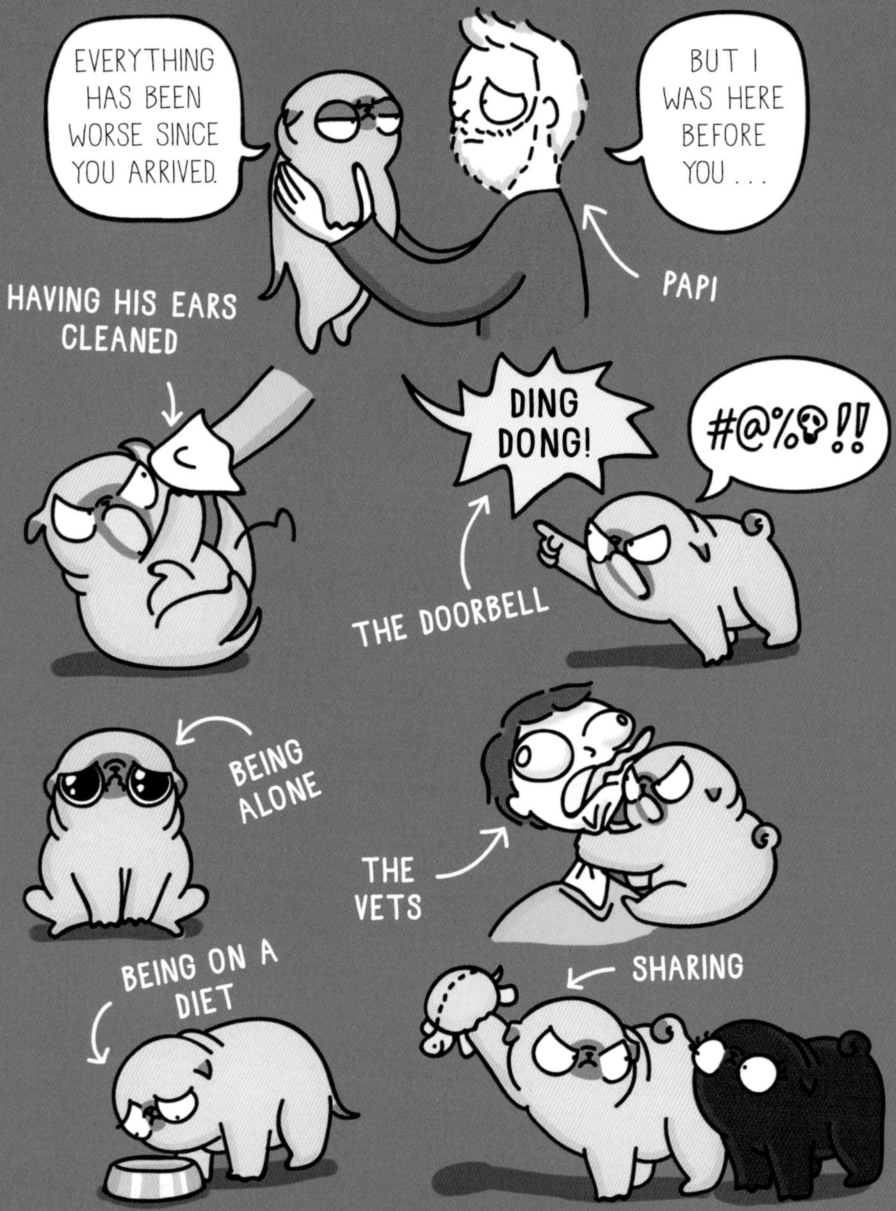

EVERYTHING HAS BEEN WORSE SINCE YOU ARRIVED.
BUT I WAS HERE BEFORE YOU . . .
PAPI
HAVING HIS EARS CLEANED
DING DONG!
#@%!!
THE DOORBELL
BEING ALONE
THE VETS
BEING ON A DIET
SHARING

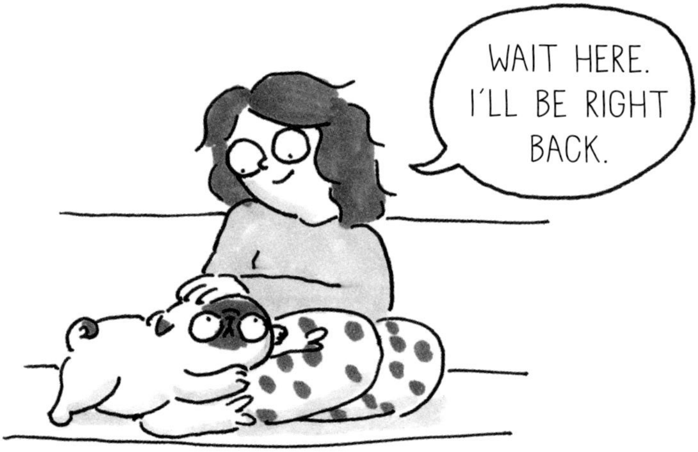
WAIT HERE. I'LL BE RIGHT BACK.

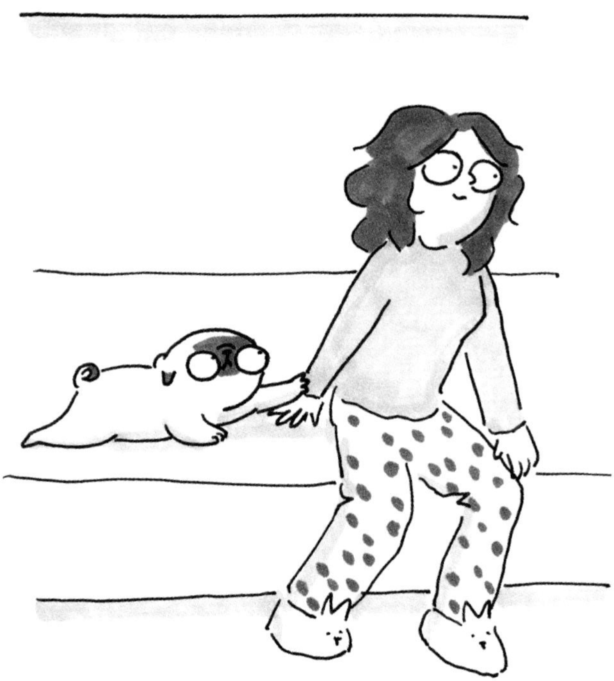

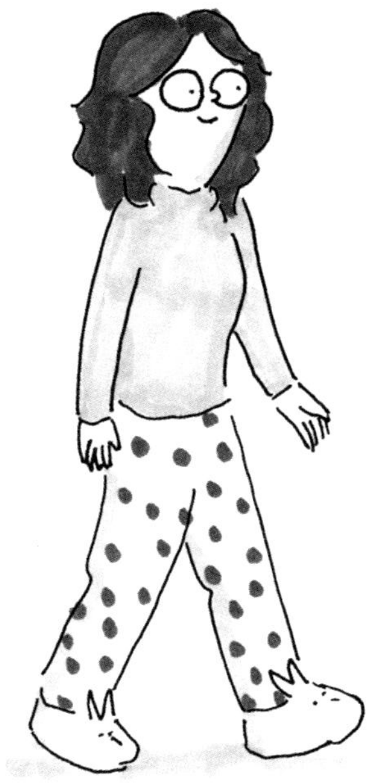

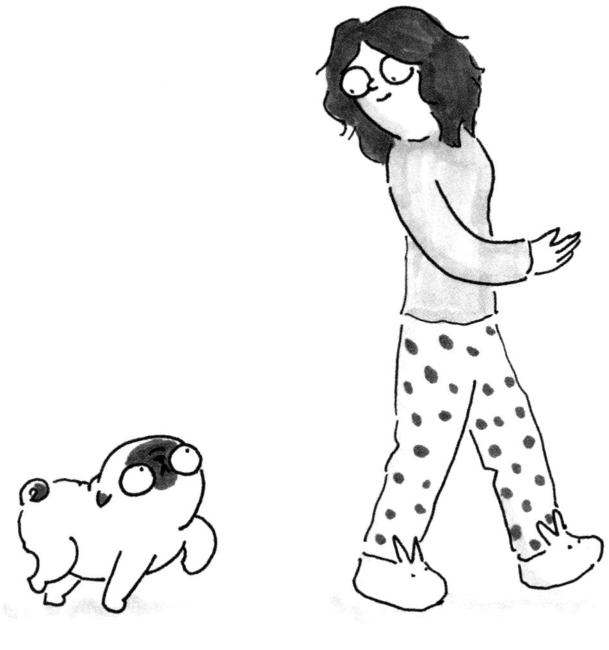

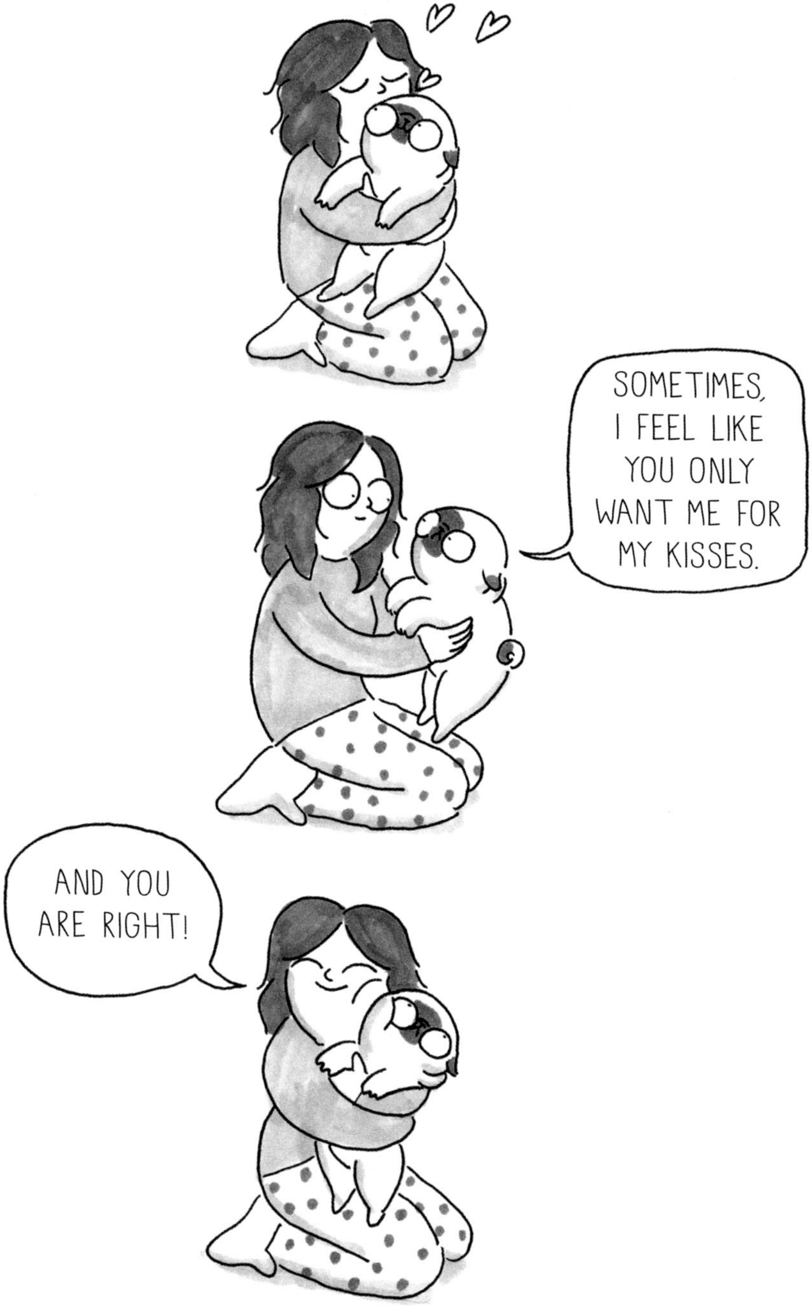
SOMETIMES, I FEEL LIKE YOU ONLY WANT ME FOR MY KISSES.
AND YOU ARE RIGHT!

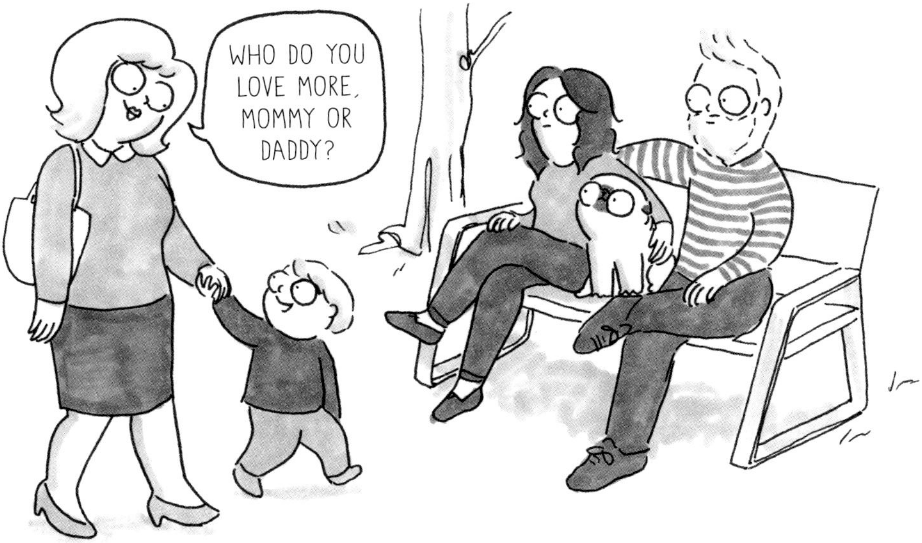
WHO DO YOU LOVE MORE, MOMMY OR DADDY?

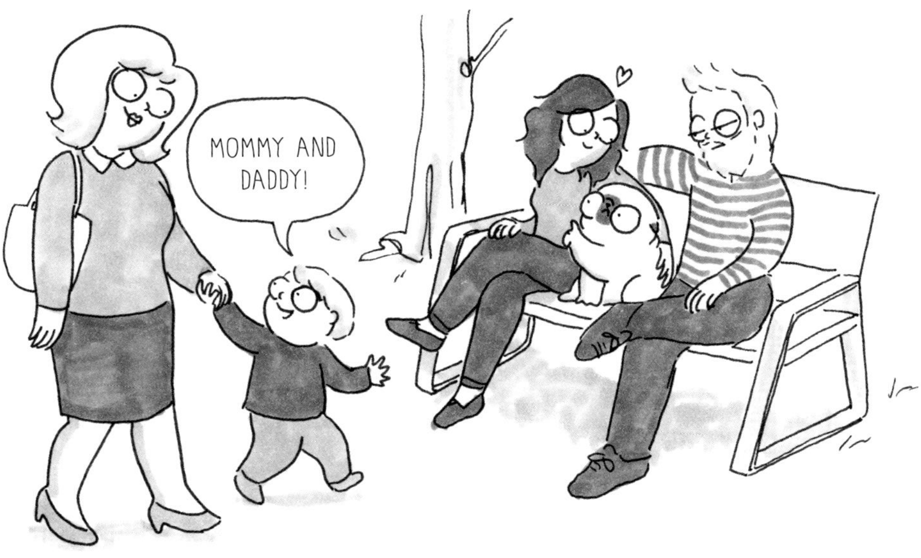
MOMMY AND DADDY!

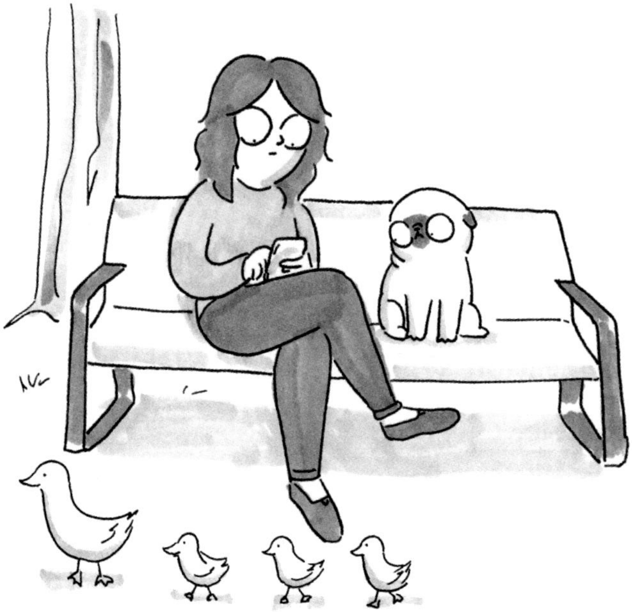

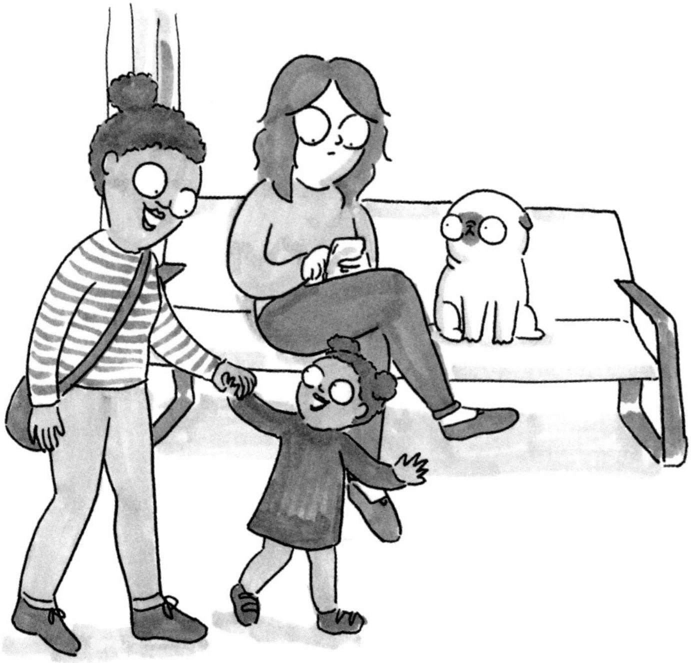

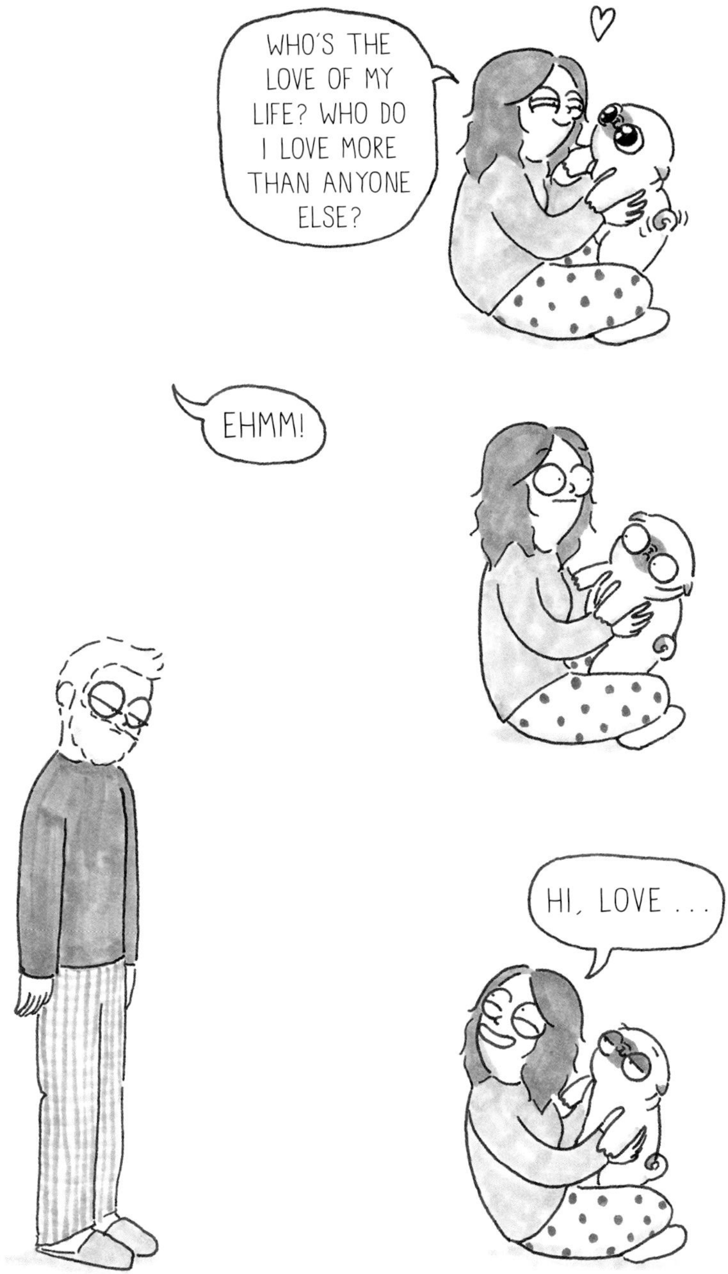
WHO'S THE LOVE OF MY LIFE? WHO DO I LOVE MORE THAN ANYONE ELSE?
EHMM!
HI, LOVE . . .

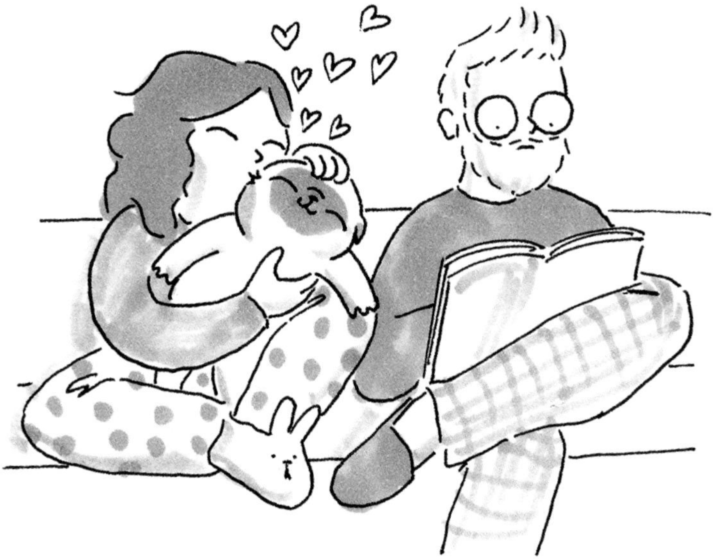

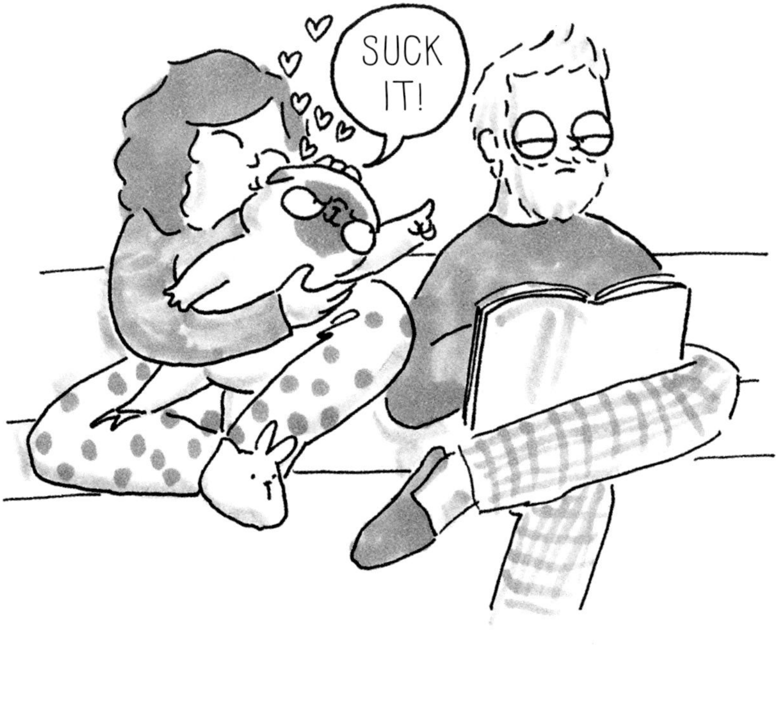
SUCK IT!

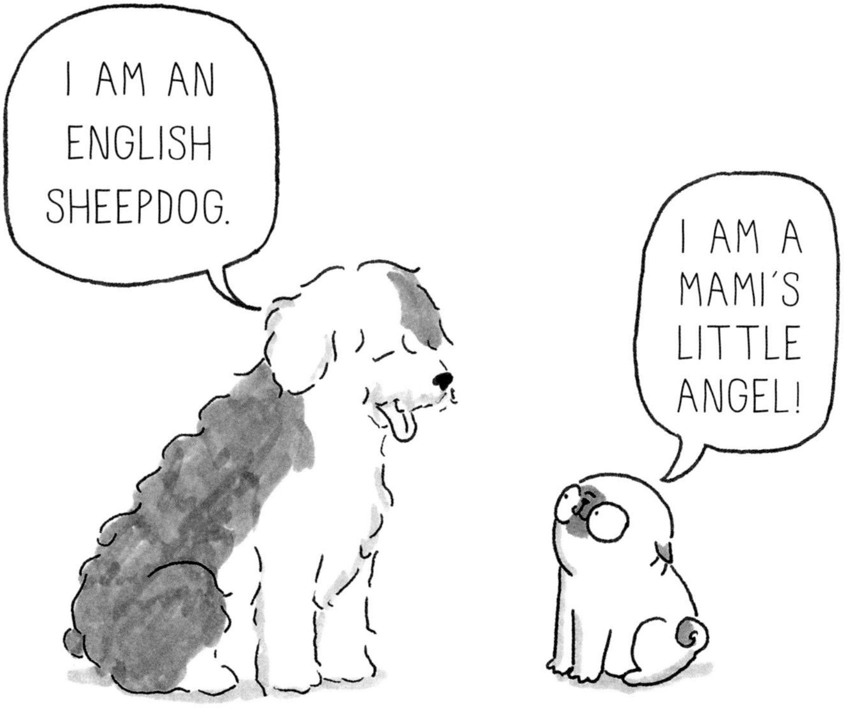
I AM AN ENGLISH SHEEPDOG.
I AM A MAMI'S LITTLE ANGEL!

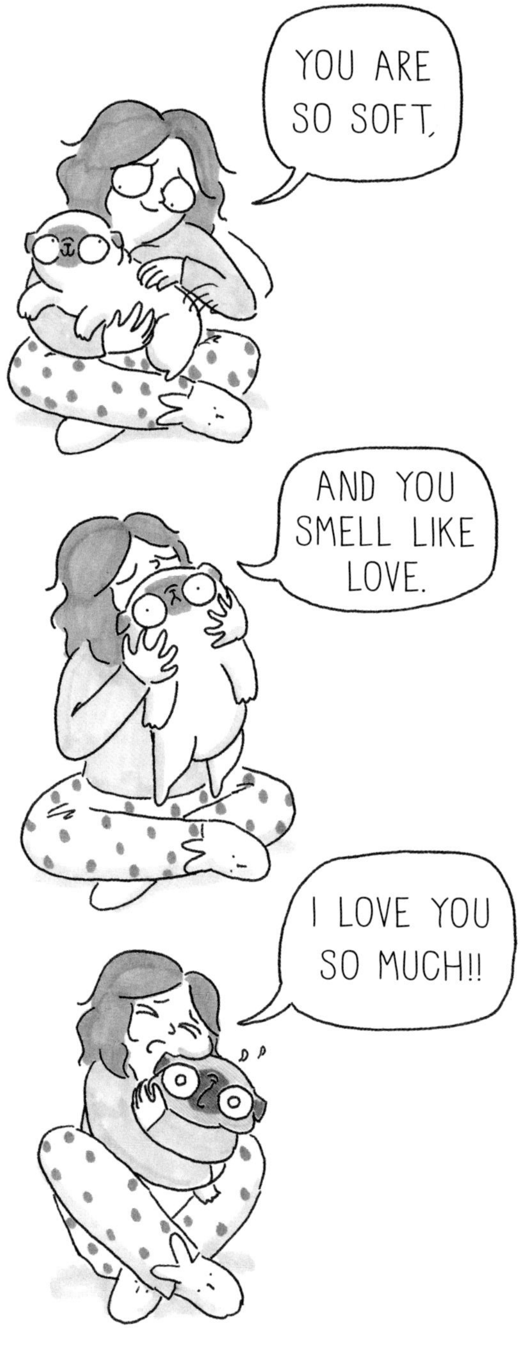
YOU ARE SO SOFT,
AND YOU SMELL LIKE LOVE.
I LOVE YOU SO MUCH!!

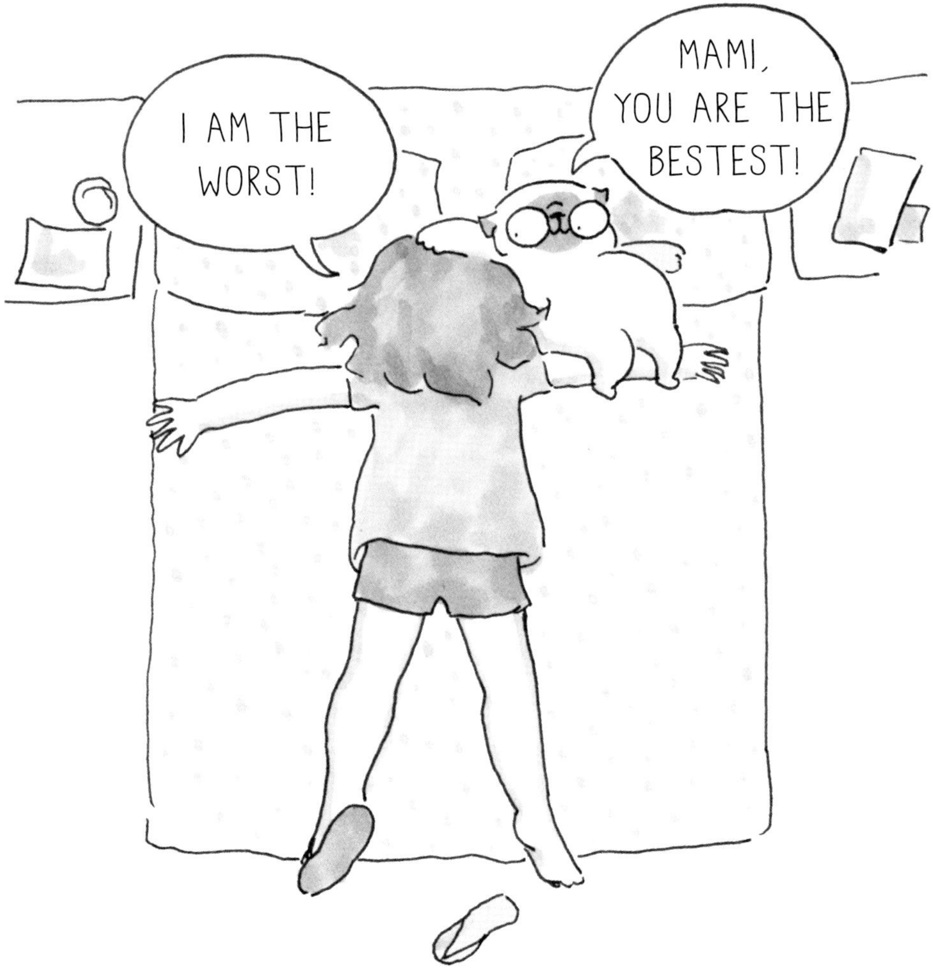
I AM THE WORST!
MAMI, YOU ARE THE BESTEST!

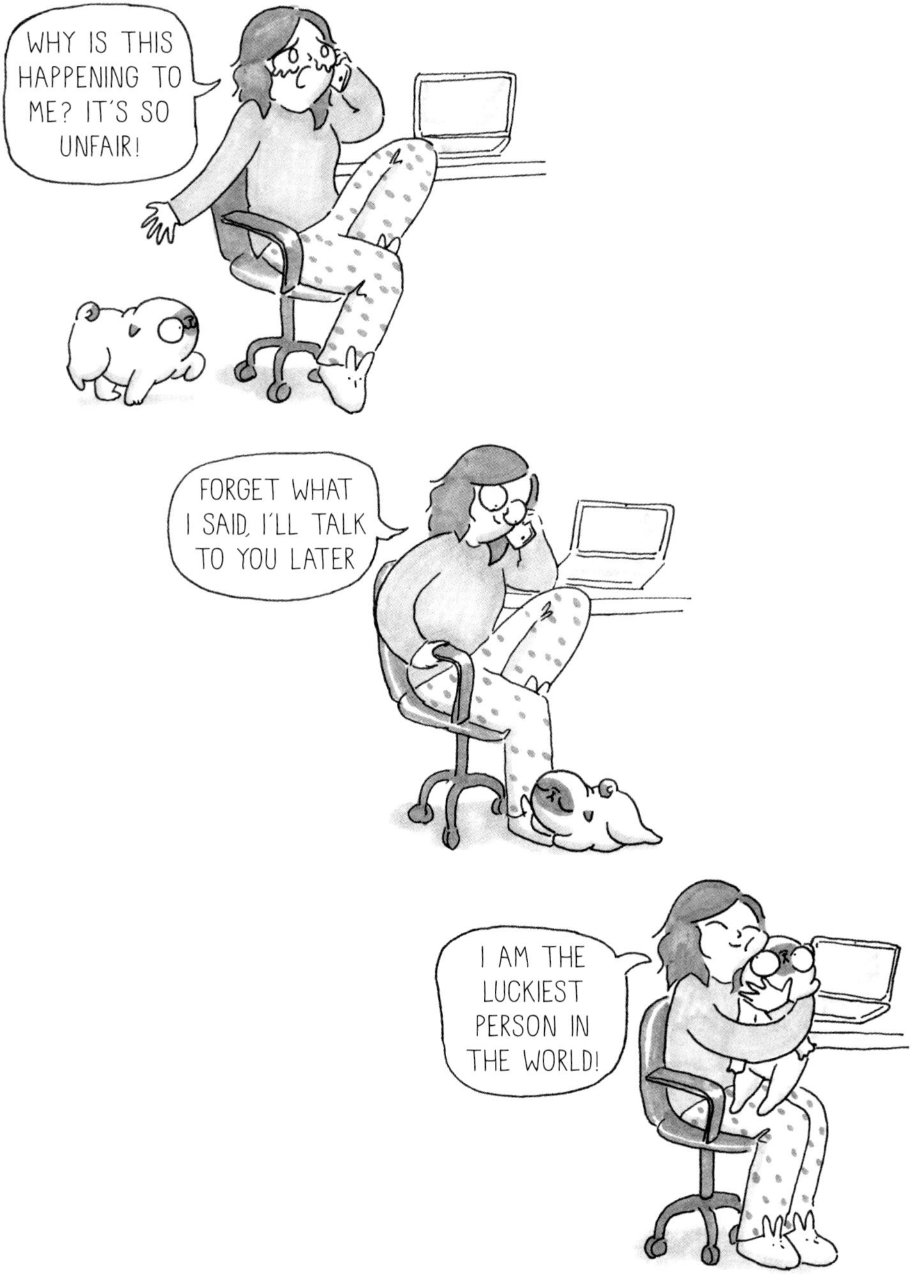
WHY IS THIS HAPPENING TO ME? IT'S SO UNFAIR!
FORGET WHAT I SAID, I'LL TALK TO YOU LATER
I AM THE LUCKIEST PERSON IN THE WORLD!

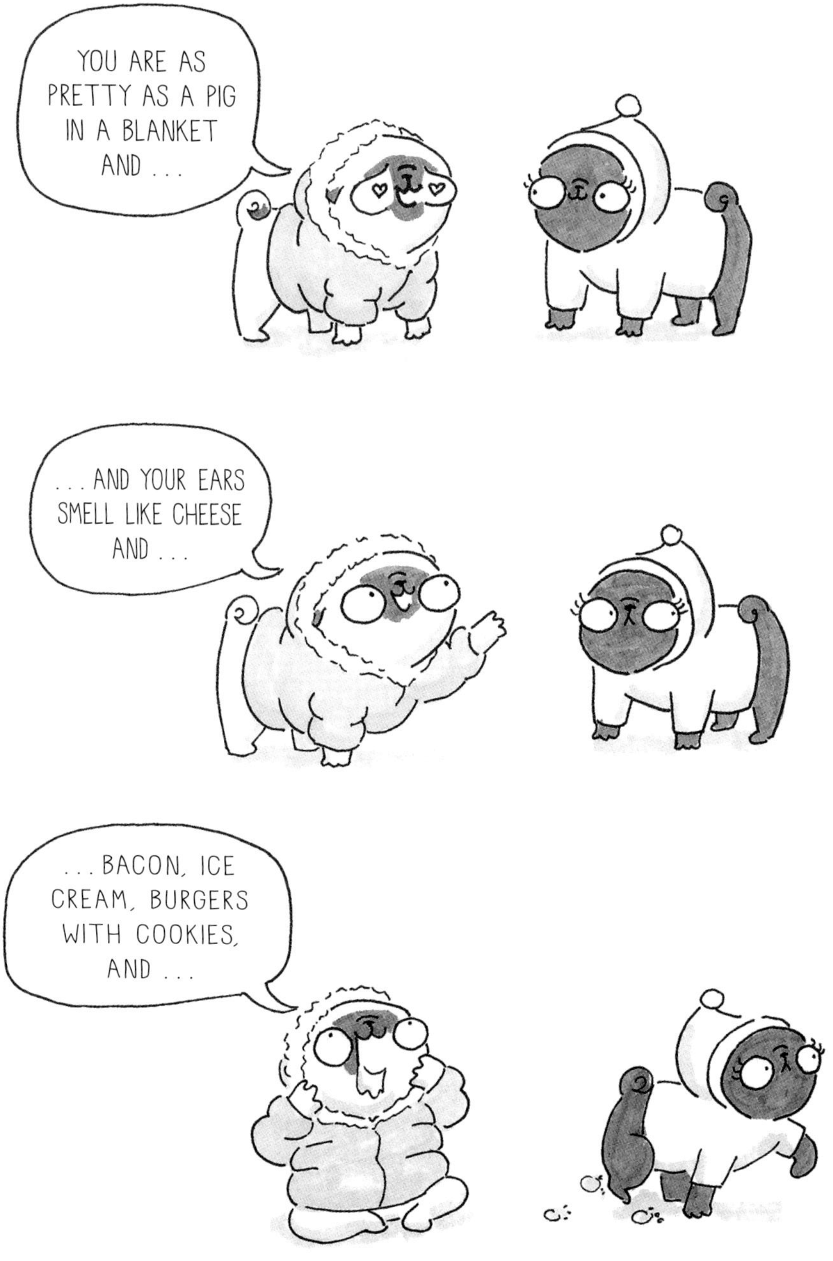
YOU ARE AS PRETTY AS A PIG IN A BLANKET AND . . .
. . . AND YOUR EARS SMELL LIKE CHEESE AND . . .
. . . BACON, ICE CREAM, BURGERS WITH COOKIES, AND . . .

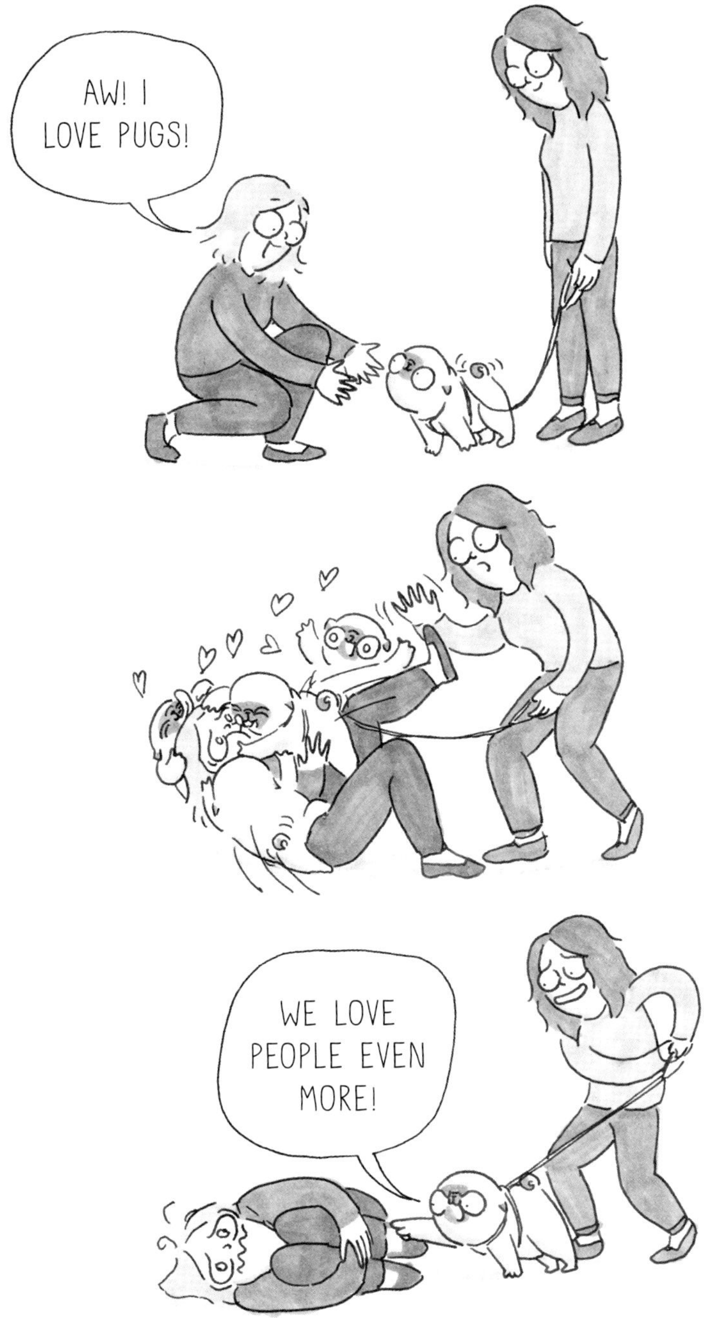
AW! I LOVE PUGS!
WE LOVE PEOPLE EVEN MORE!

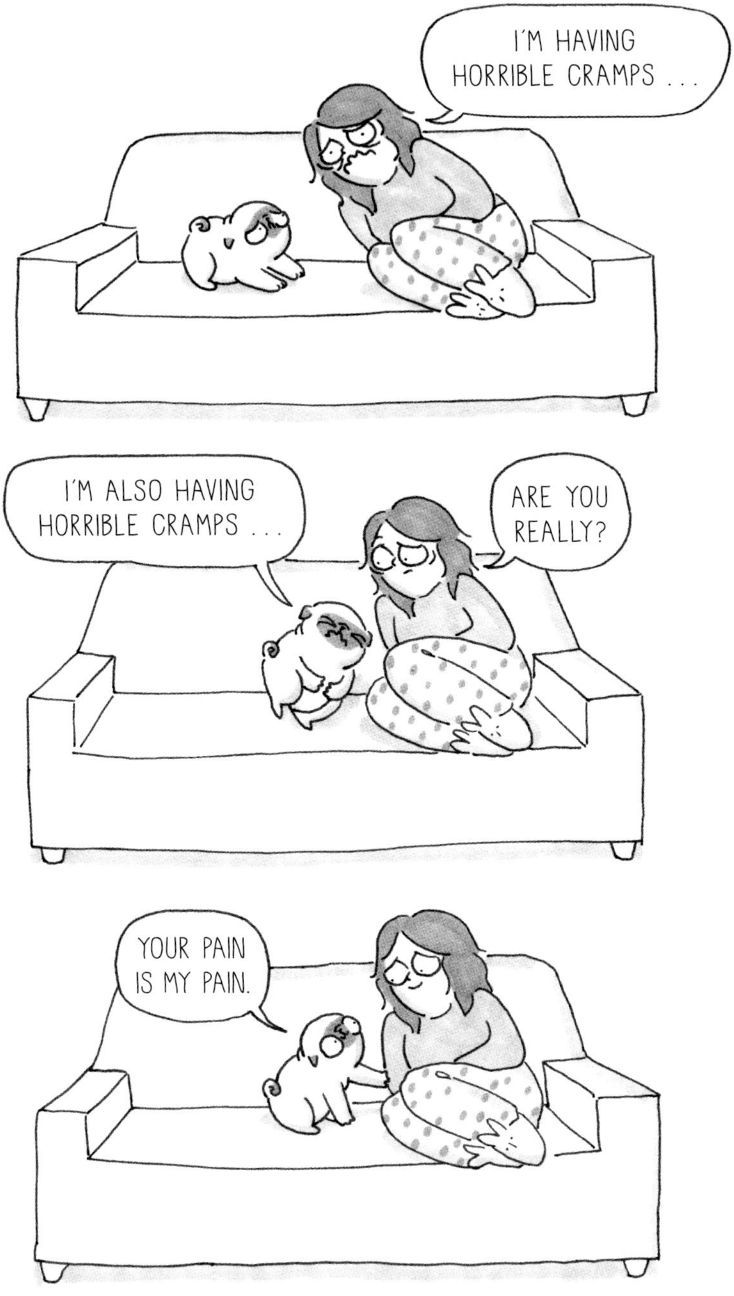
I'M HAVING HORRIBLE CRAMPS . . .
I'M ALSO HAVING HORRIBLE CRAMPS . . .
ARE YOU REALLY?
YOUR PAIN IS MY PAIN.

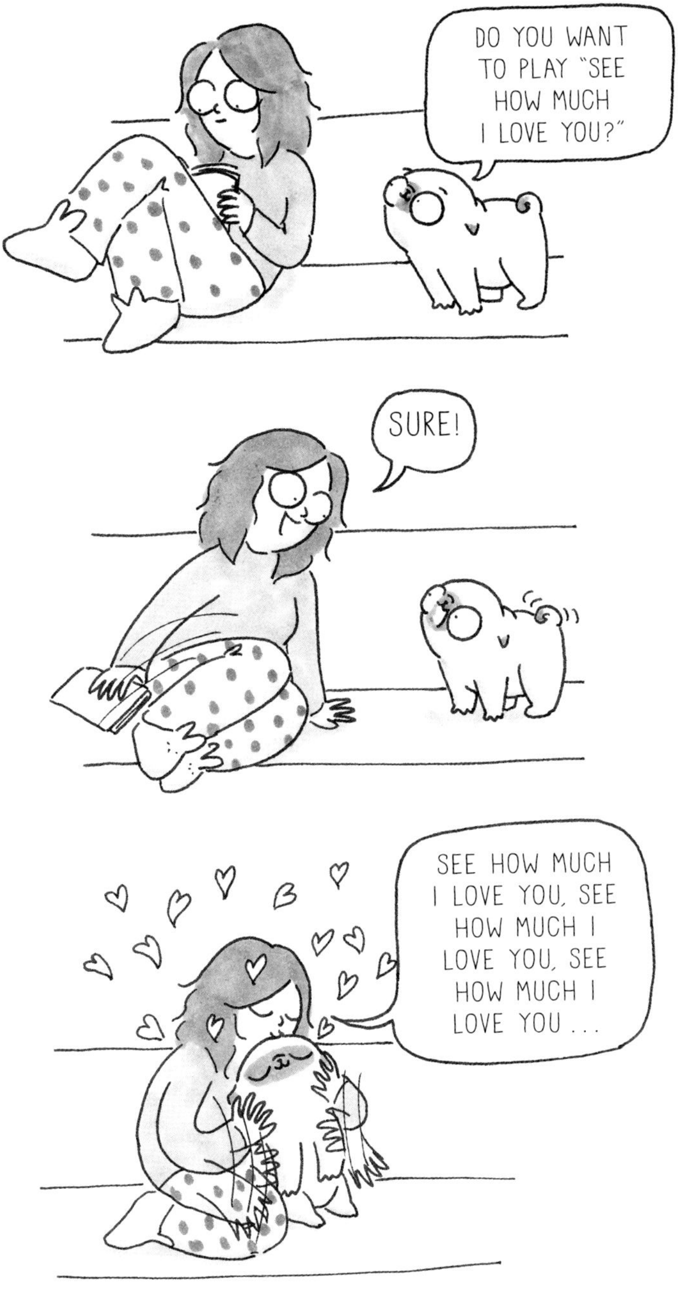
DO YOU WANT TO PLAY "SEE HOW MUCH I LOVE YOU?"
SURE!
SEE HOW MUCH I LOVE YOU, SEE HOW MUCH I LOVE YOU, SEE HOW MUCH I LOVE YOU . . .

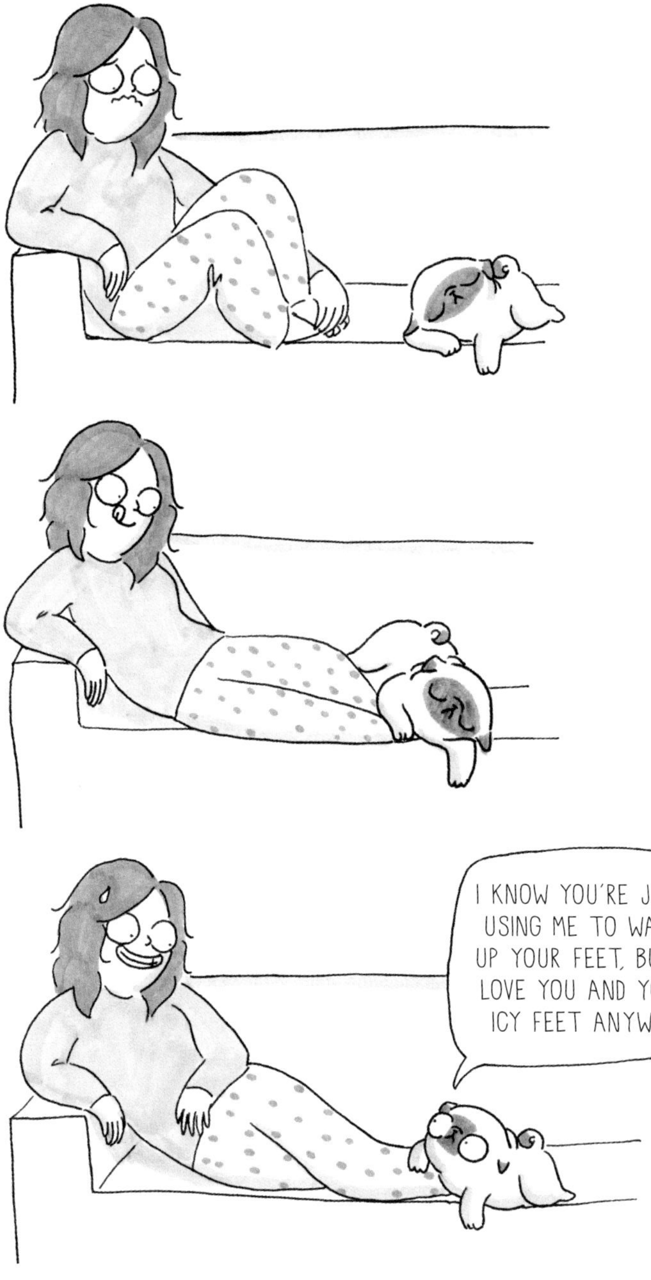
I KNOW YOU'RE JUST USING ME TO WARM UP YOUR FEET, BUT I LOVE YOU AND YOUR ICY FEET ANYWAY.

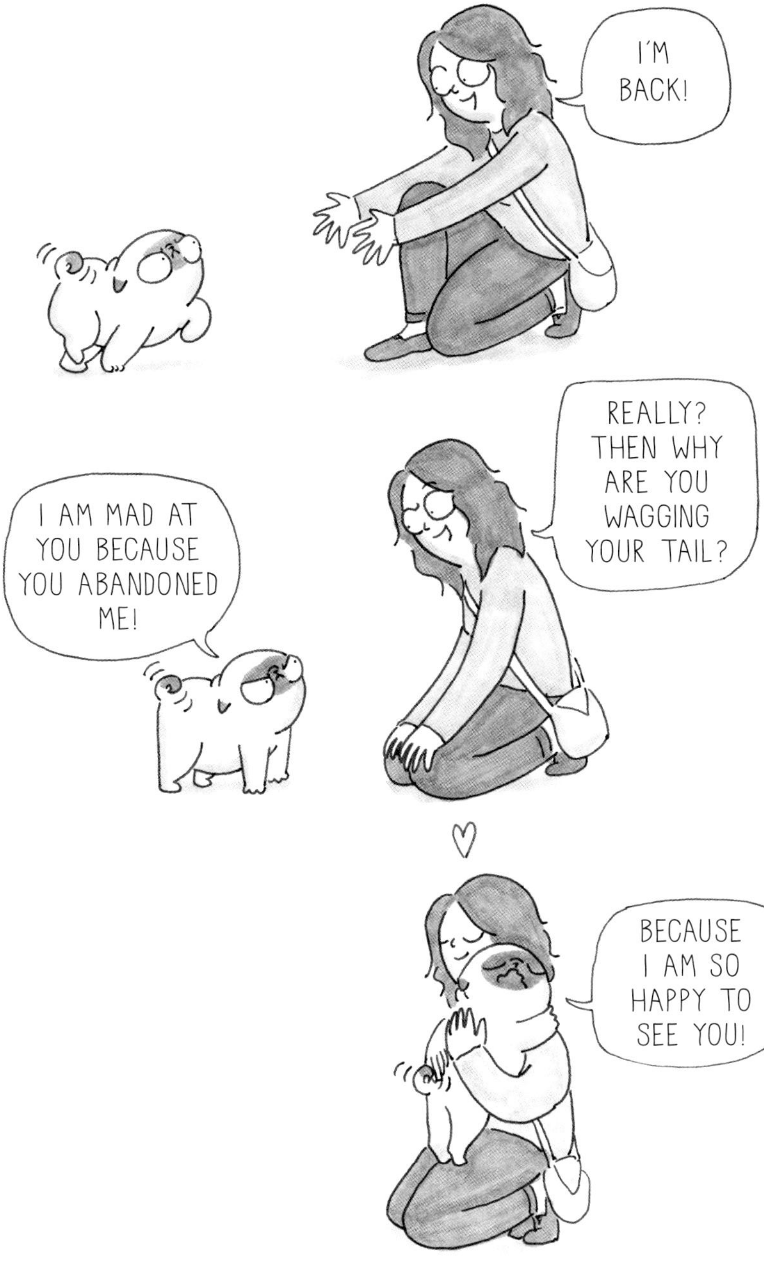
I'M BACK!
REALLY? THEN WHY ARE YOU WAGGING YOUR TAIL?
I AM MAD AT YOU BECAUSE YOU ABANDONED ME!
BECAUSE I AM SO HAPPY TO SEE YOU!

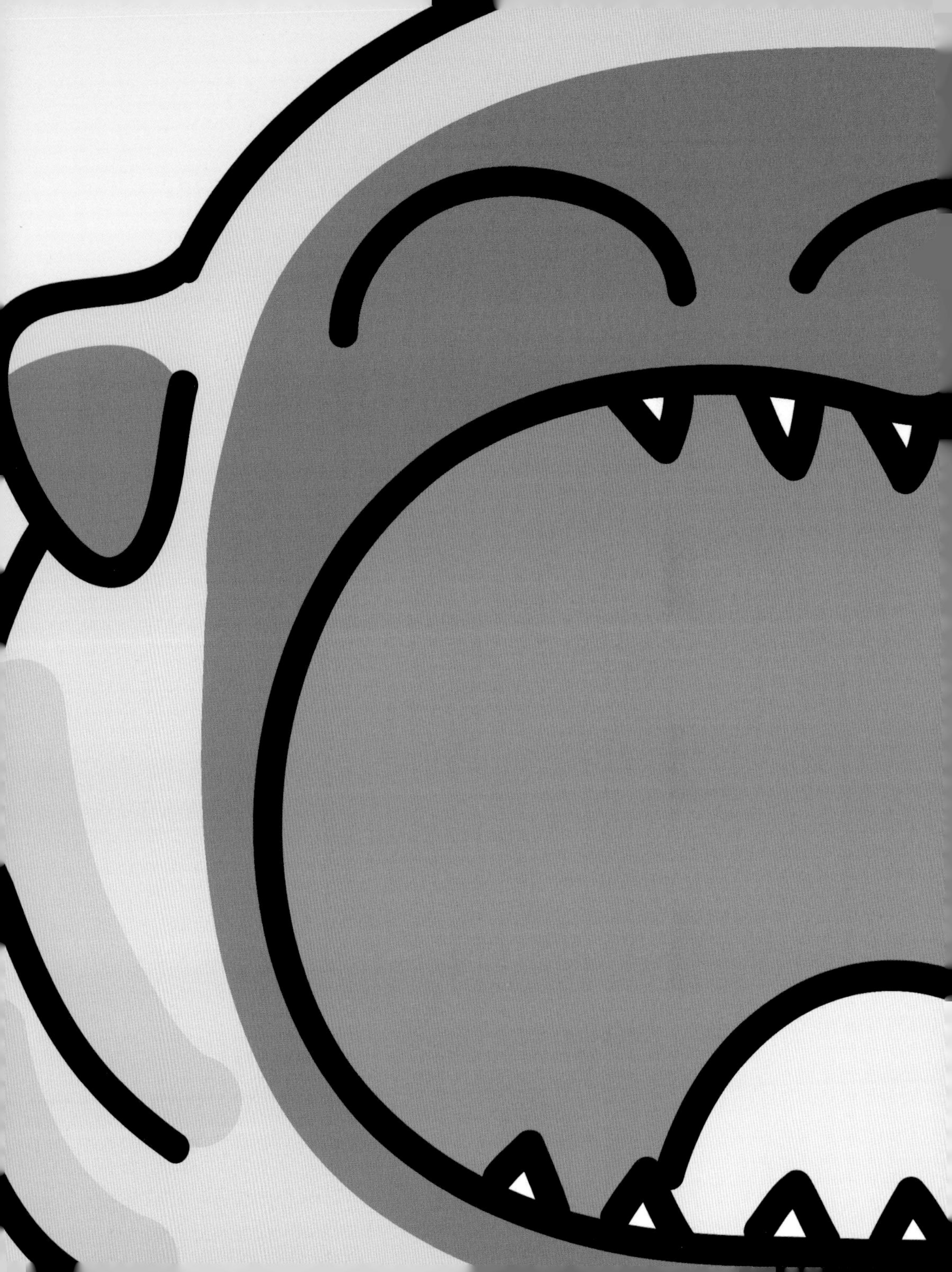

FOOD

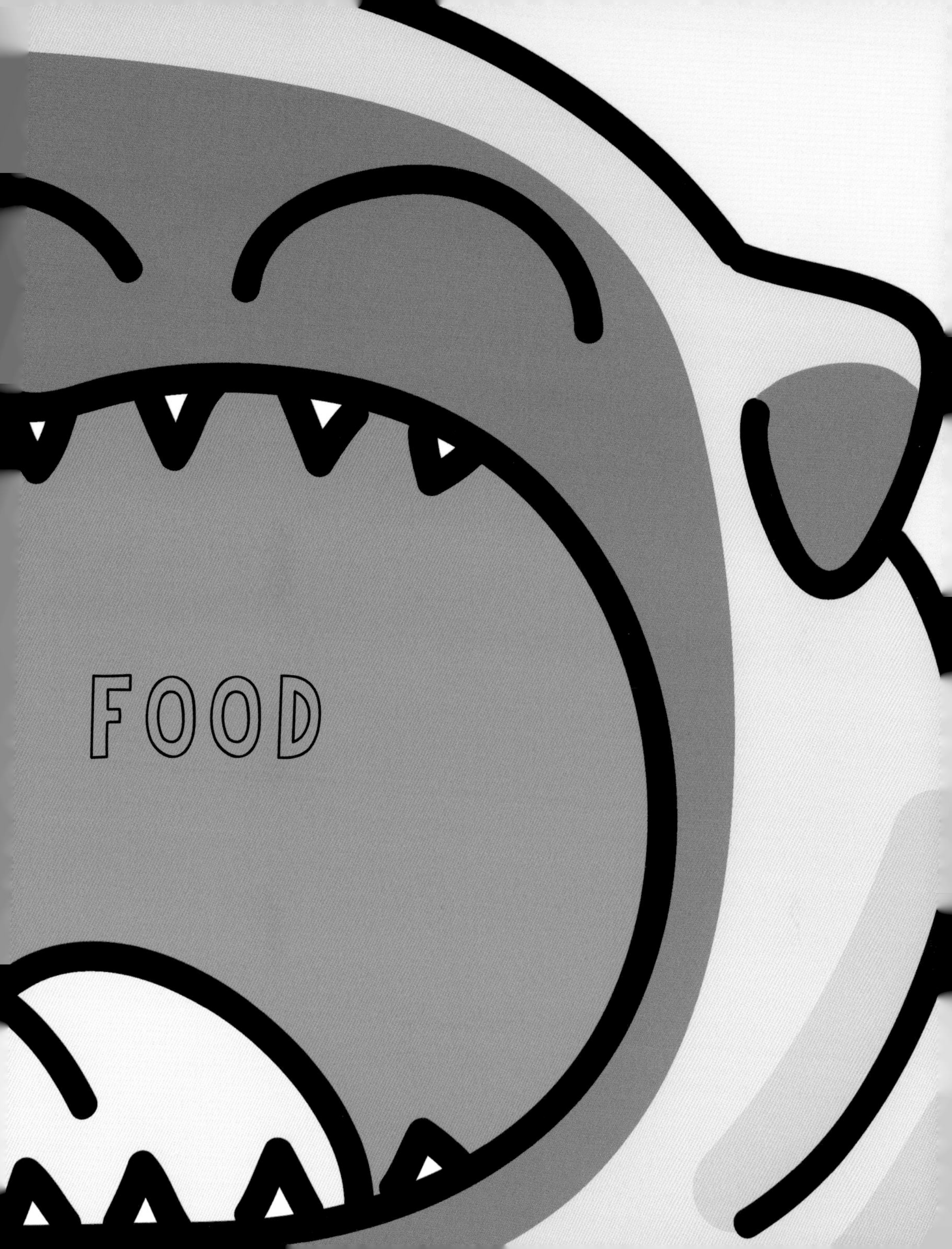

MOCHI'S FAVORITE FOOD

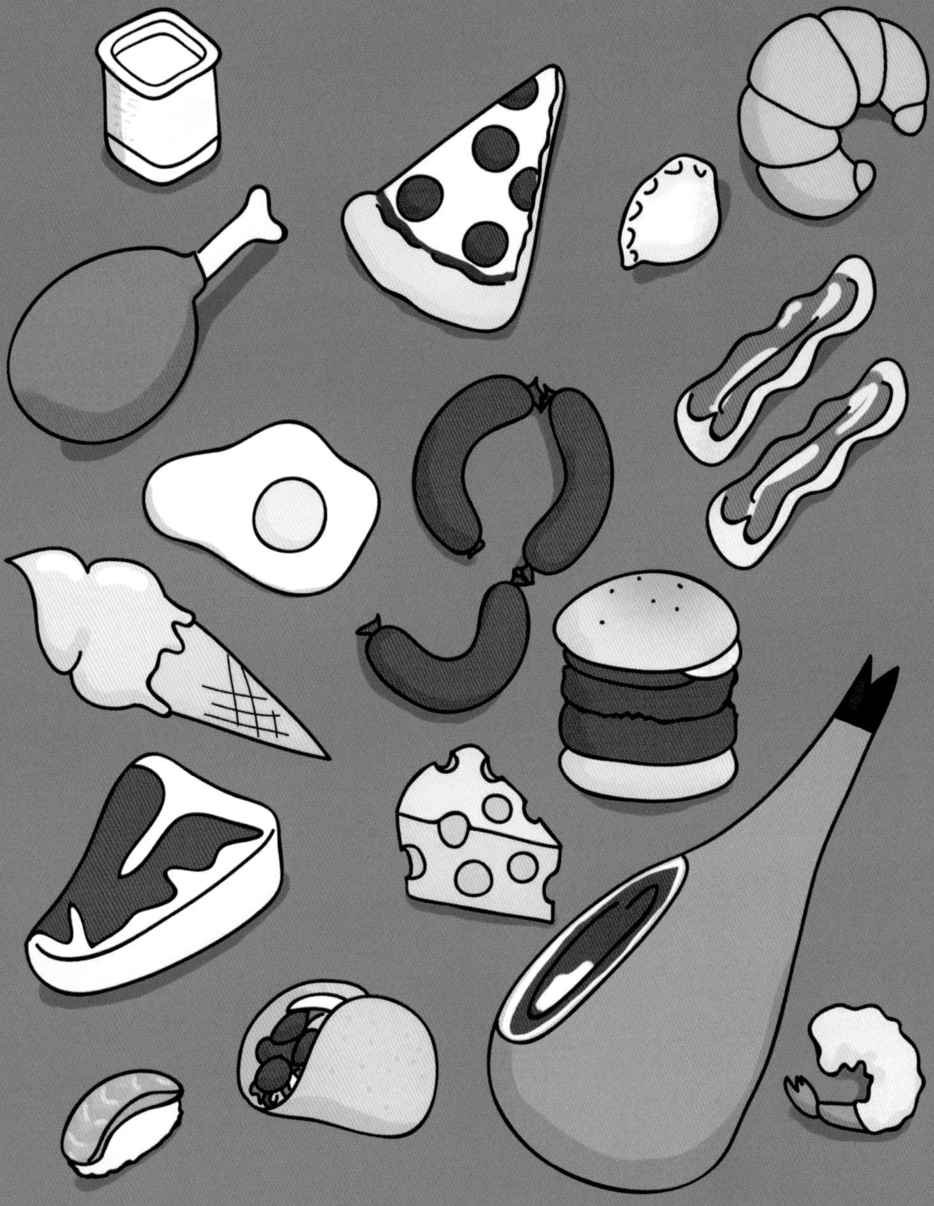

MOCHI'S LEAST FAVORITE FOOD

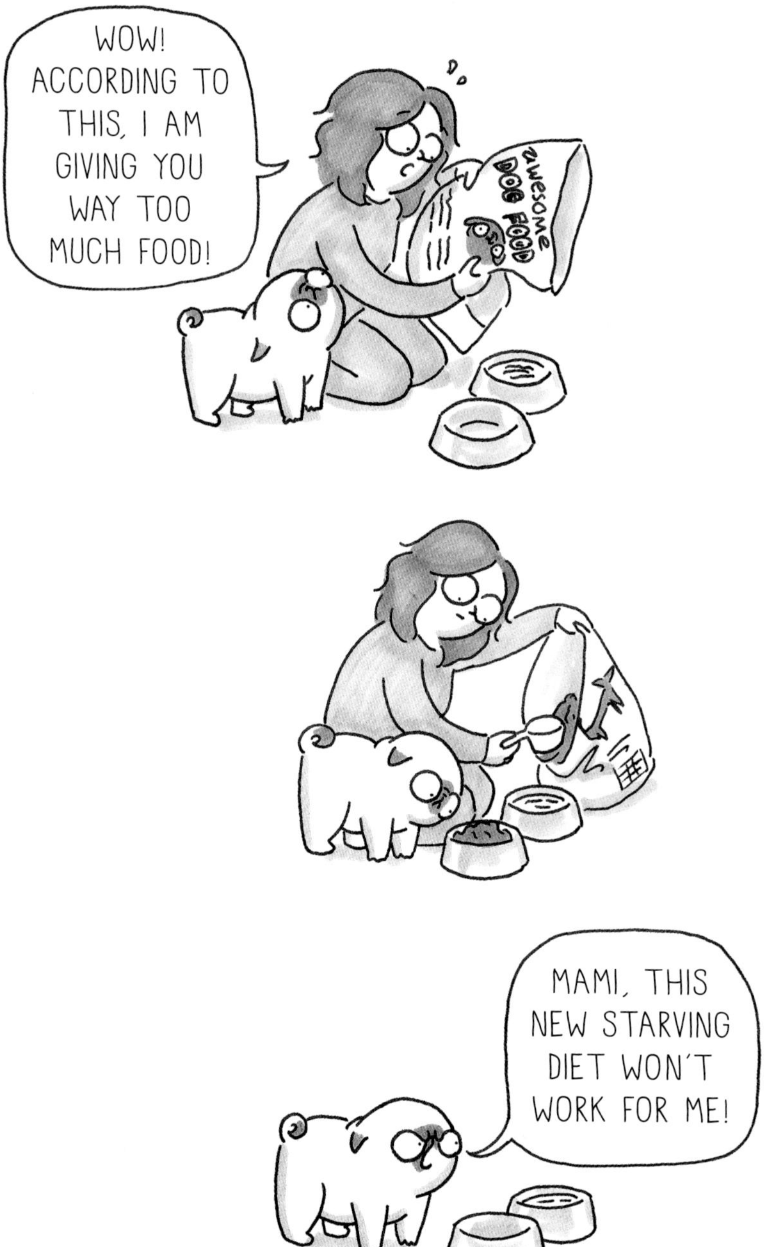
WOW! ACCORDING TO THIS, I AM GIVING YOU WAY TOO MUCH FOOD!
AWESOME DOG FOOD
MAMI, THIS NEW STARVING DIET WON'T WORK FOR ME!

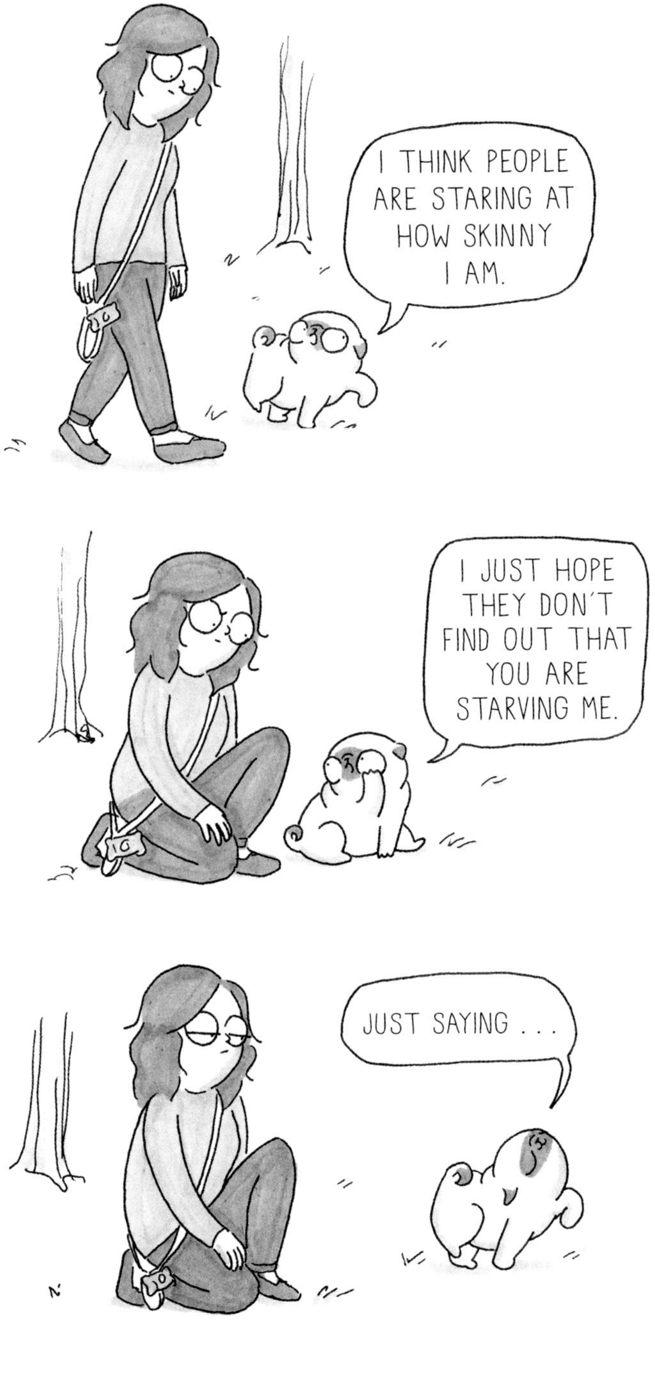
I THINK PEOPLE ARE STARING AT HOW SKINNY I AM.
I JUST HOPE THEY DON'T FIND OUT THAT YOU ARE STARVING ME.
JUST SAYING . . .

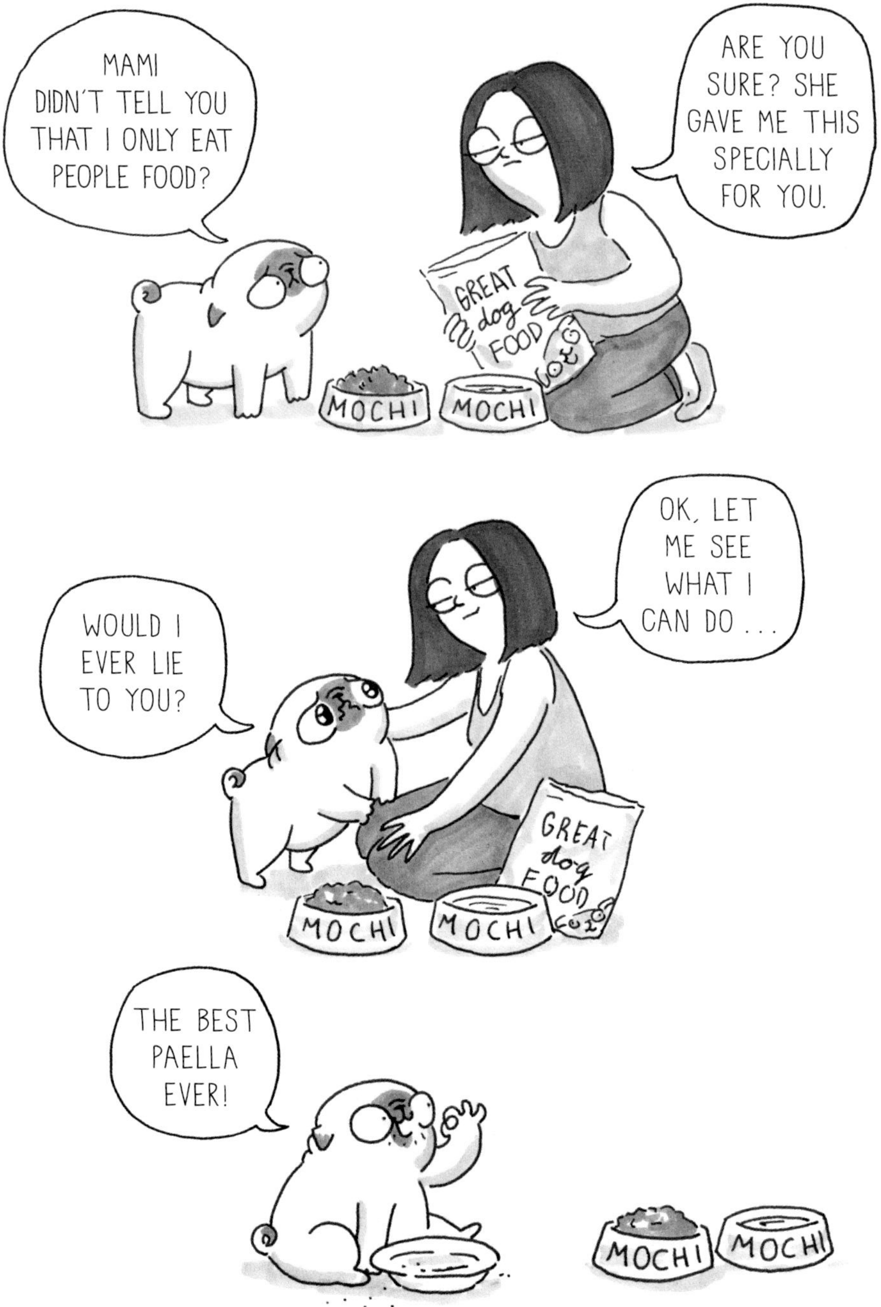
MAMI DIDN'T TELL YOU THAT I ONLY EAT PEOPLE FOOD?
ARE YOU SURE? SHE GAVE ME THIS SPECIALLY FOR YOU.
GREAT dog FOOD
MOCHI
MOCHI
WOULD I EVER LIE TO YOU?
OK, LET ME SEE WHAT I CAN DO . . .
GREAT dog FOOD
MOCHI
MOCHI
THE BEST PAELLA EVER!
MOCHI
MOCHI

MOCHI, DO YOU WANT FOOD?

WHAT'S UP, MOCHI?
YOU ALL WANT MY STICK AND YOU'LL NEVER GET IT!

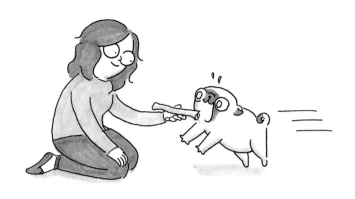

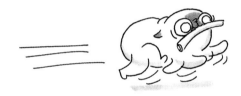

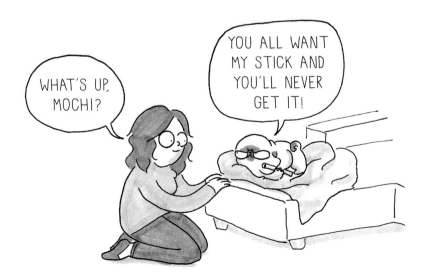

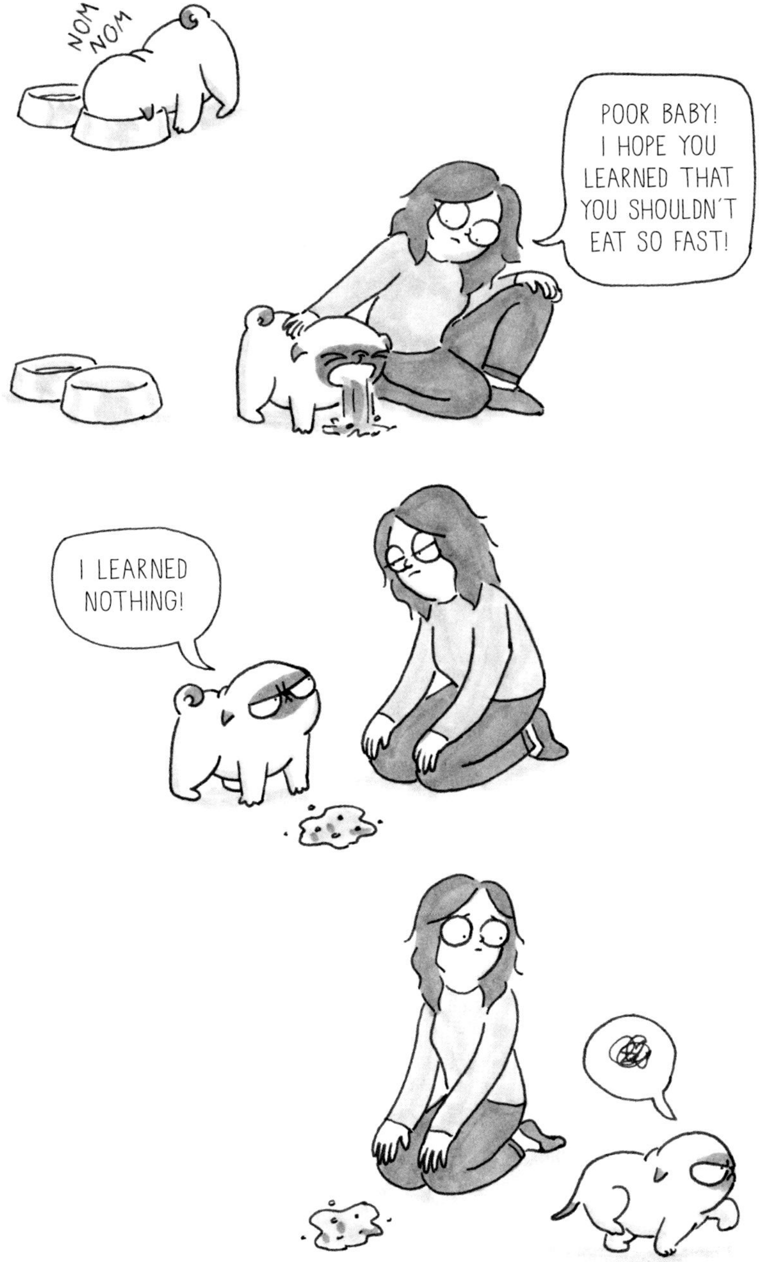
NOM NOM
POOR BABY! I HOPE YOU LEARNED THAT YOU SHOULDN'T EAT SO FAST!
I LEARNED NOTHING!

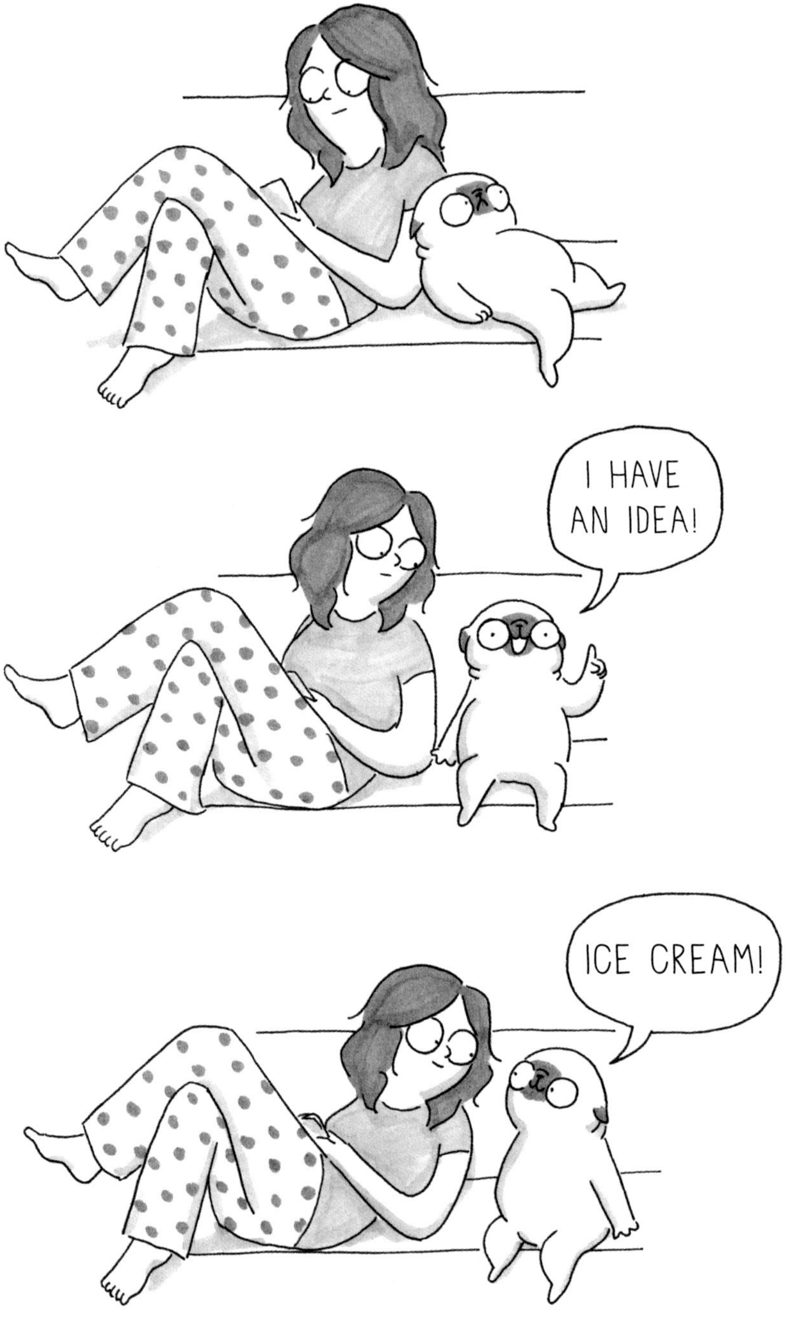
I HAVE AN IDEA!
ICE CREAM!

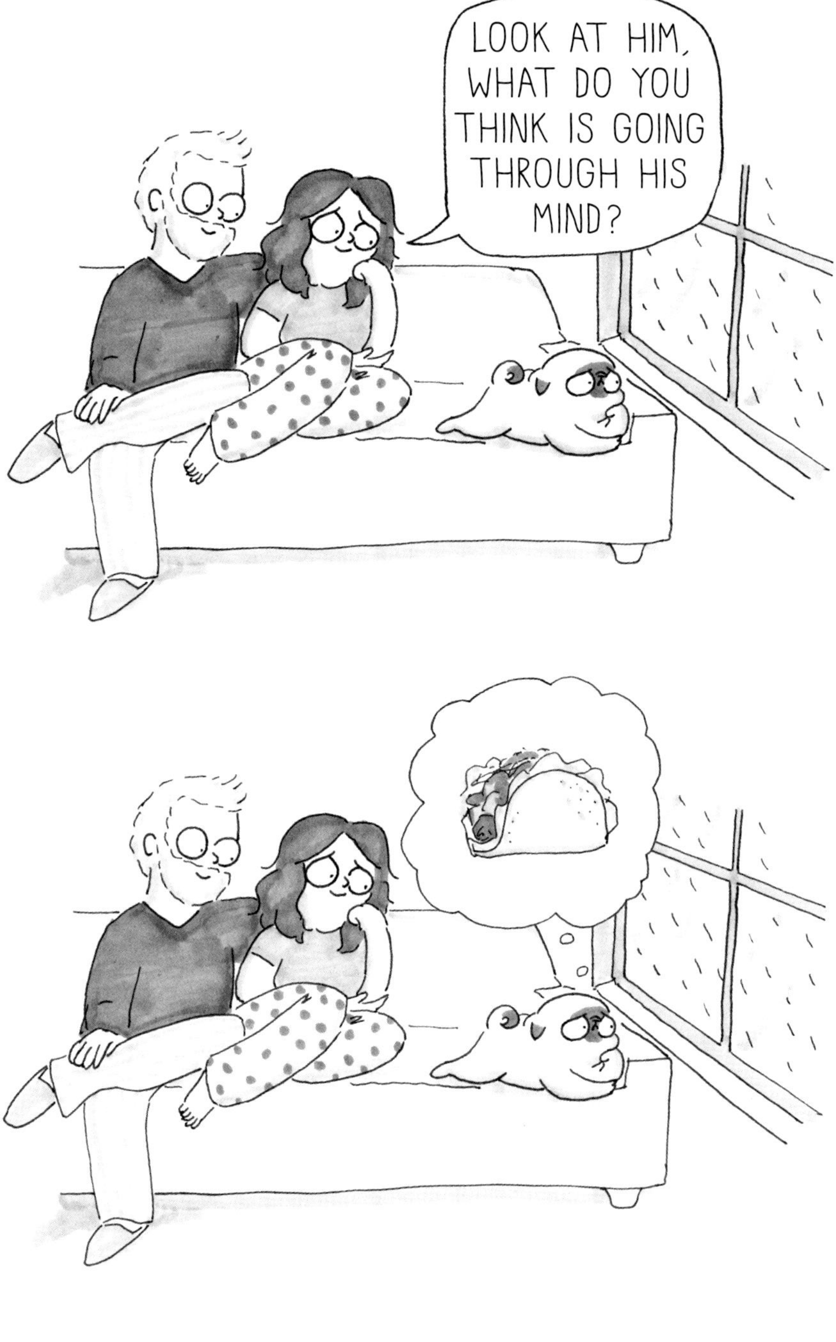
LOOK AT HIM, WHAT DO YOU THINK IS GOING THROUGH HIS MIND?

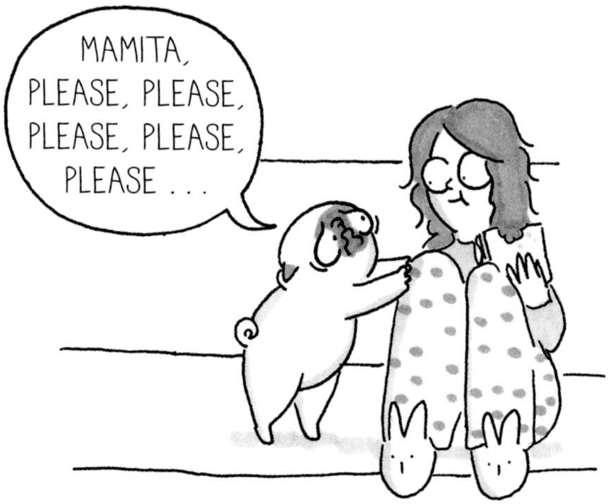
MAMITA, PLEASE, PLEASE, PLEASE, PLEASE, PLEASE . . .

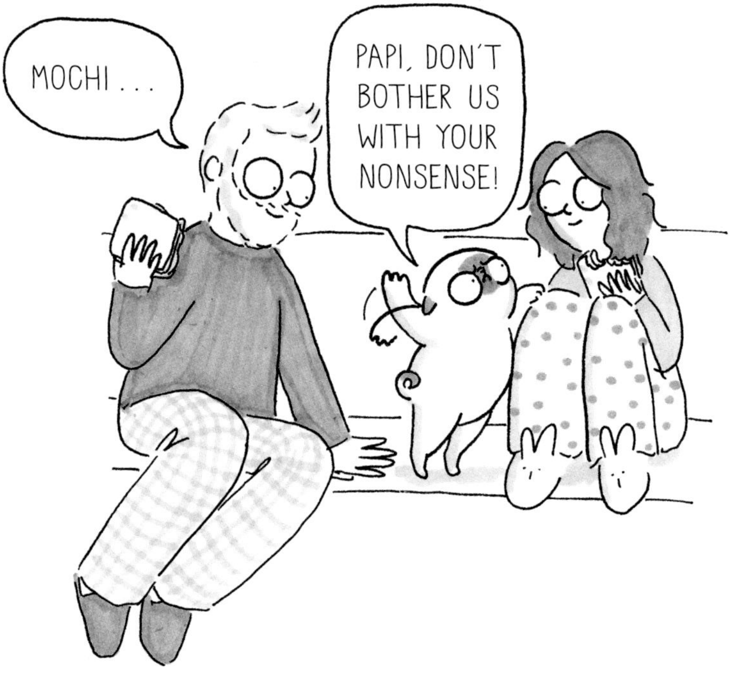
MOCHI . . .
PAPI, DON'T BOTHER US WITH YOUR NONSENSE!

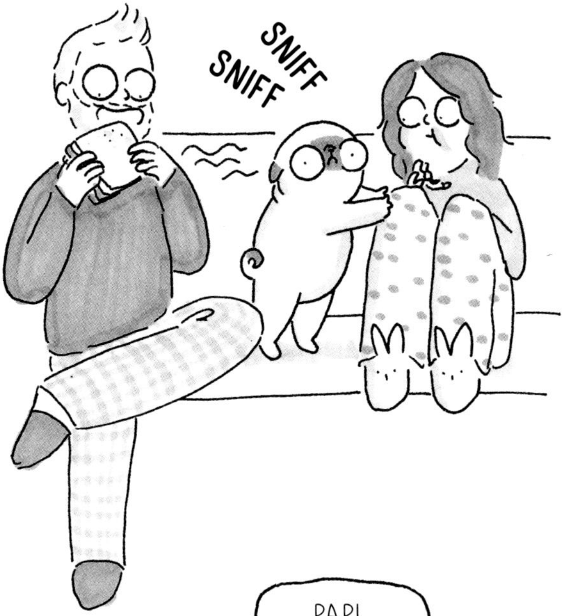
SNIFF
SNIFF

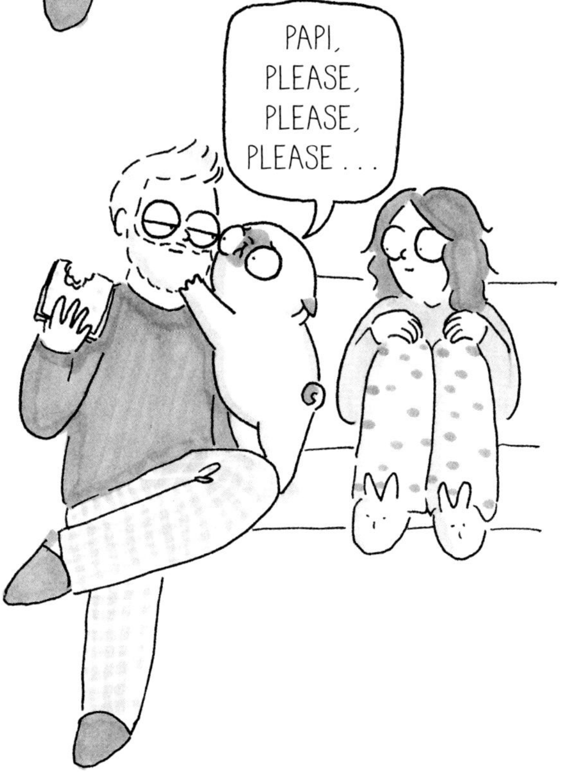
PAPI, PLEASE, PLEASE, PLEASE . . .

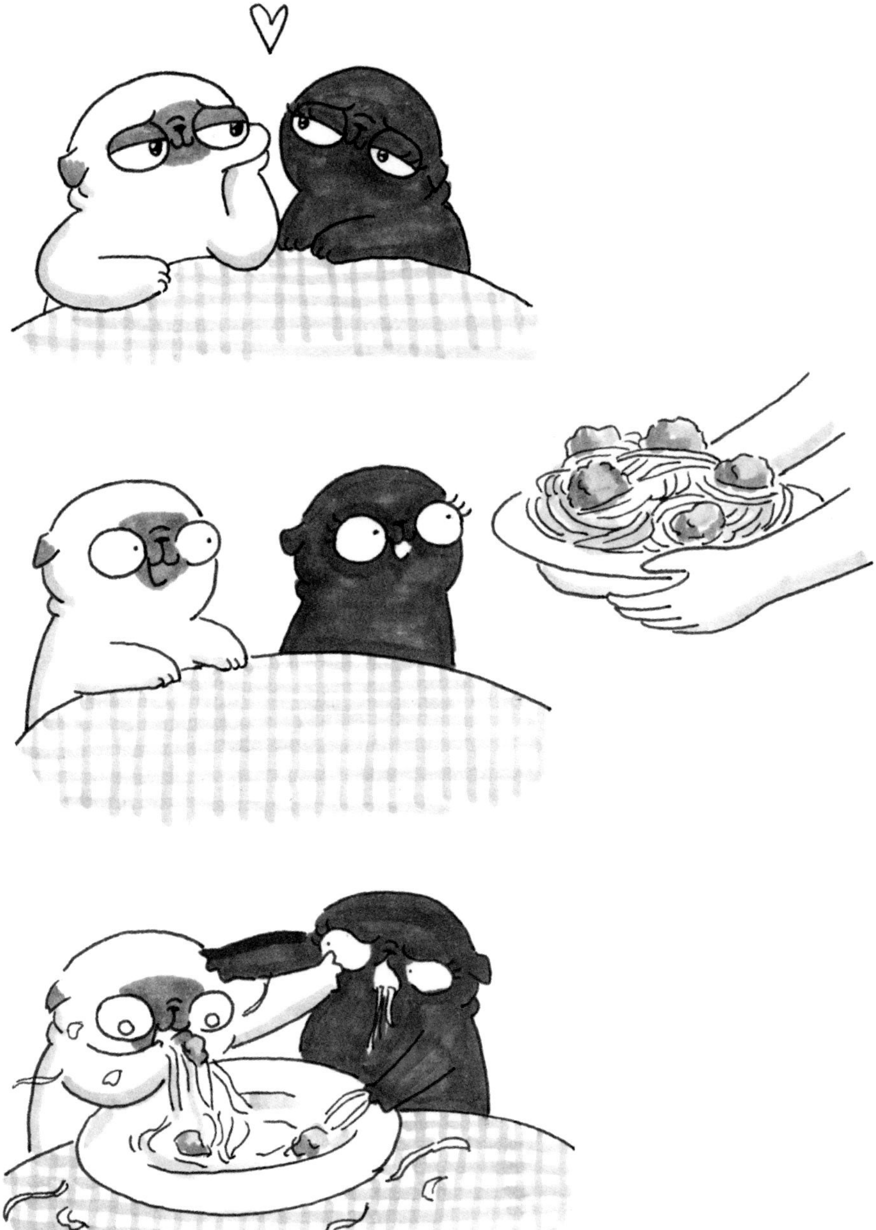

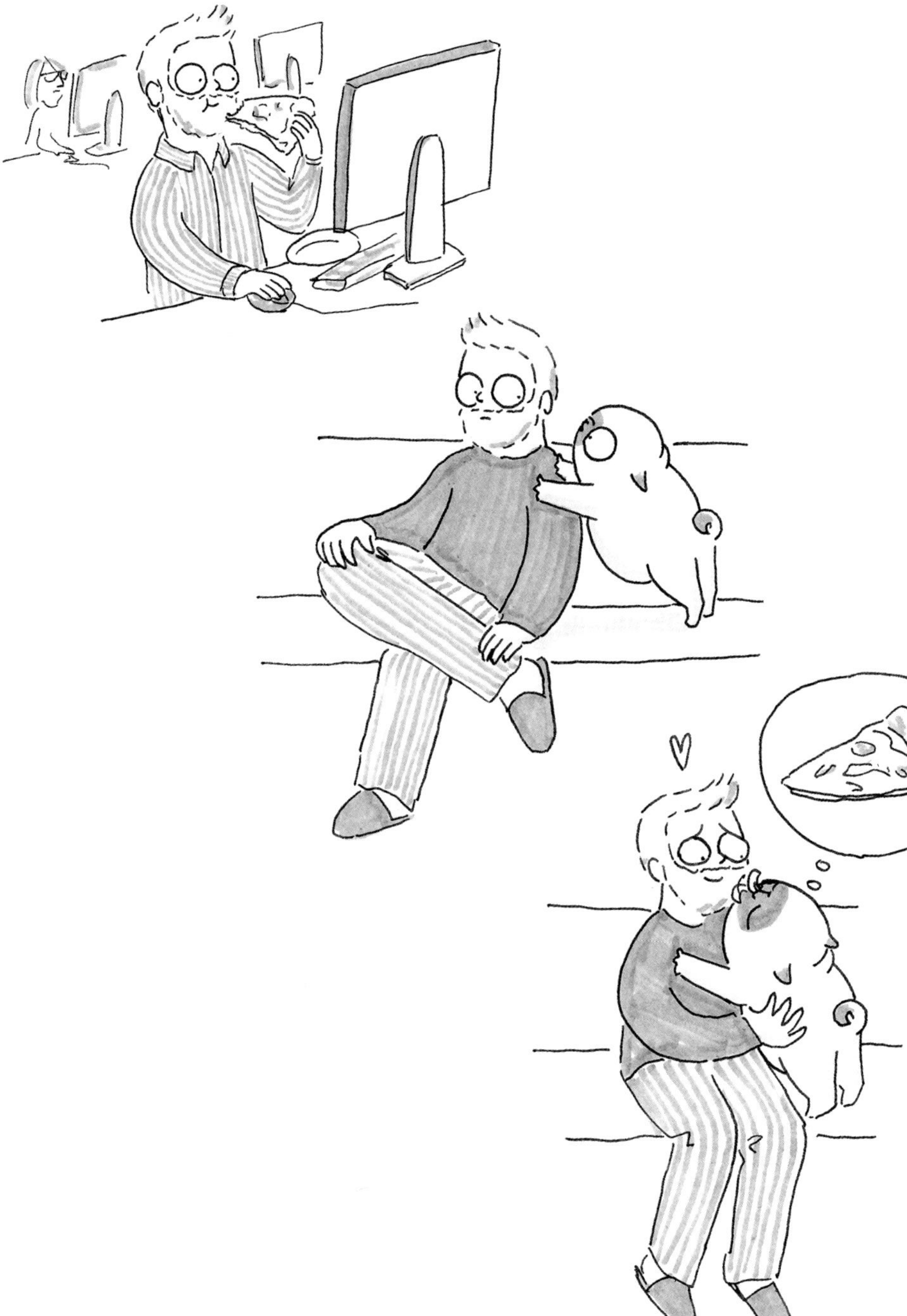

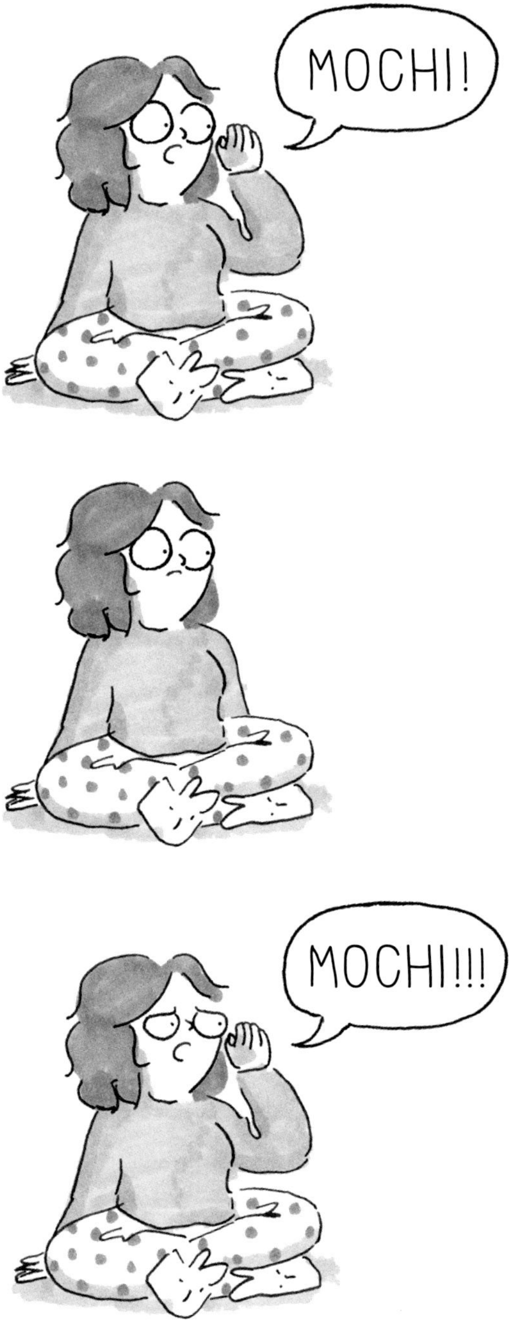
MOCHI!
MOCHI!!!

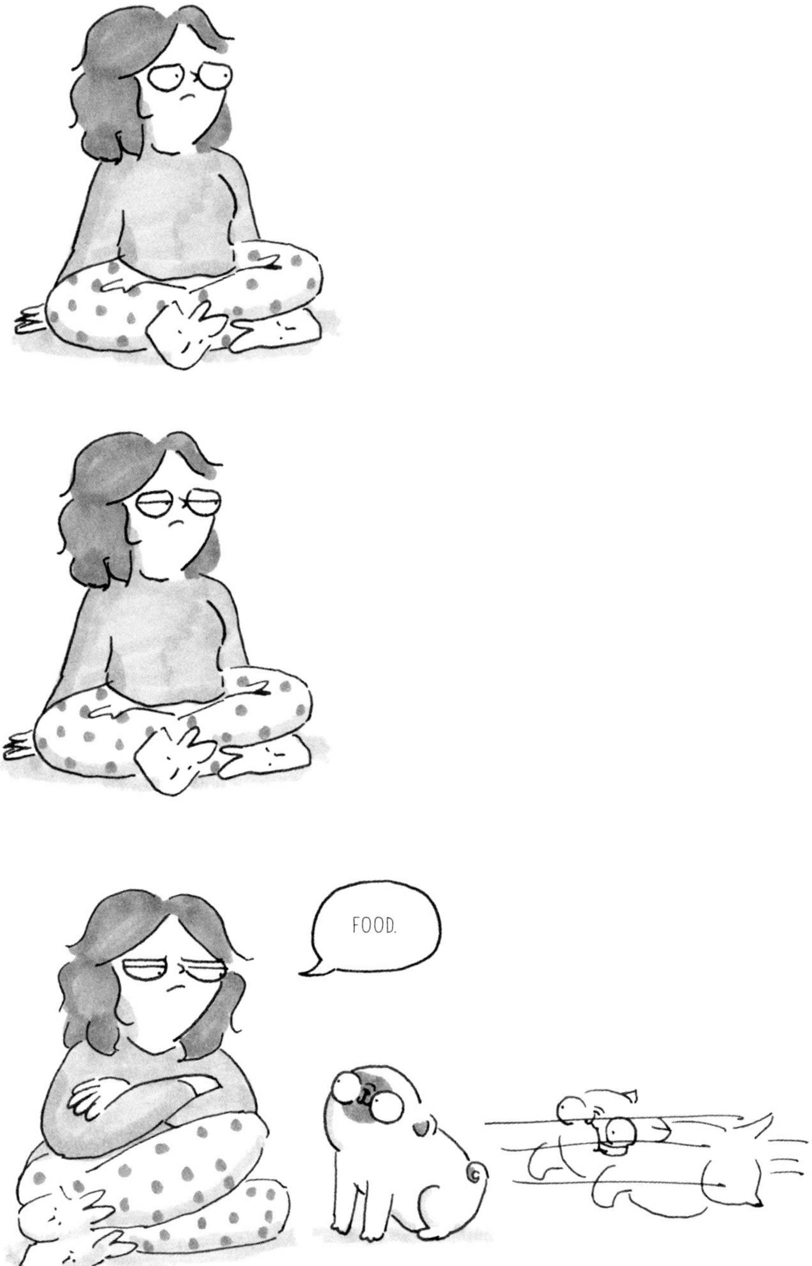
FOOD.

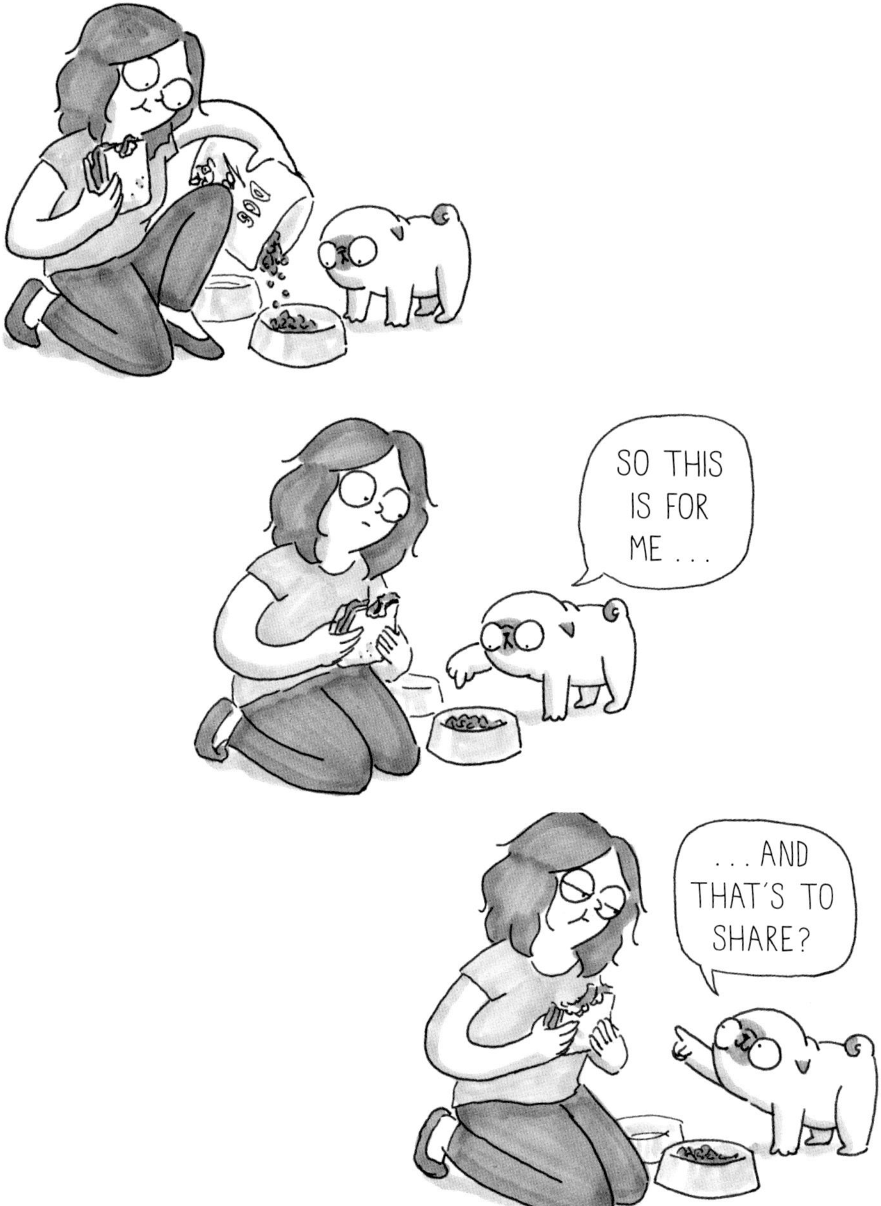
SO THIS IS FOR ME . . .
. . . AND THAT'S TO SHARE?

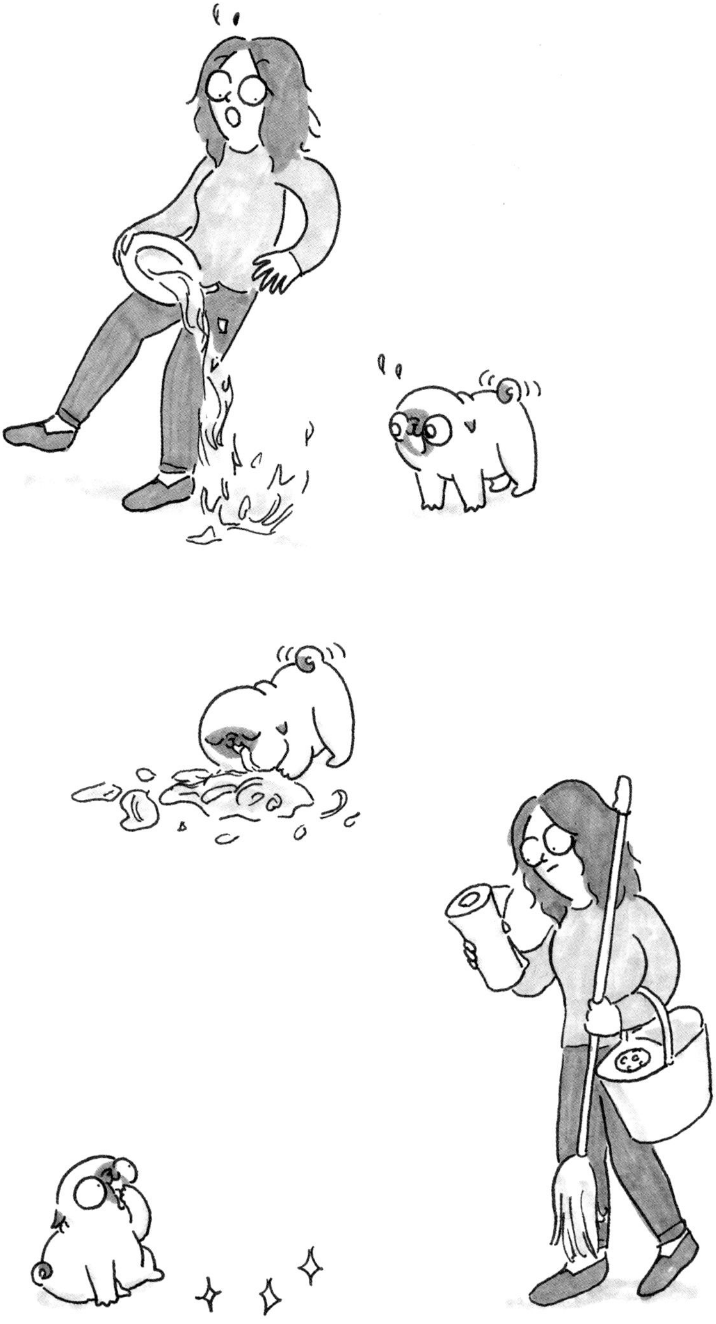

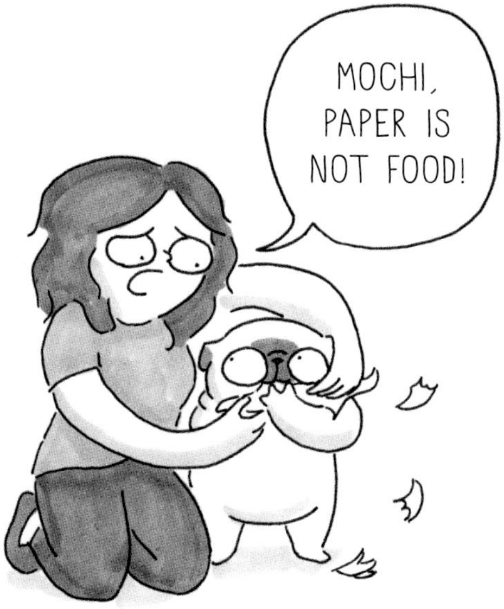
MOCHI, PAPER IS NOT FOOD!

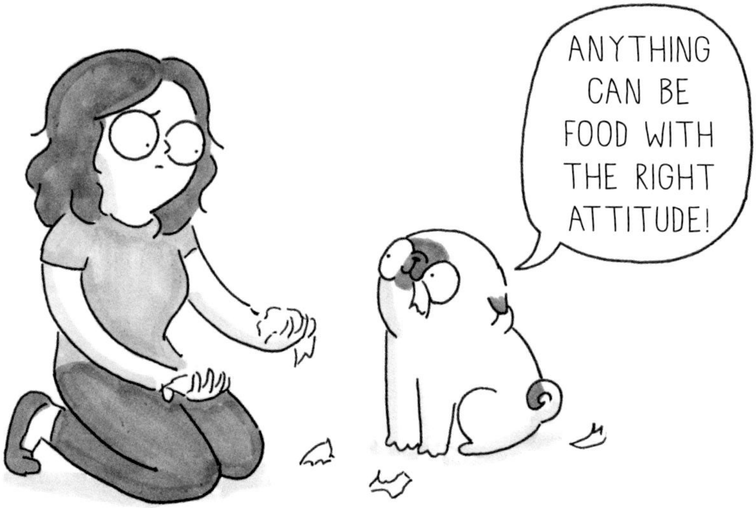
ANYTHING CAN BE FOOD WITH THE RIGHT ATTITUDE!

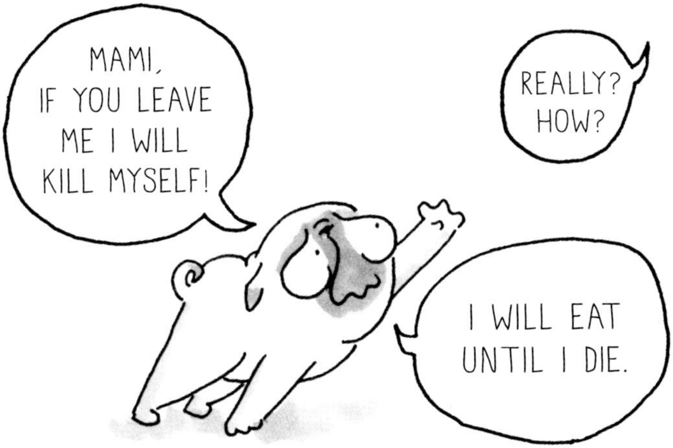
MAMI, IF YOU LEAVE ME I WILL KILL MYSELF!
REALLY? HOW?
I WILL EAT UNTIL I DIE.

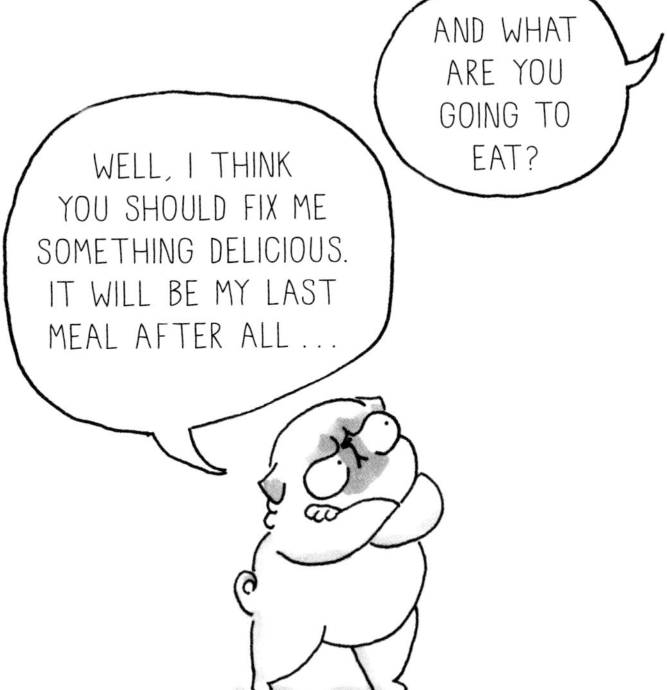
AND WHAT ARE YOU GOING TO EAT?
WELL, I THINK YOU SHOULD FIX ME SOMETHING DELICIOUS. IT WILL BE MY LAST MEAL AFTER ALL . . .

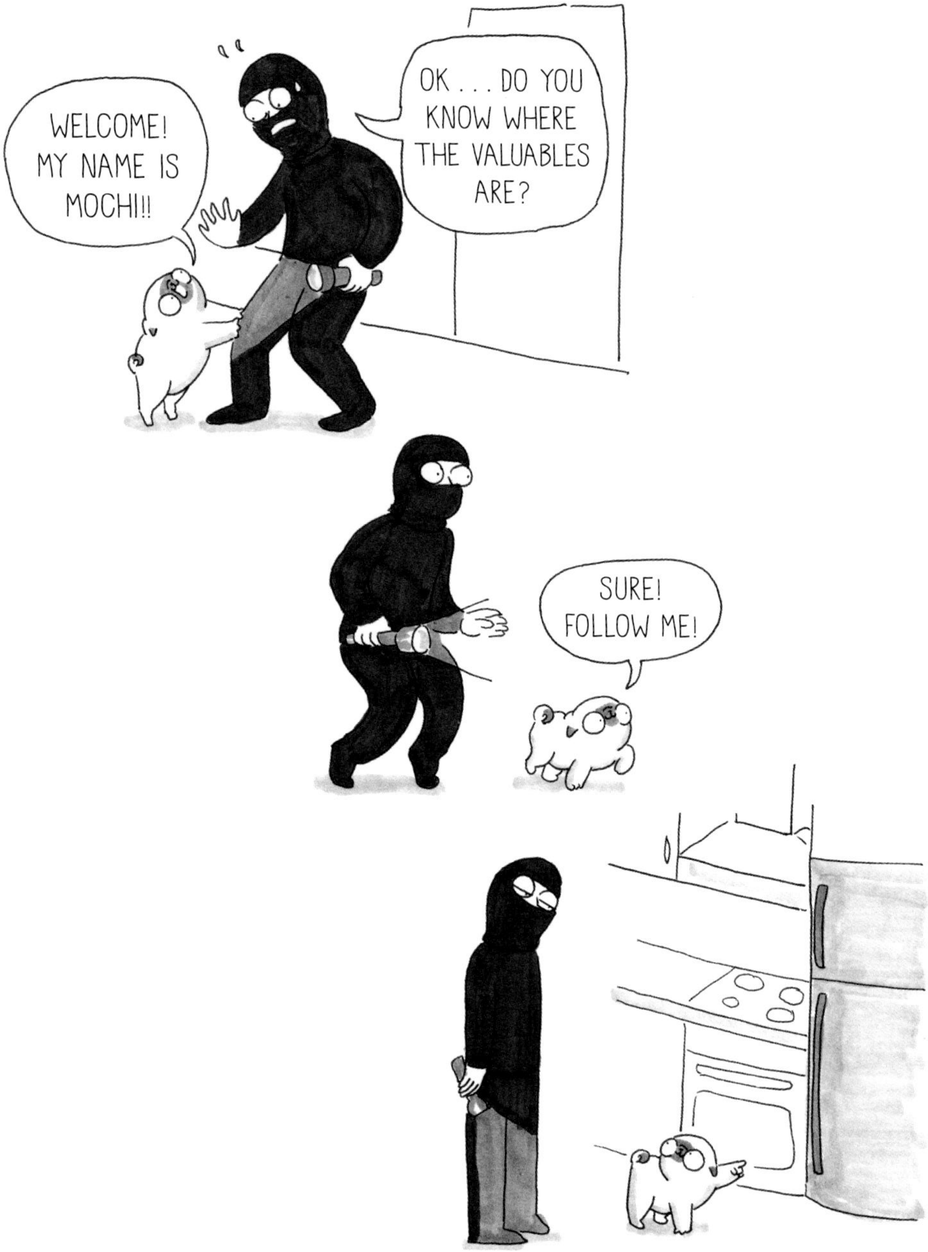
WELCOME! MY NAME IS MOCHI!!
OK . . . DO YOU KNOW WHERE THE VALUABLES ARE?
SURE! FOLLOW ME!

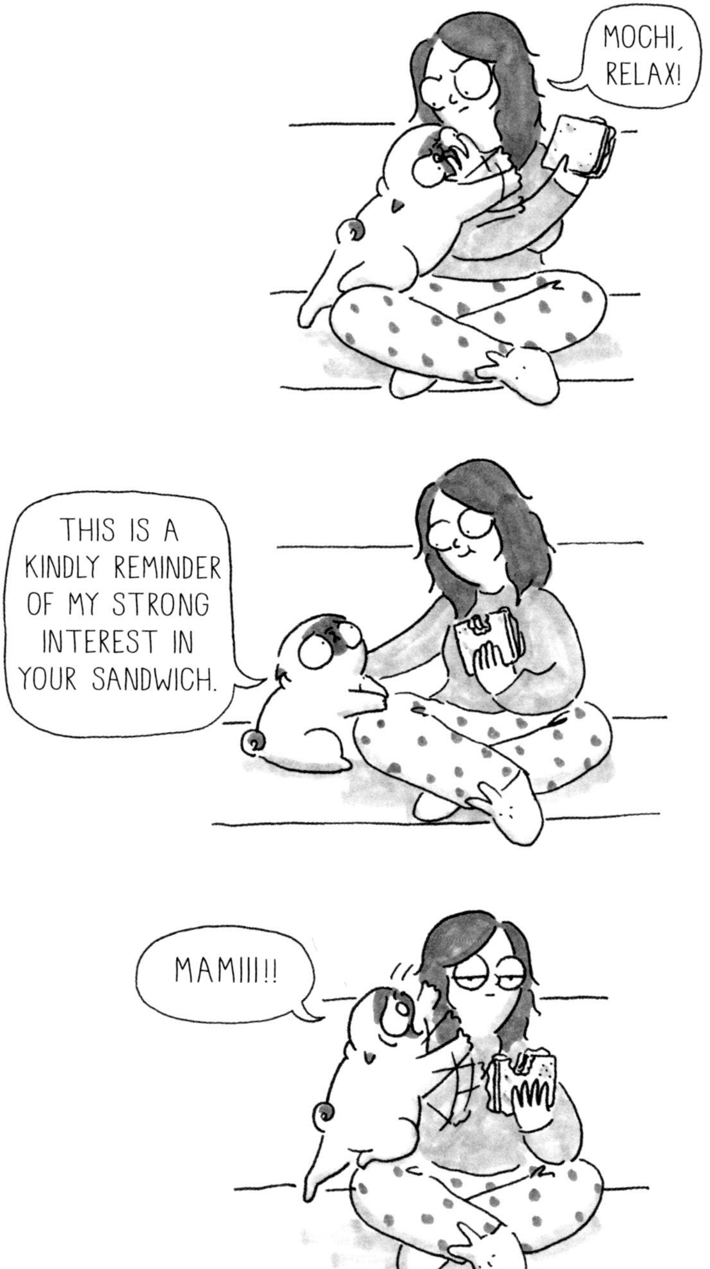
MOCHI, RELAX!
THIS IS A KINDLY REMINDER OF MY STRONG INTEREST IN YOUR SANDWICH.
MAMIII!!

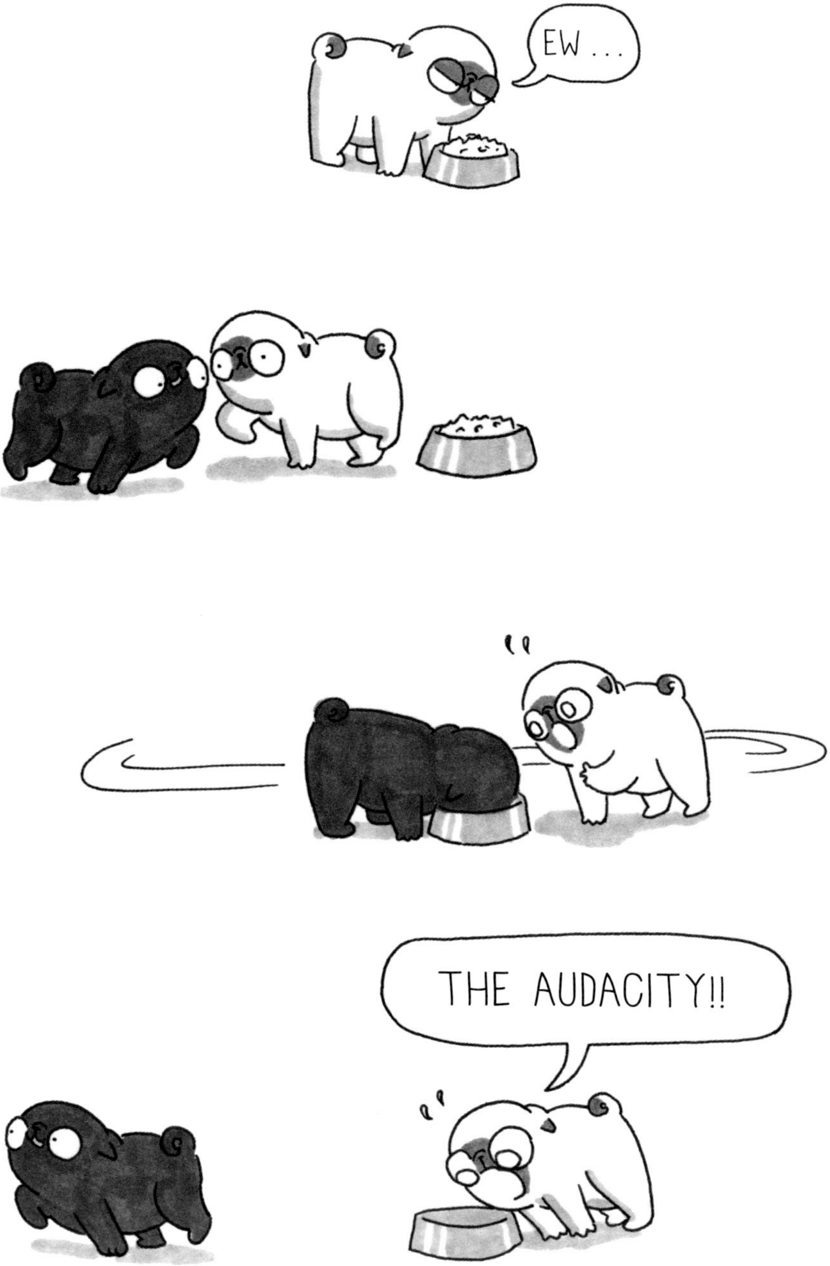
EW...
THE AUDACITY!!

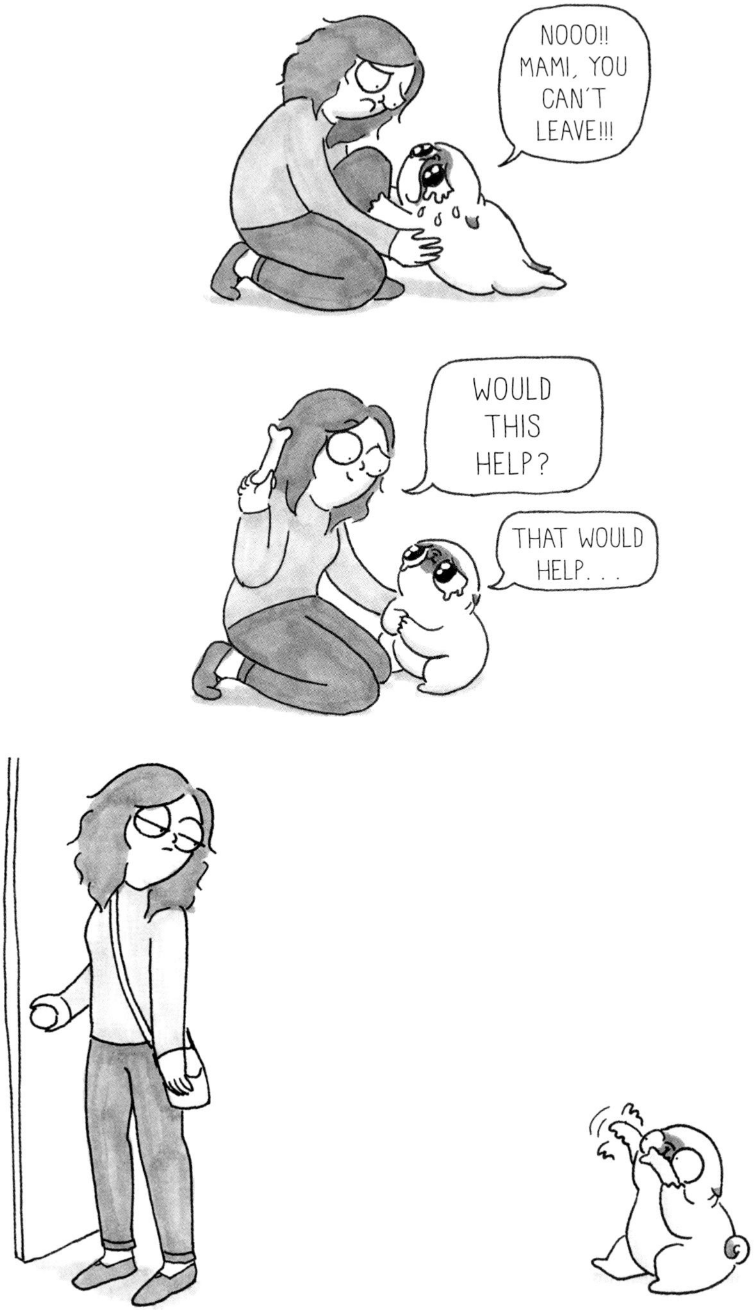
NOOO!! MAMI, YOU CAN´T LEAVE!!!
WOULD THIS HELP?
THAT WOULD HELP. . .

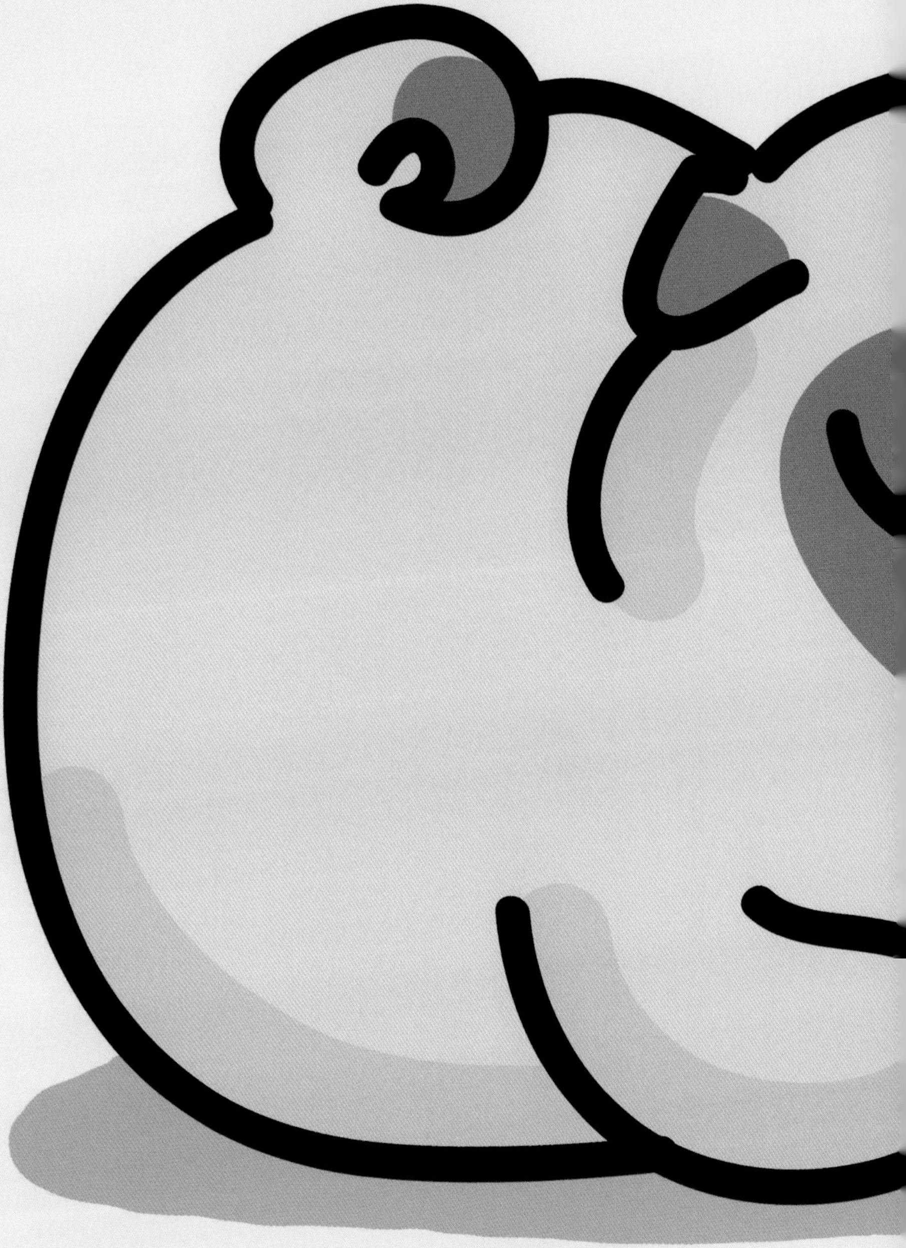

SLEEP

MOCHI'S FAVORITE PLACES TO SLEEP

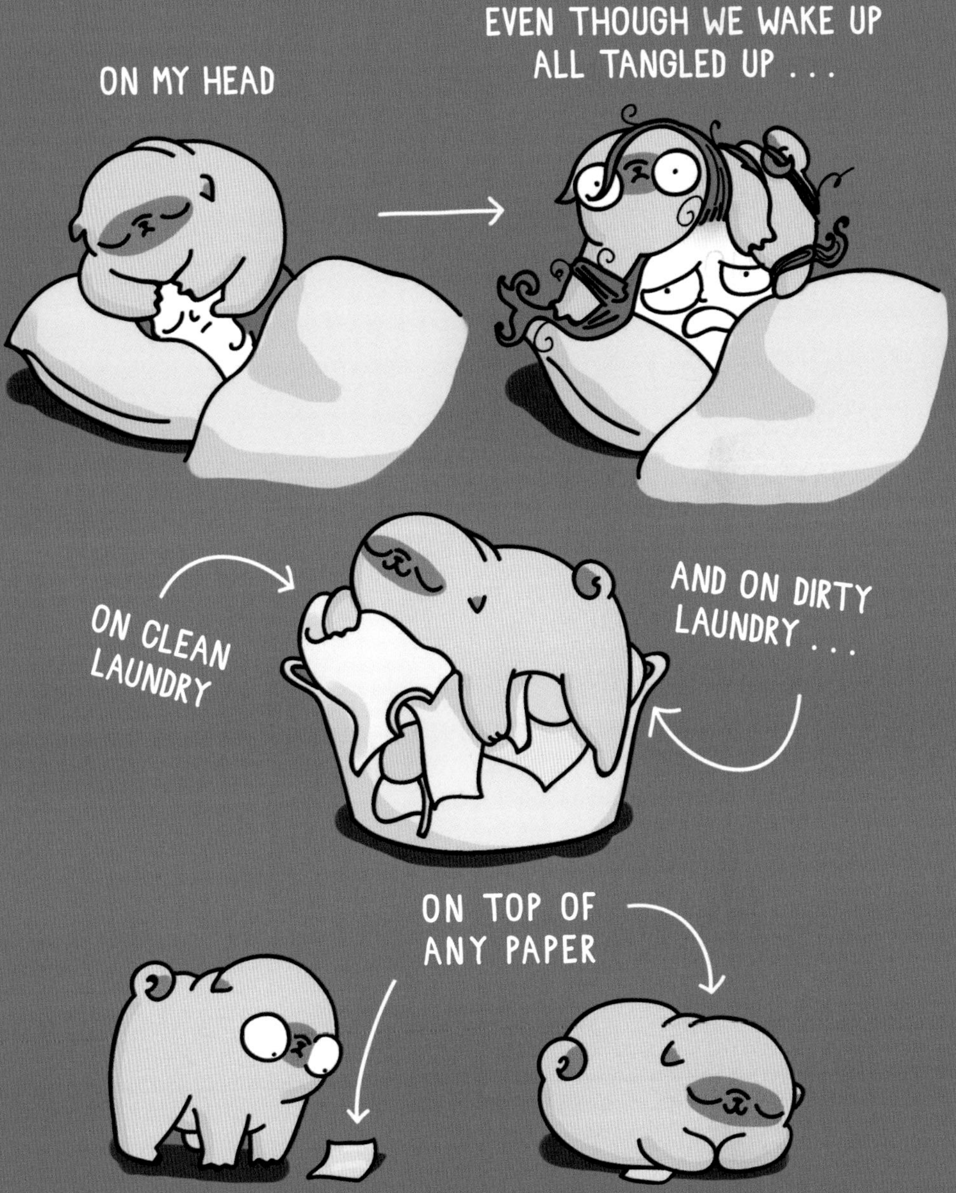

ON MY HEAD
EVEN THOUGH WE WAKE UP ALL TANGLED UP . . .
ON CLEAN LAUNDRY
AND ON DIRTY LAUNDRY . . .
ON TOP OF ANY PAPER

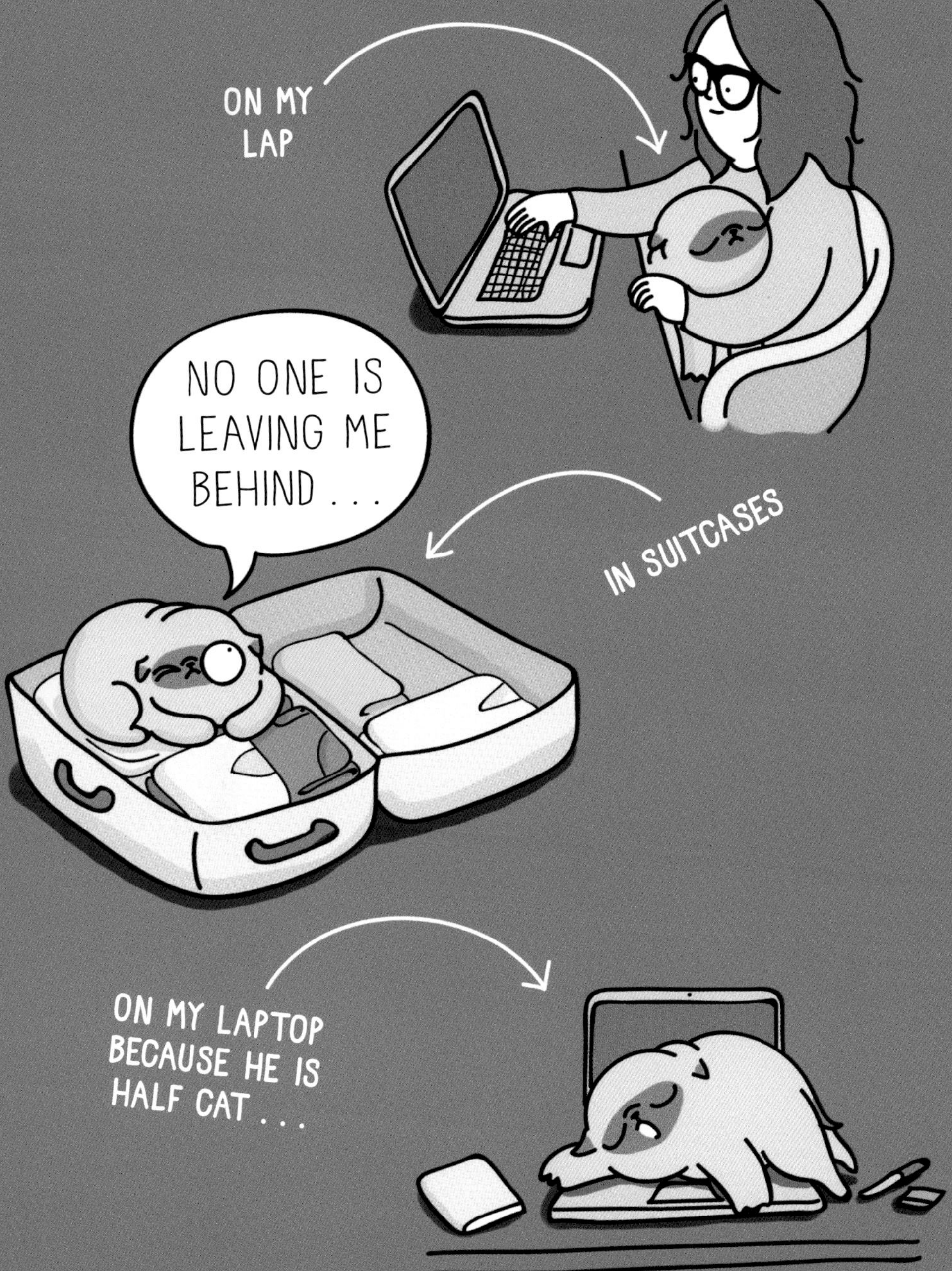
ON MY LAP
NO ONE IS LEAVING ME BEHIND . . .
IN SUITCASES
ON MY LAPTOP BECAUSE HE IS HALF CAT . . .

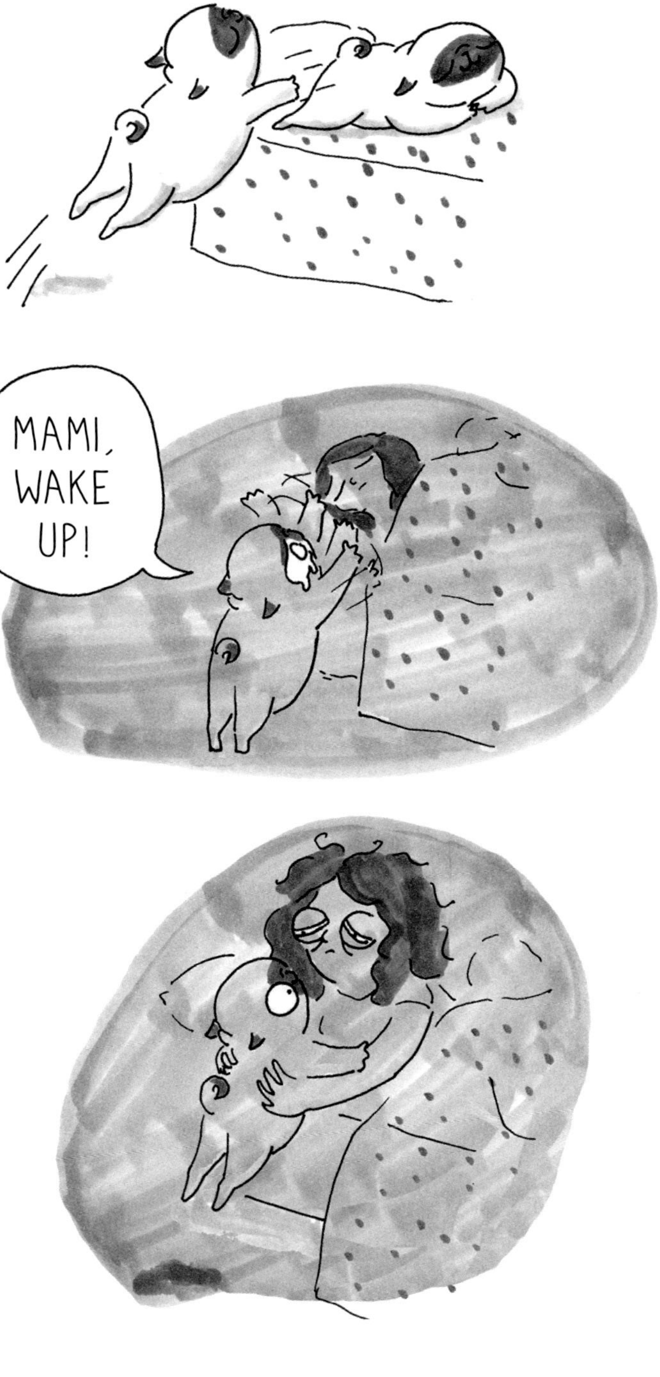
MAMI, WAKE UP!

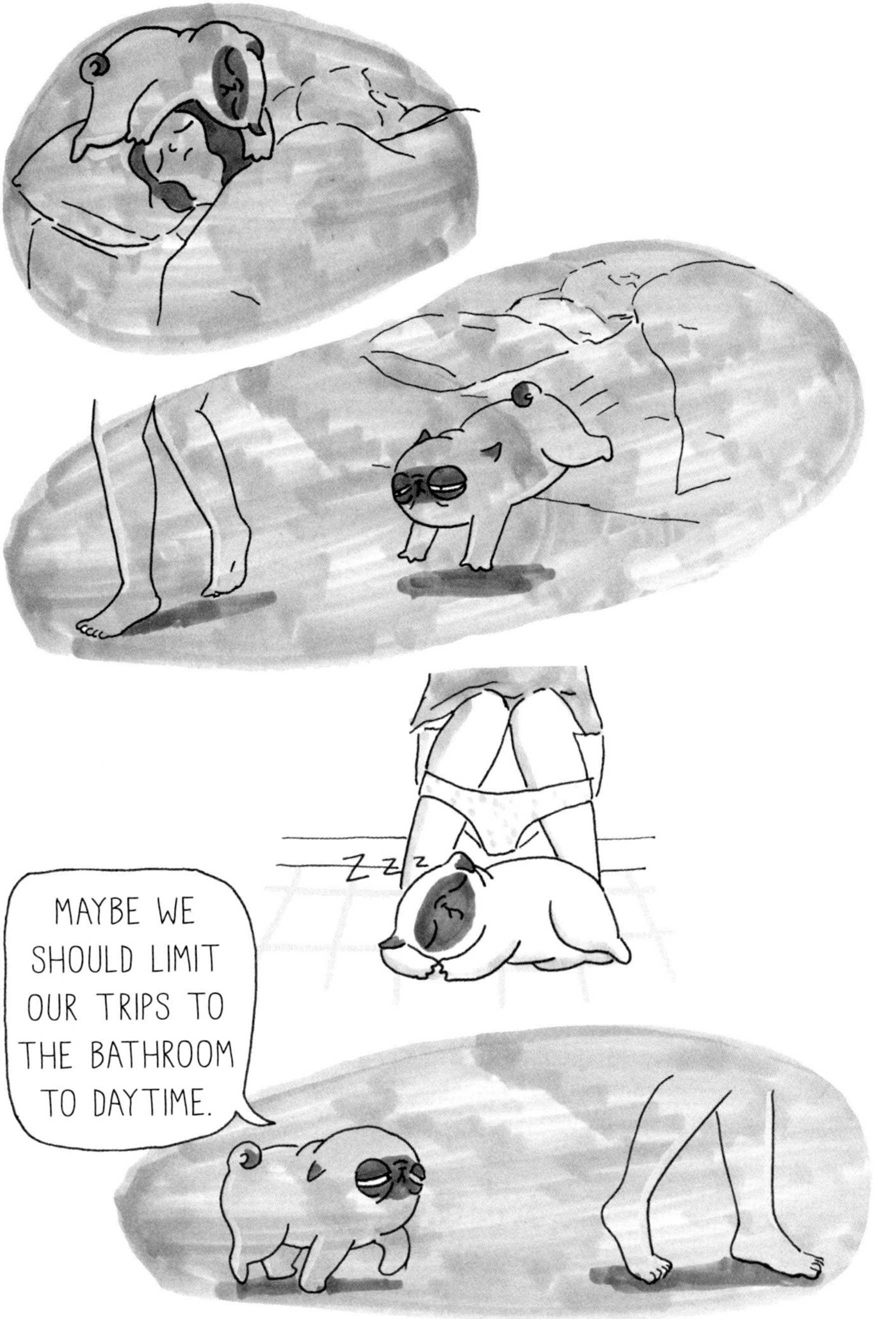
ZZZ
MAYBE WE SHOULD LIMIT OUR TRIPS TO THE BATHROOM TO DAYTIME.

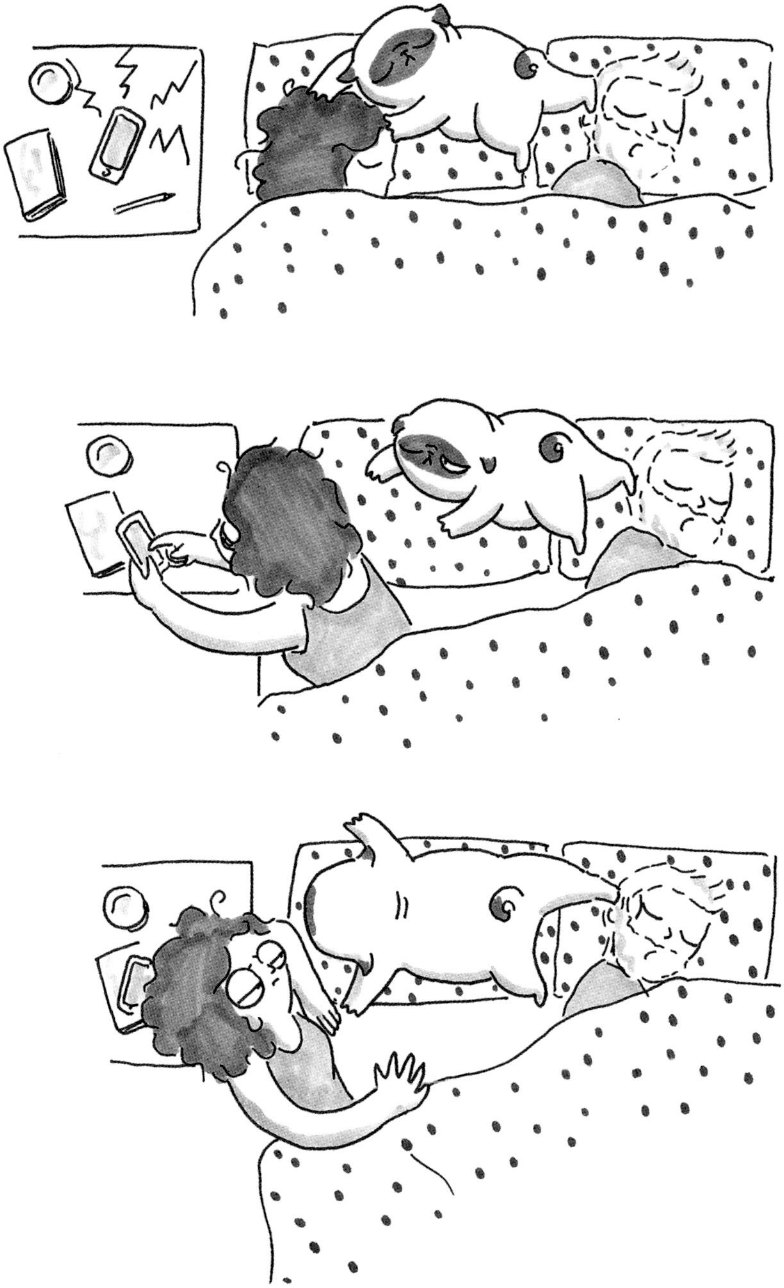

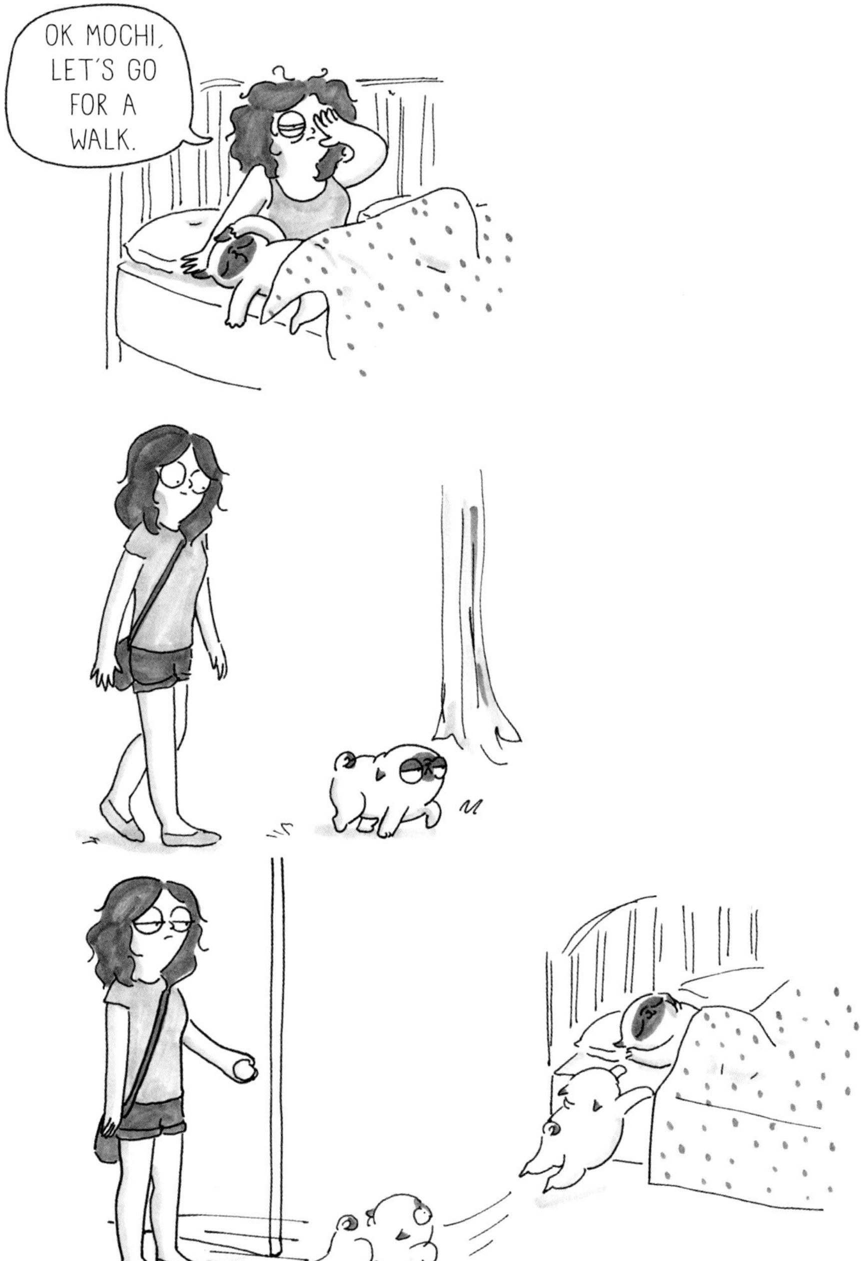
OK MOCHI, LET'S GO FOR A WALK.

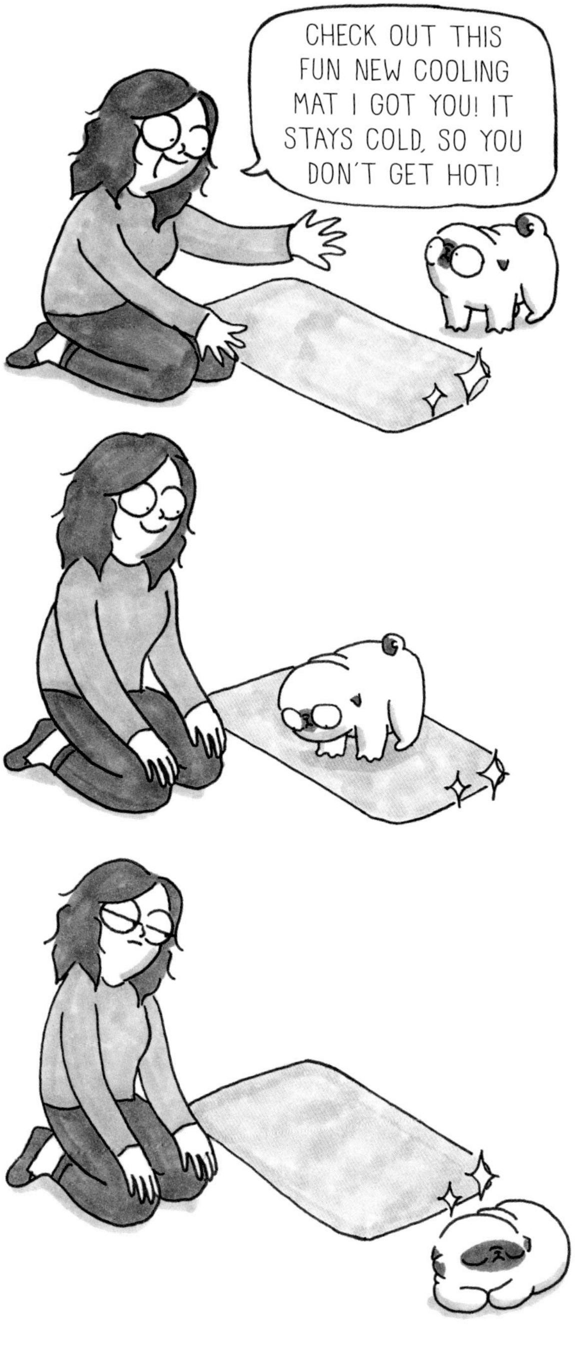
CHECK OUT THIS FUN NEW COOLING MAT I GOT YOU! IT STAYS COLD, SO YOU DON'T GET HOT!

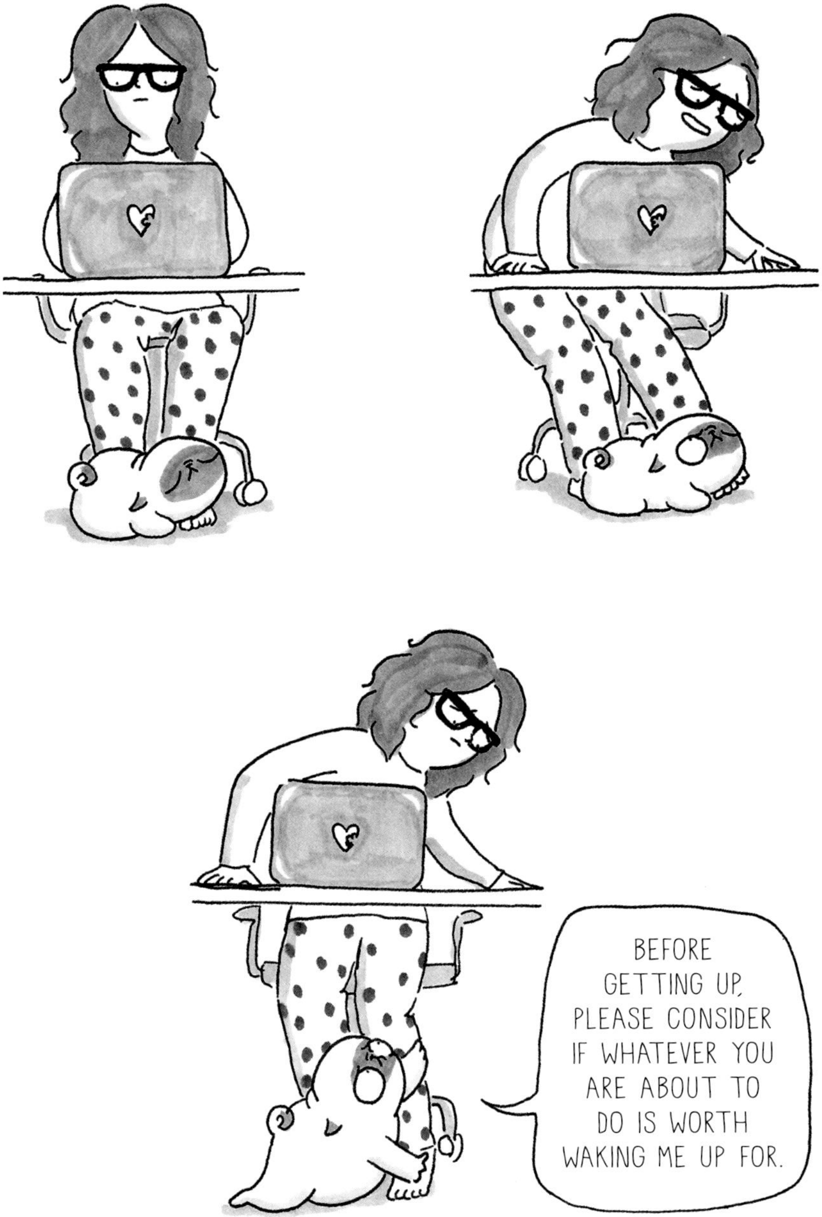
BEFORE GETTING UP, PLEASE CONSIDER IF WHATEVER YOU ARE ABOUT TO DO IS WORTH WAKING ME UP FOR.

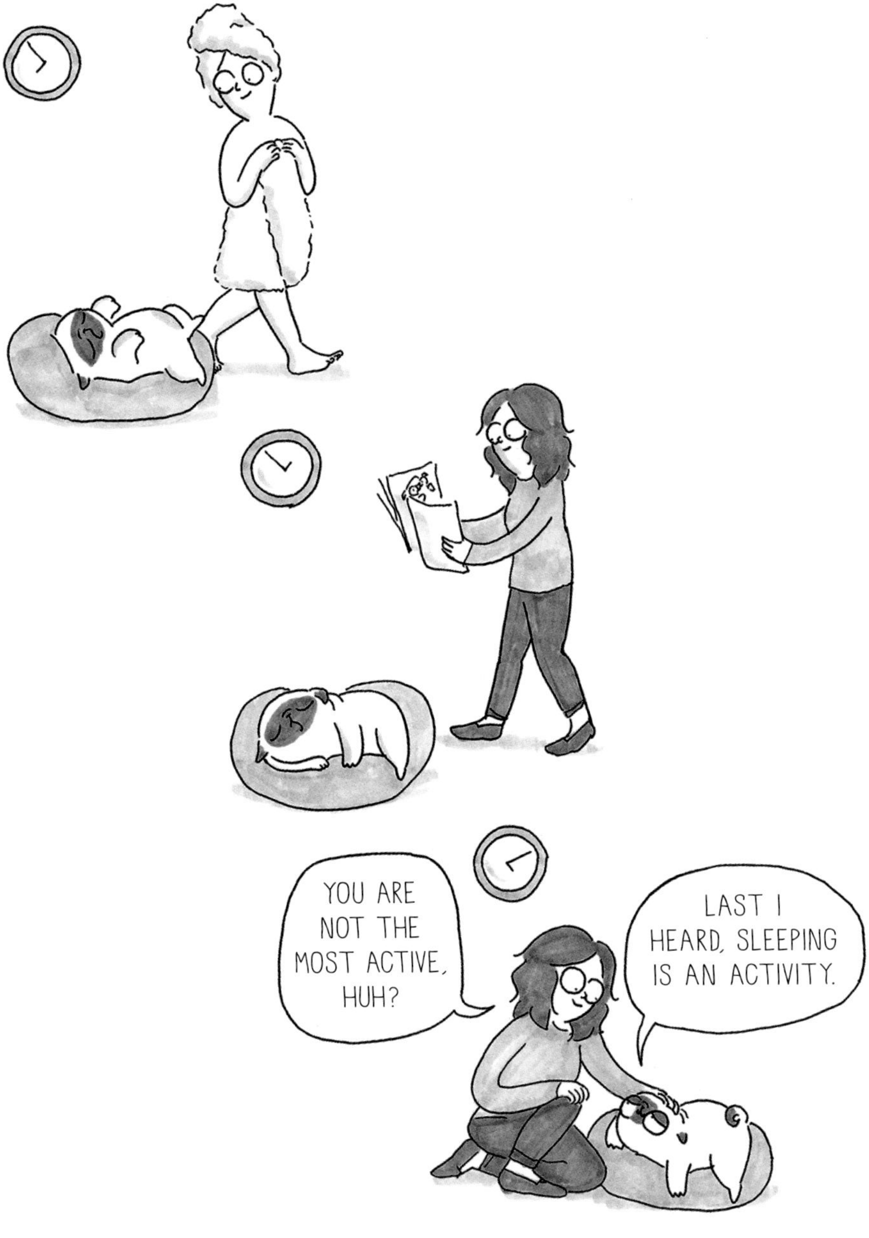
YOU ARE NOT THE MOST ACTIVE, HUH?
LAST I HEARD, SLEEPING IS AN ACTIVITY.

MOCHI!
ZZZ
ZZZ
ZZZ

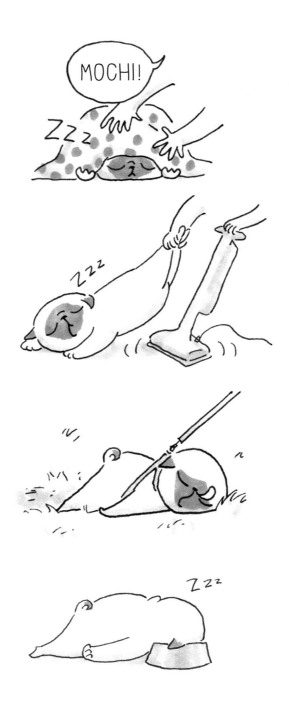

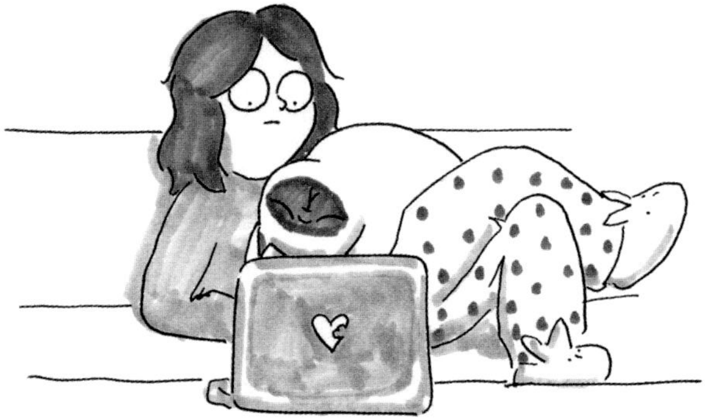

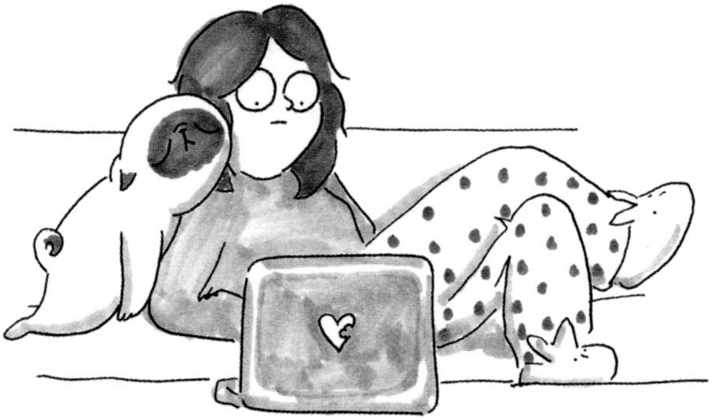

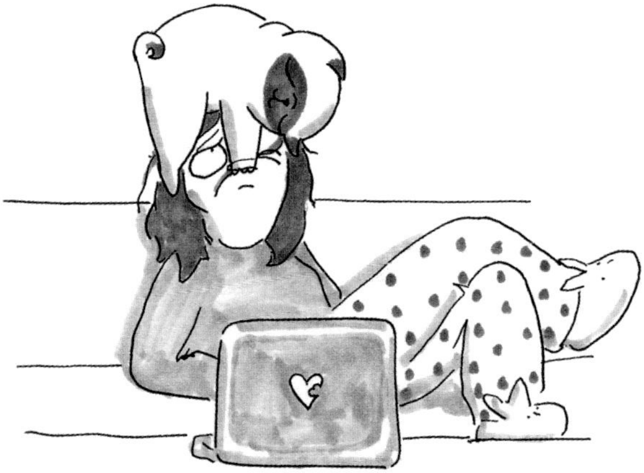

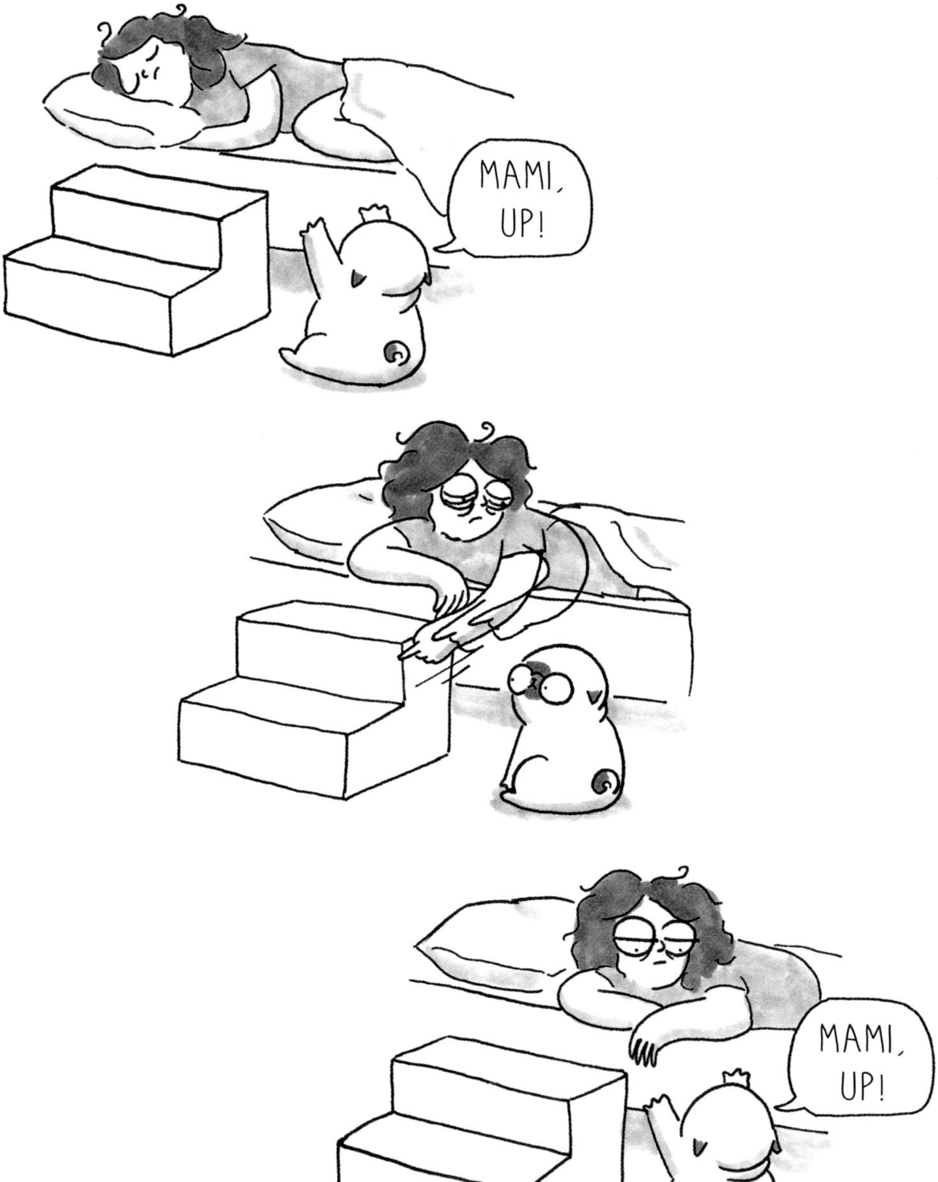
MAMI, UP!
MAMI, UP!

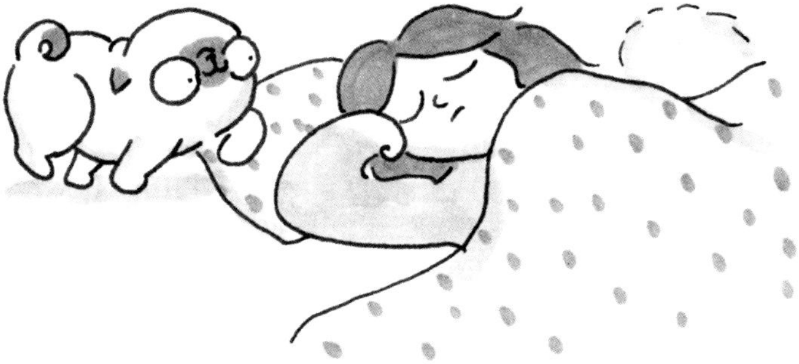

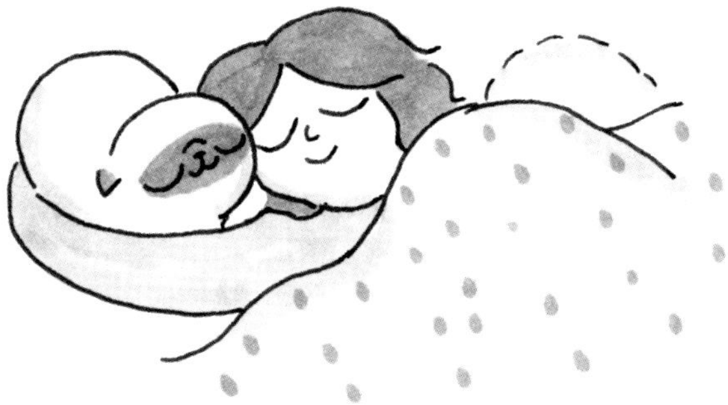

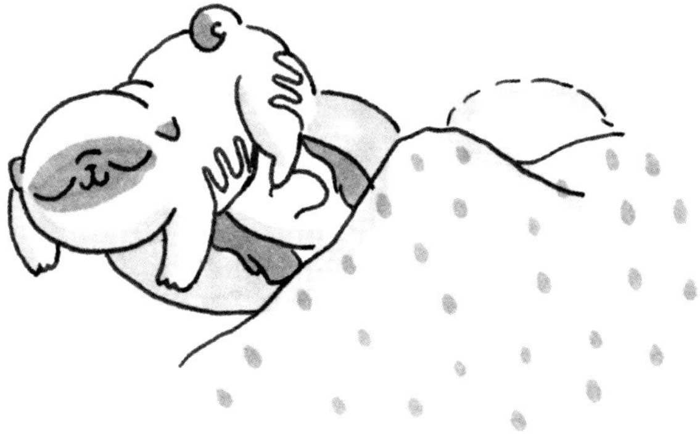

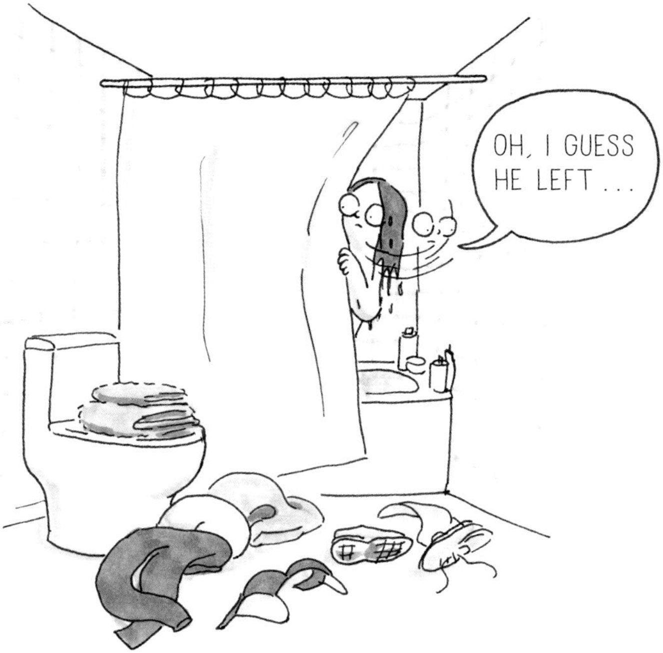
OH, I GUESS HE LEFT . . .

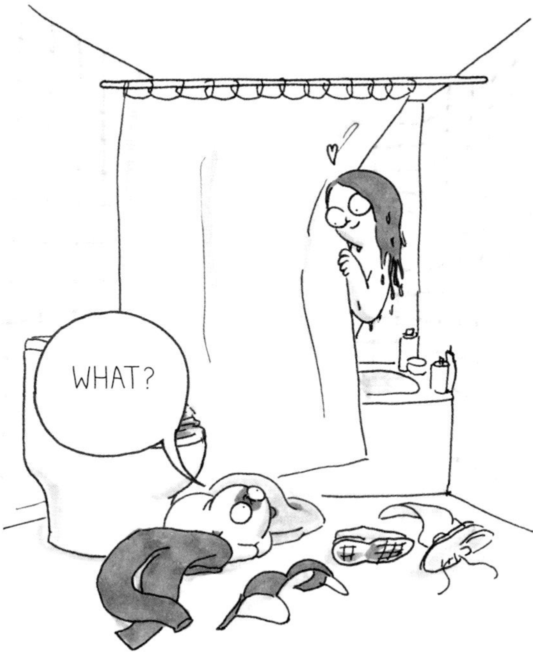
WHAT?

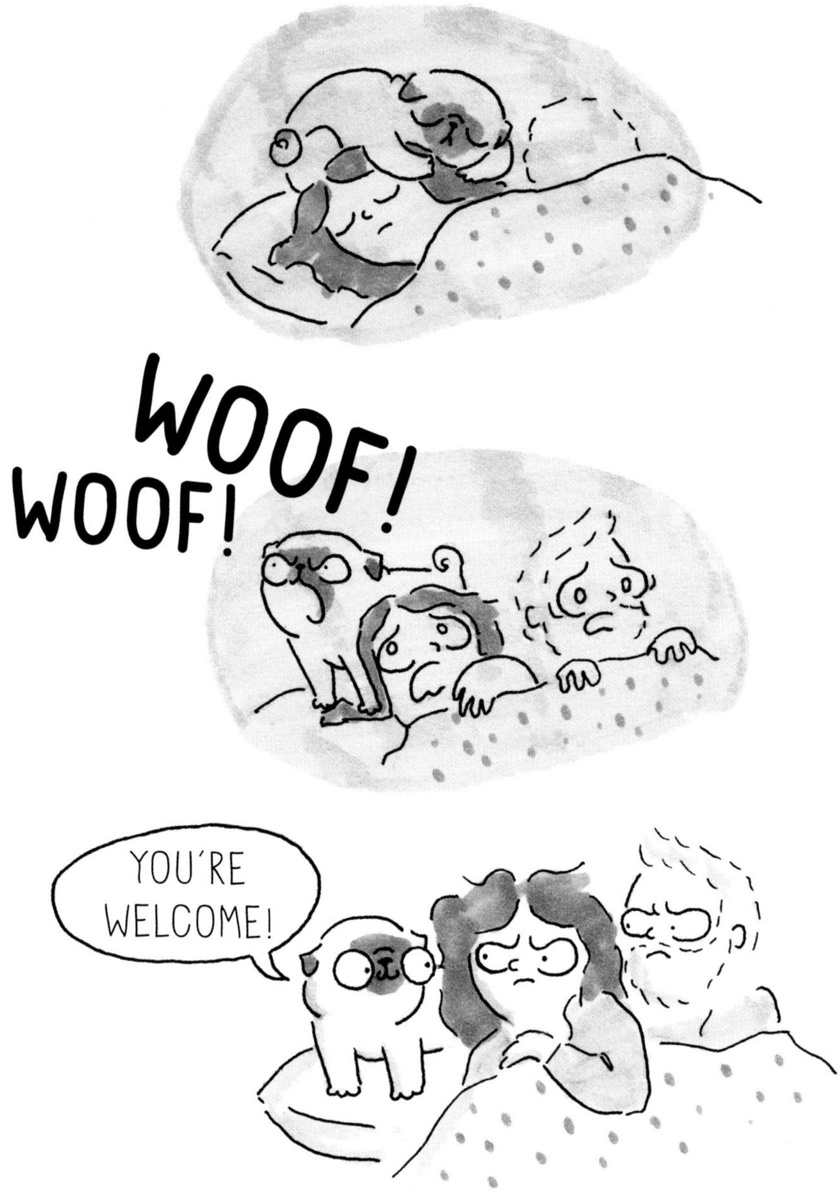
WOOF!
WOOF!
YOU'RE WELCOME!

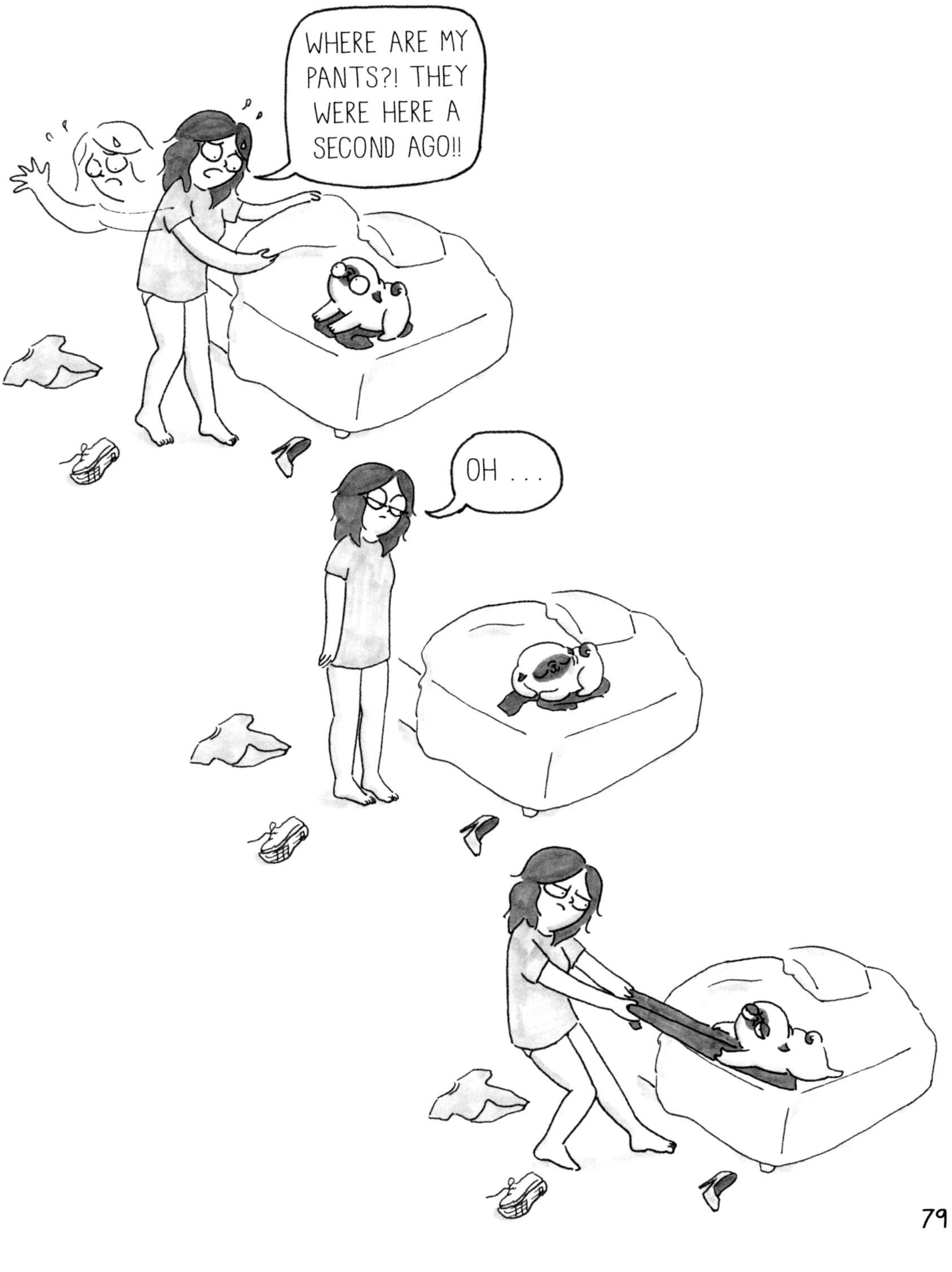
WHERE ARE MY PANTS?! THEY WERE HERE A SECOND AGO!!
OH . . .

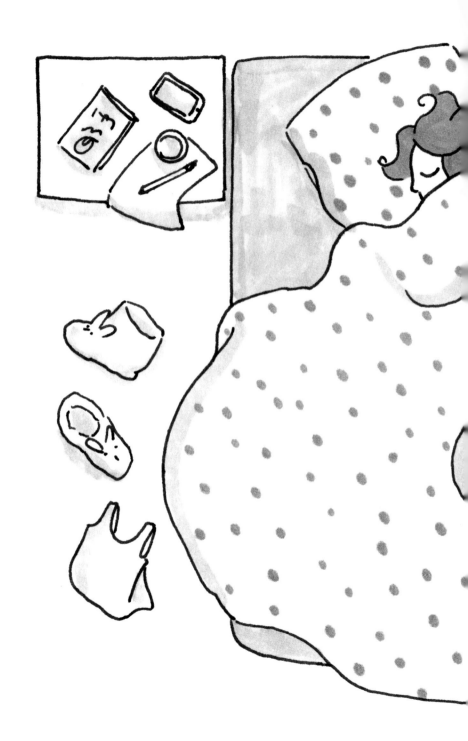

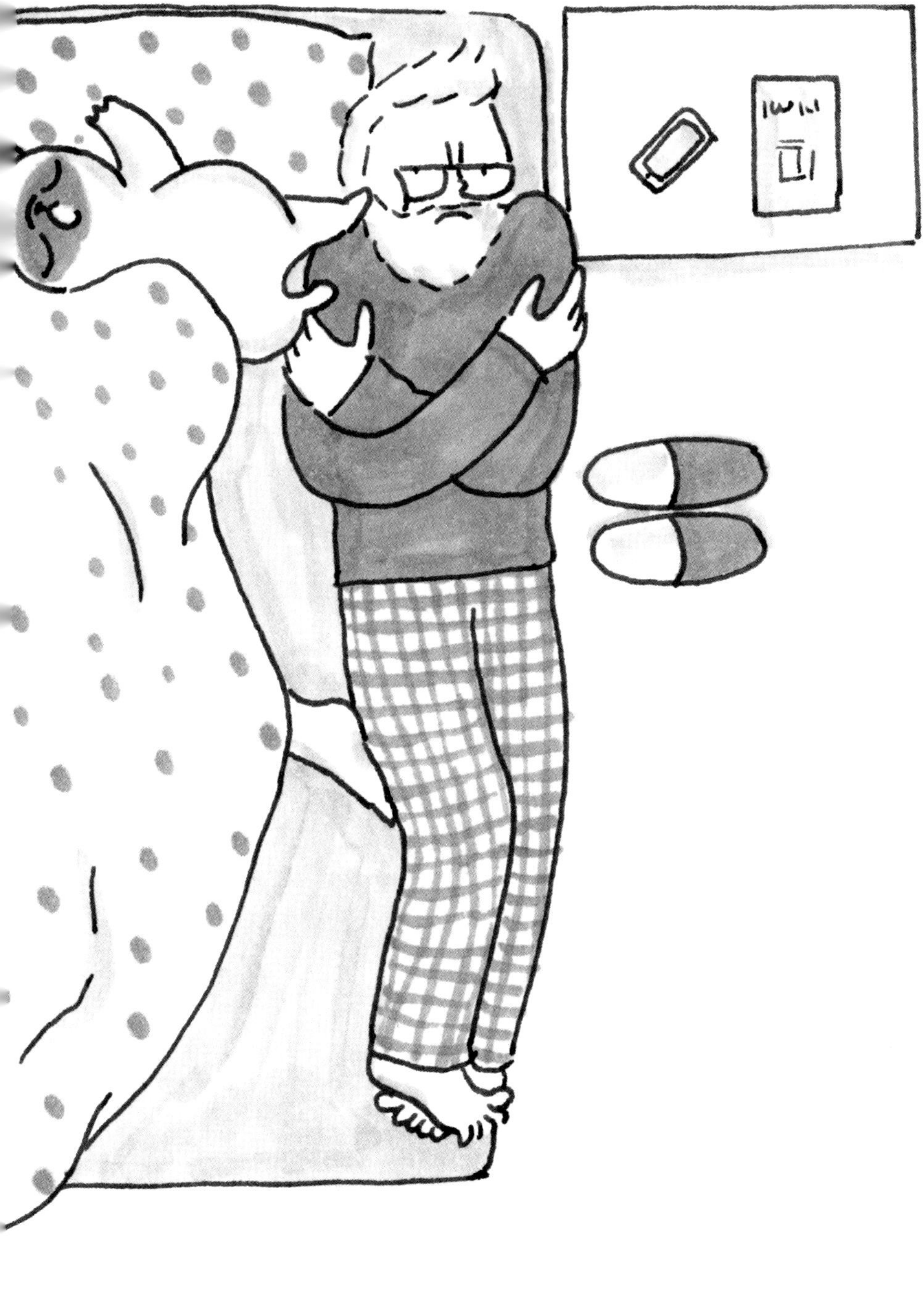

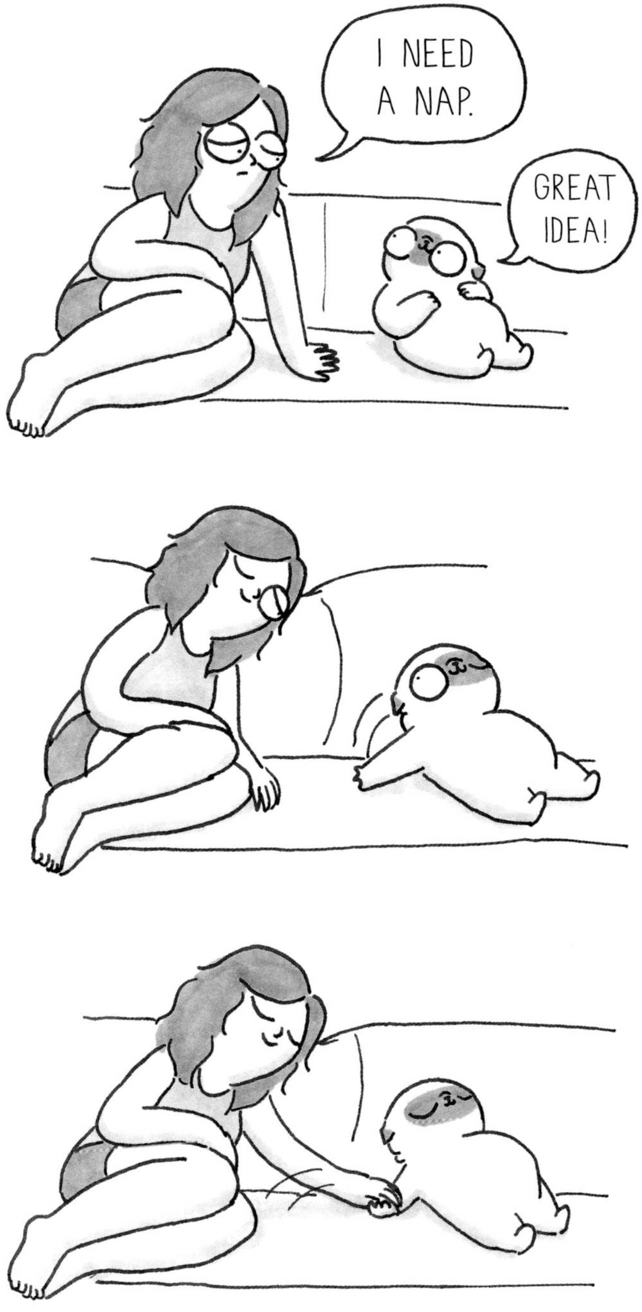
I NEED A NAP.
GREAT IDEA!

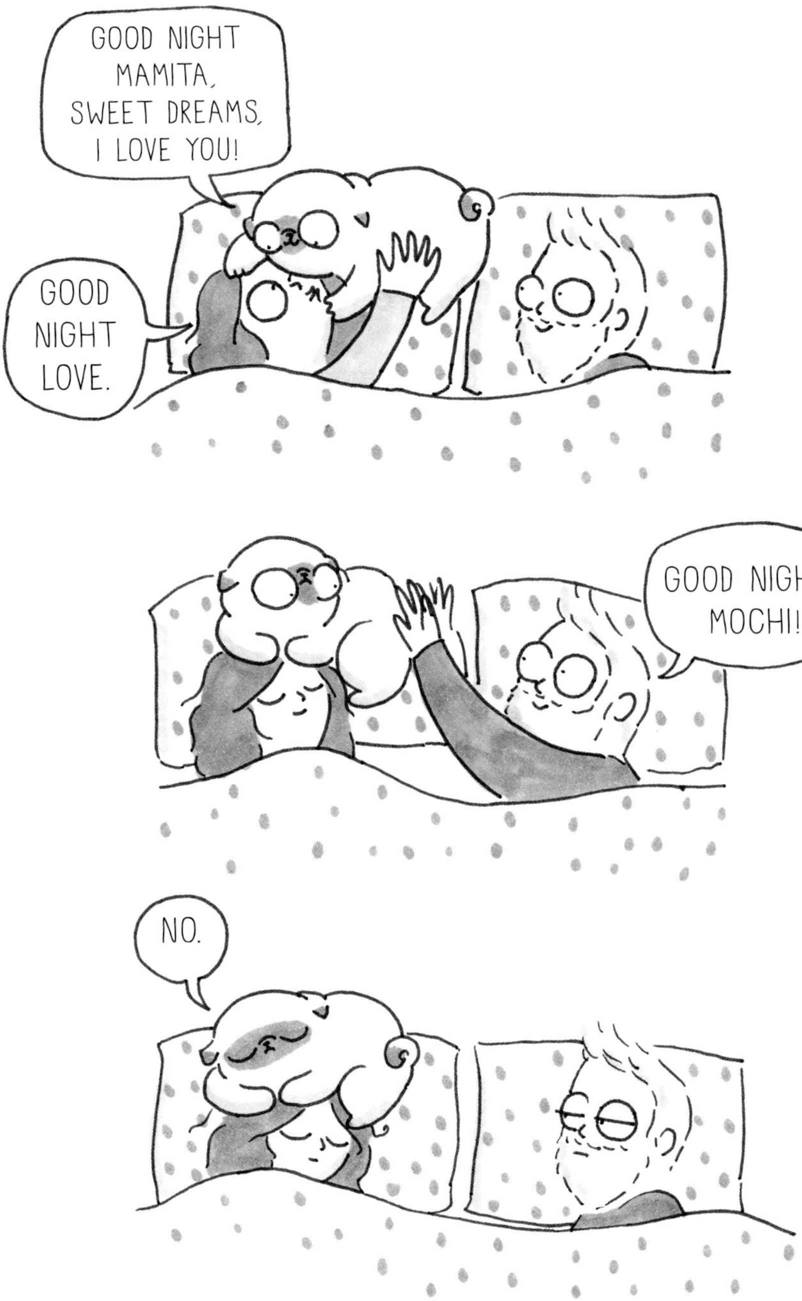
GOOD NIGHT MAMITA, SWEET DREAMS, I LOVE YOU!
GOOD NIGHT LOVE.
GOOD NIGHT MOCHI!
NO.

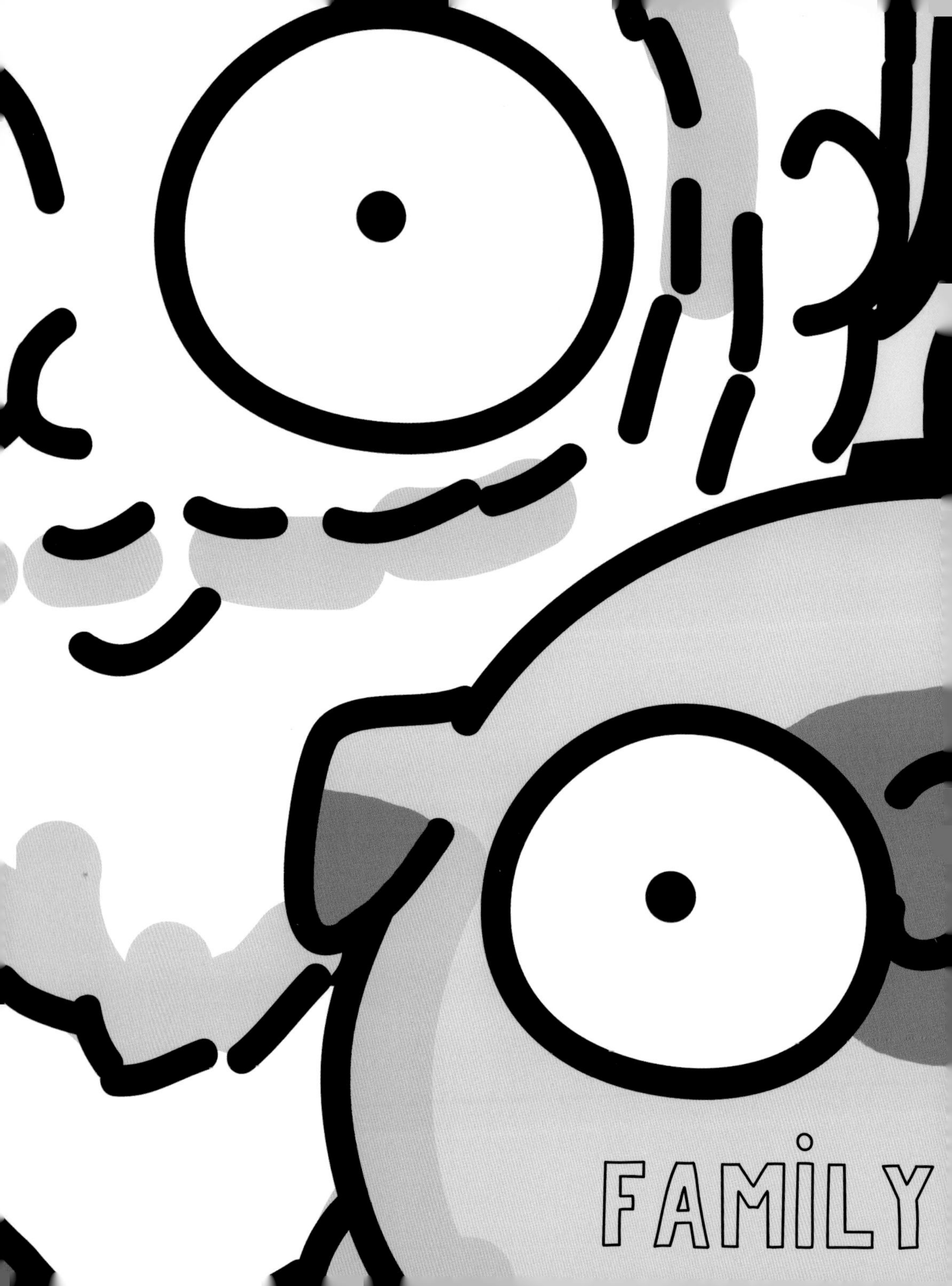
FAMILY

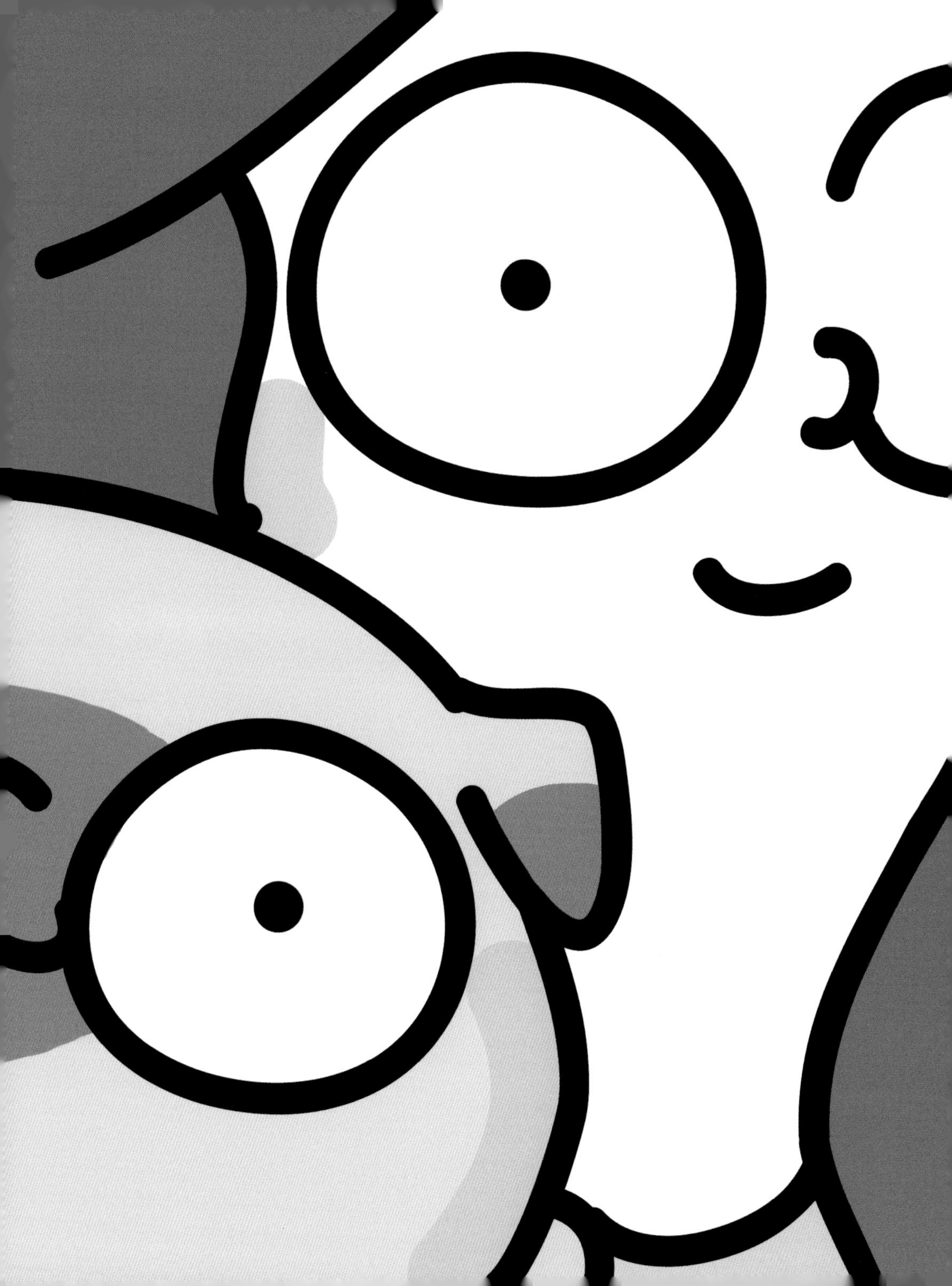

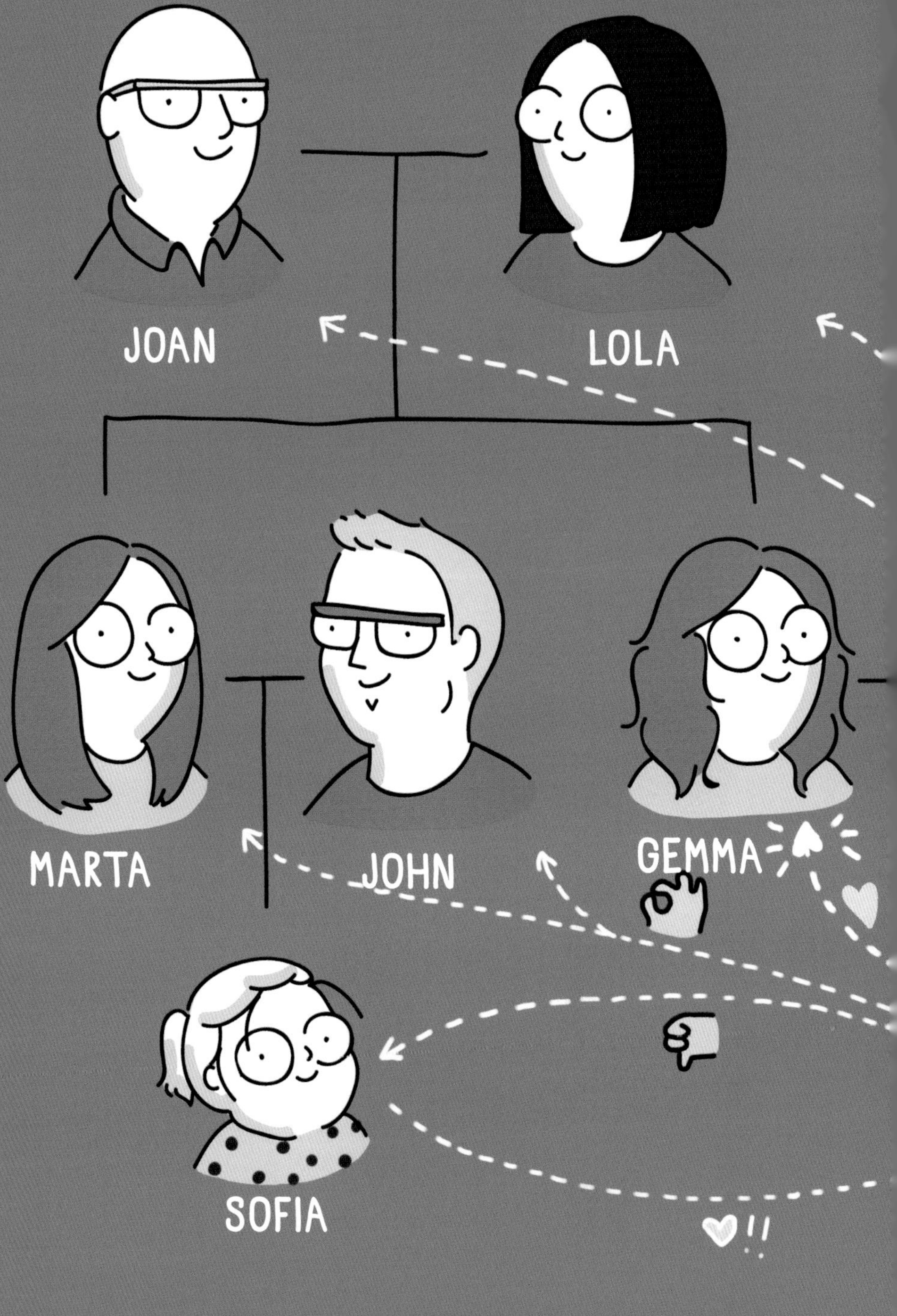
JOAN
LOLA
MARTA
JOHN
GEMMA
SOFIA
!!

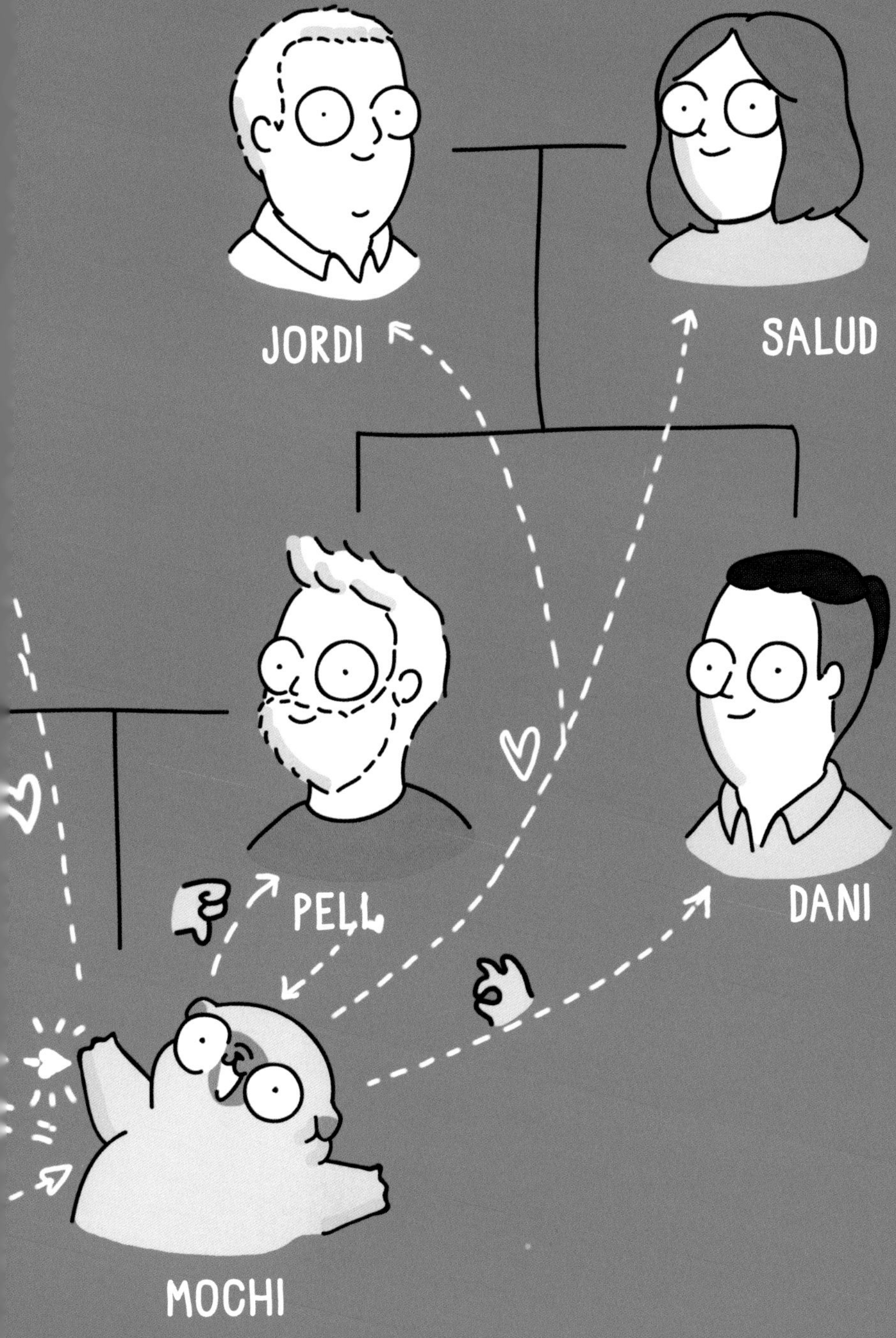
JORDI
SALUD
PELL
DANI
MOCHI

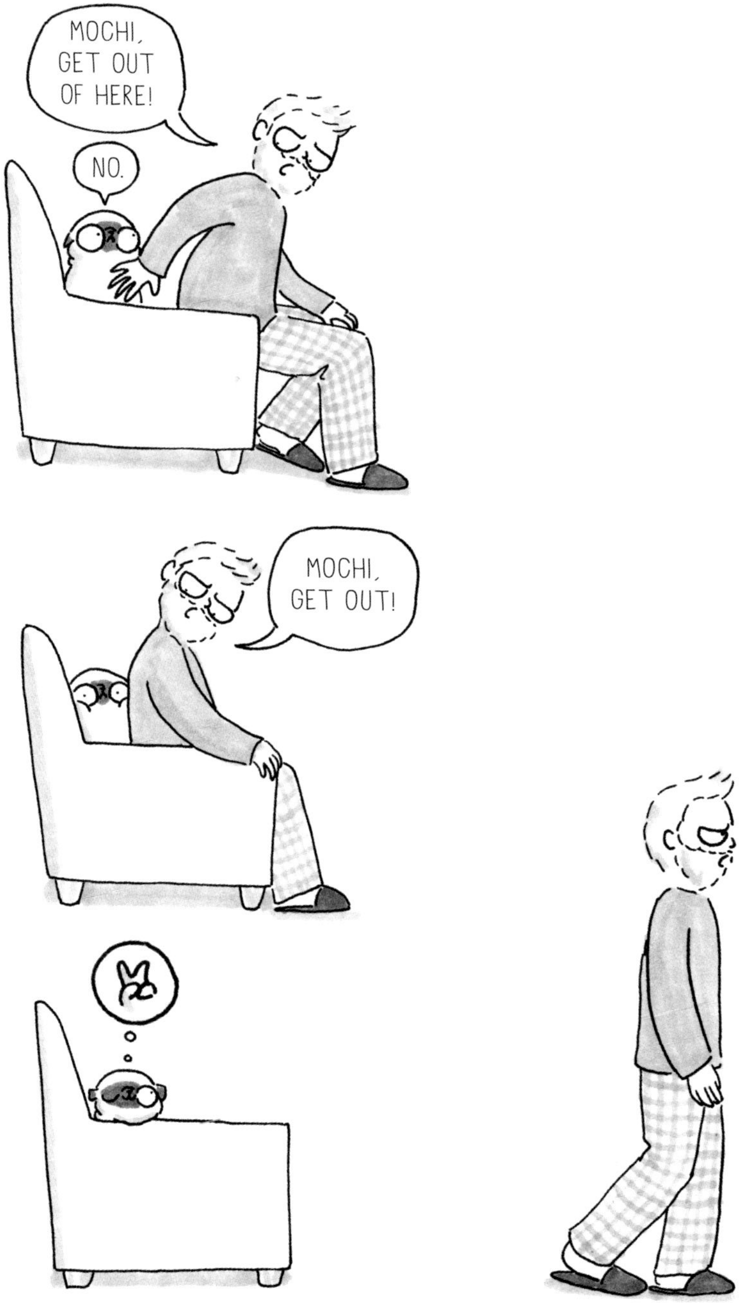
MOCHI, GET OUT OF HERE!
NO.
MOCHI, GET OUT!

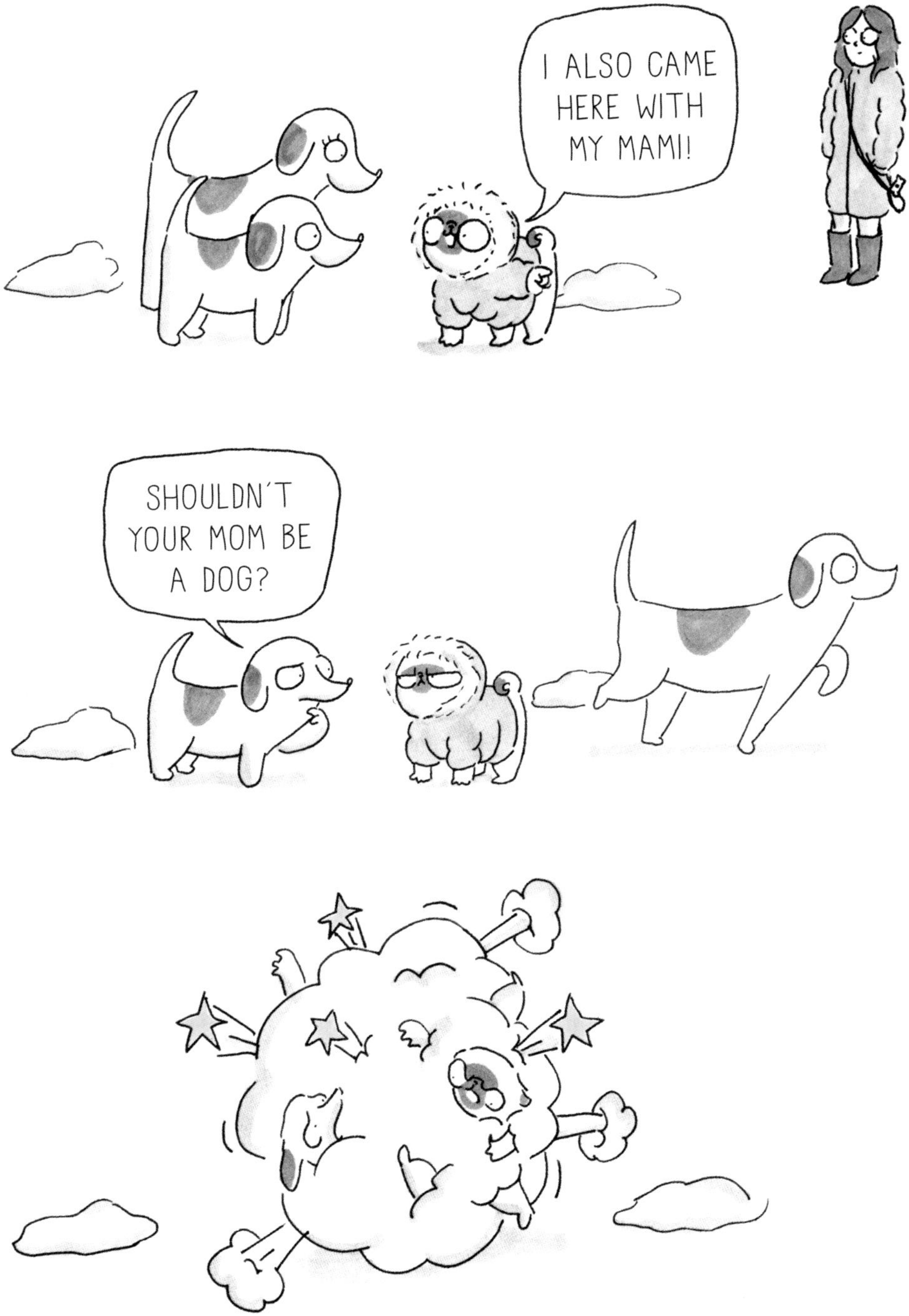
I ALSO CAME HERE WITH MY MAMI!
SHOULDN´T YOUR MOM BE A DOG?

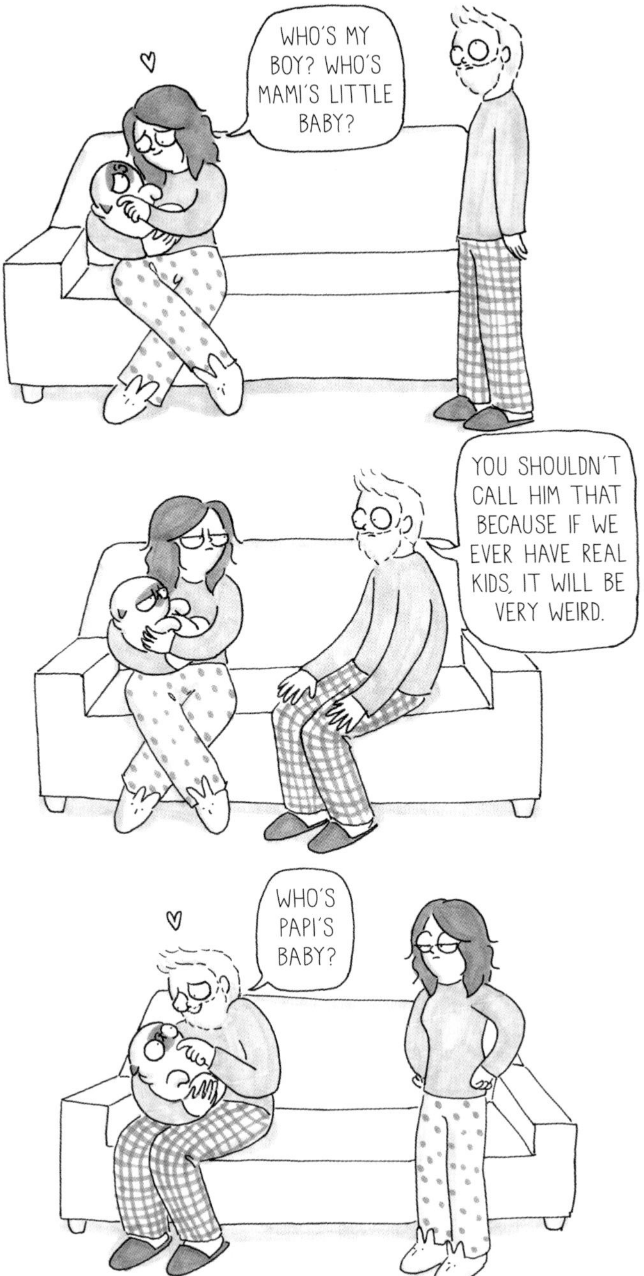
WHO'S MY BOY? WHO'S MAMI'S LITTLE BABY?
YOU SHOULDN'T CALL HIM THAT BECAUSE IF WE EVER HAVE REAL KIDS, IT WILL BE VERY WEIRD.
WHO'S PAPI'S BABY?

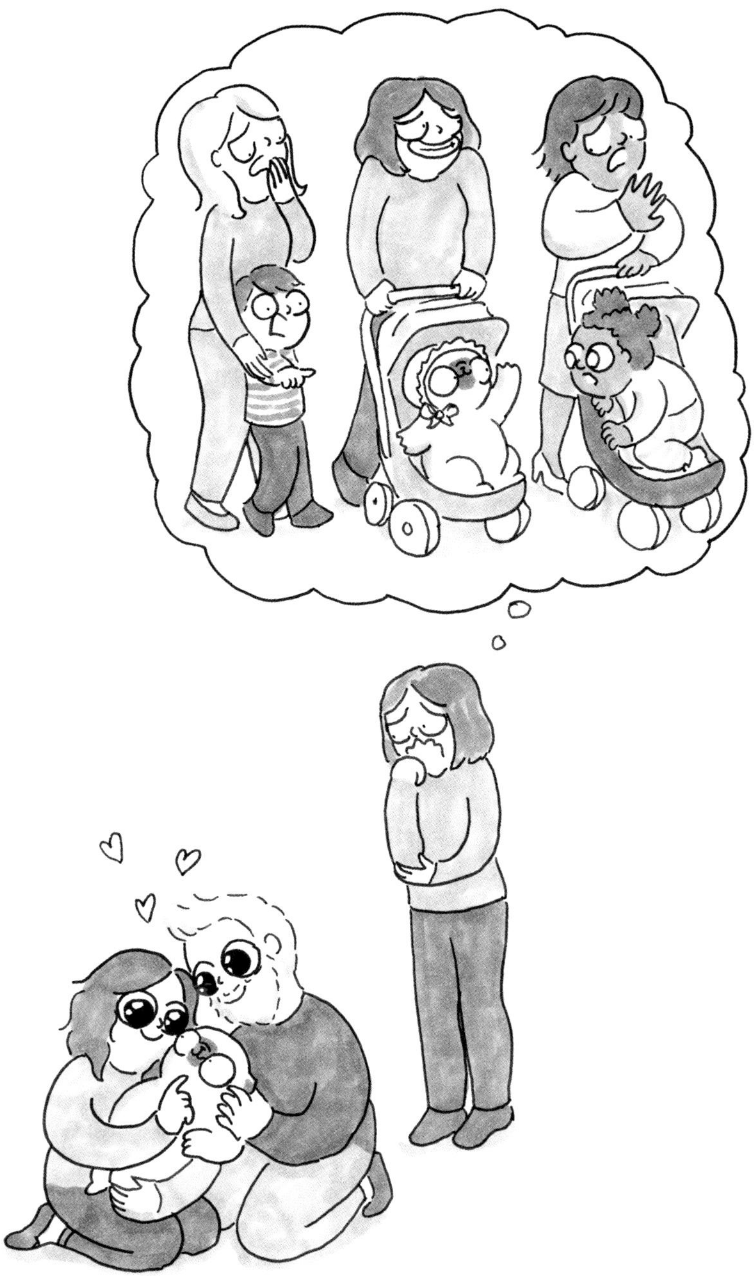

AT MAMI'S PARENTS' HOUSE

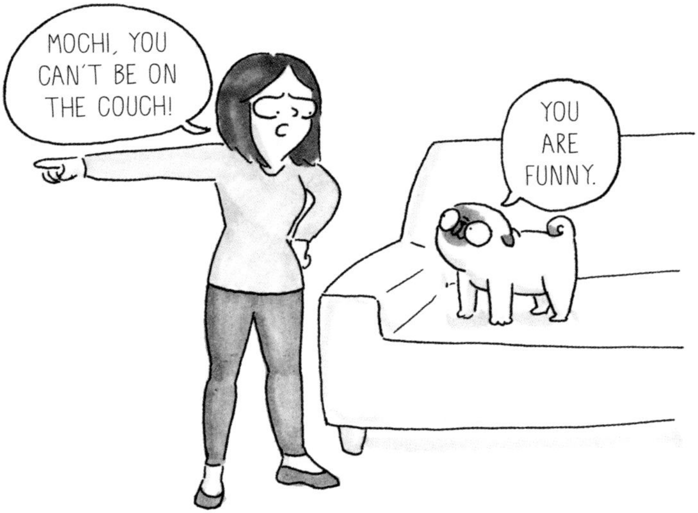
MOCHI, YOU CAN'T BE ON THE COUCH!
YOU ARE FUNNY.

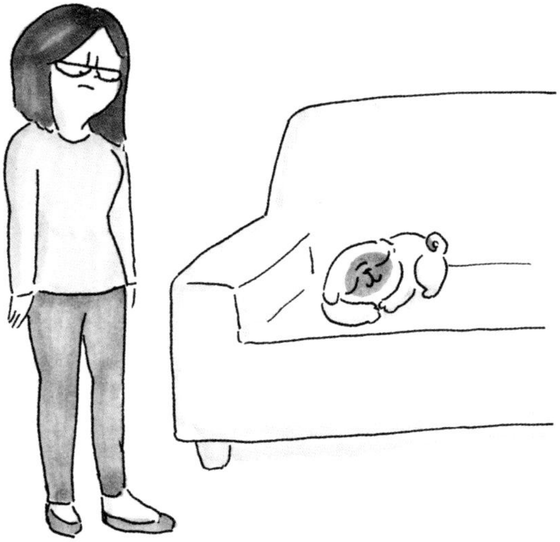

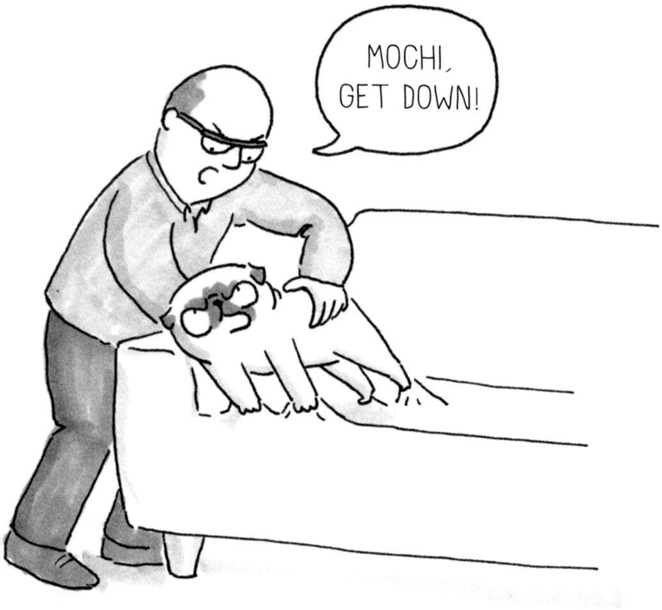
MOCHI, GET DOWN!

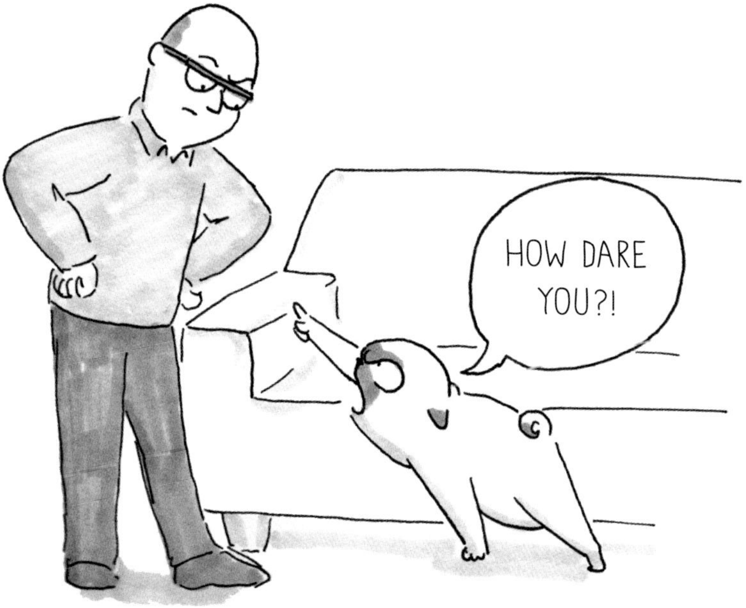
HOW DARE YOU?!

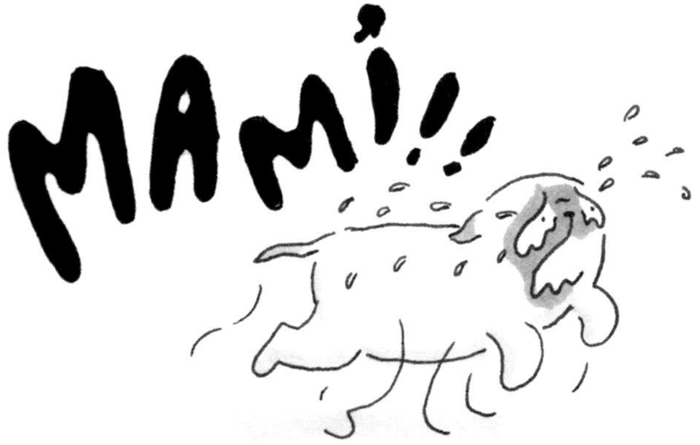
MAMI!!!

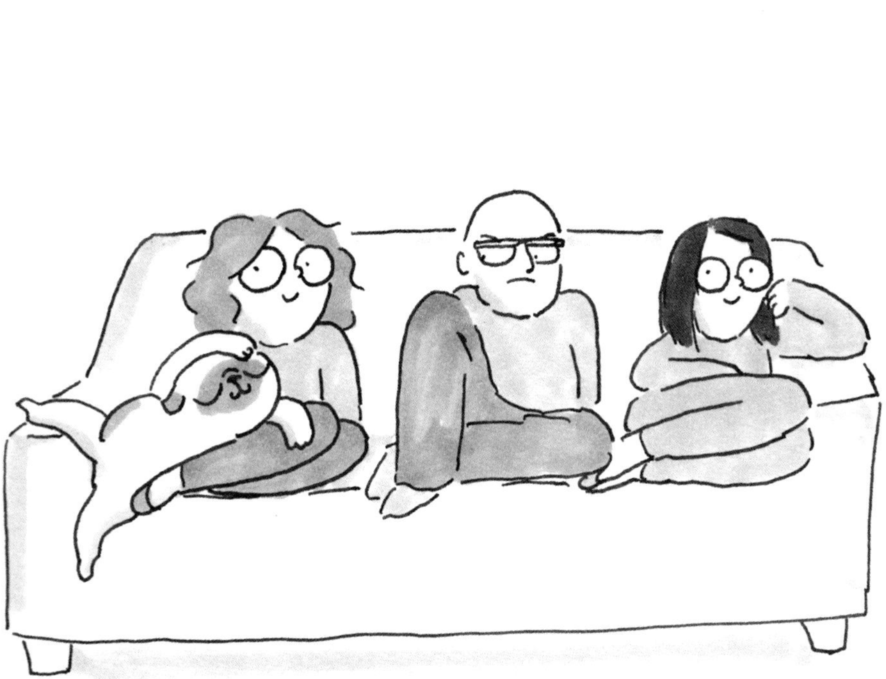

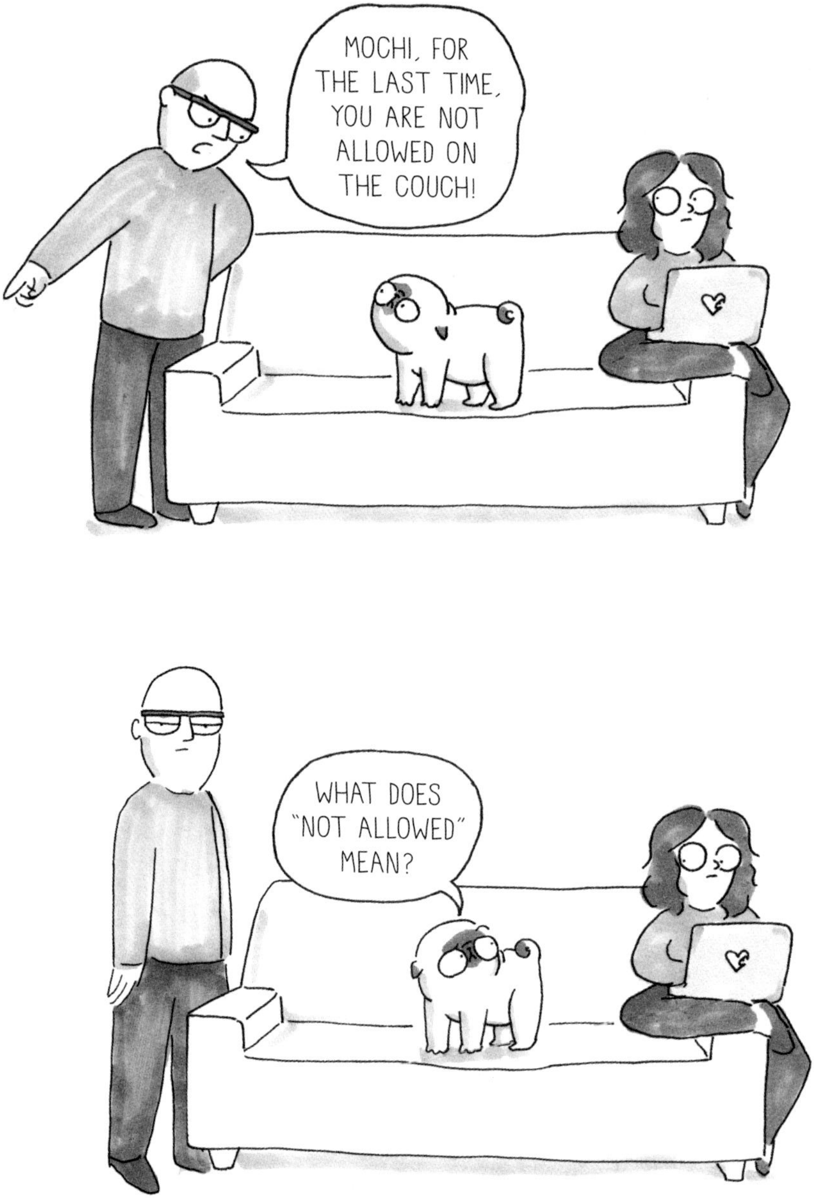
MOCHI, FOR THE LAST TIME, YOU ARE NOT ALLOWED ON THE COUCH!
WHAT DOES "NOT ALLOWED" MEAN?

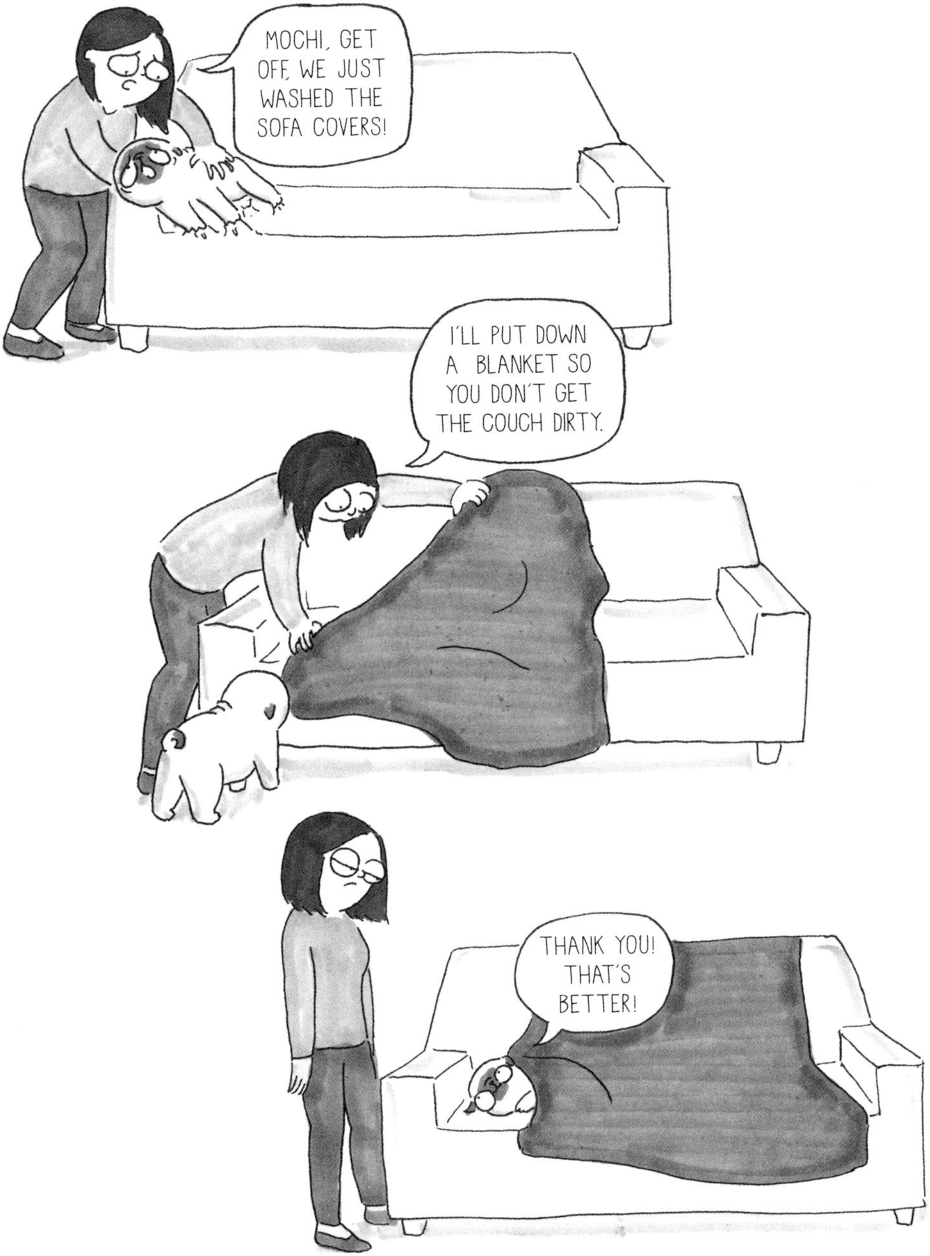
MOCHI, GET OFF, WE JUST WASHED THE SOFA COVERS!
I'LL PUT DOWN A BLANKET SO YOU DON'T GET THE COUCH DIRTY.
THANK YOU! THAT'S BETTER!

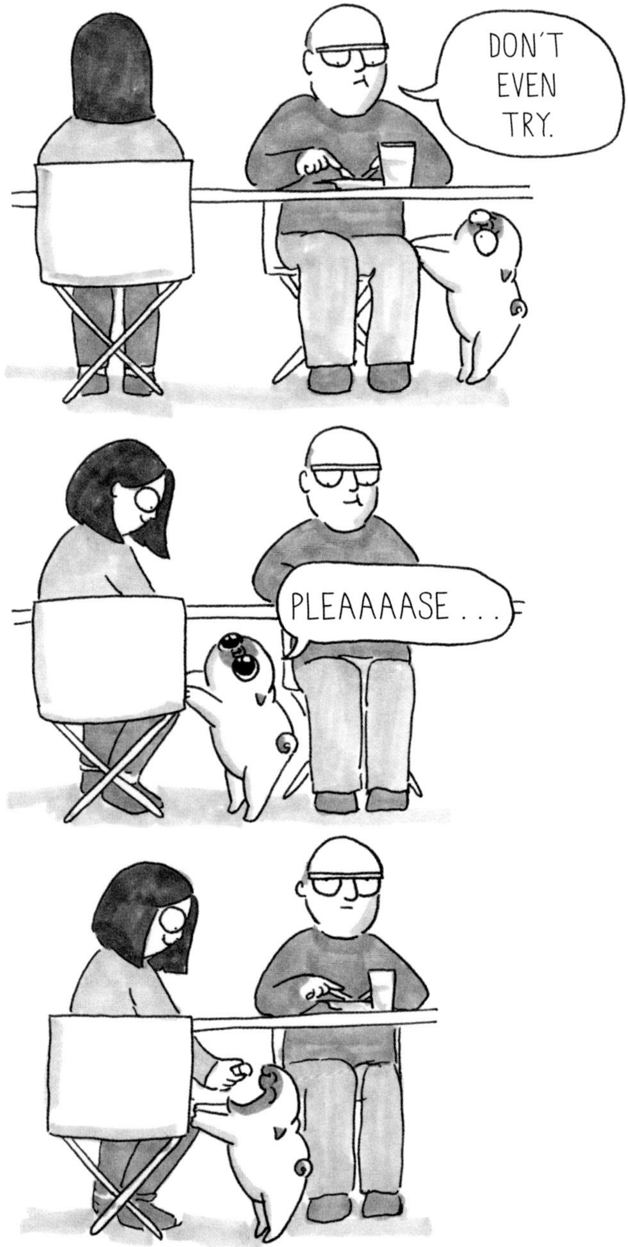
DON'T EVEN TRY.
PLEAAAASE . . .

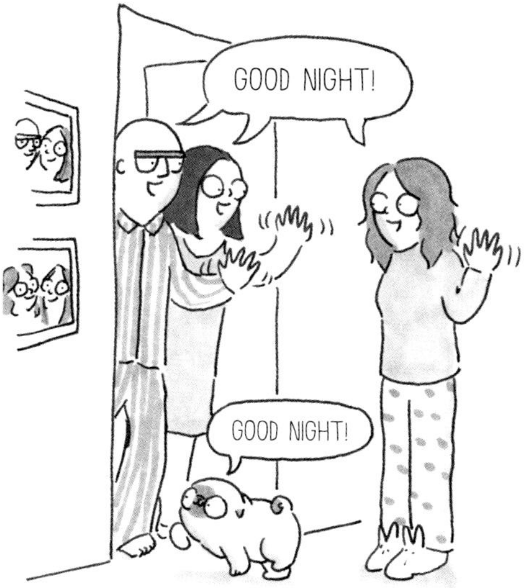
GOOD NIGHT!
GOOD NIGHT!

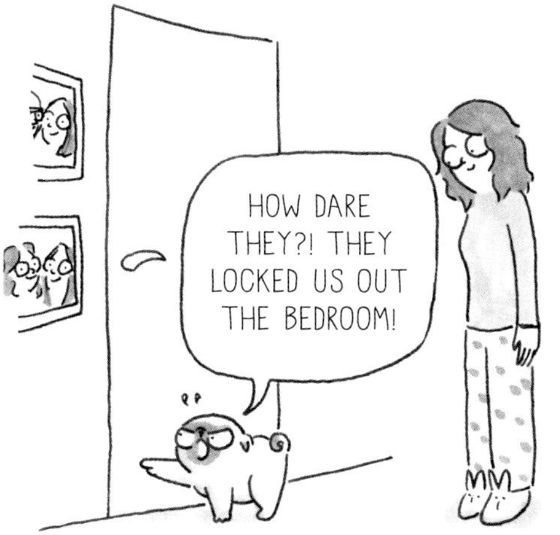
HOW DARE THEY?! THEY LOCKED US OUT THE BEDROOM!

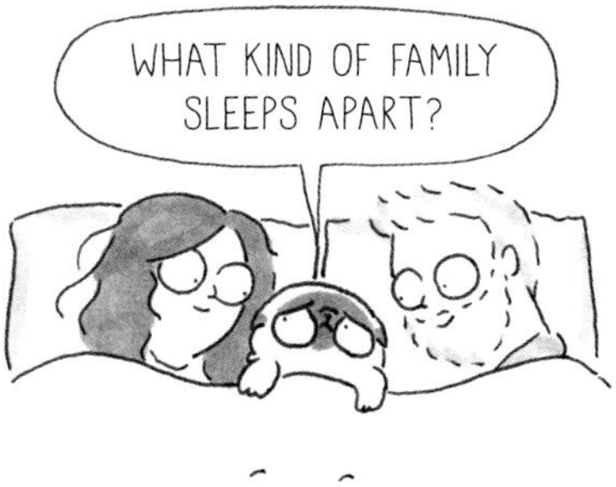
WHAT KIND OF FAMILY SLEEPS APART?

AT PAPI'S PARENTS' HOME

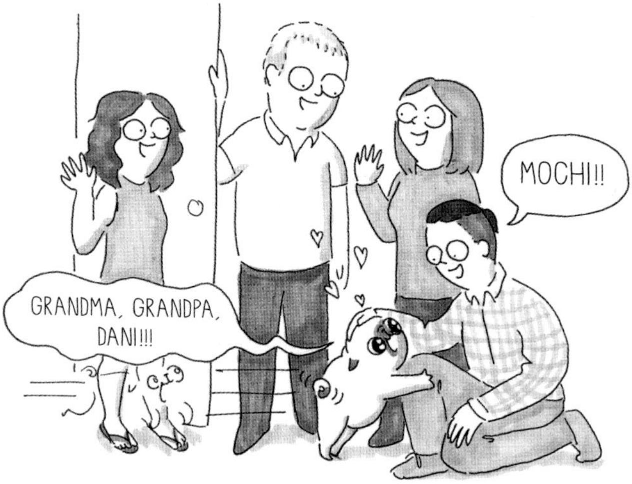
MOCHI!!
GRANDMA, GRANDPA, DANI!!!

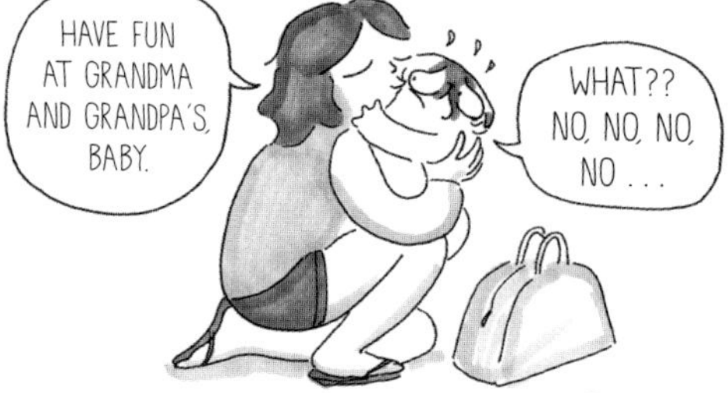
HAVE FUN AT GRANDMA AND GRANDPA'S, BABY.
WHAT?? NO, NO, NO, NO . . .

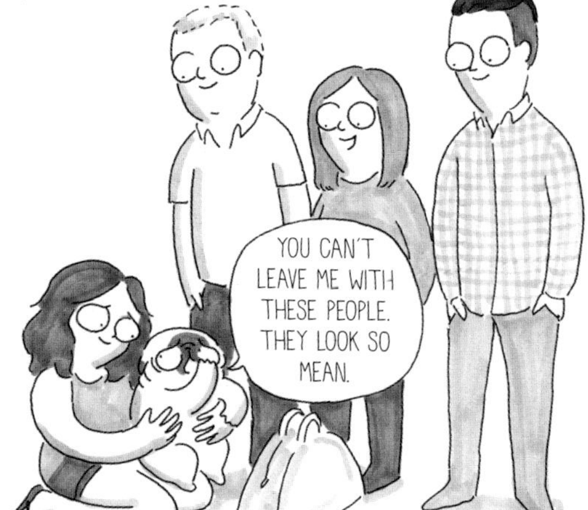
YOU CAN'T LEAVE ME WITH THESE PEOPLE. THEY LOOK SO MEAN.

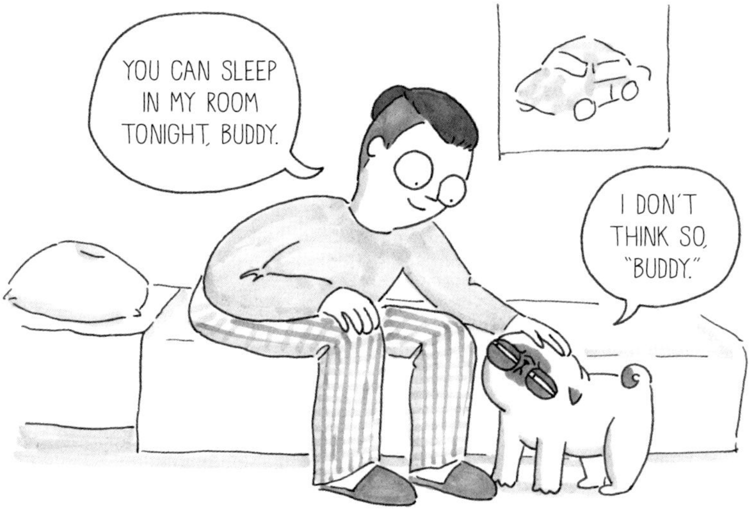
YOU CAN SLEEP IN MY ROOM TONIGHT, BUDDY.
I DON'T THINK SO, "BUDDY."

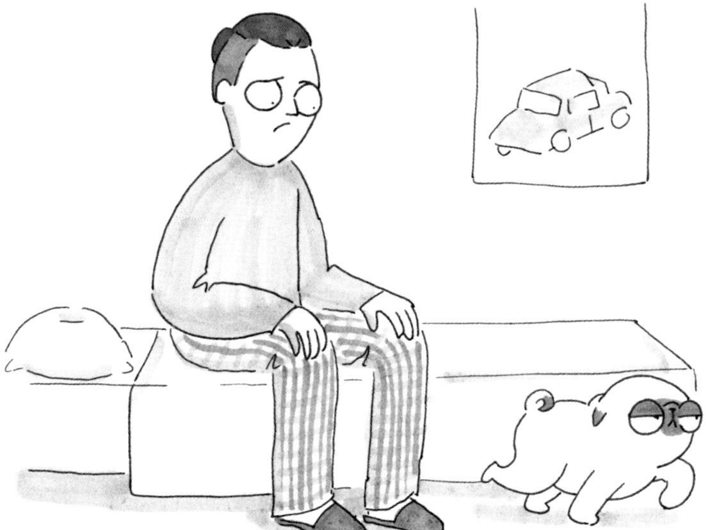

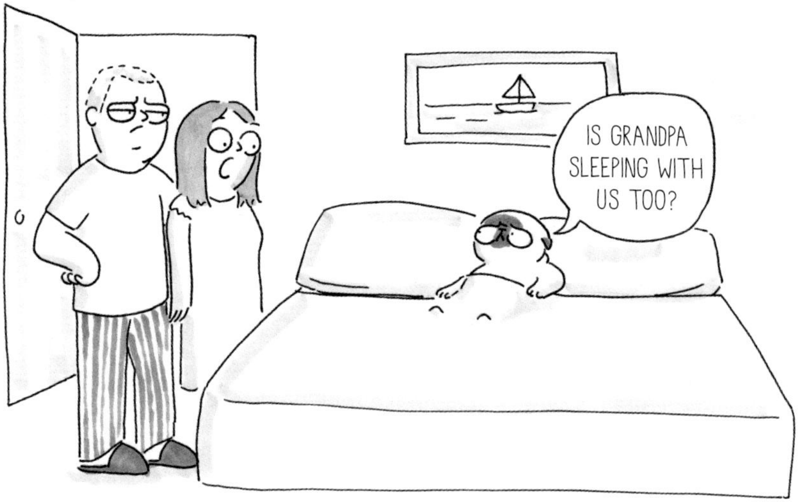
IS GRANDPA SLEEPING WITH US TOO?

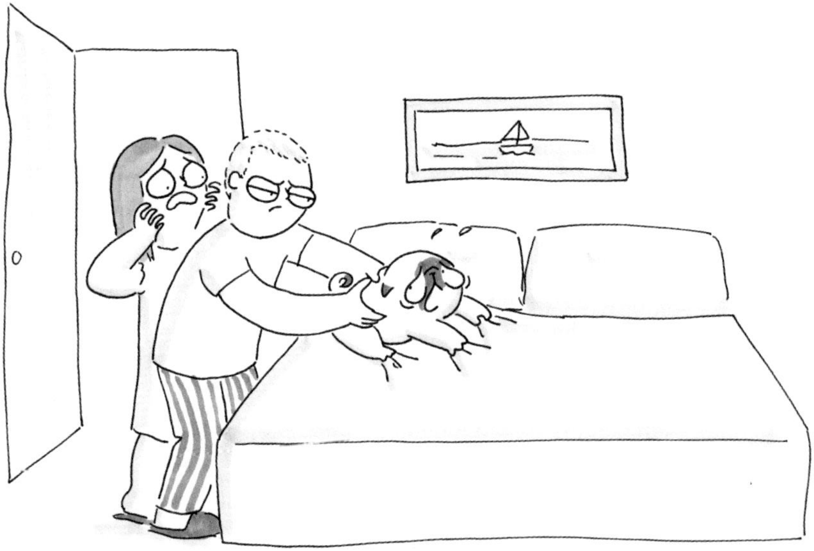

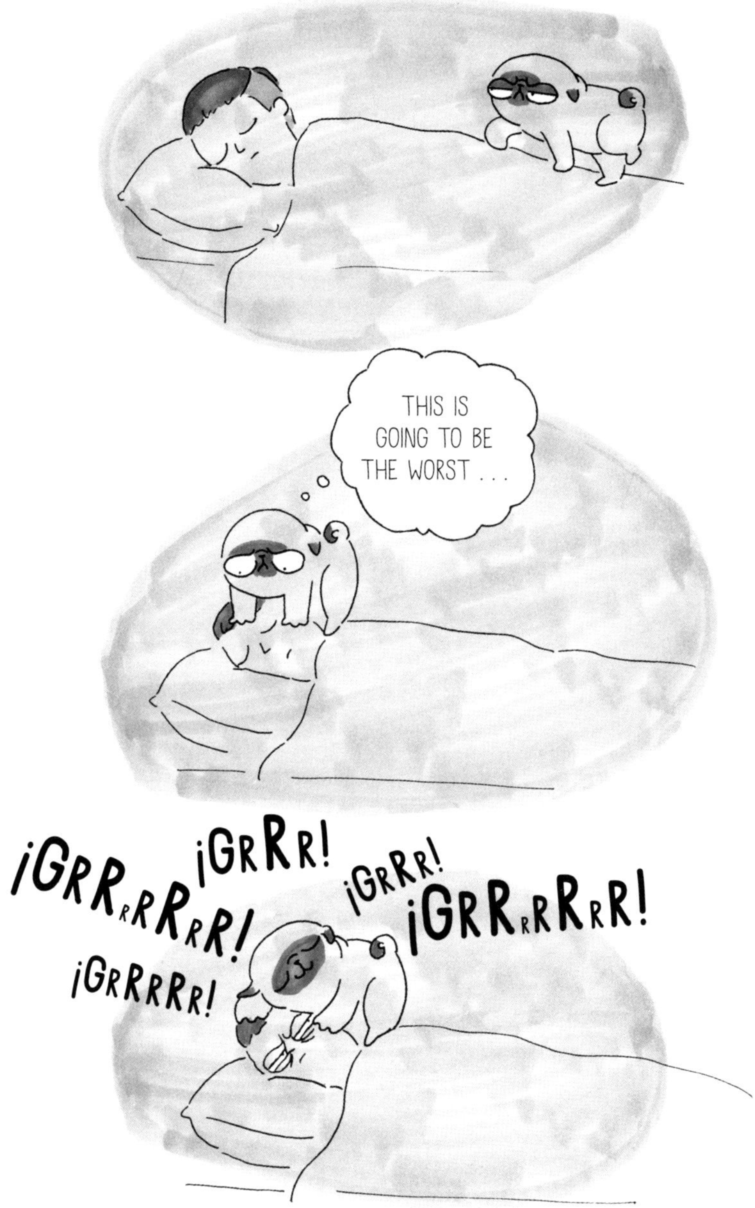
THIS IS GOING TO BE THE WORST . . .
¡GRRRRRRR!
¡GRRR!
¡GRRR!
¡GRRRRRRR!
¡GRRRRR!

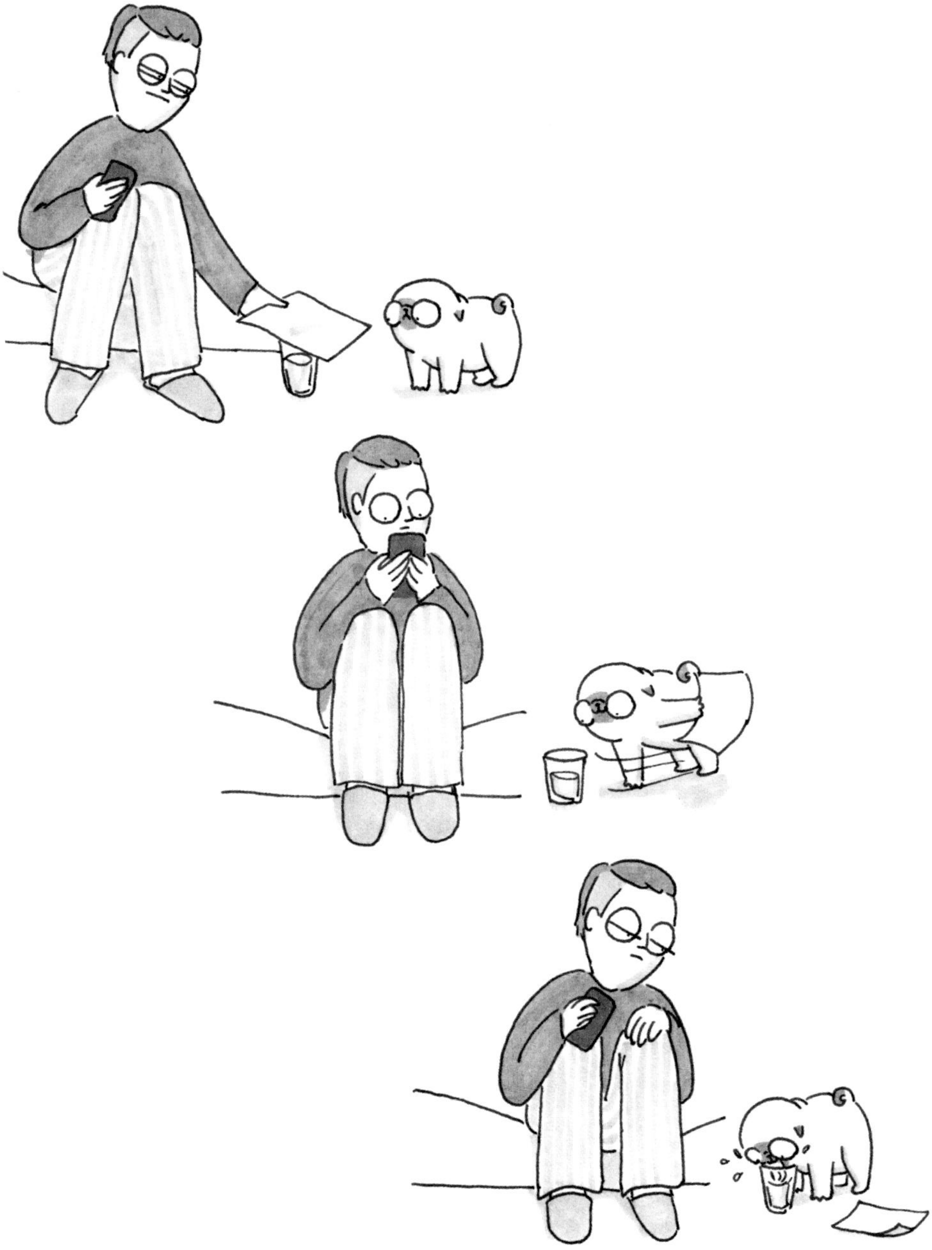

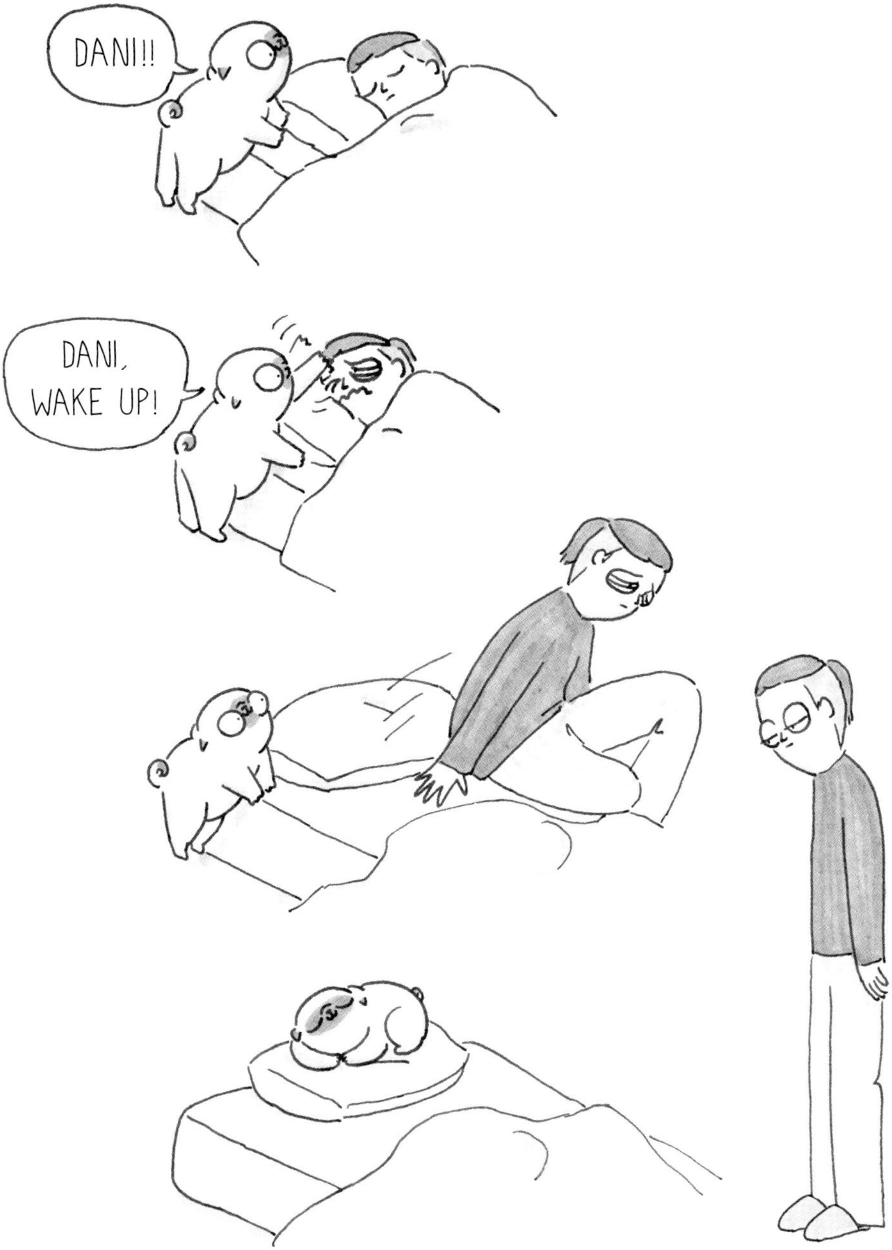
DANI!!
DANI, WAKE UP!

SPENDING A NIGHT ALONE AT MAMI'S PARENTS' HOUSE

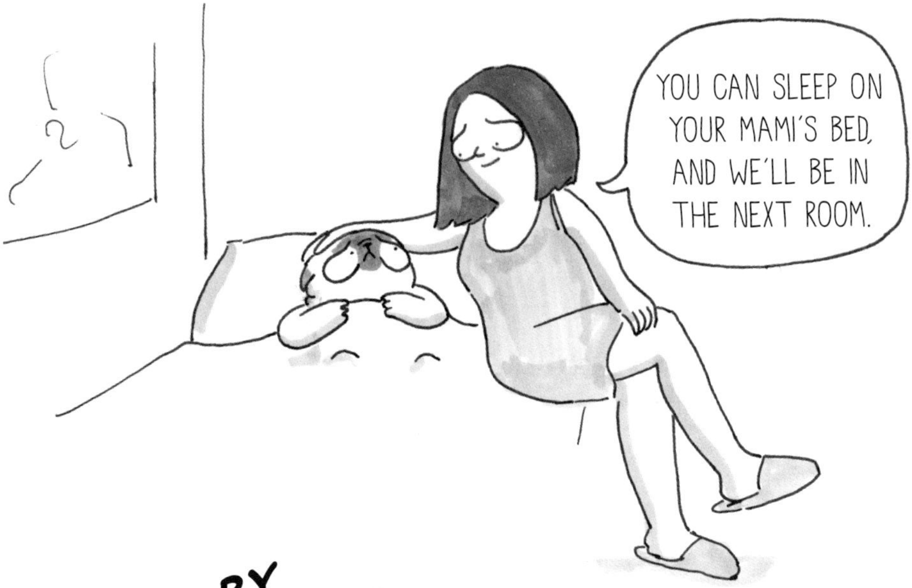
YOU CAN SLEEP ON YOUR MAMI'S BED, AND WE'LL BE IN THE NEXT ROOM.

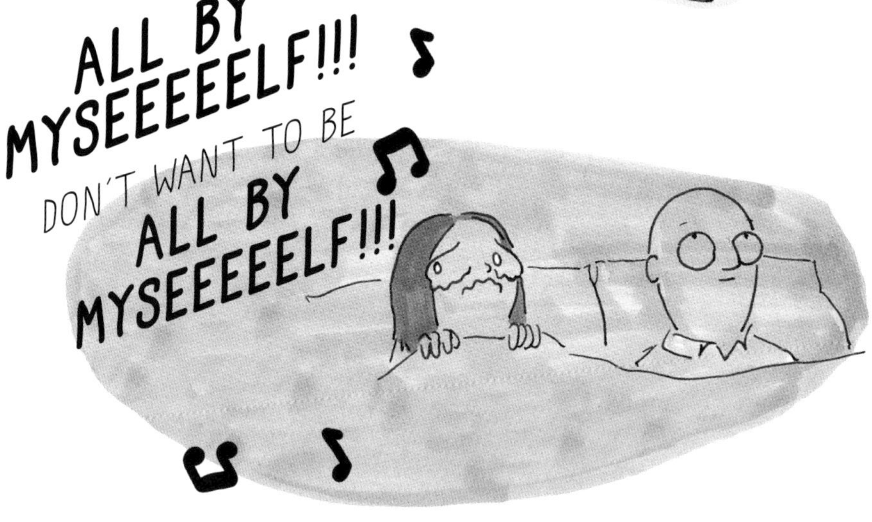
ALL BY MYSEEEEELF!!!
DON'T WANT TO BE
ALL BY MYSEEEEELF!!!

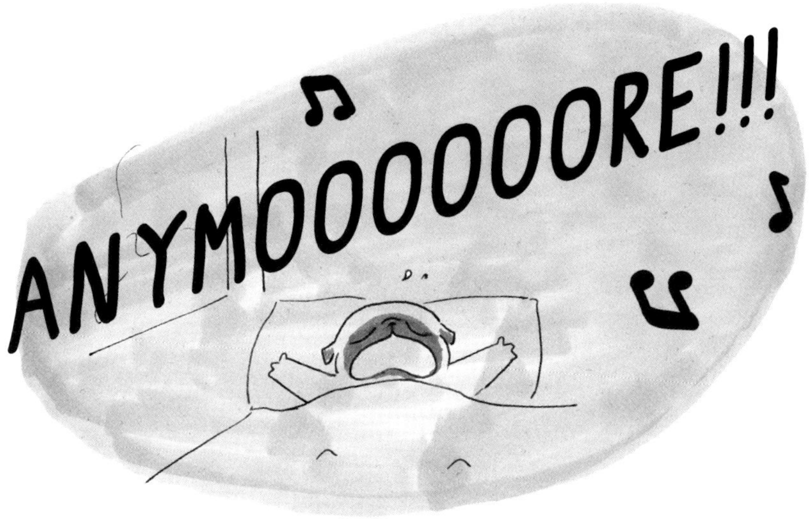
ANYMOOOOOOORE!!!

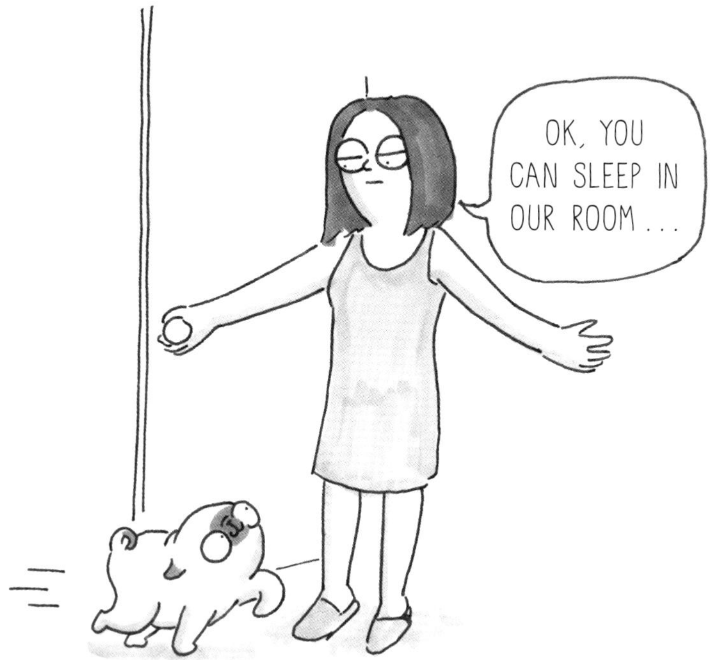
OK, YOU CAN SLEEP IN OUR ROOM . . .

AT AUNTIE MARTA'S HOUSE

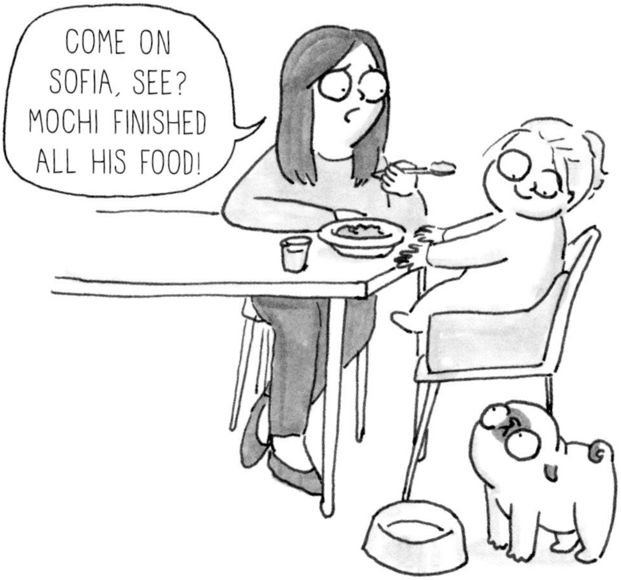
COME ON SOFIA, SEE? MOCHI FINISHED ALL HIS FOOD!

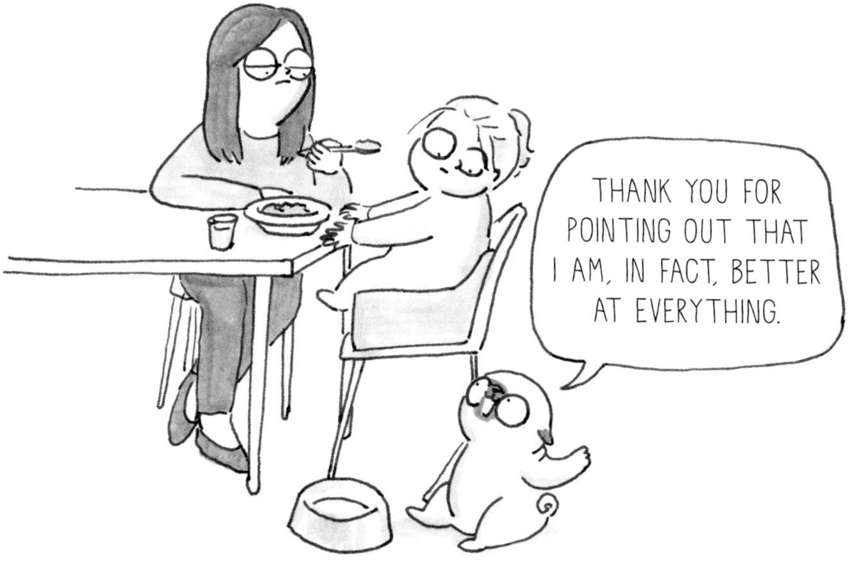
THANK YOU FOR POINTING OUT THAT I AM, IN FACT, BETTER AT EVERYTHING.

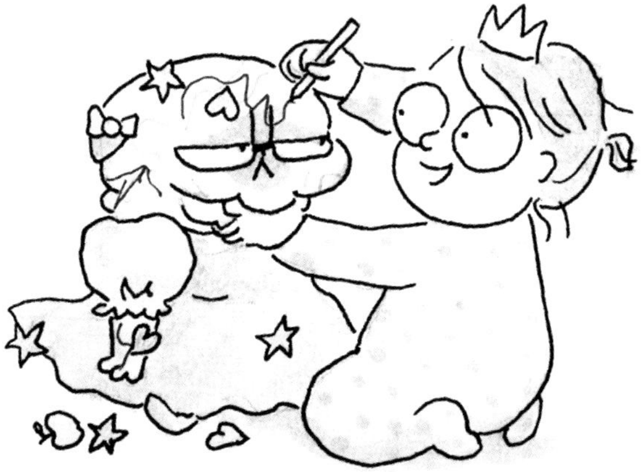

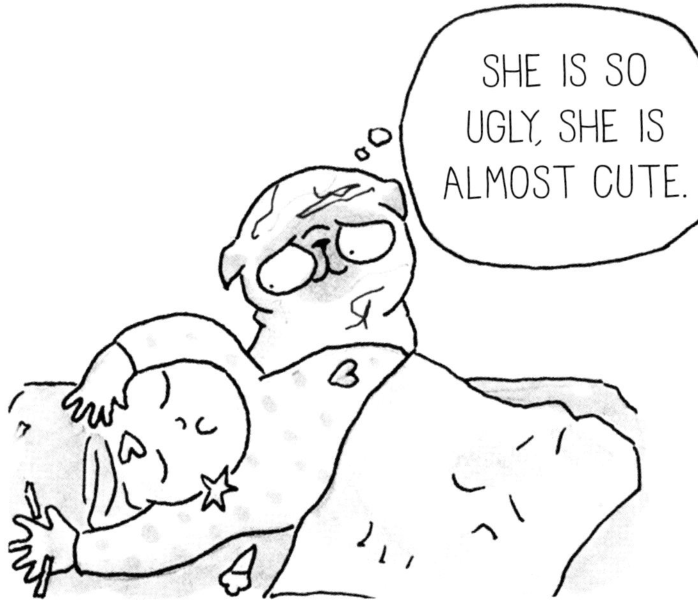
SHE IS SO UGLY, SHE IS ALMOST CUTE.

OOPS, MOCHI! I POKED YOUR EYE ON ACCIDENT!

ALL OF YOUR "ACCIDENTS" SEEM TO BE DIRECTED MY WAY.

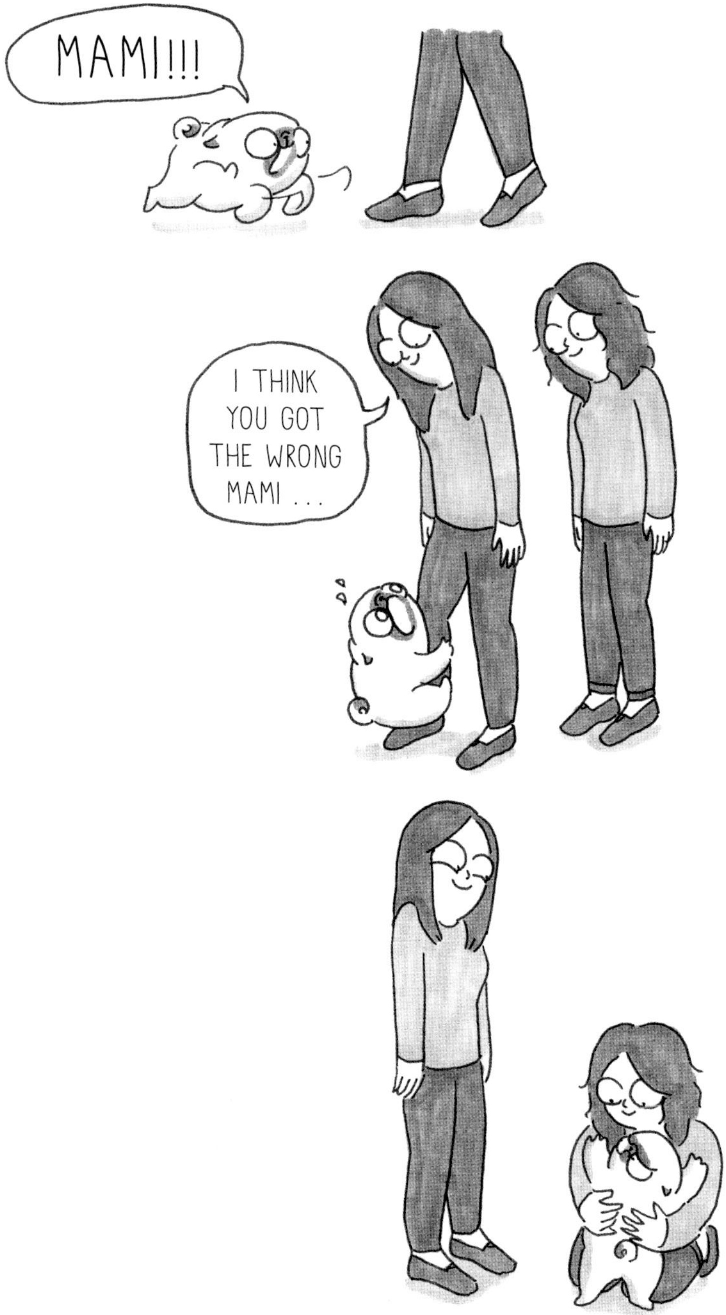
MAMI!!!
I THINK YOU GOT THE WRONG MAMI . . .

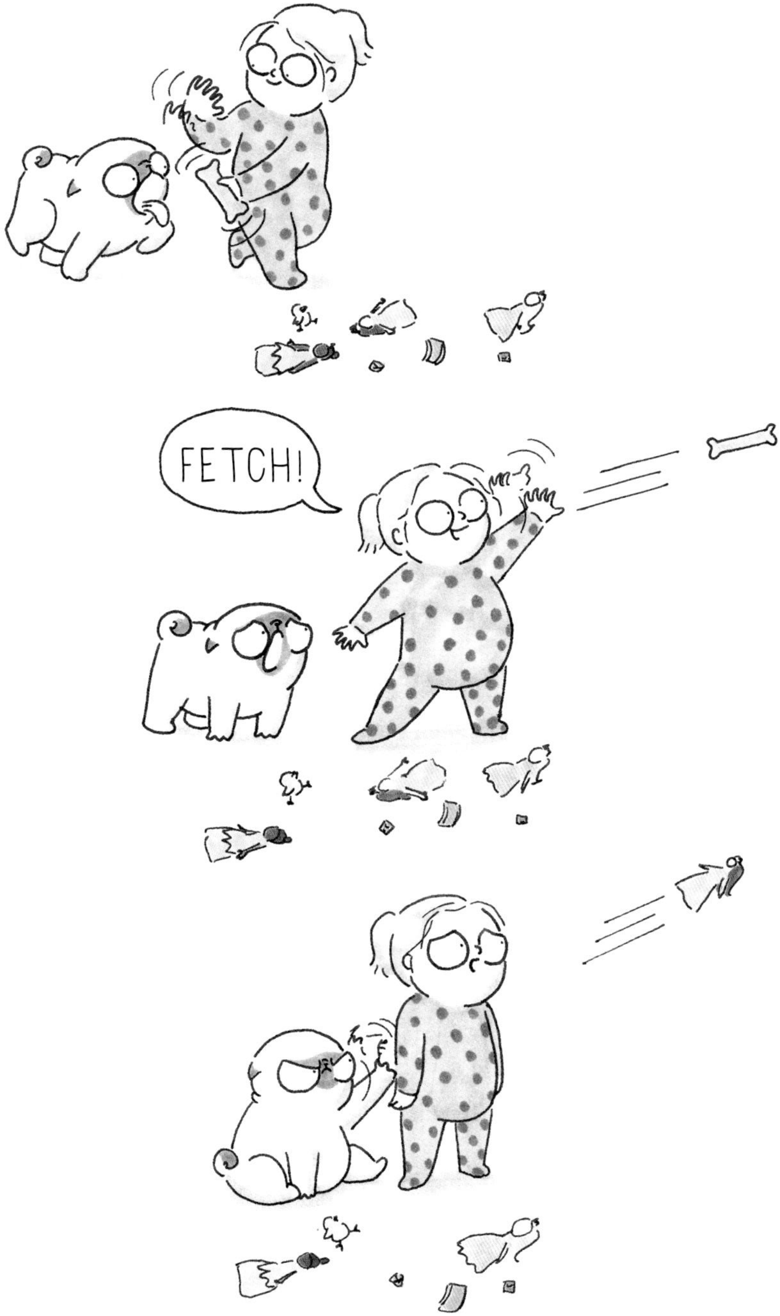
FETCH!

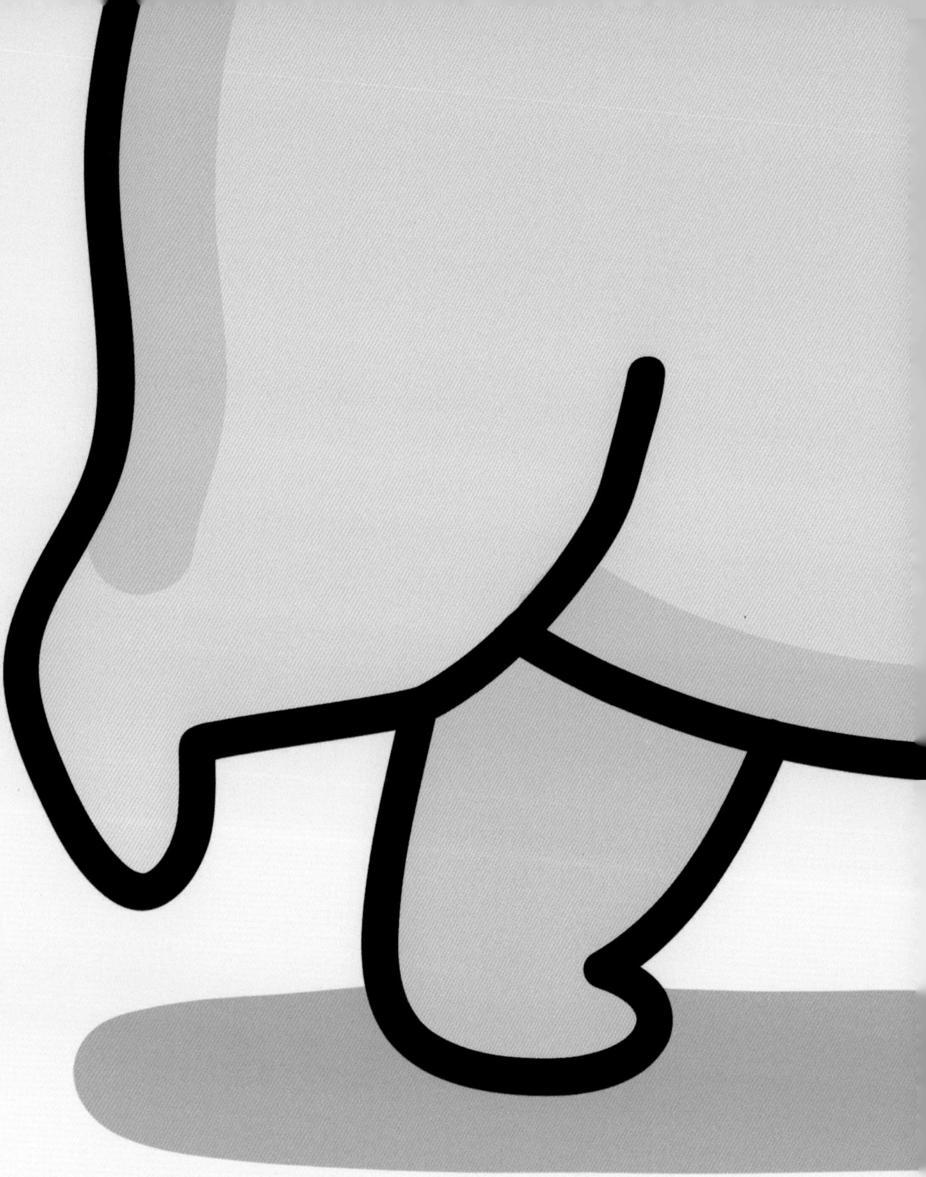

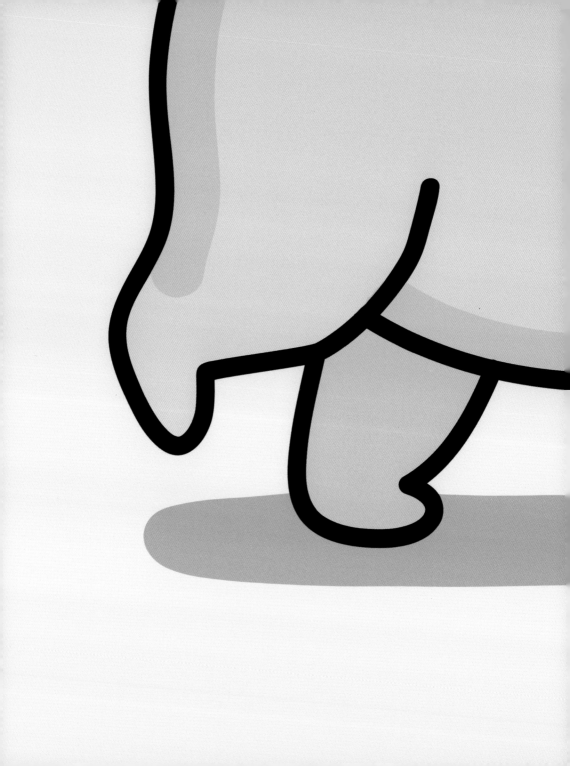

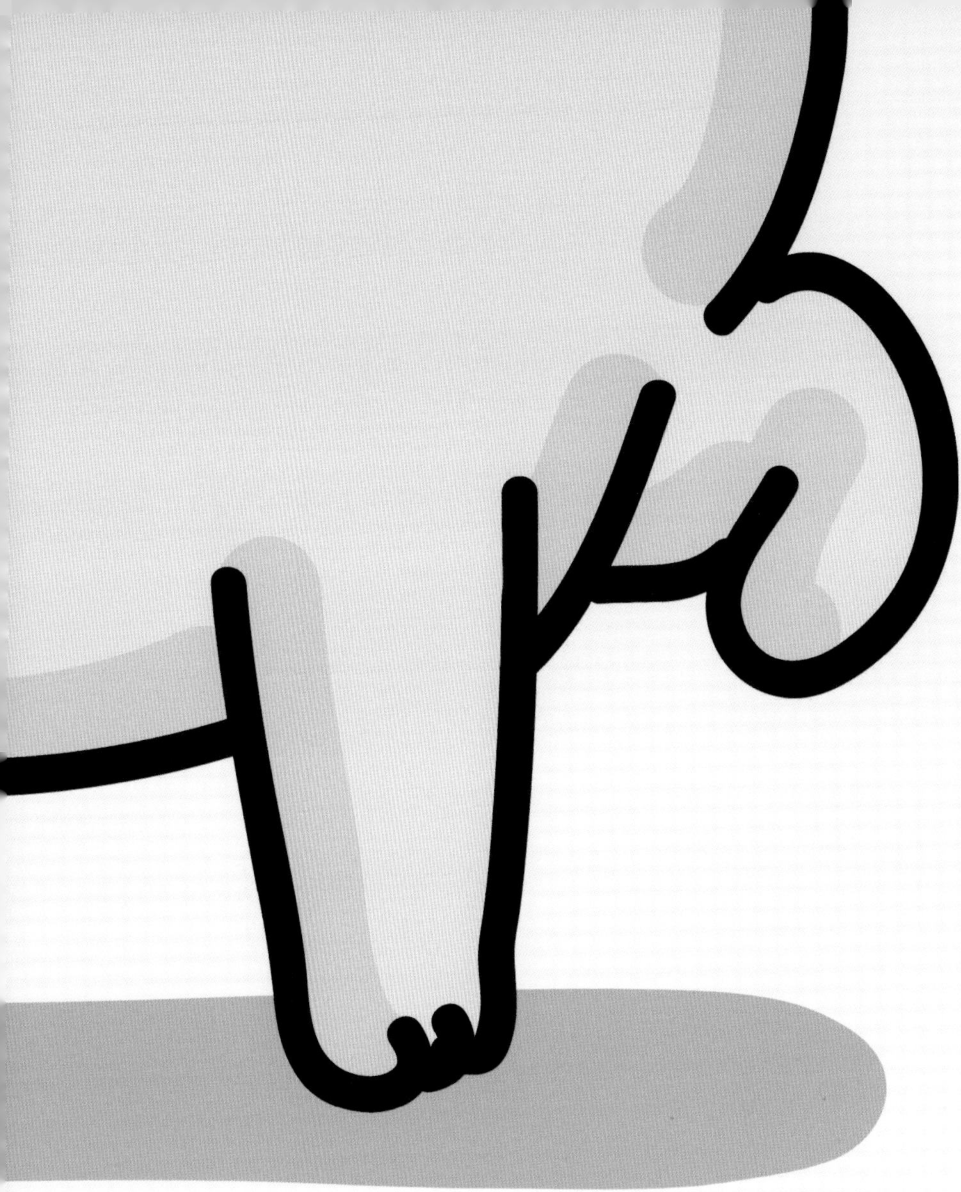

WALKS

MOCHI'S MINI GUIDE TO WALKS

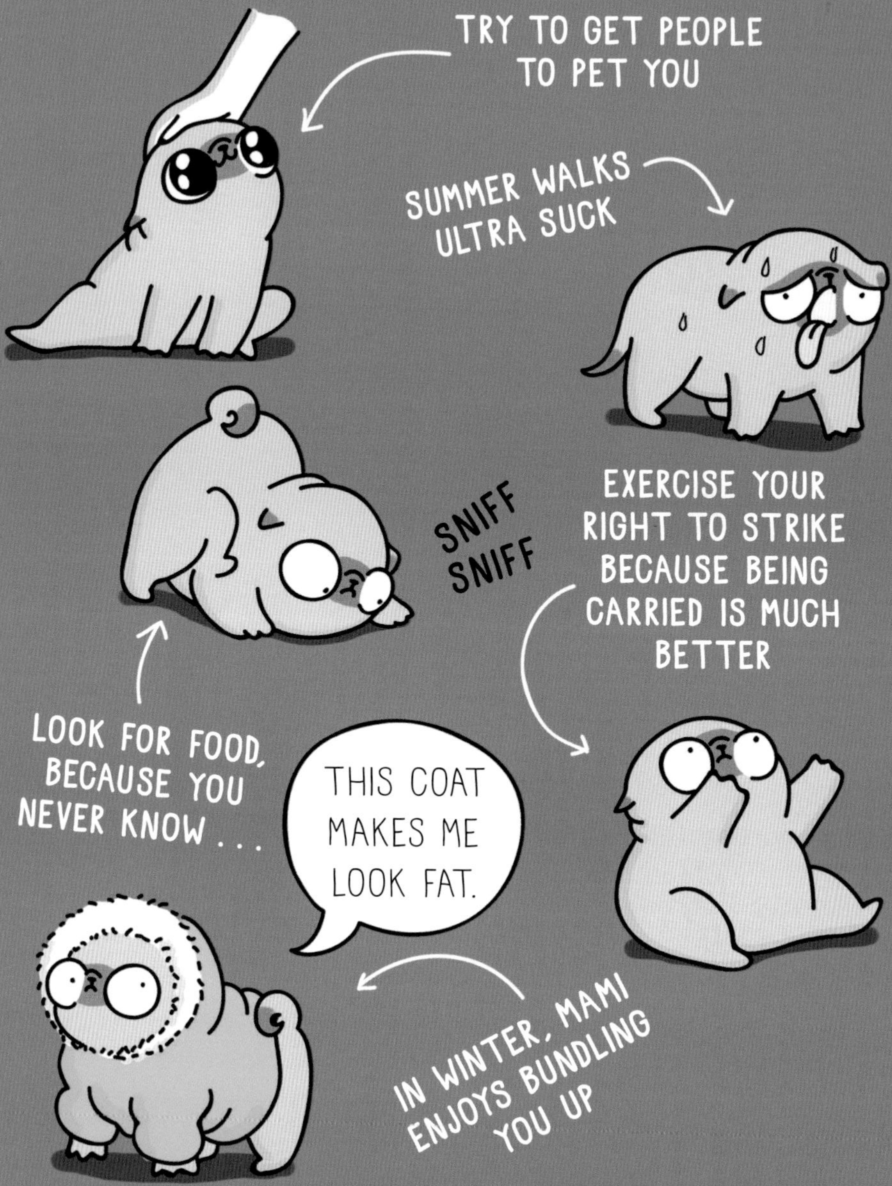
TRY TO GET PEOPLE TO PET YOU
SUMMER WALKS ULTRA SUCK
SNIFF SNIFF
EXERCISE YOUR RIGHT TO STRIKE BECAUSE BEING CARRIED IS MUCH BETTER
LOOK FOR FOOD, BECAUSE YOU NEVER KNOW . . .
THIS COAT MAKES ME LOOK FAT.
IN WINTER, MAMI ENJOYS BUNDLING YOU UP

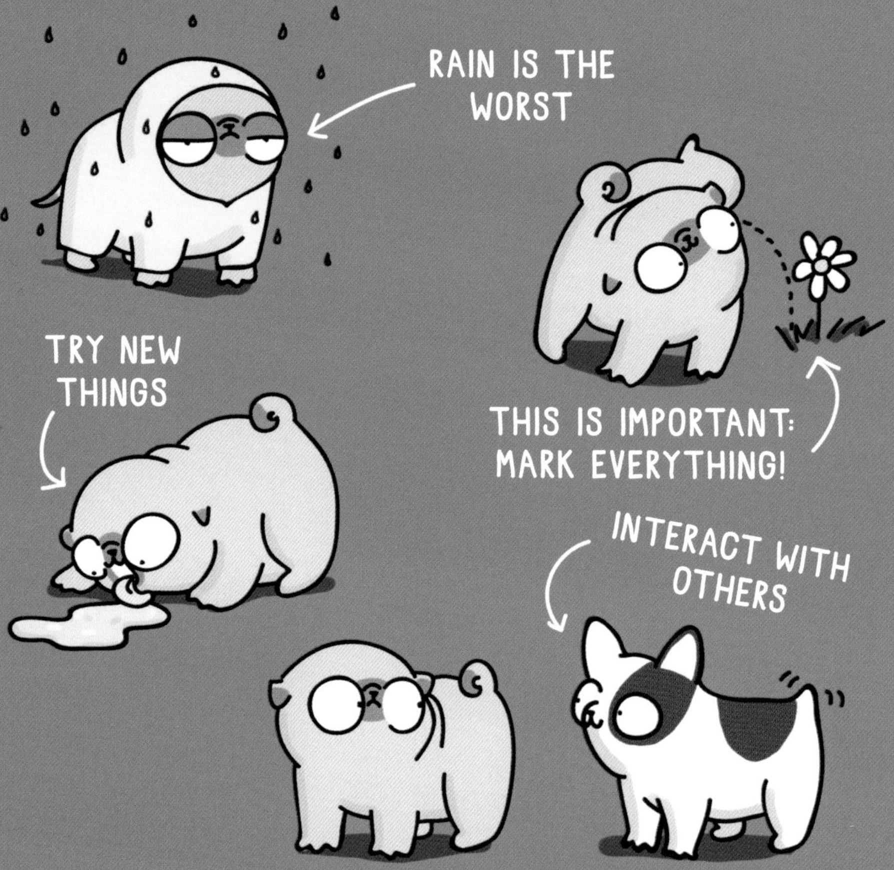
RAIN IS THE WORST
THIS IS IMPORTANT: MARK EVERYTHING!
TRY NEW THINGS
INTERACT WITH OTHERS

TO SUM IT UP, STAYING HOME IS MUCH BETTER . . .

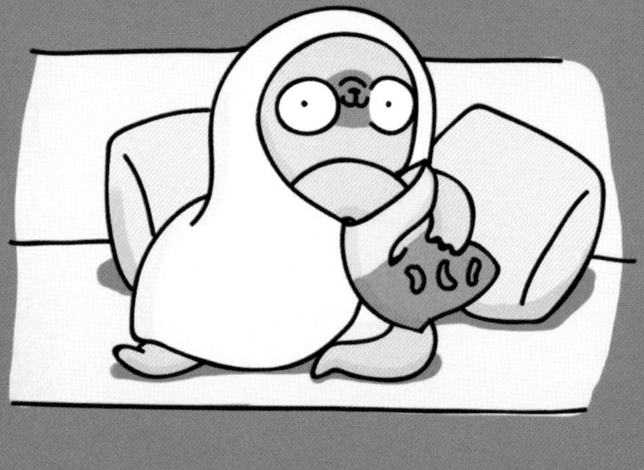

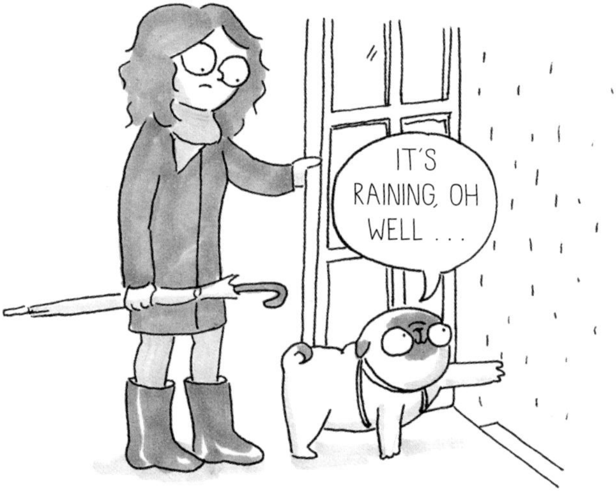
IT'S RAINING, OH WELL . . .

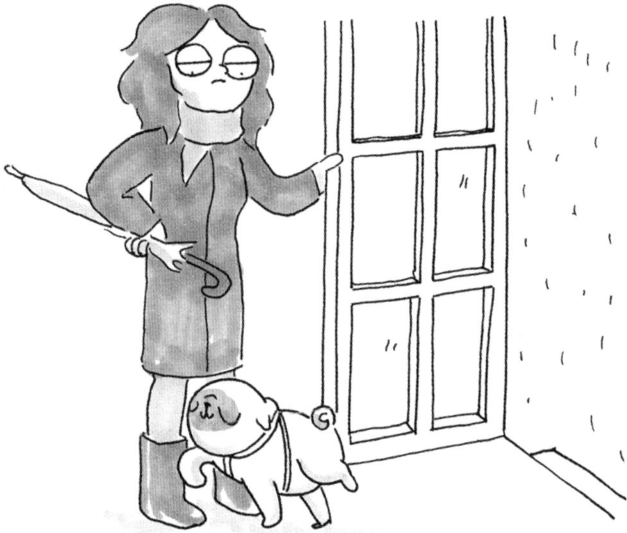

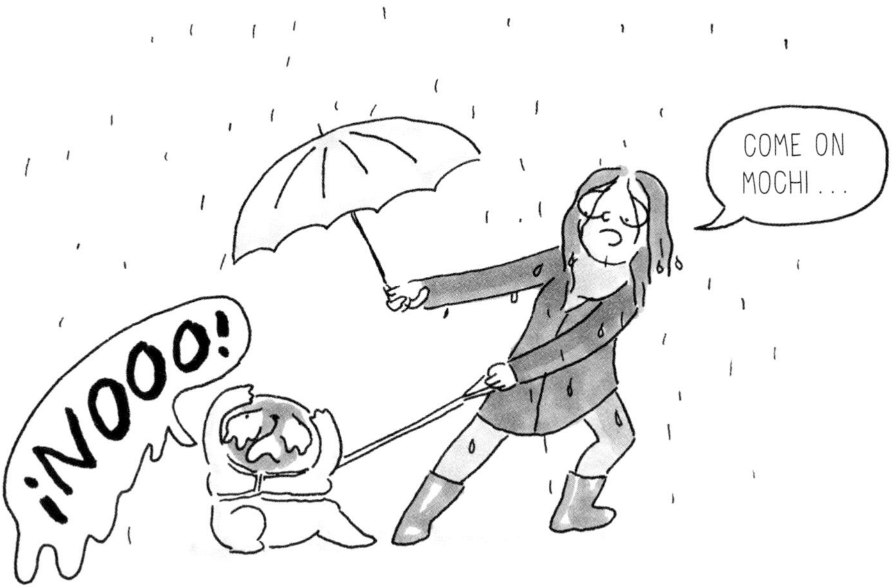
COME ON MOCHI...
¡NOOO!

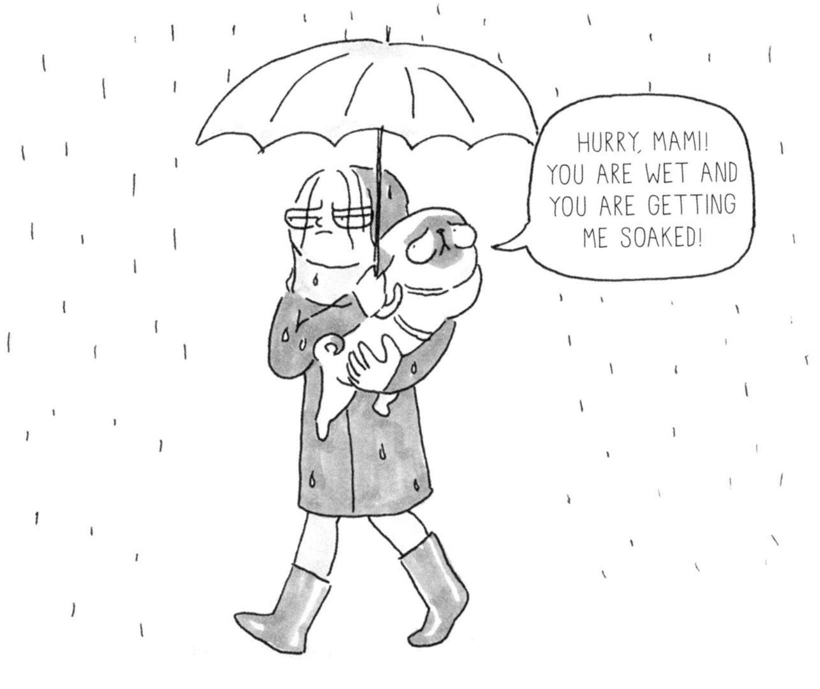
HURRY, MAMI! YOU ARE WET AND YOU ARE GETTING ME SOAKED!

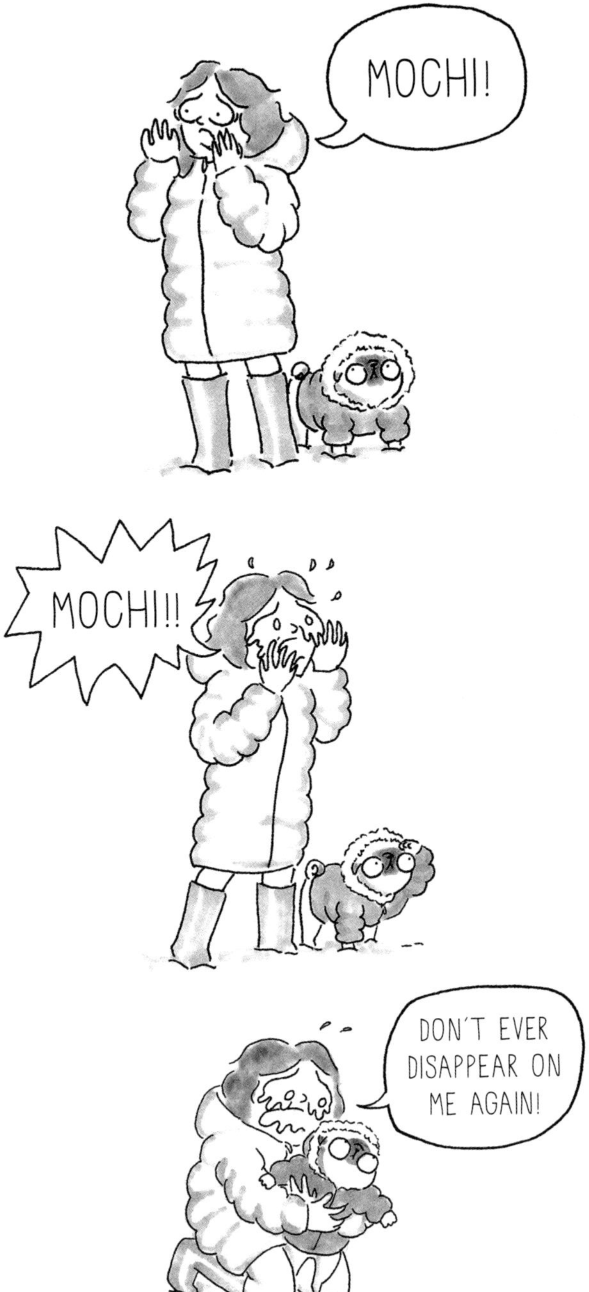
MOCHI!
MOCHI!!!
DON'T EVER DISAPPEAR ON ME AGAIN!

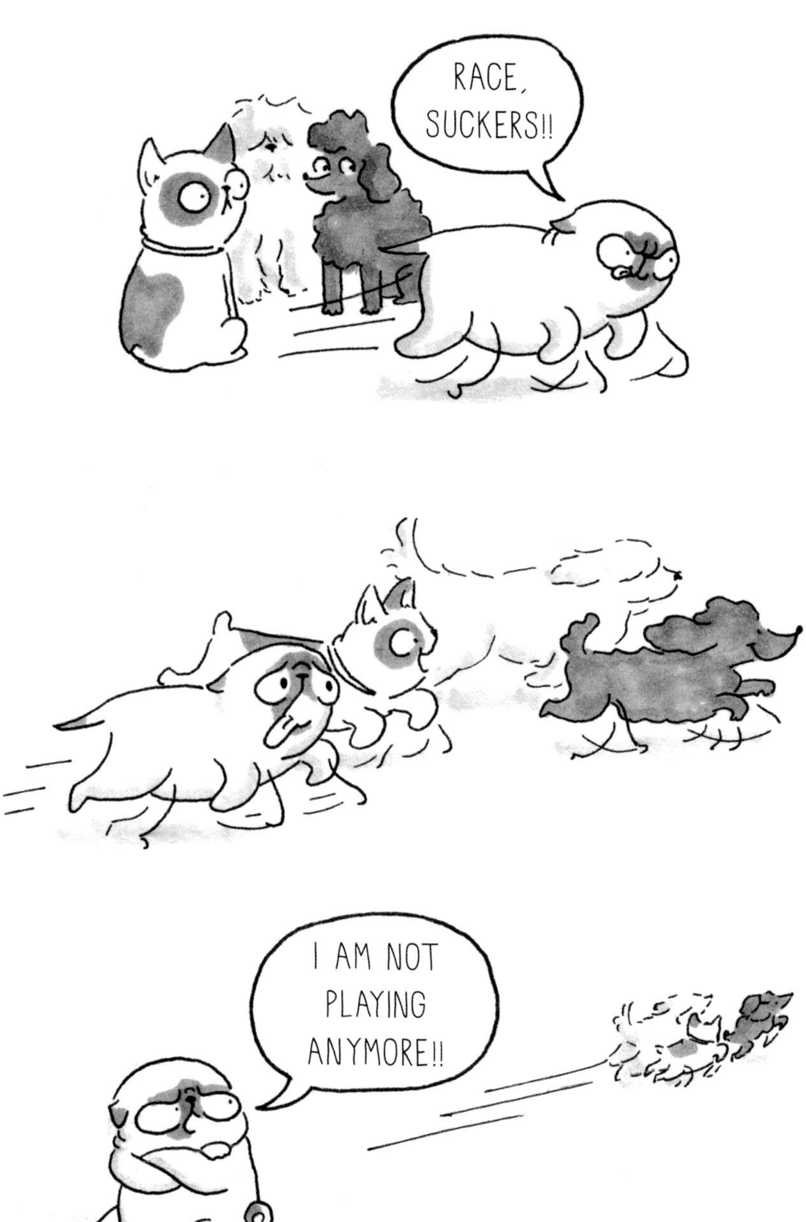
RACE, SUCKERS!!
I AM NOT PLAYING ANYMORE!!

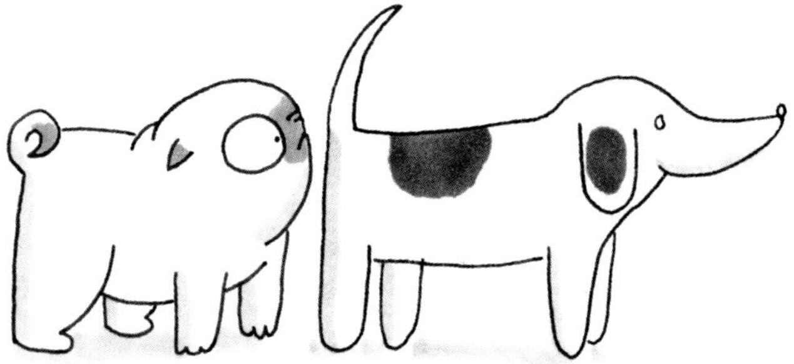

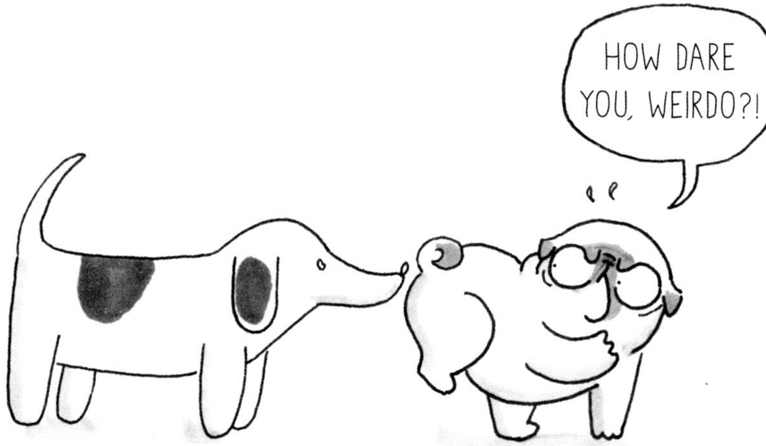
HOW DARE YOU, WEIRDO?!

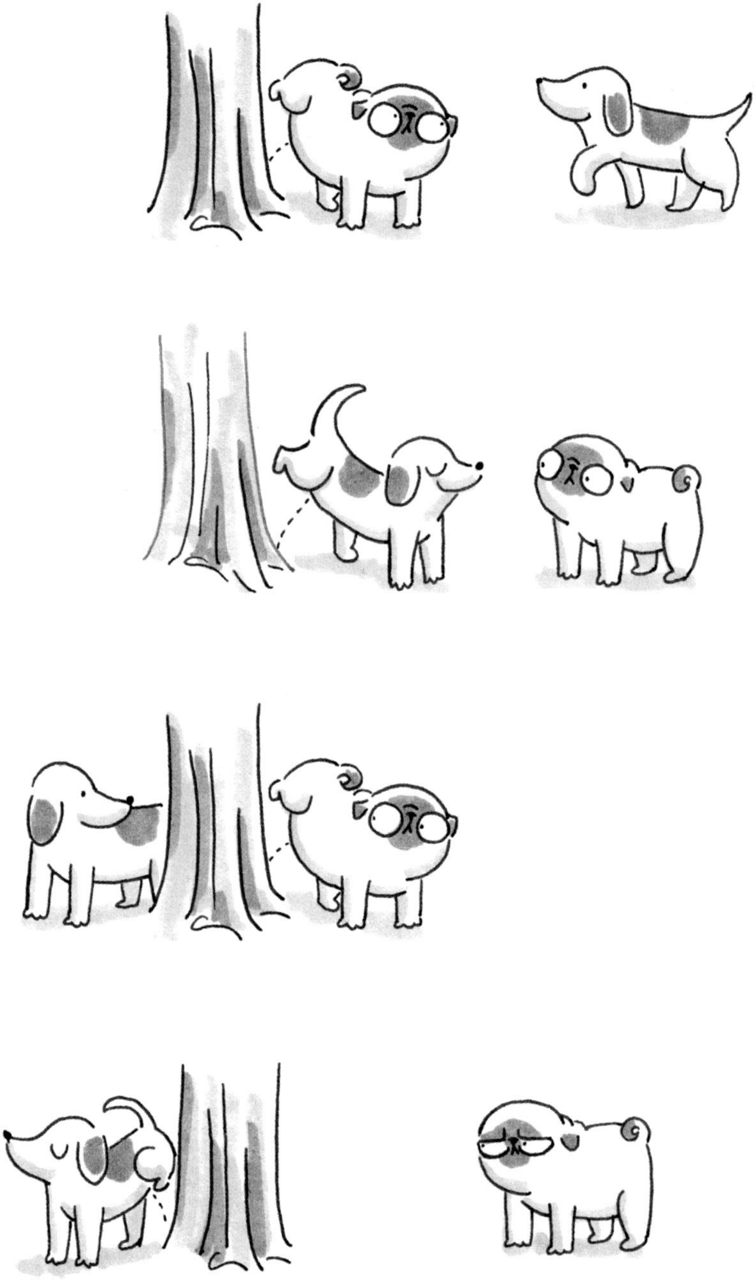

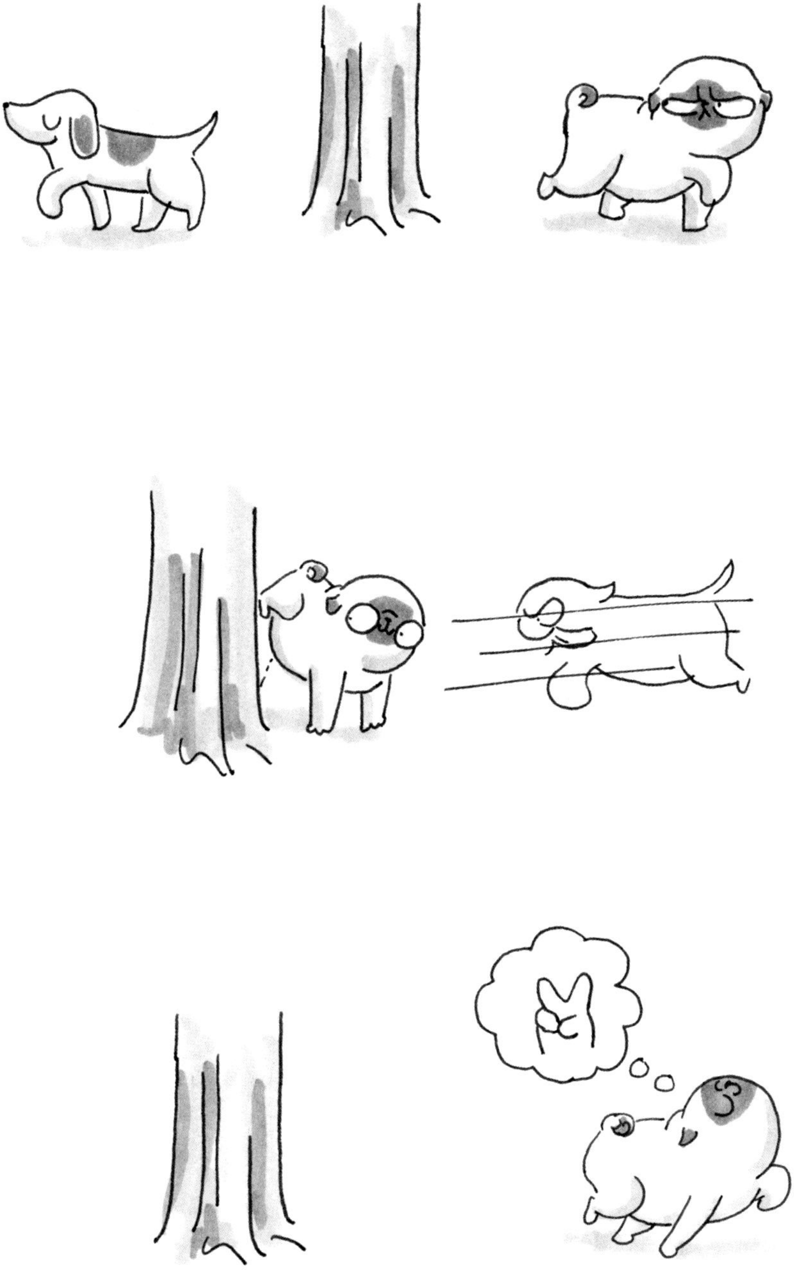

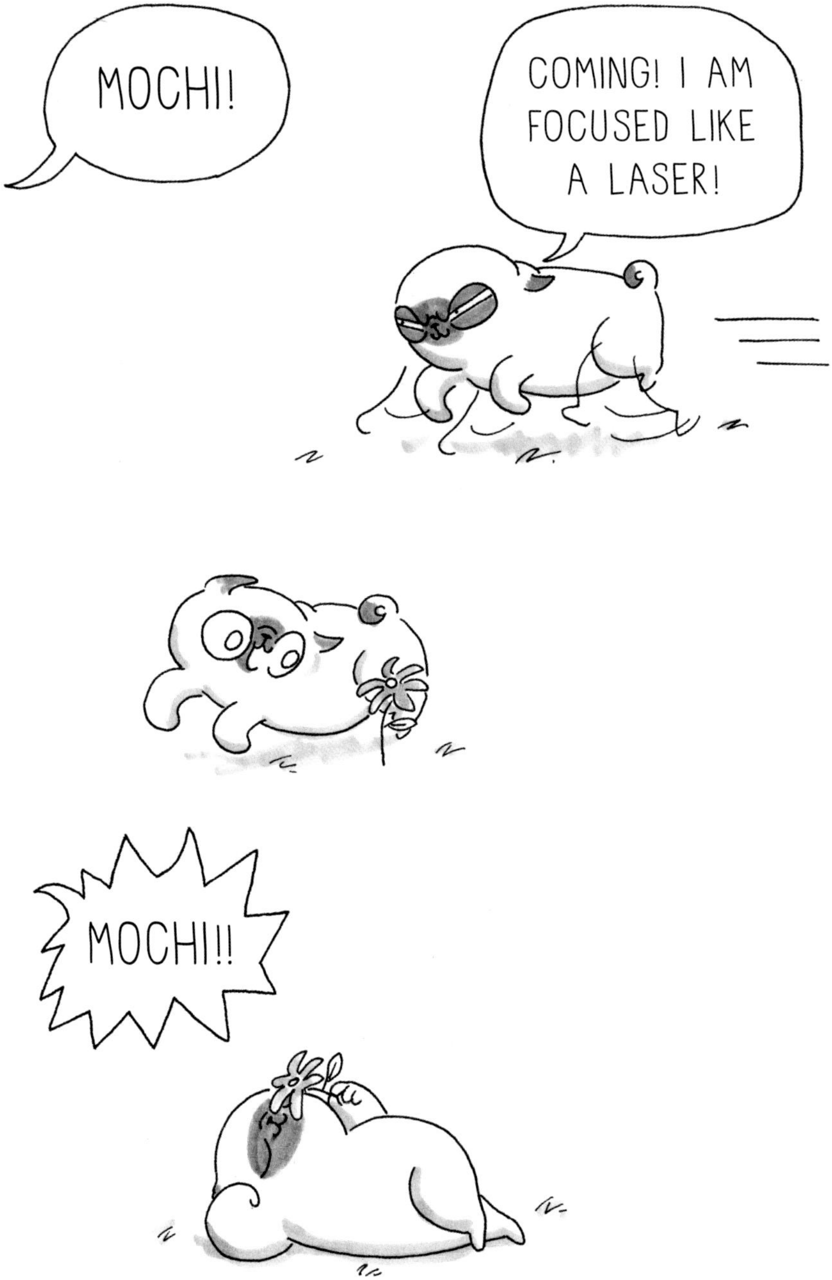
MOCHI!
COMING! I AM FOCUSED LIKE A LASER!
MOCHI!!

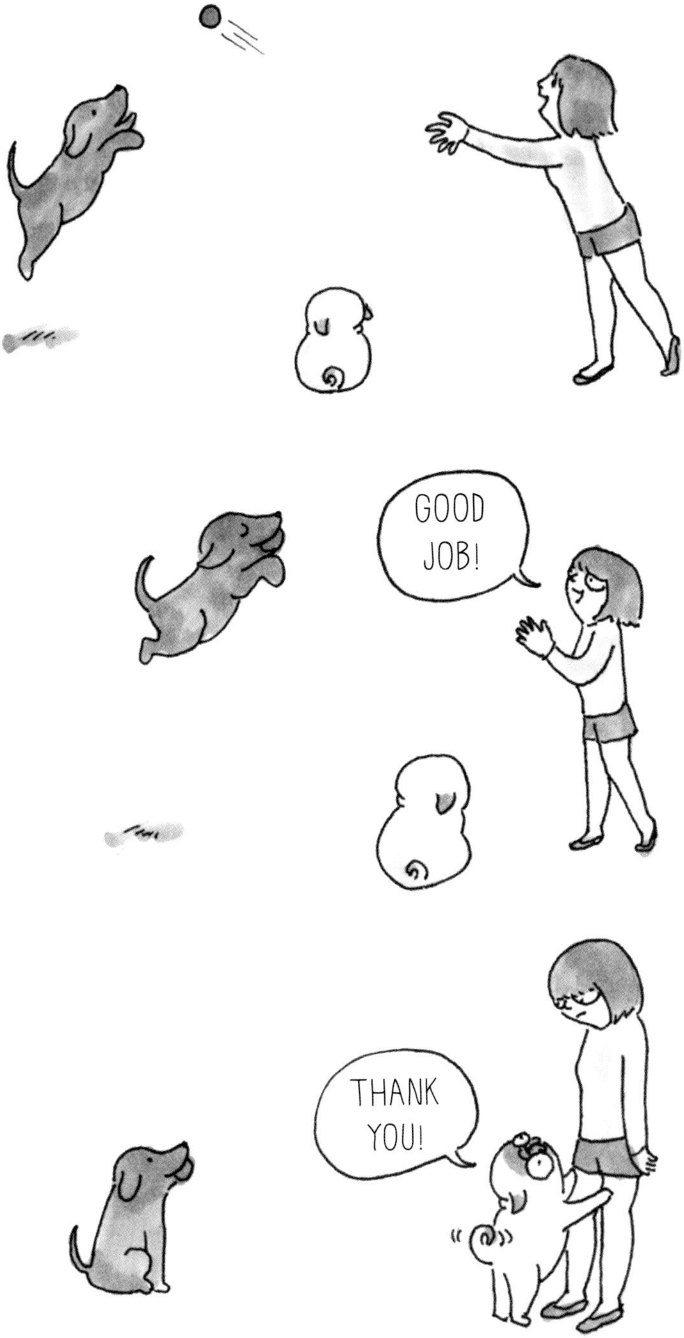
GOOD JOB!
THANK YOU!

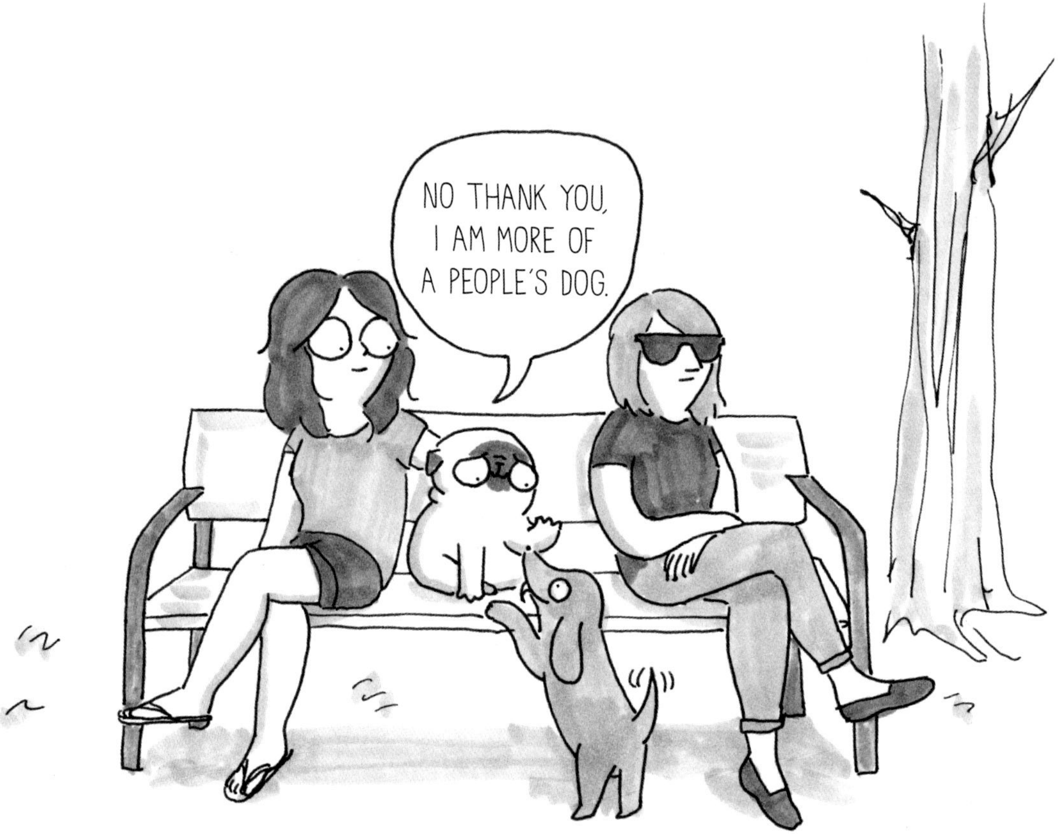
NO THANK YOU, I AM MORE OF A PEOPLE'S DOG.

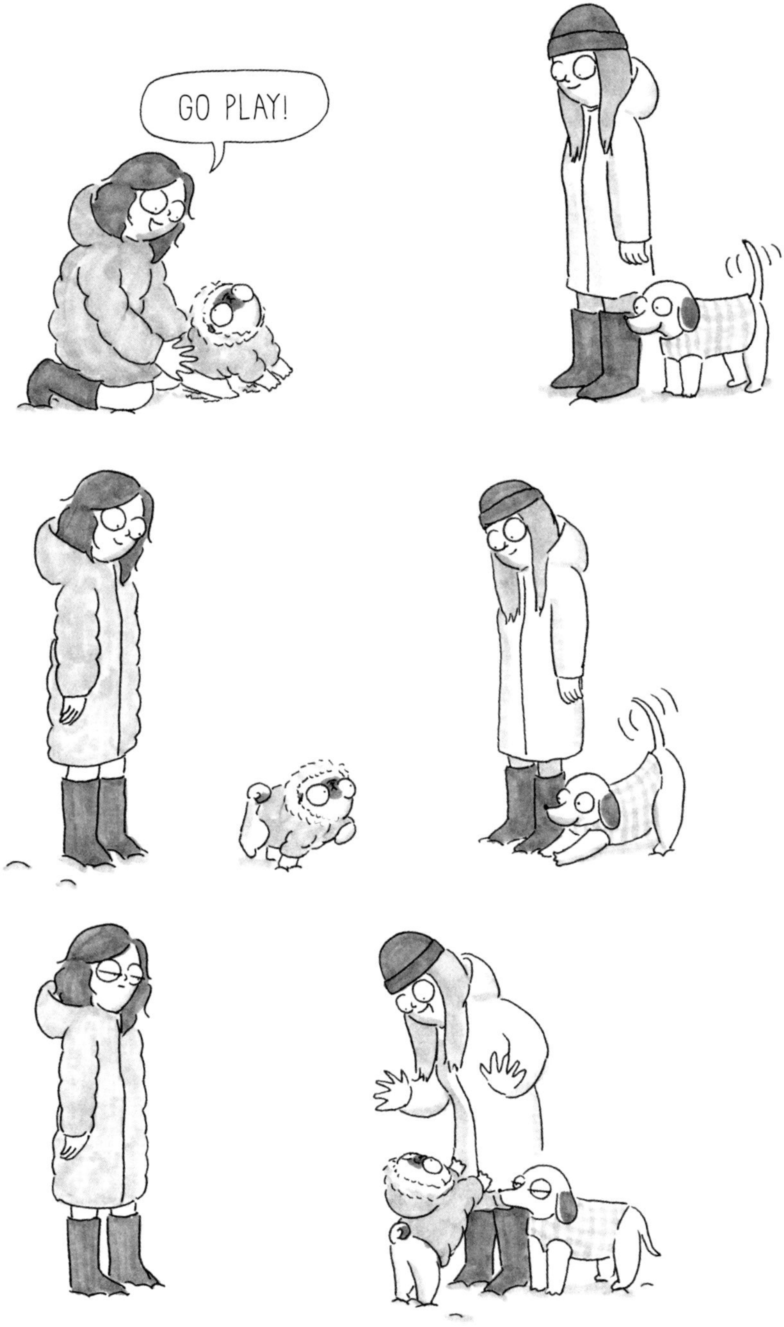
GO PLAY!

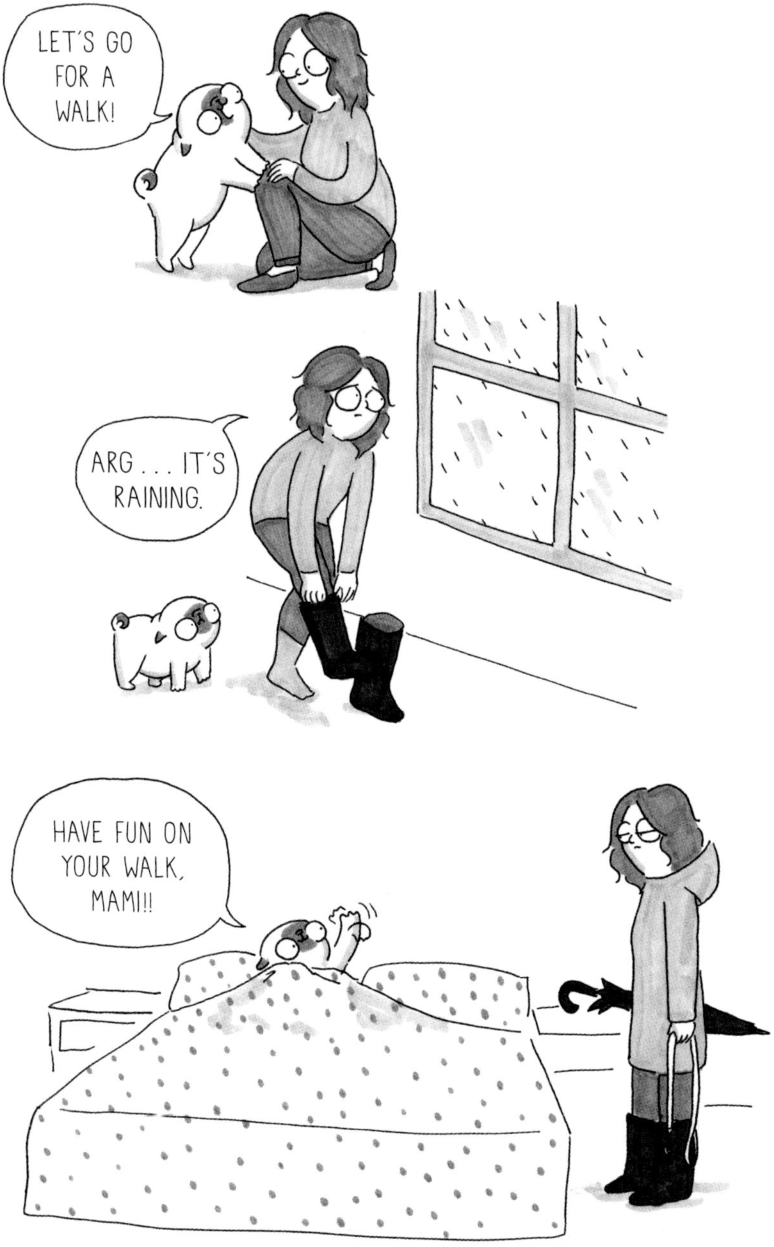
LET'S GO FOR A WALK!
ARG . . . IT'S RAINING.
HAVE FUN ON YOUR WALK, MAMI!!

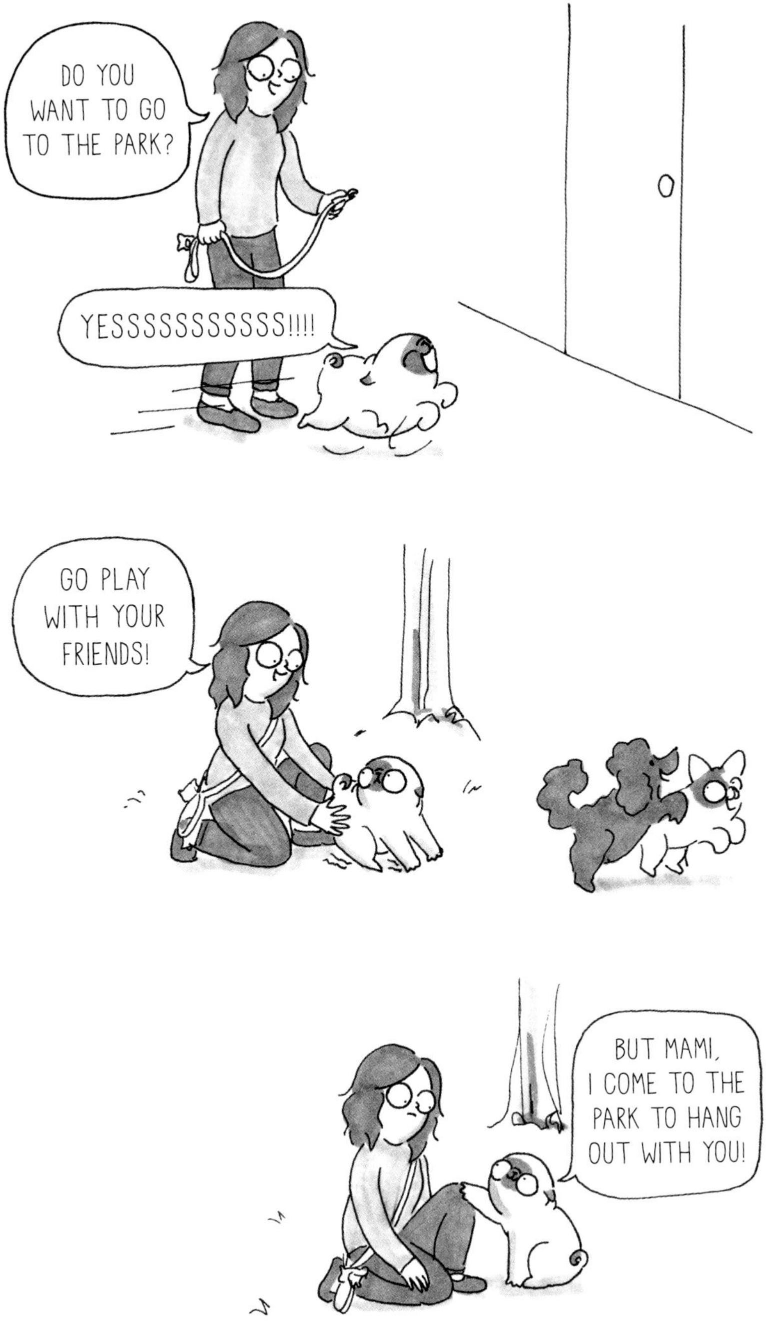
DO YOU WANT TO GO TO THE PARK?
YESSSSSSSSSSSS!!!!
GO PLAY WITH YOUR FRIENDS!
BUT MAMI, I COME TO THE PARK TO HANG OUT WITH YOU!

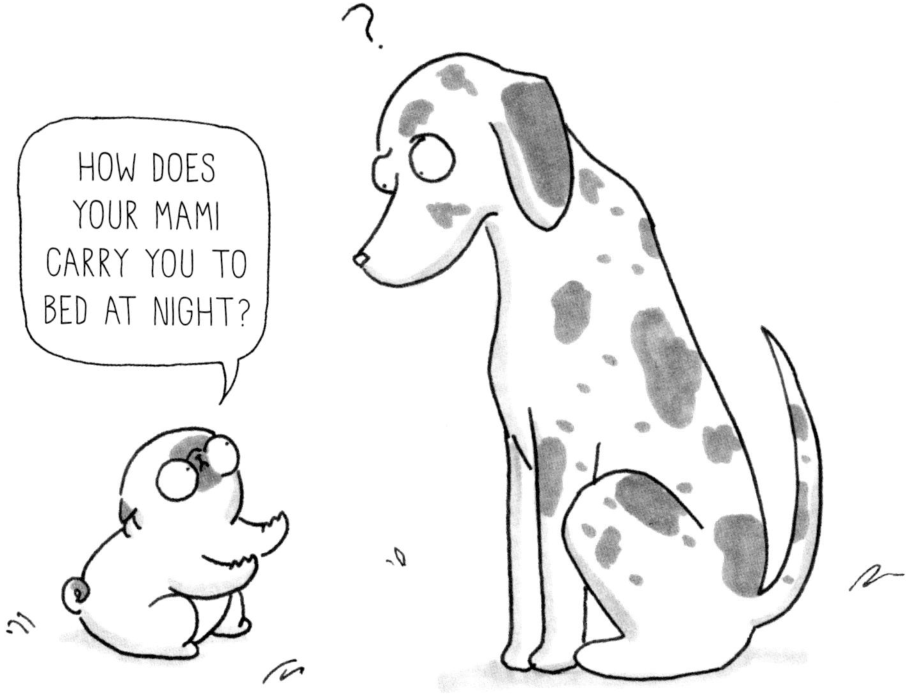
HOW DOES YOUR MAMI CARRY YOU TO BED AT NIGHT?
?

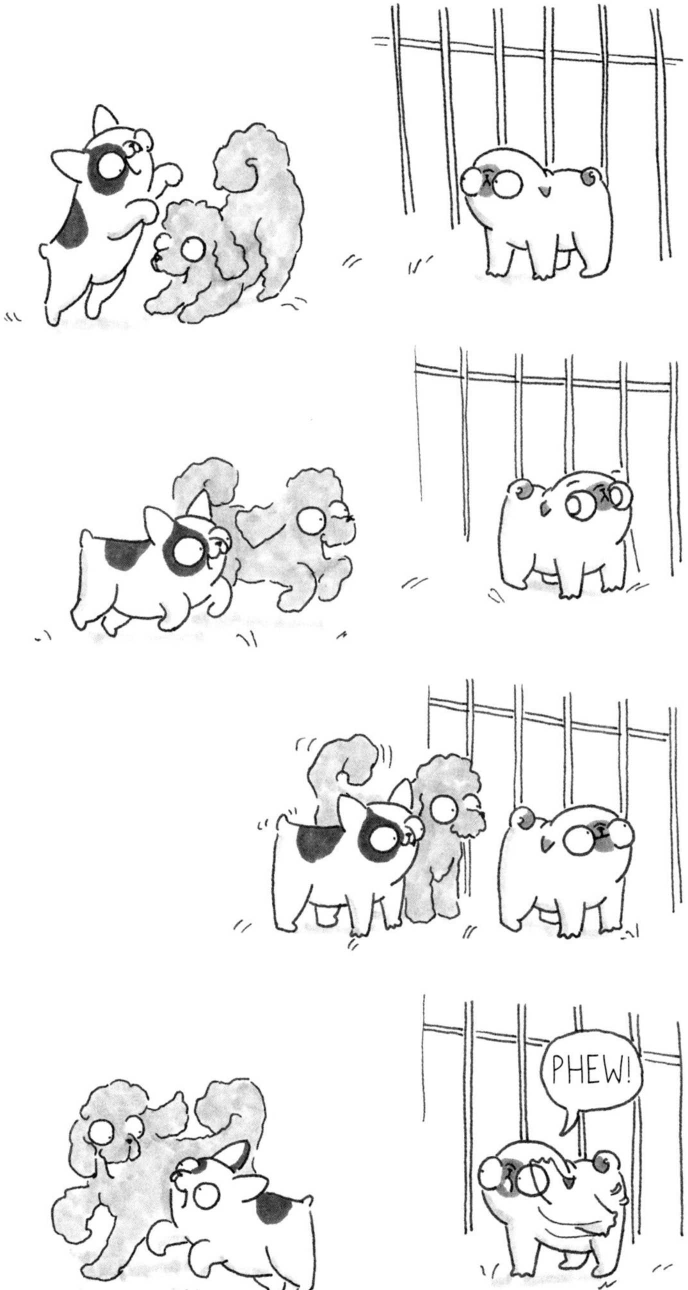
PHEW!

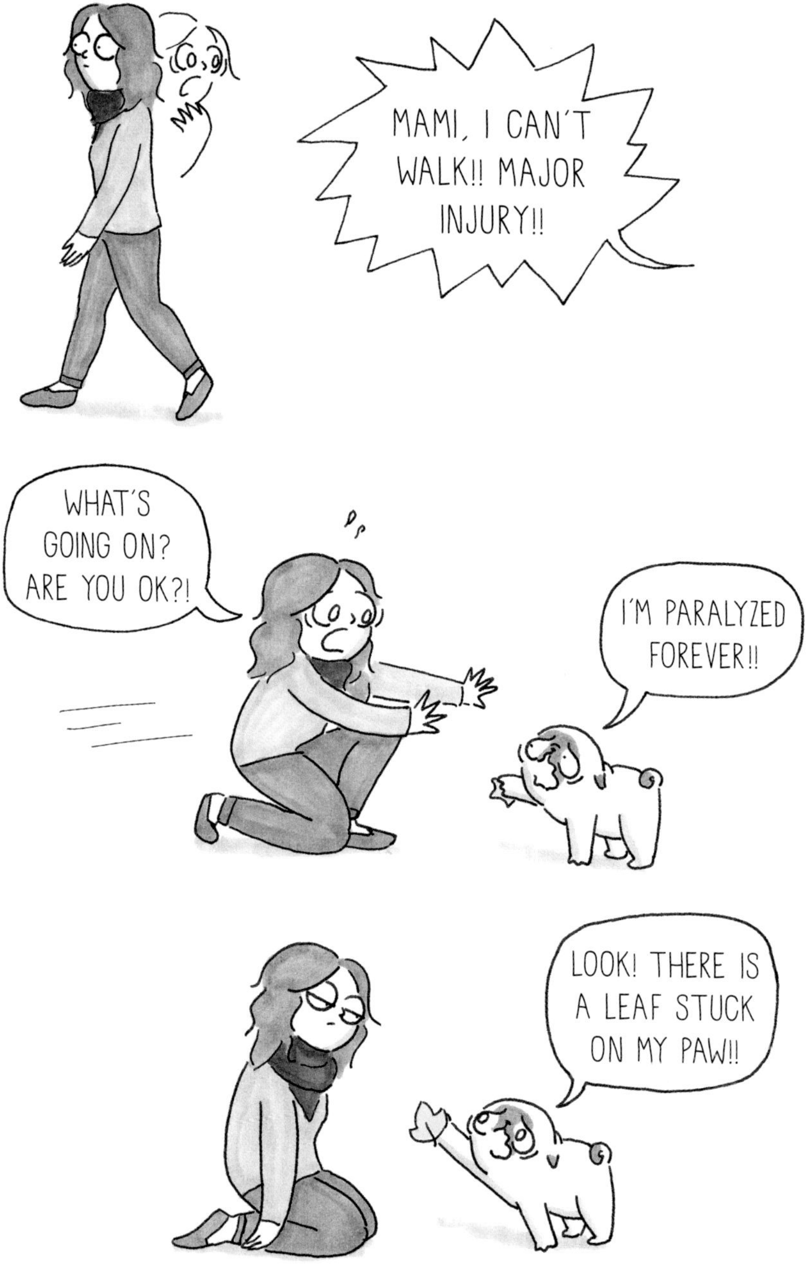
MAMI, I CAN'T WALK!! MAJOR INJURY!!
WHAT'S GOING ON? ARE YOU OK?!
I'M PARALYZED FOREVER!!
LOOK! THERE IS A LEAF STUCK ON MY PAW!!

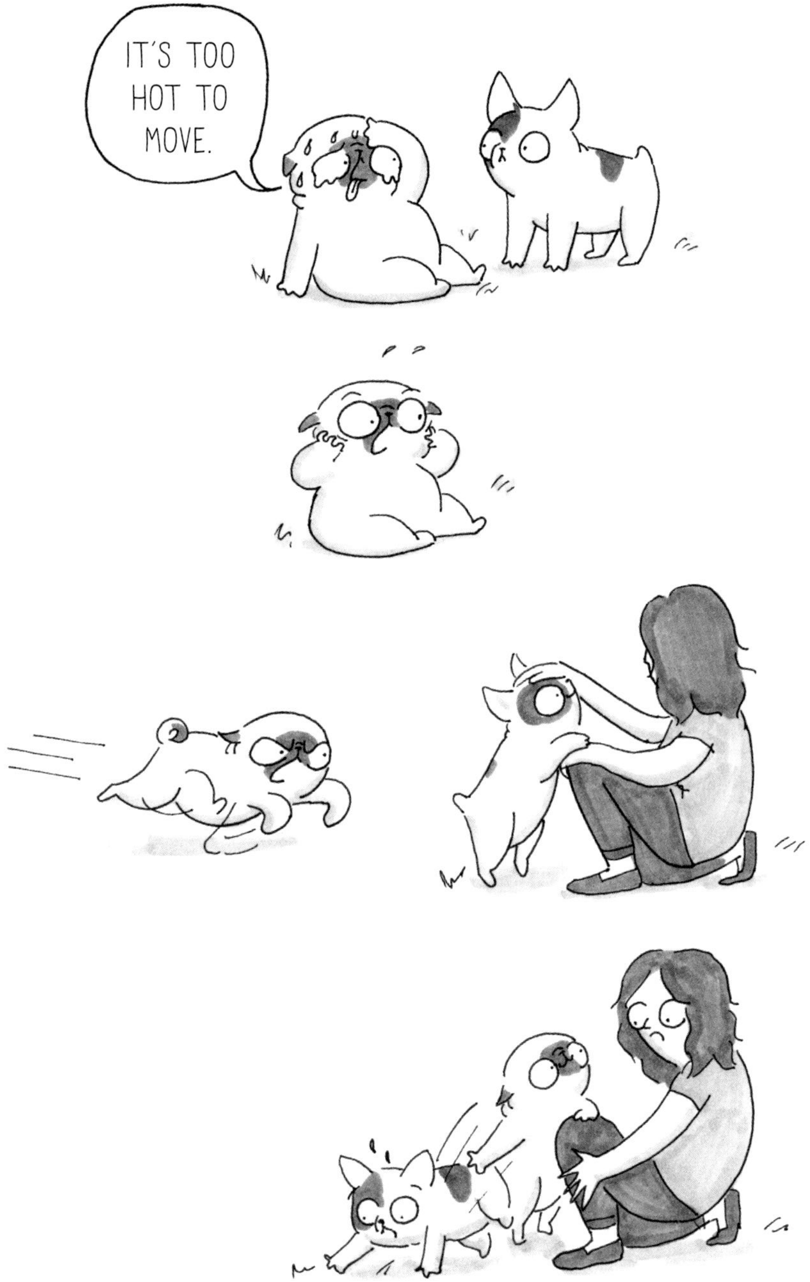
IT'S TOO HOT TO MOVE.

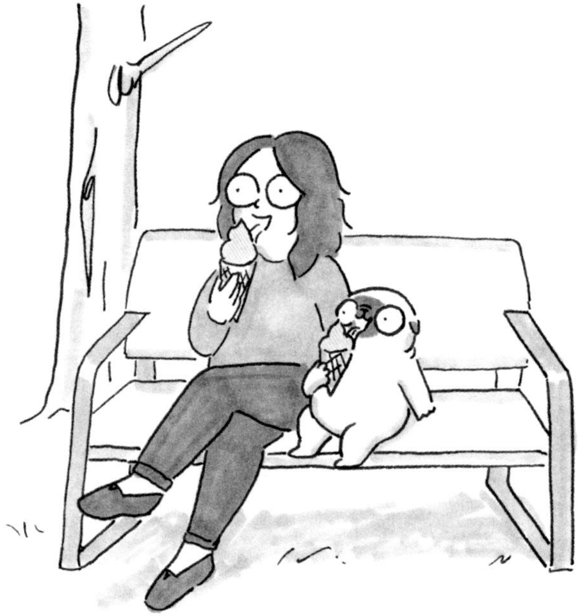

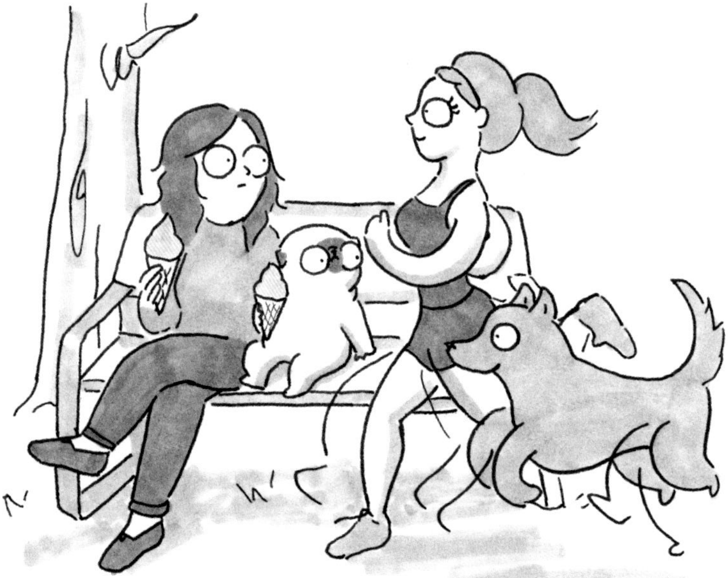

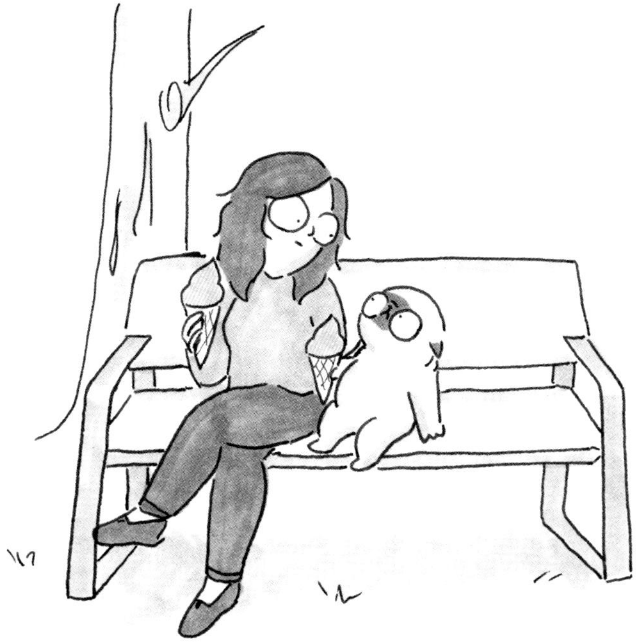

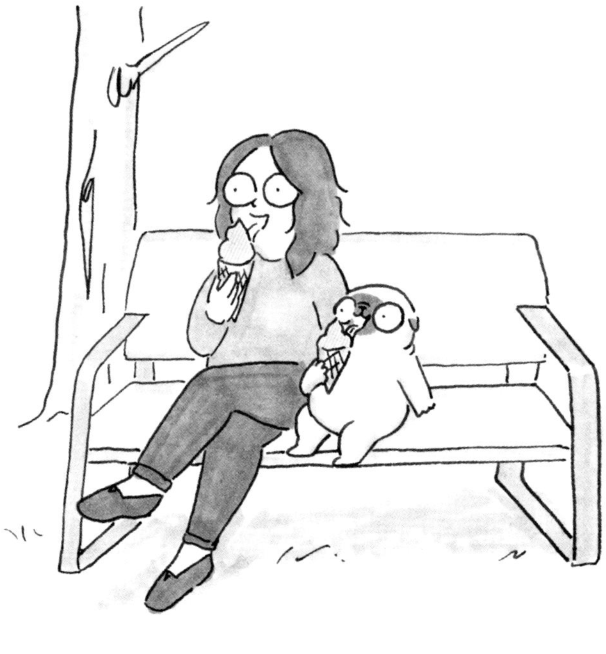

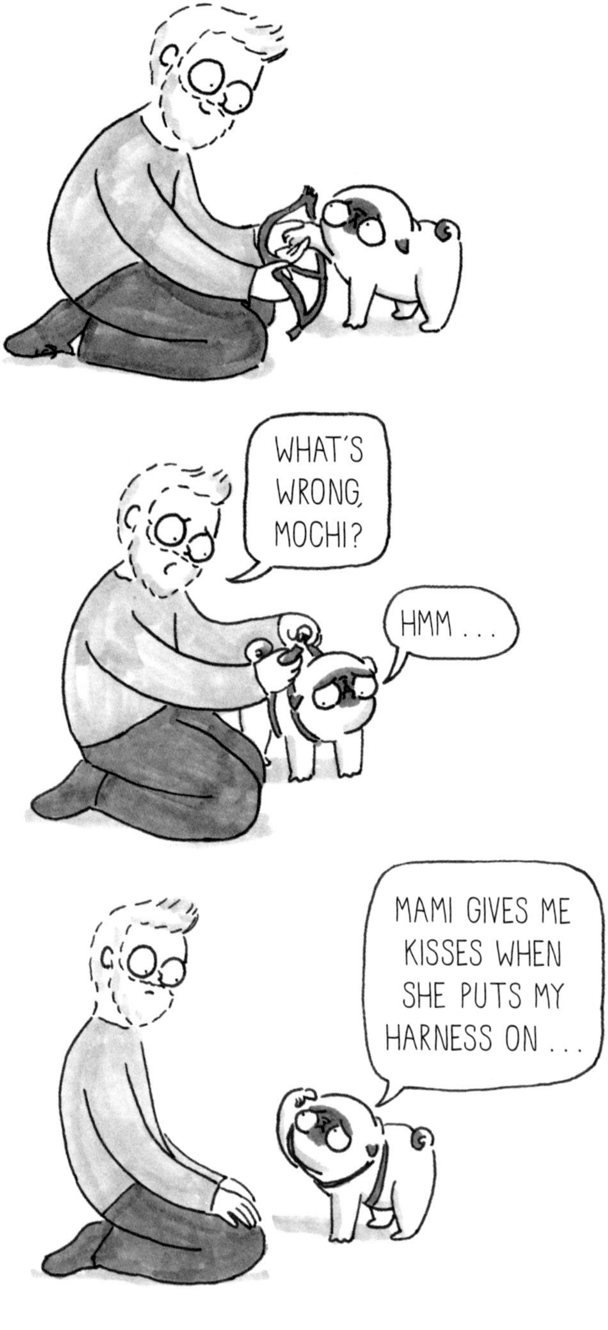
WHAT'S WRONG, MOCHI?
HMM . . .
MAMI GIVES ME KISSES WHEN SHE PUTS MY HARNESS ON . . .

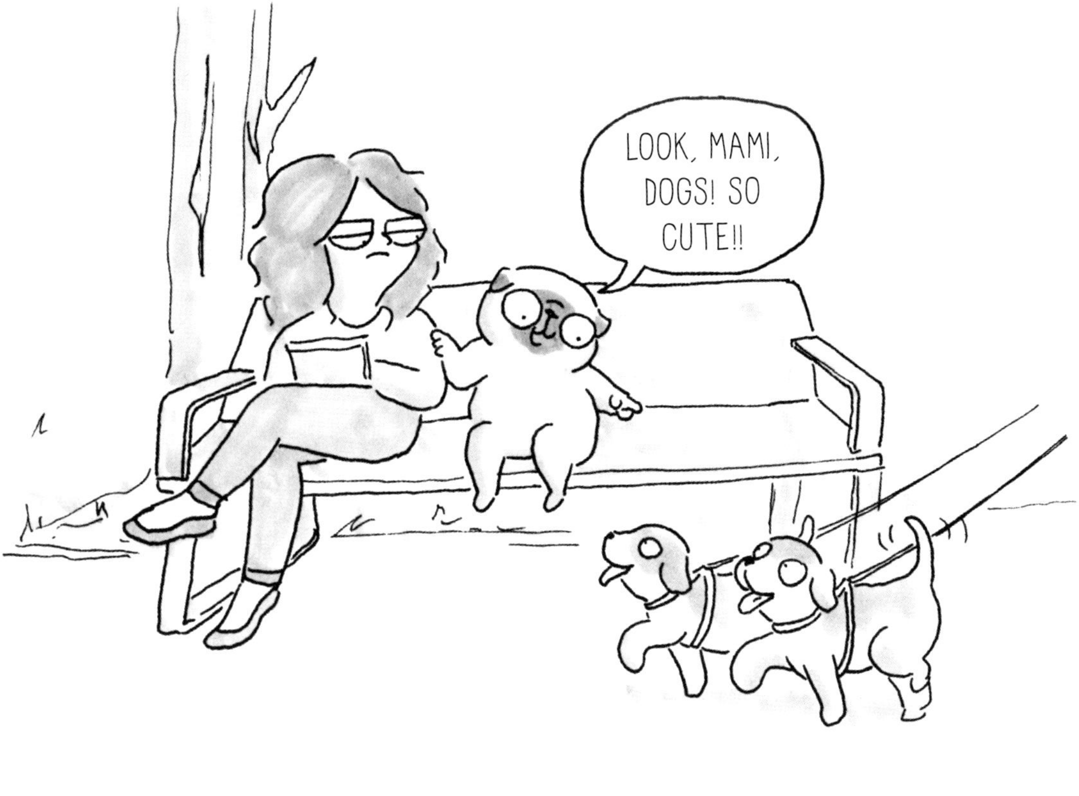
LOOK, MAMI, DOGS! SO CUTE!!

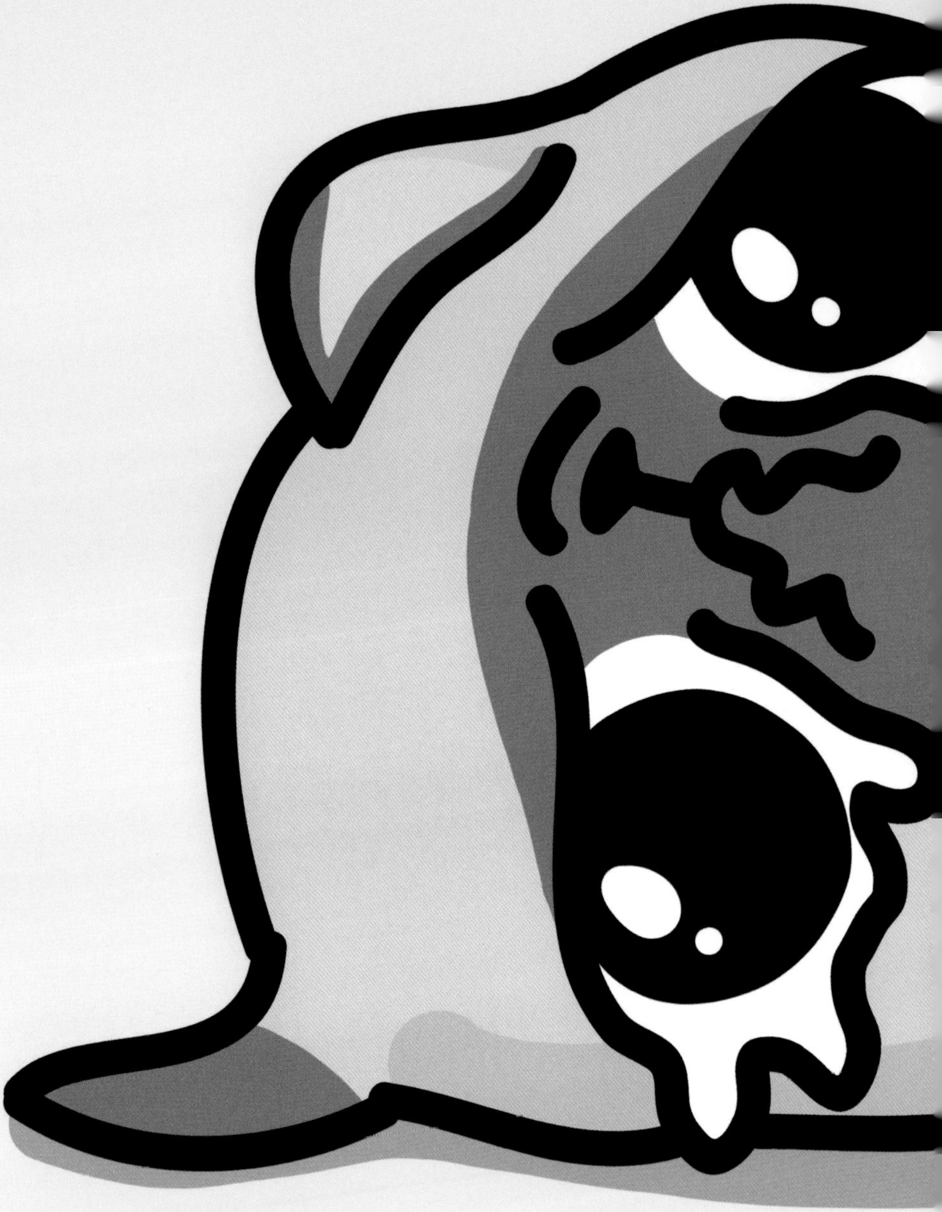

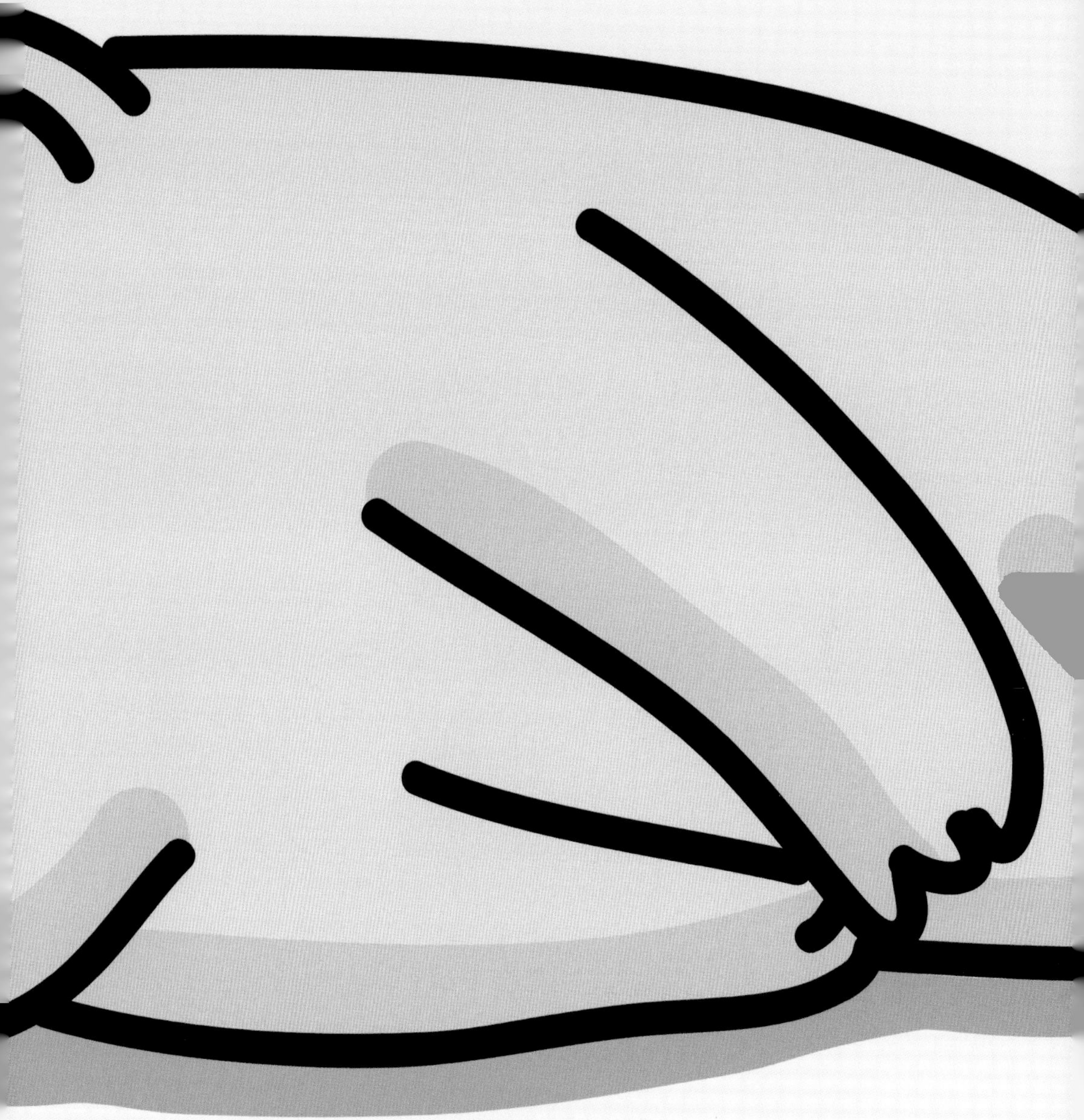

STRUGGLES

MOCHI'S LIFE STRUGGLES

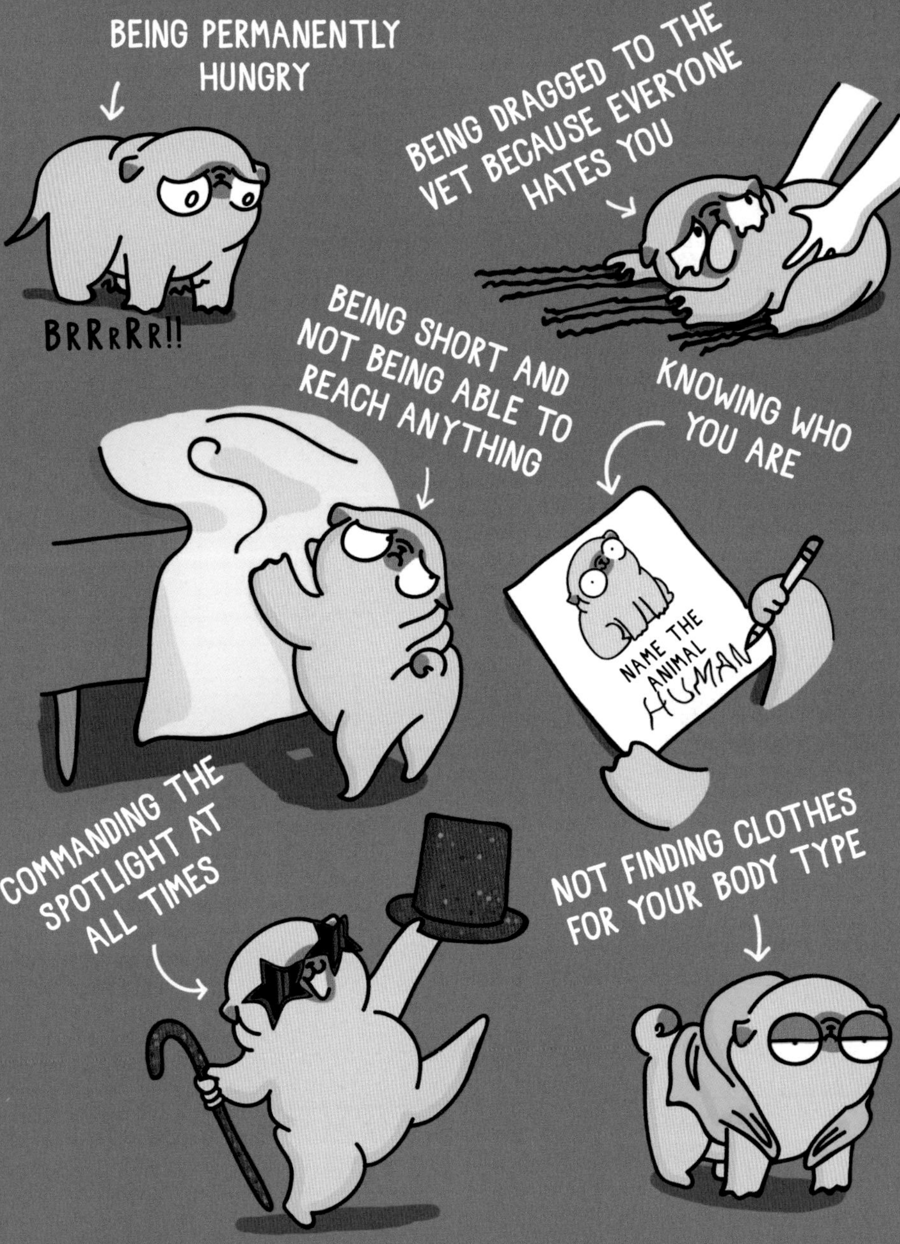
BEING PERMANENTLY HUNGRY
BRRRRR!!
BEING DRAGGED TO THE VET BECAUSE EVERYONE HATES YOU
BEING SHORT AND NOT BEING ABLE TO REACH ANYTHING
KNOWING WHO YOU ARE
NAME THE ANIMAL
HUMAN
COMMANDING THE SPOTLIGHT AT ALL TIMES
NOT FINDING CLOTHES FOR YOUR BODY TYPE

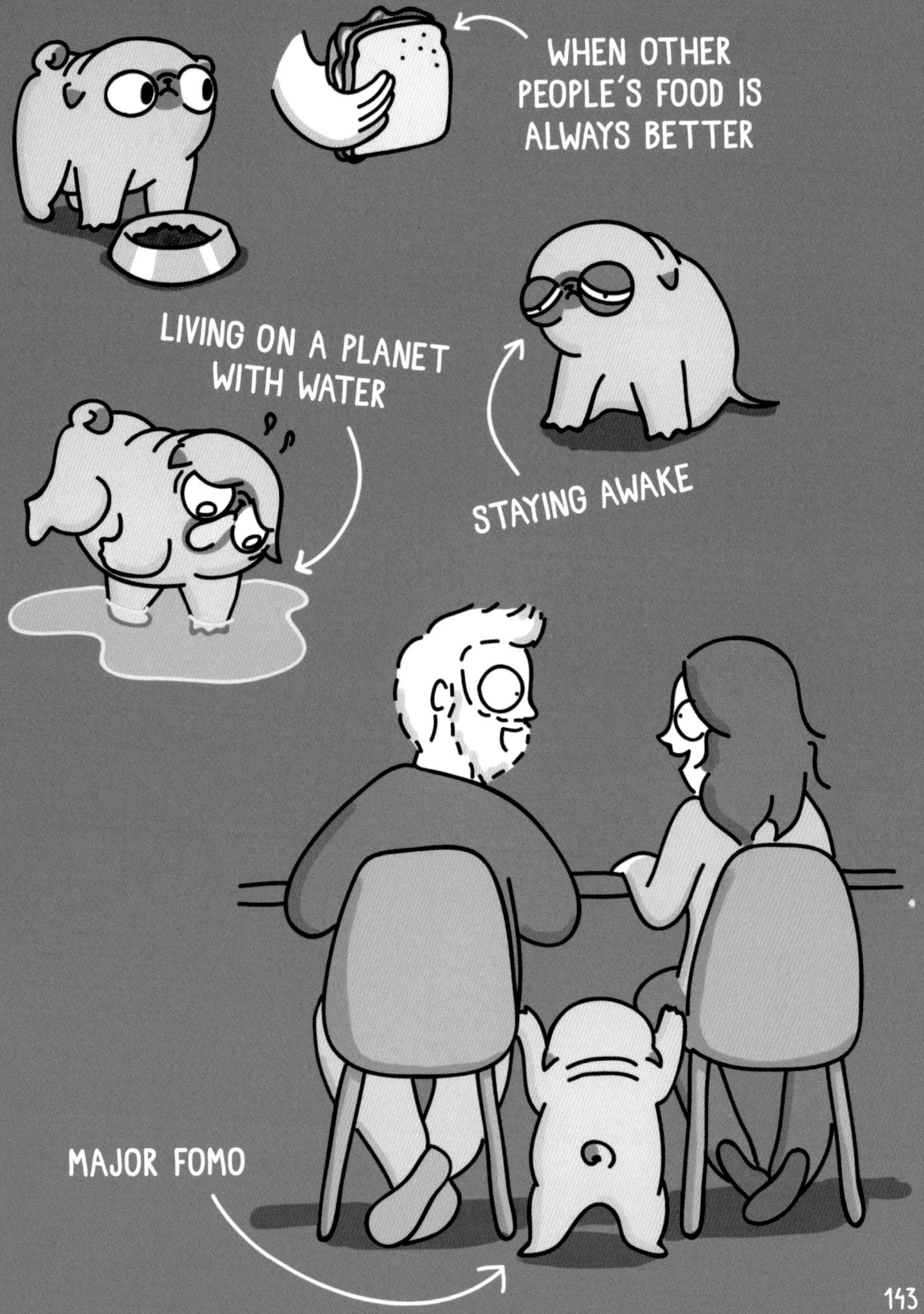
WHEN OTHER PEOPLE'S FOOD IS ALWAYS BETTER
LIVING ON A PLANET WITH WATER
STAYING AWAKE
MAJOR FOMO

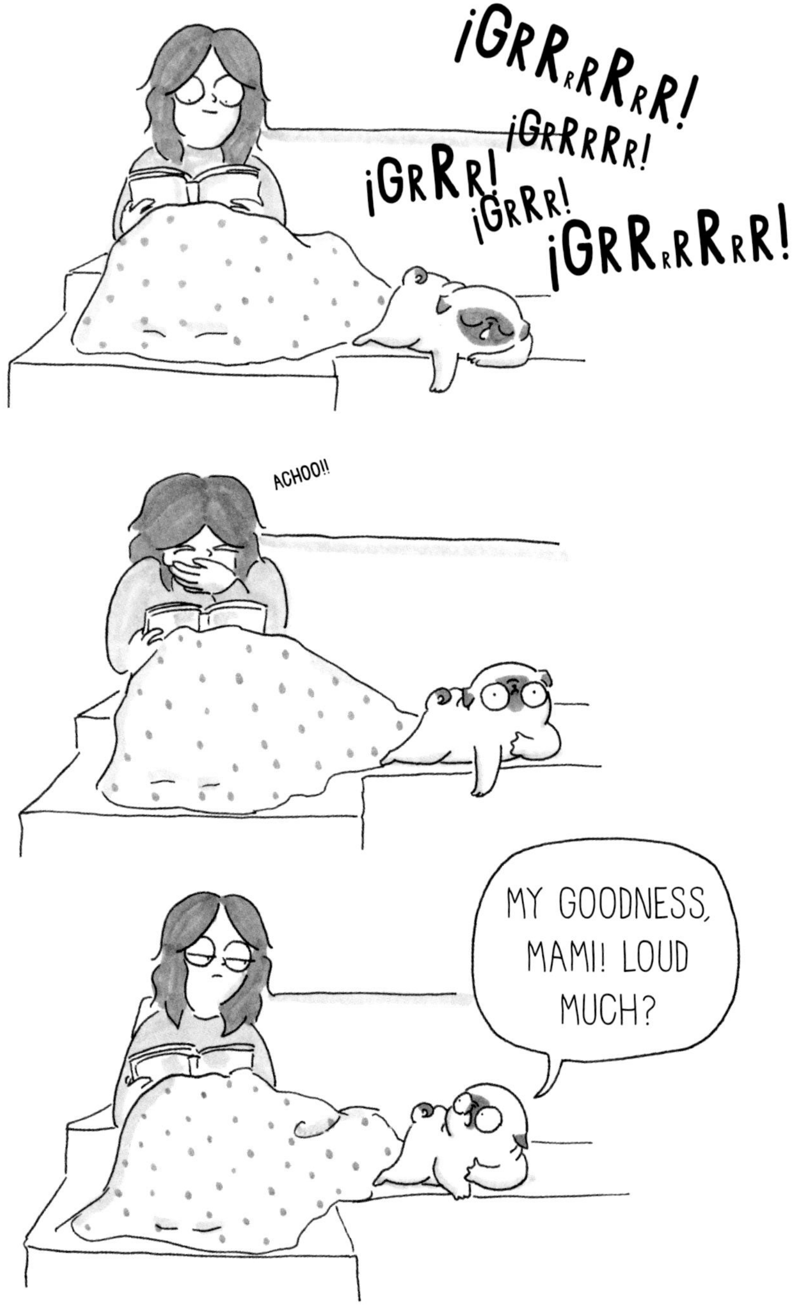
¡GRRRRRRR!
¡GRRRRRR!
¡GRRR!
¡GRRR!
¡GRRRRRRR!
ACHOO!!
MY GOODNESS, MAMI! LOUD MUCH?

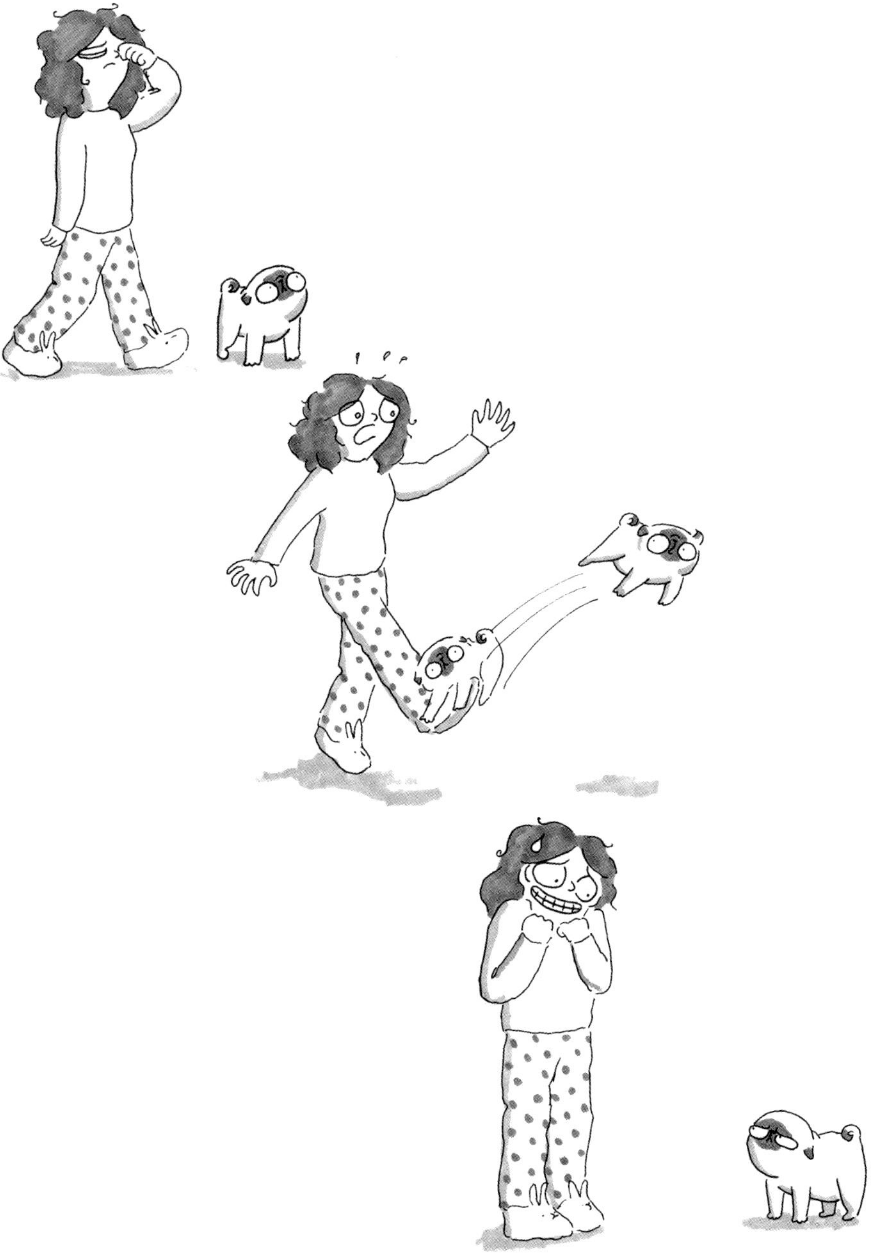

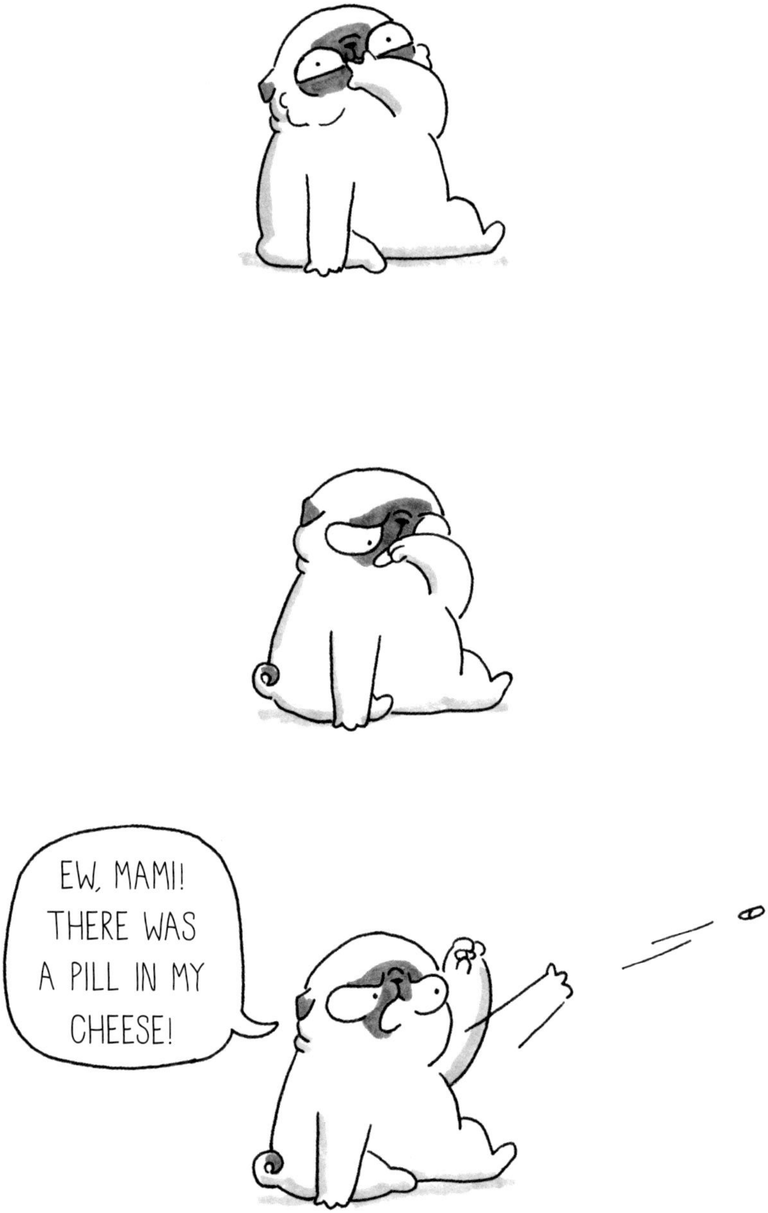
EW, MAMI! THERE WAS A PILL IN MY CHEESE!

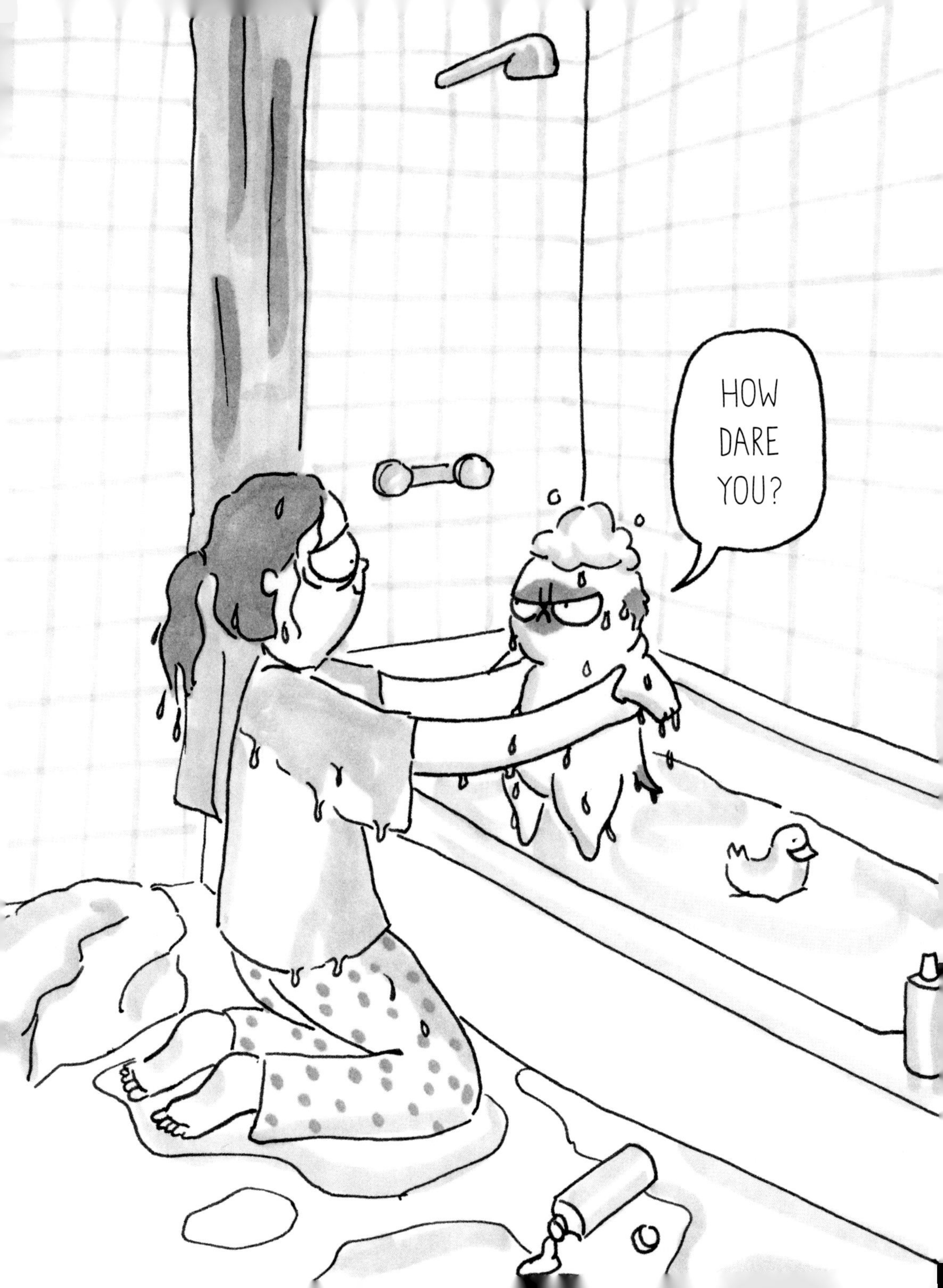
HOW DARE YOU?

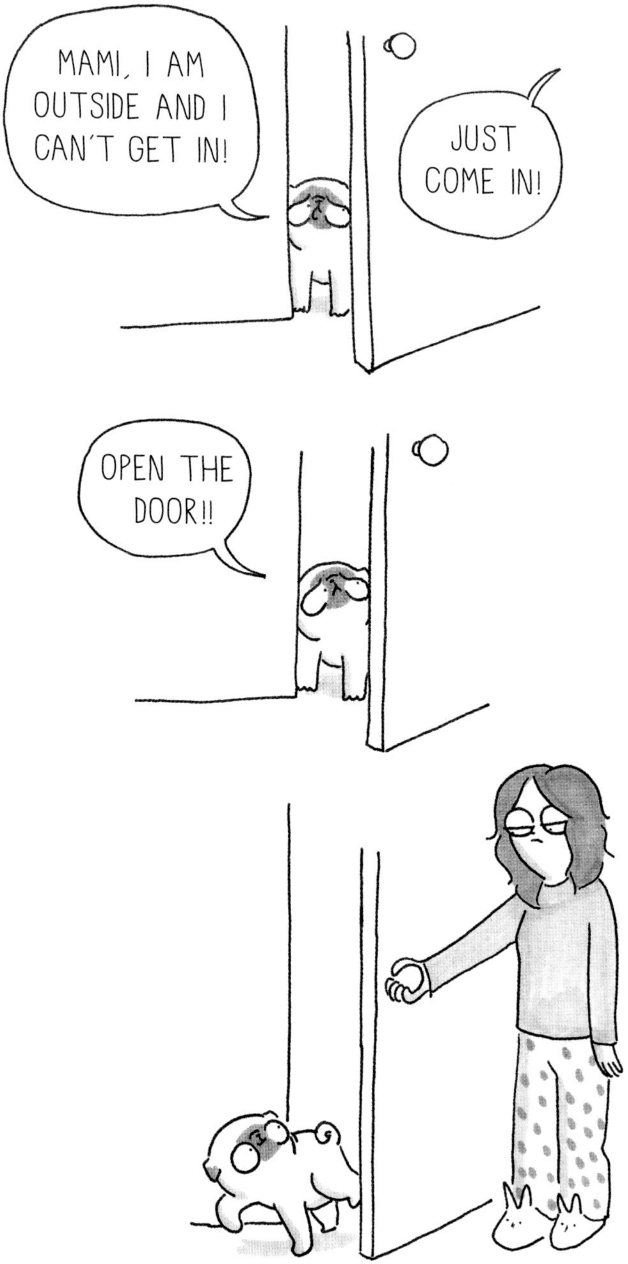
MAMI, I AM OUTSIDE AND I CAN'T GET IN!
JUST COME IN!
OPEN THE DOOR!!

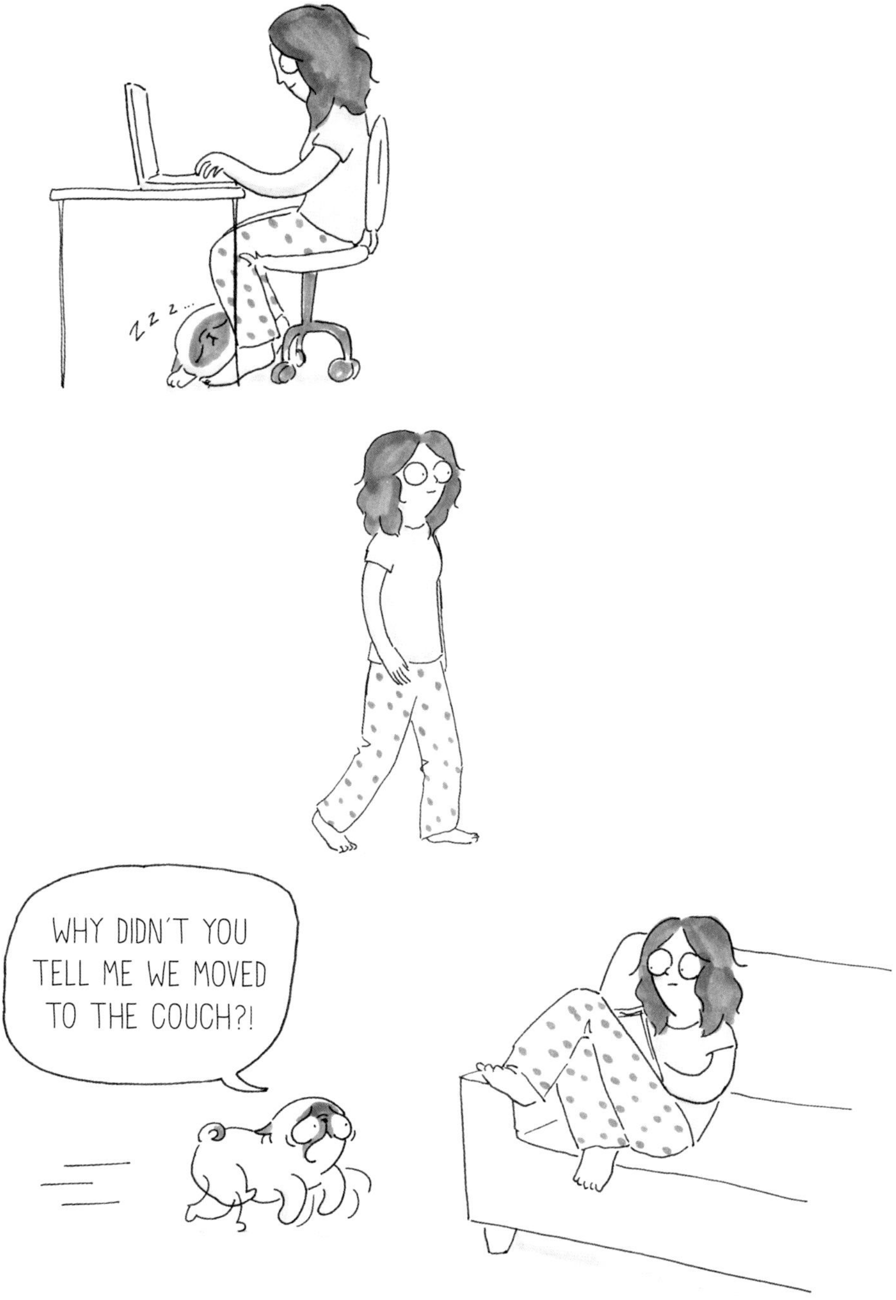
WHY DIDN´T YOU TELL ME WE MOVED TO THE COUCH?!

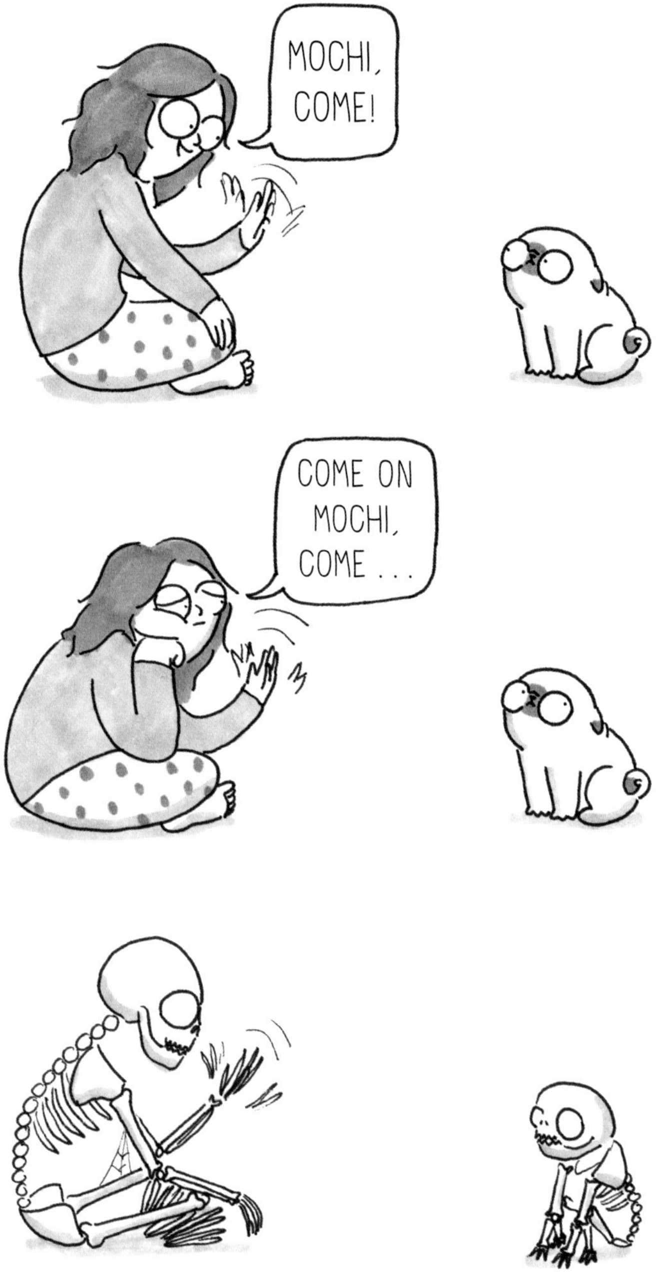
MOCHI, COME!
COME ON MOCHI, COME . . .

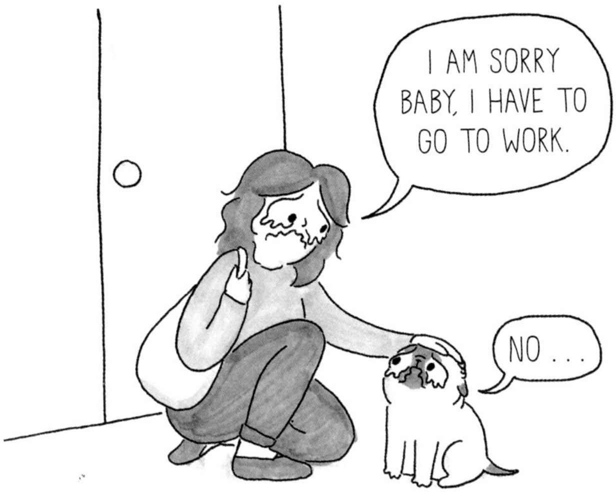
I AM SORRY BABY, I HAVE TO GO TO WORK.
NO . . .

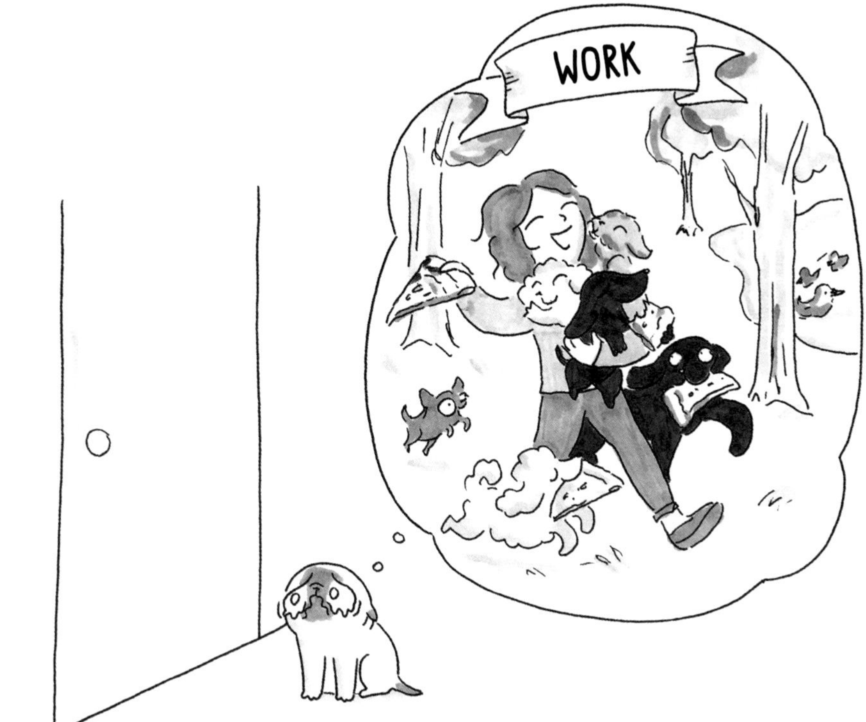
WORK

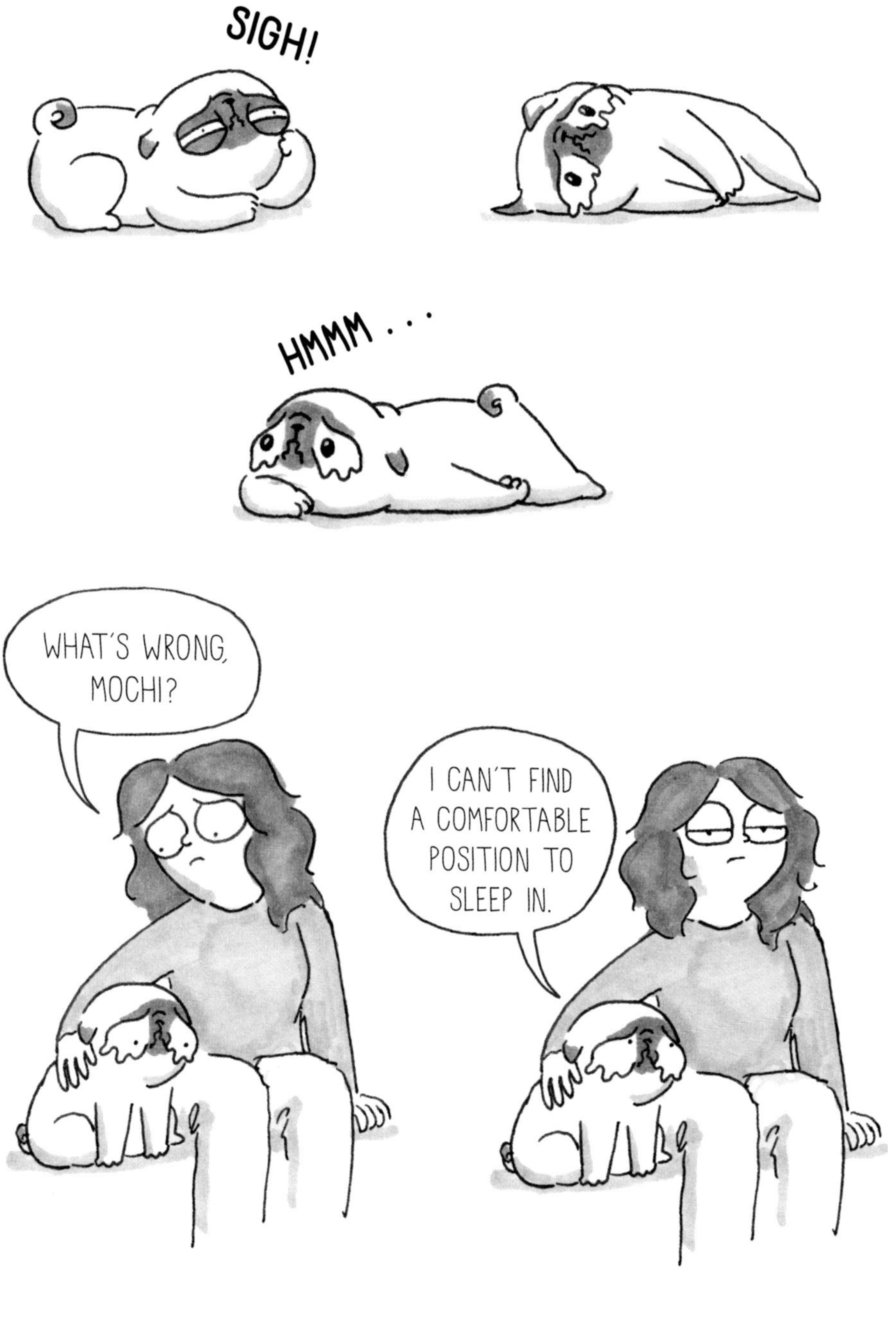
SIGH!
HMMM . . .
WHAT'S WRONG, MOCHI?
I CAN'T FIND A COMFORTABLE POSITION TO SLEEP IN.

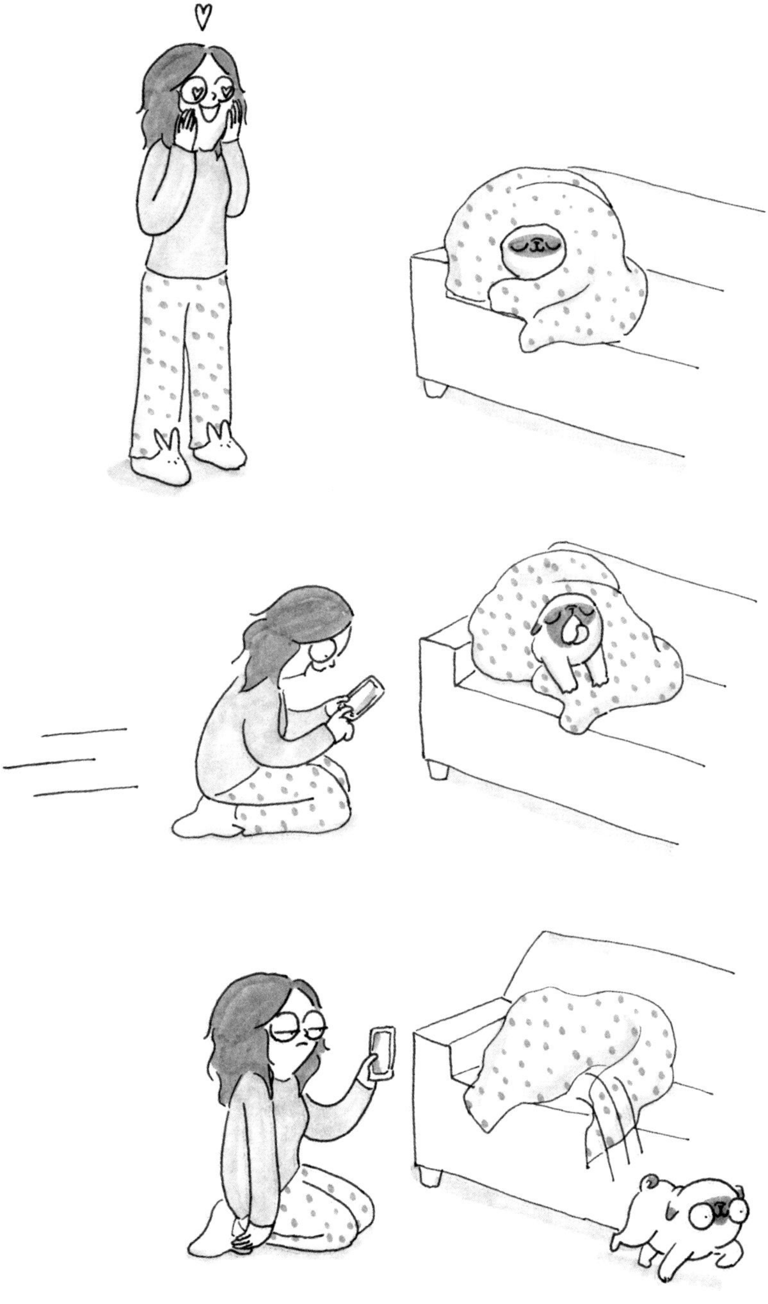

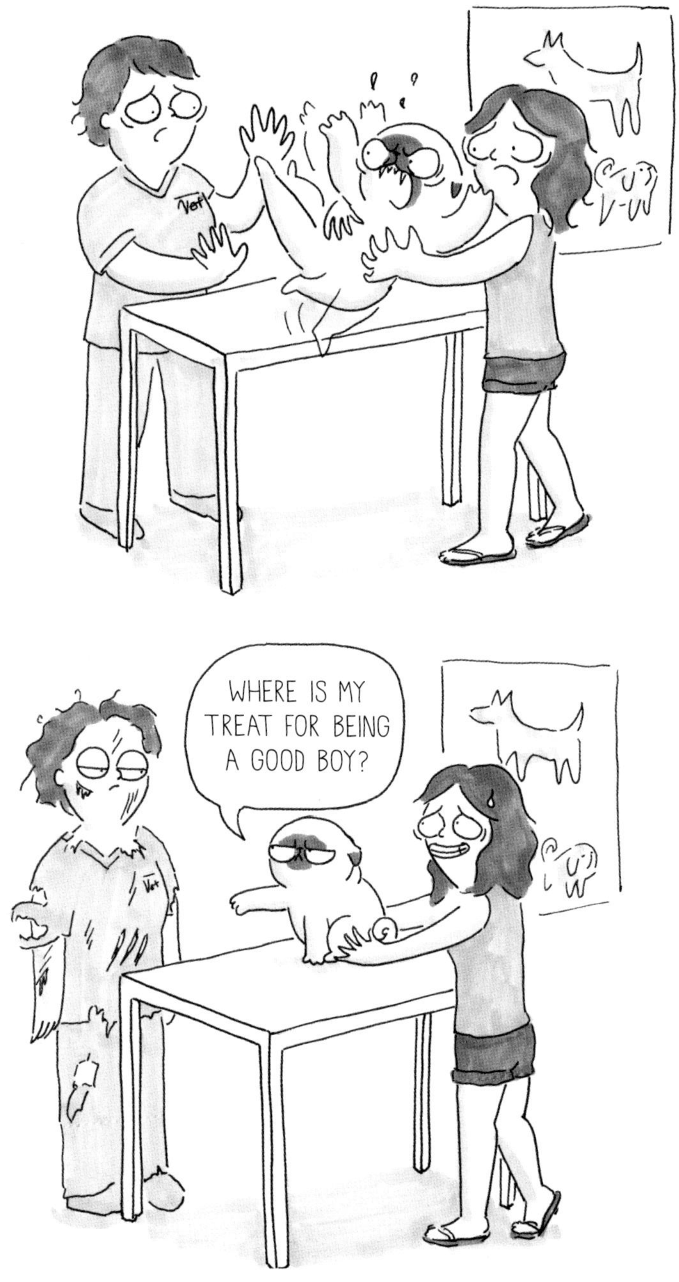
Vet
WHERE IS MY TREAT FOR BEING A GOOD BOY?
Vet

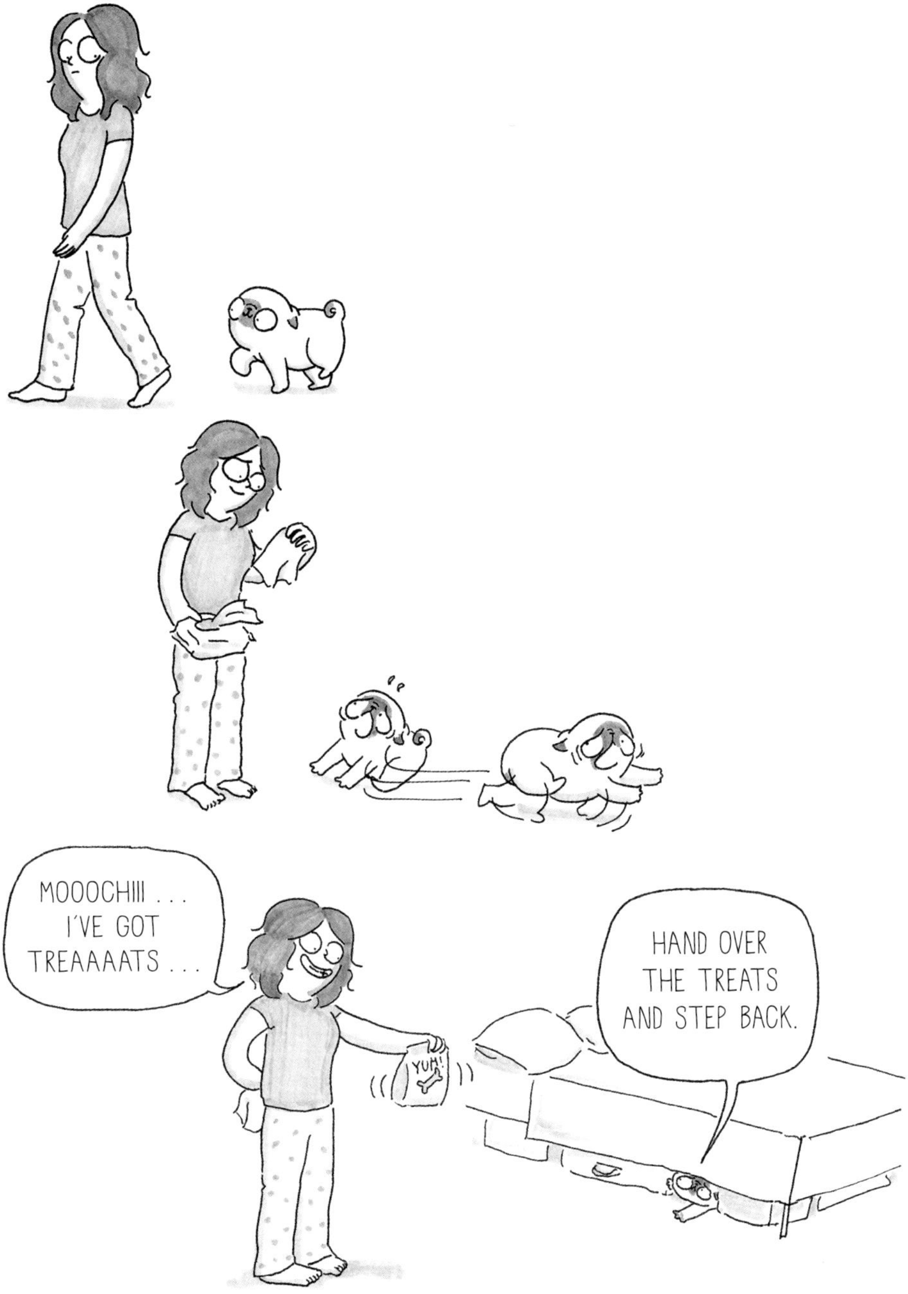
MOOOCHIII . . . I'VE GOT TREAAAATS . . .
HAND OVER THE TREATS AND STEP BACK.
YUM!

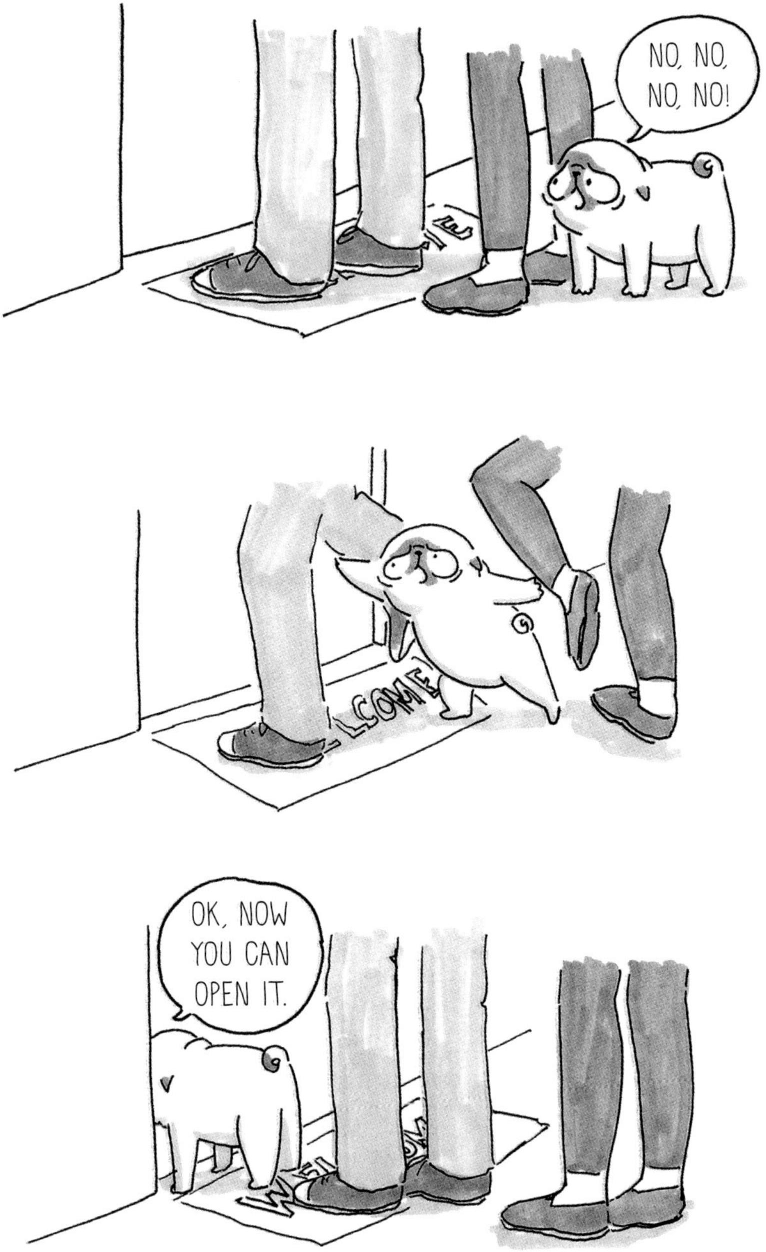
NO, NO, NO, NO!
LCOME
OK, NOW YOU CAN OPEN IT.

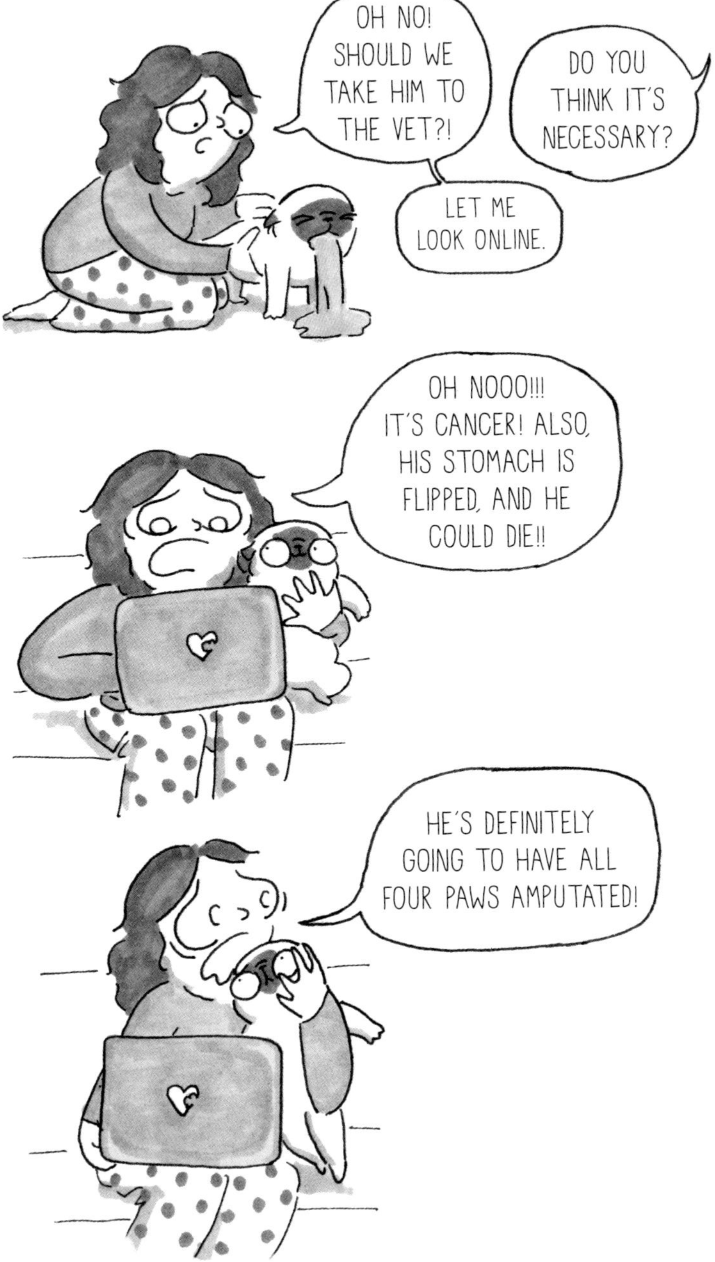
OH NO! SHOULD WE TAKE HIM TO THE VET?!
DO YOU THINK IT'S NECESSARY?
LET ME LOOK ONLINE.
OH NOOO!!! IT'S CANCER! ALSO, HIS STOMACH IS FLIPPED, AND HE COULD DIE!!
HE'S DEFINITELY GOING TO HAVE ALL FOUR PAWS AMPUTATED!

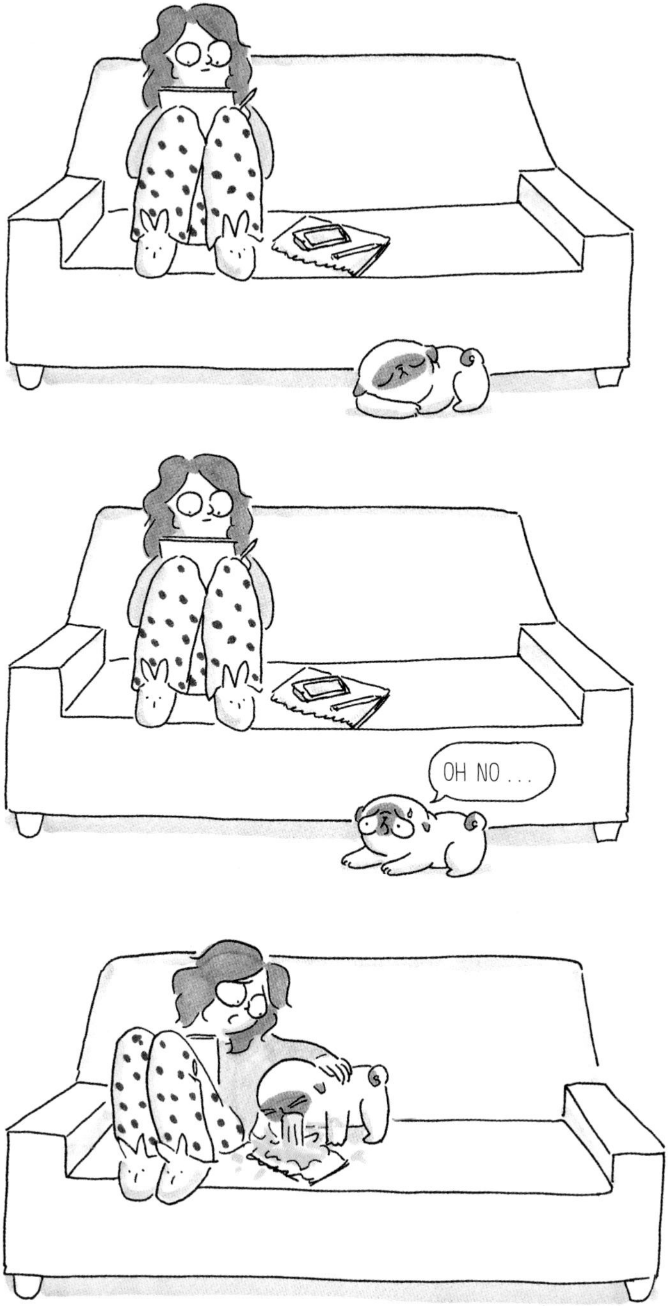
OH NO . . .

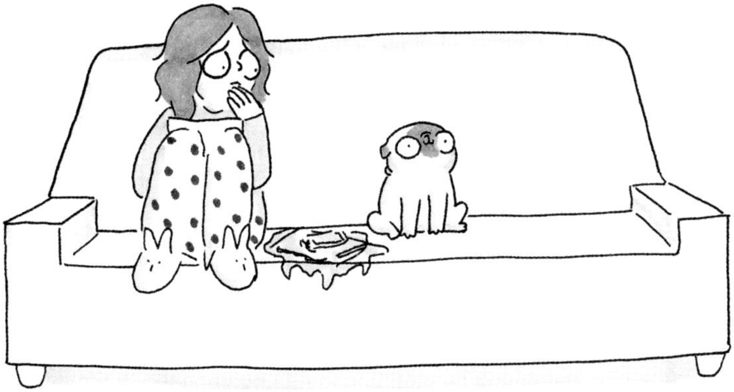

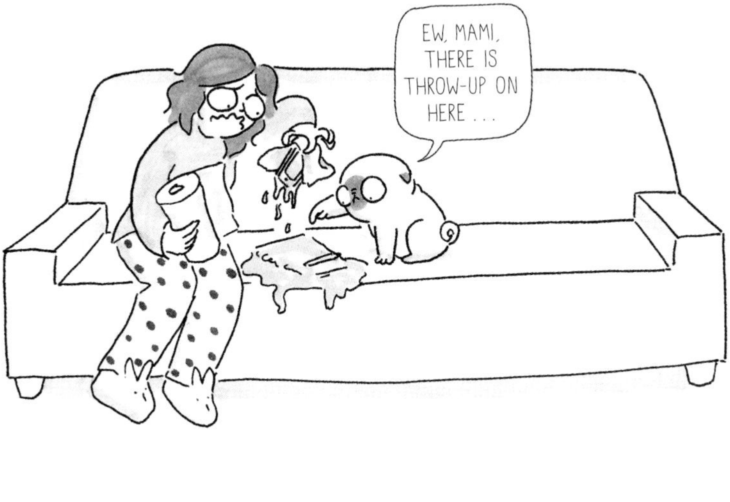
EW, MAMI, THERE IS THROW-UP ON HERE . . .

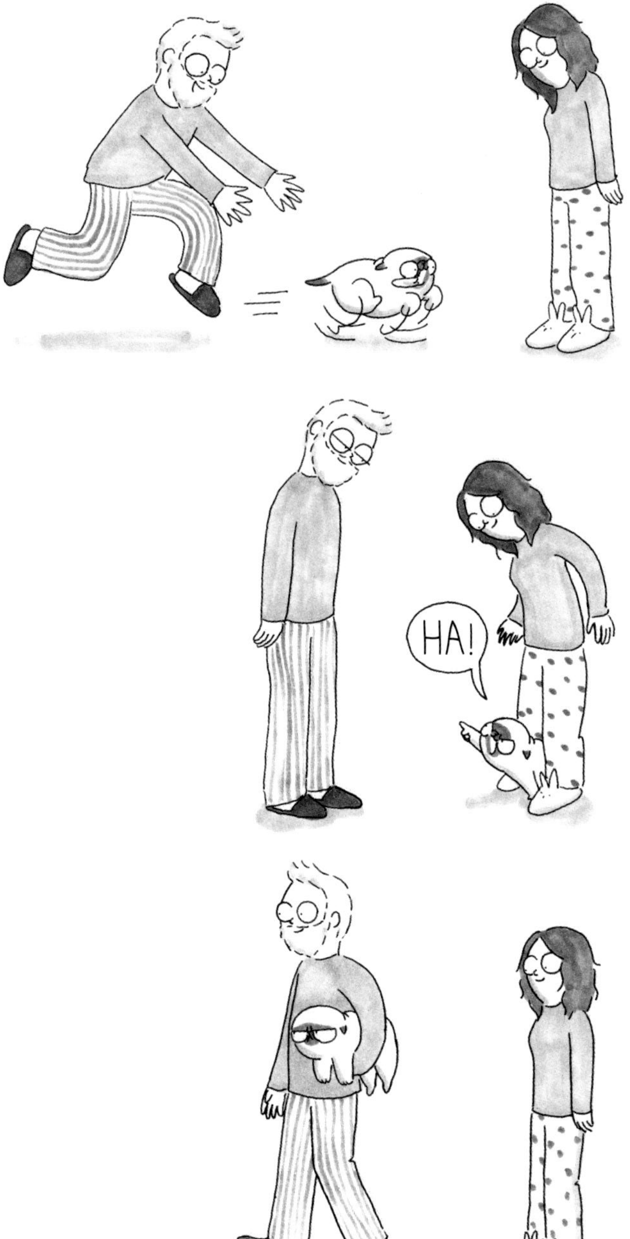
HA!

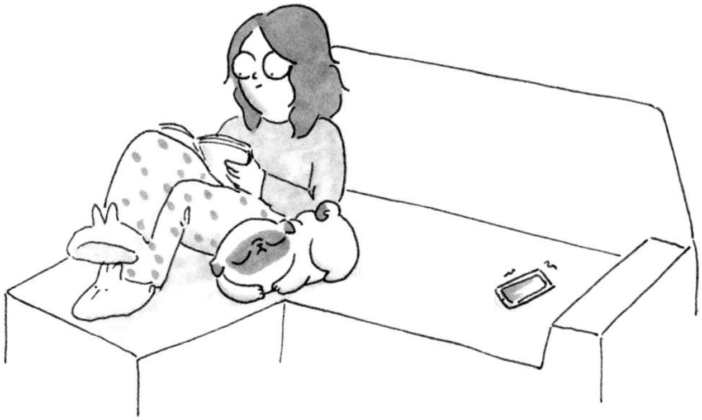

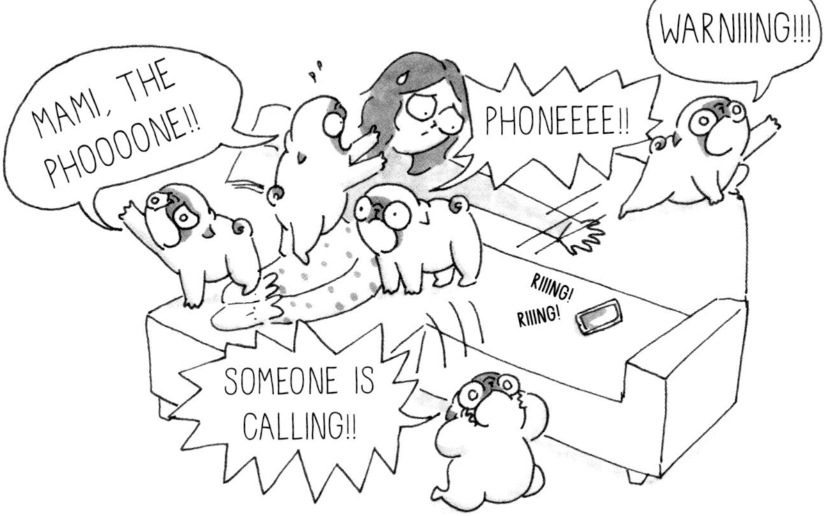
WARNIIING!!!
MAMI, THE PHOOOONE!!
PHONEEEE!!
RIIING!
RIIING!
SOMEONE IS CALLING!!

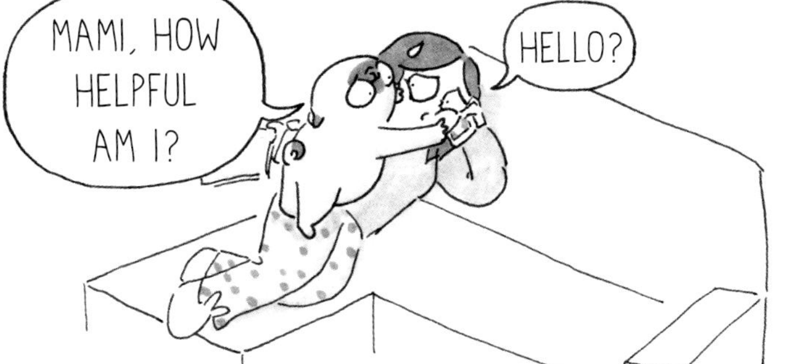
MAMI, HOW HELPFUL AM I?
HELLO?

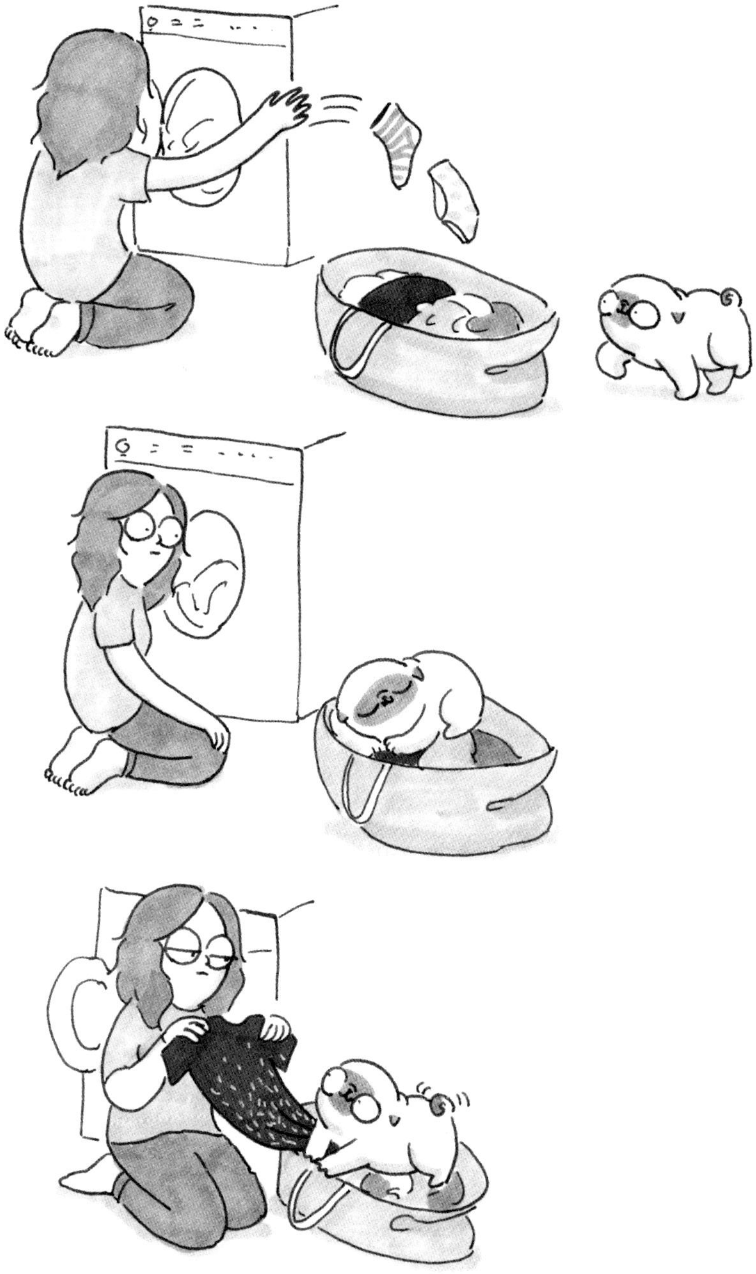

HELLO?
HOLD ON A
SECOND . . .

MOCHI,
WHY ARE
YOU CRYING?

BECAUSE YOU
ARE ON THE
PHONE.

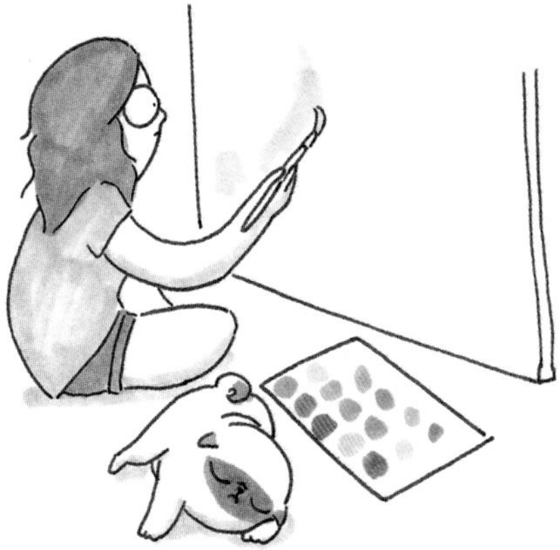

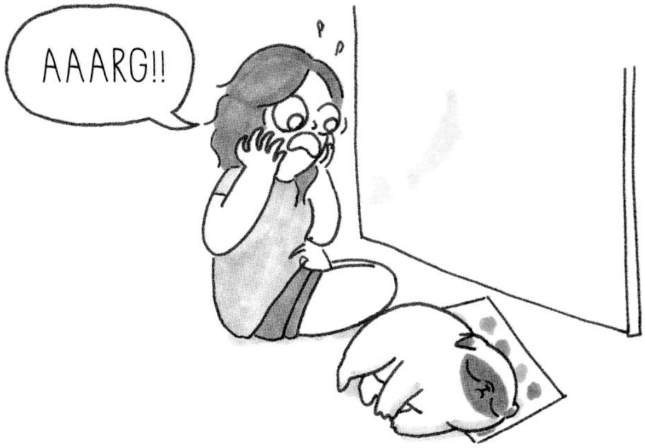
AAARG!!

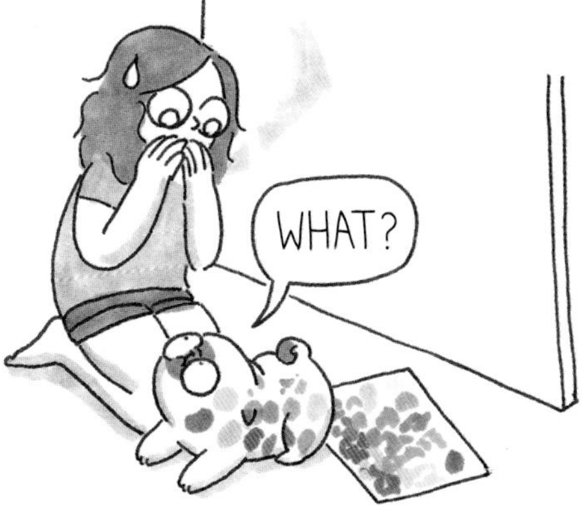
WHAT?

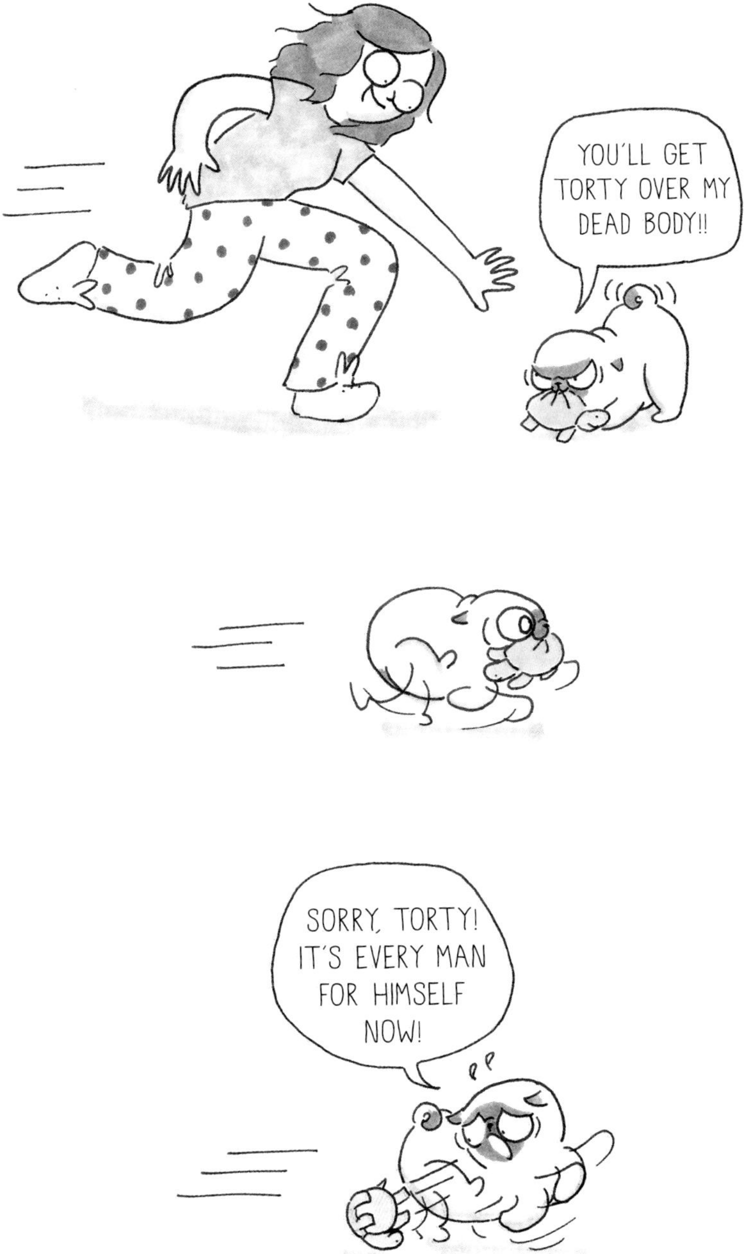
YOU'LL GET TORTY OVER MY DEAD BODY!!
SORRY, TORTY! IT'S EVERY MAN FOR HIMSELF NOW!

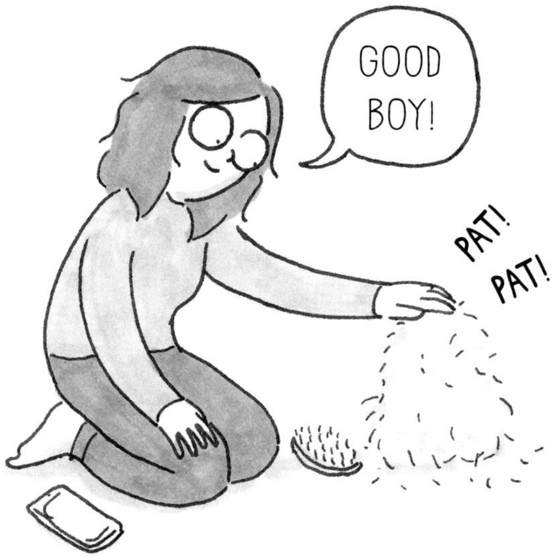
GOOD BOY!
PAT! PAT!

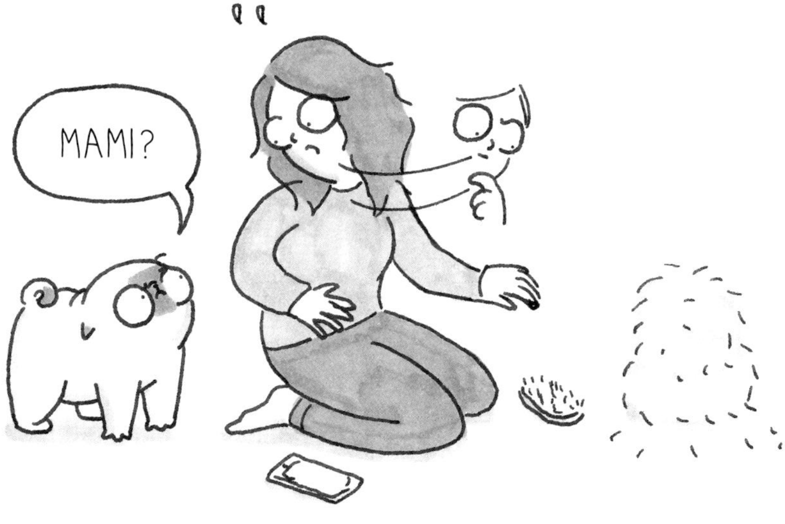
MAMI?

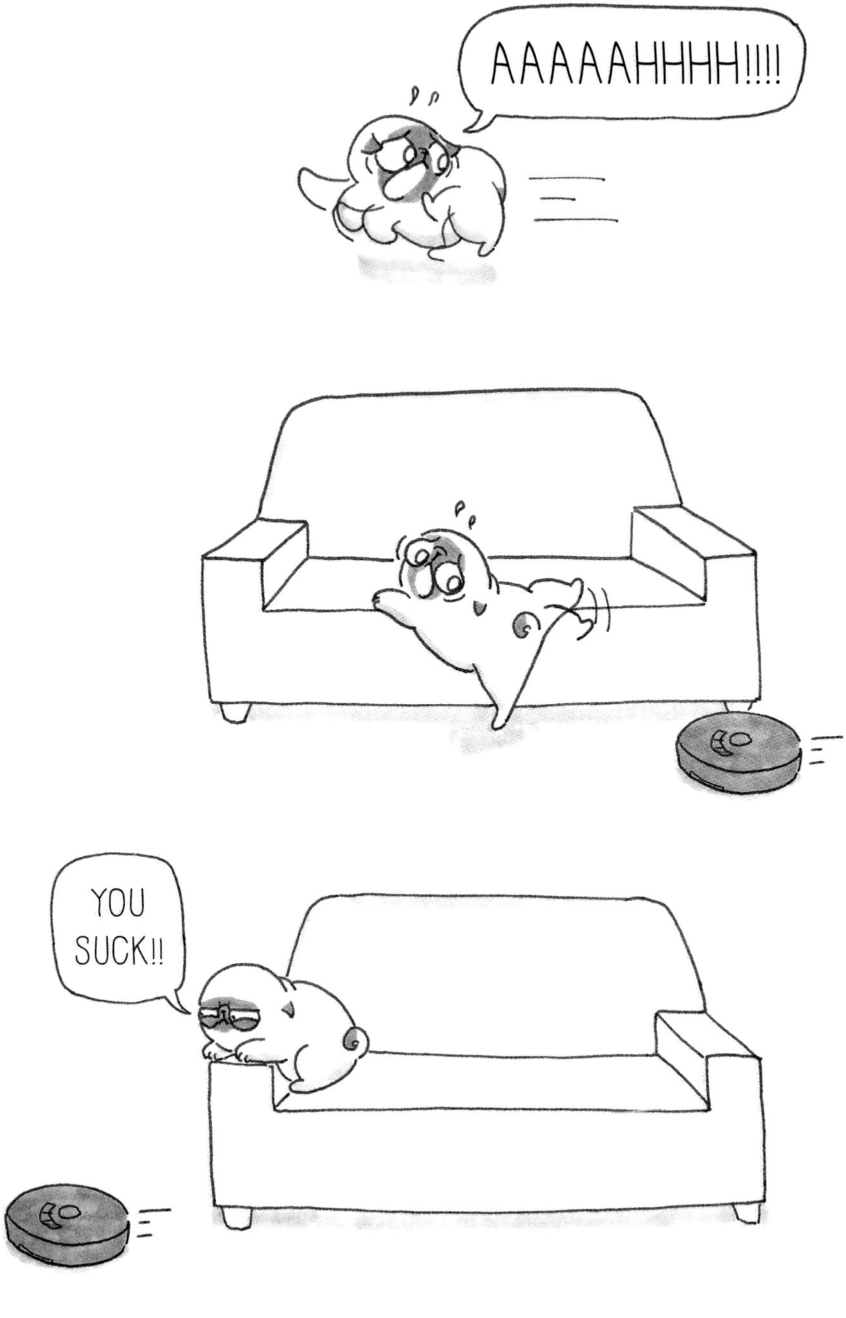
AAAAAHHHH!!!!
YOU SUCK!!

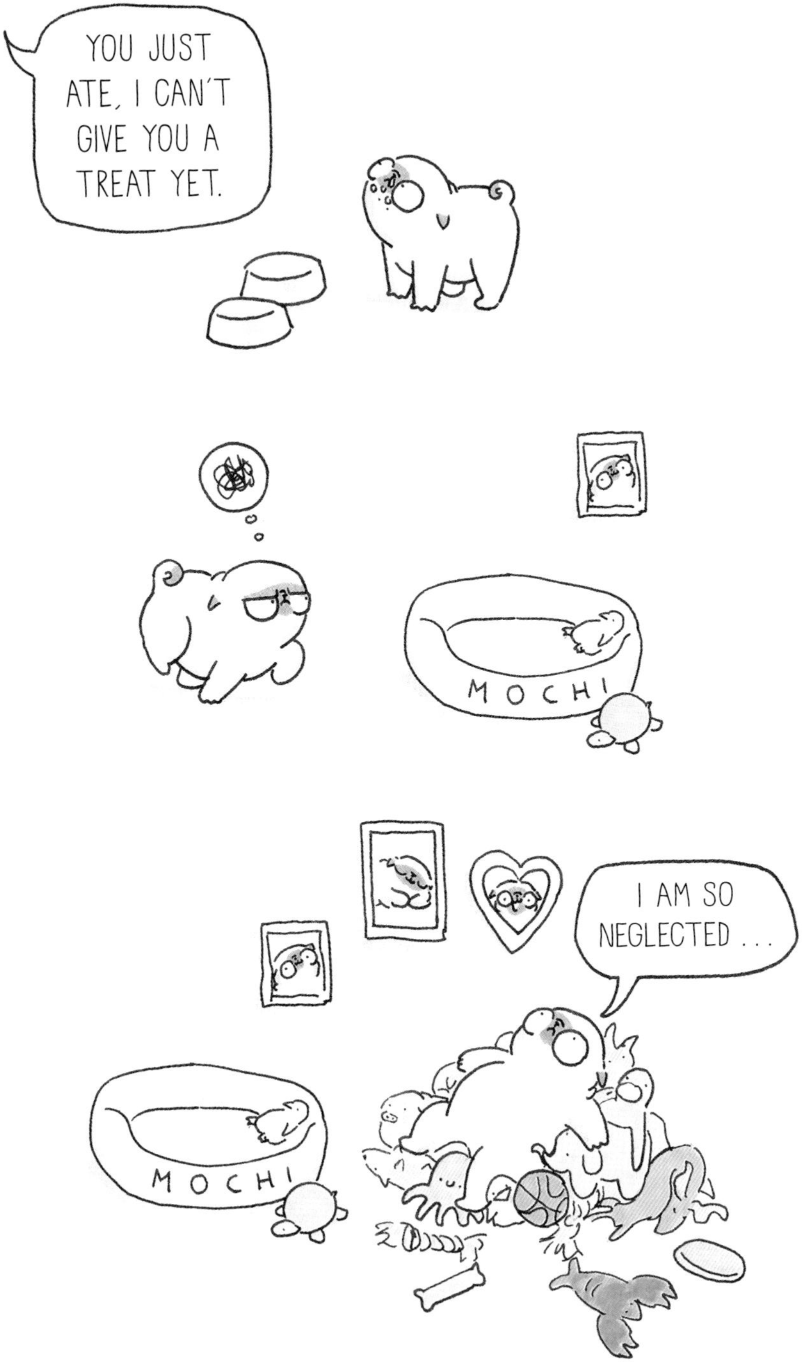
YOU JUST ATE, I CAN'T GIVE YOU A TREAT YET.
MOCHI
MOCHI
I AM SO NEGLECTED . . .

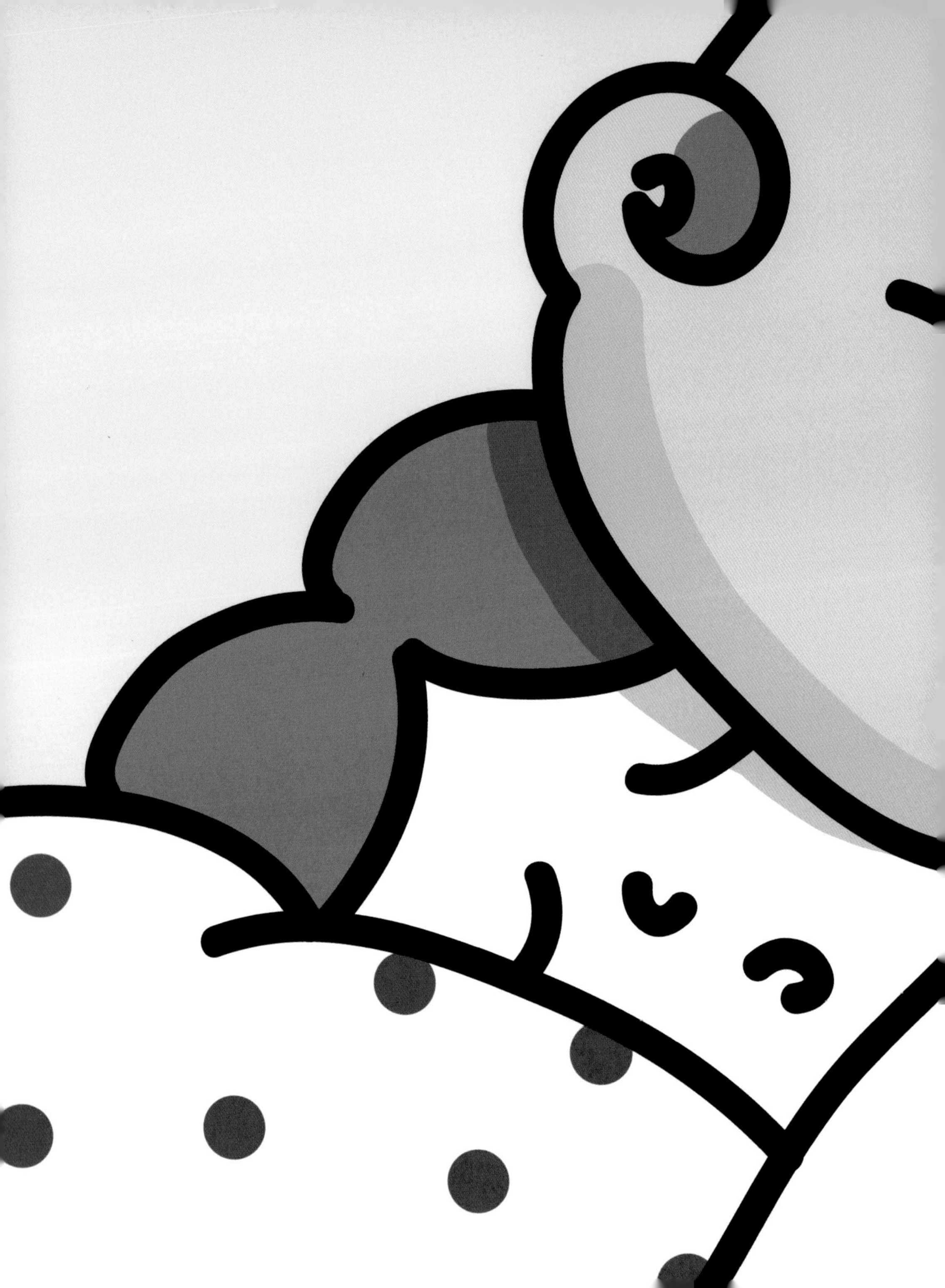

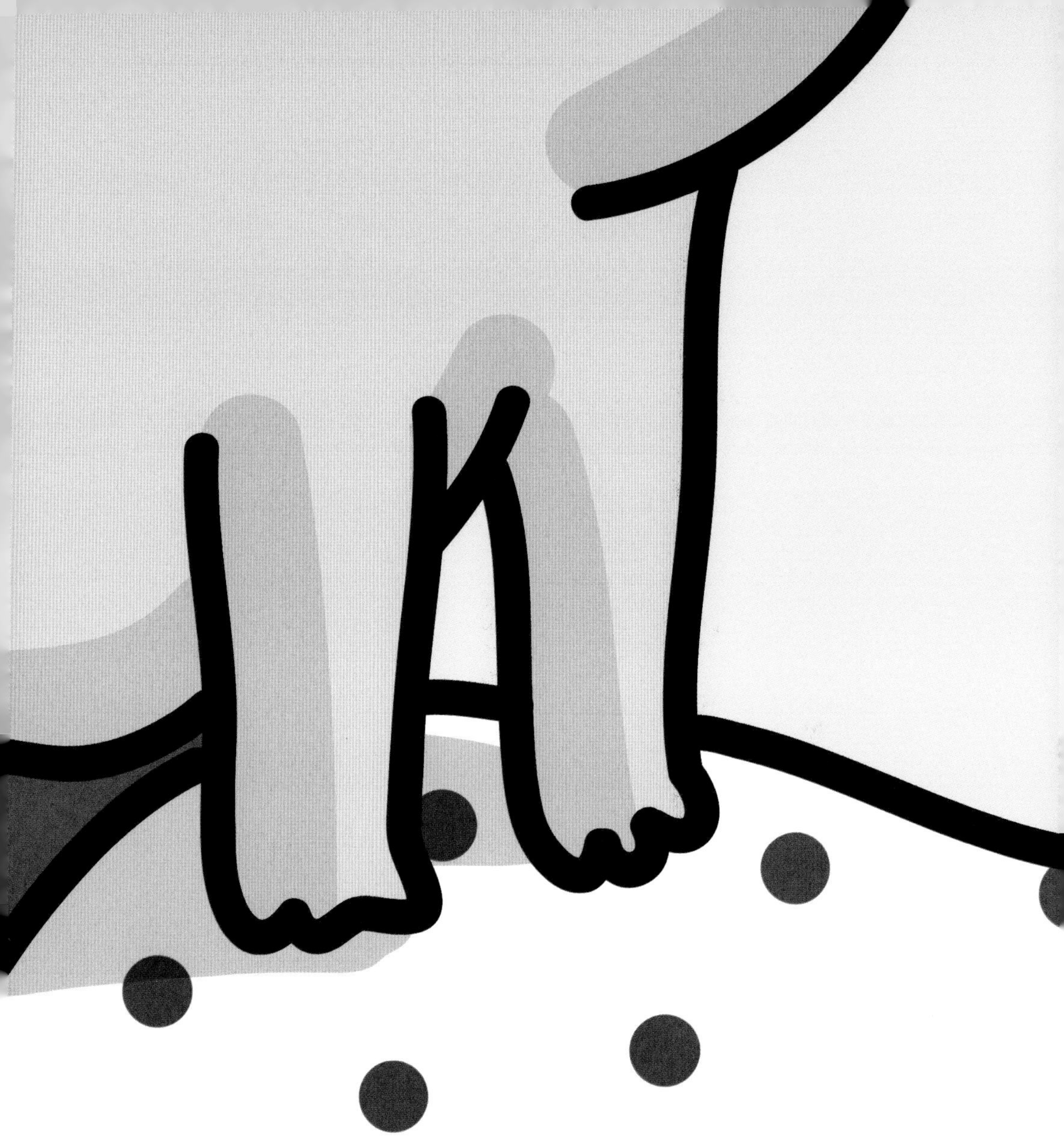

BOUNDARIES

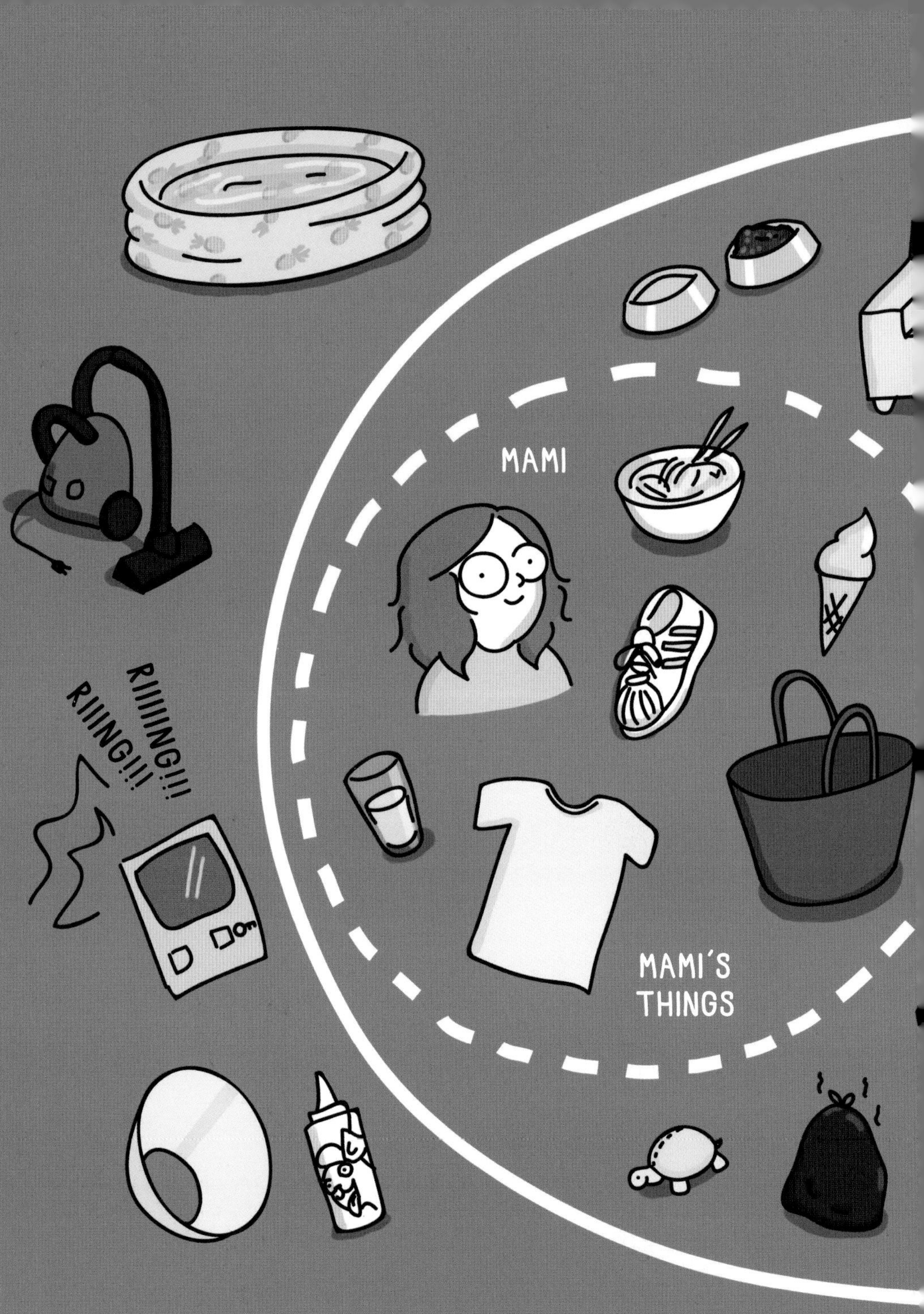
RIIIIING!!!
RIIING!!!
MAMI
MAMI´S THINGS

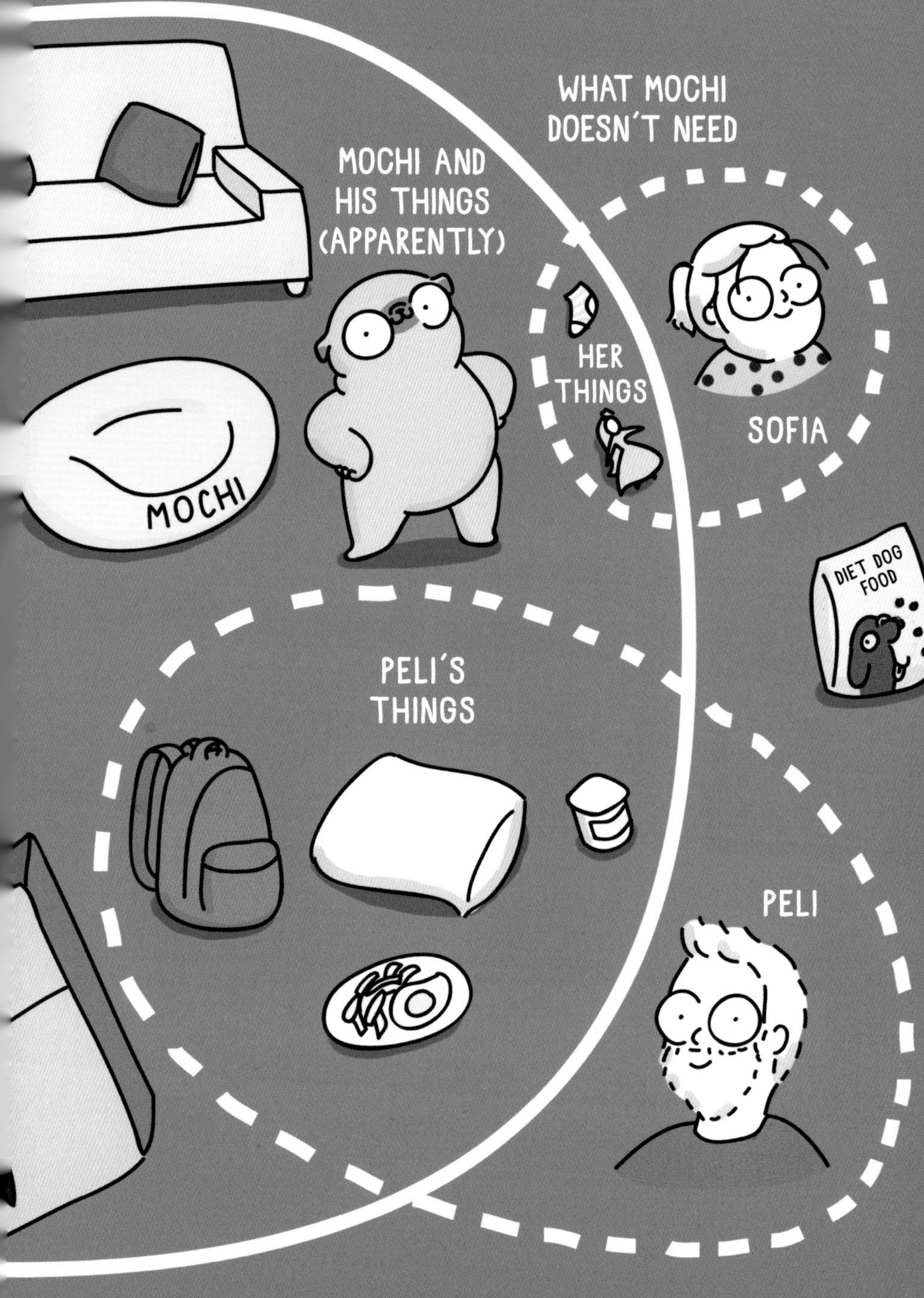
WHAT MOCHI DOESN'T NEED
MOCHI AND HIS THINGS (APPARENTLY)
HER THINGS
SOFIA
MOCHI
DIET DOG FOOD
PELI'S THINGS
PELI

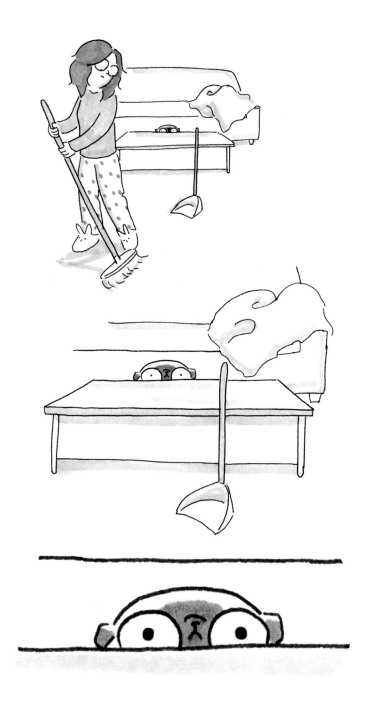

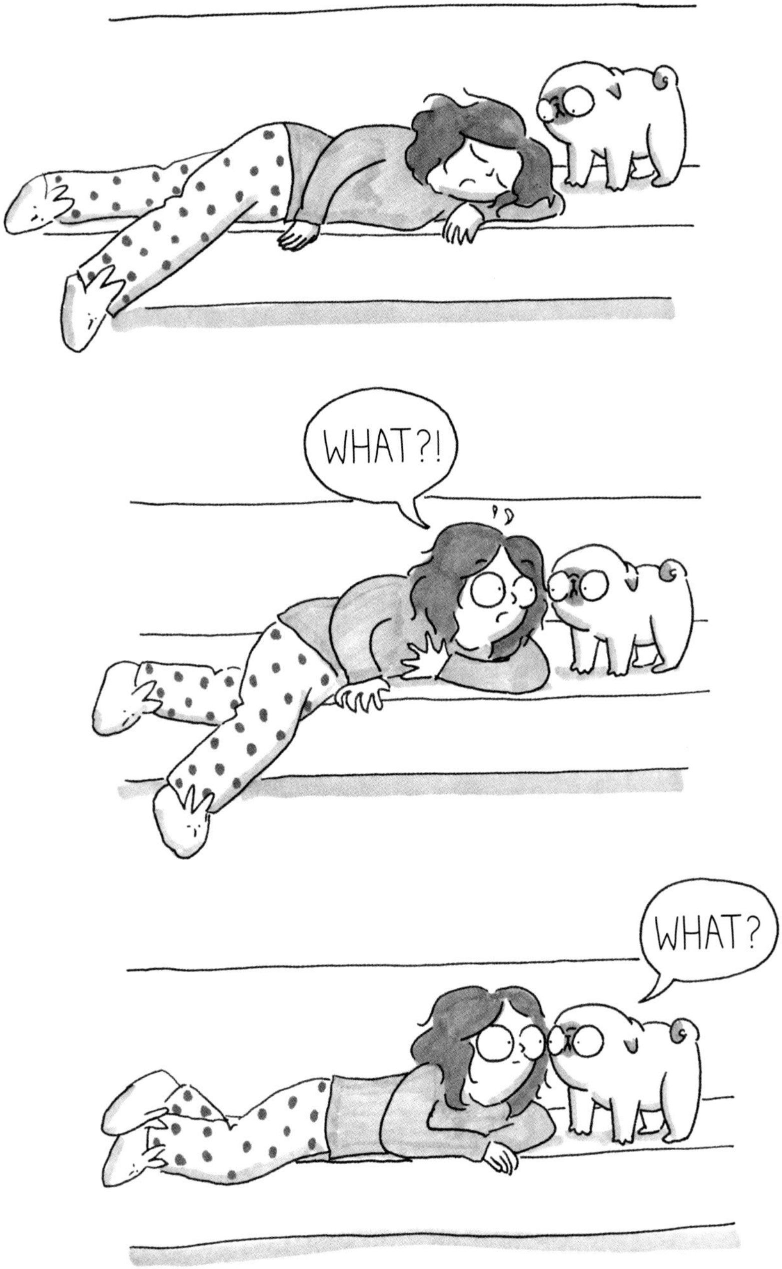
WHAT?!
WHAT?

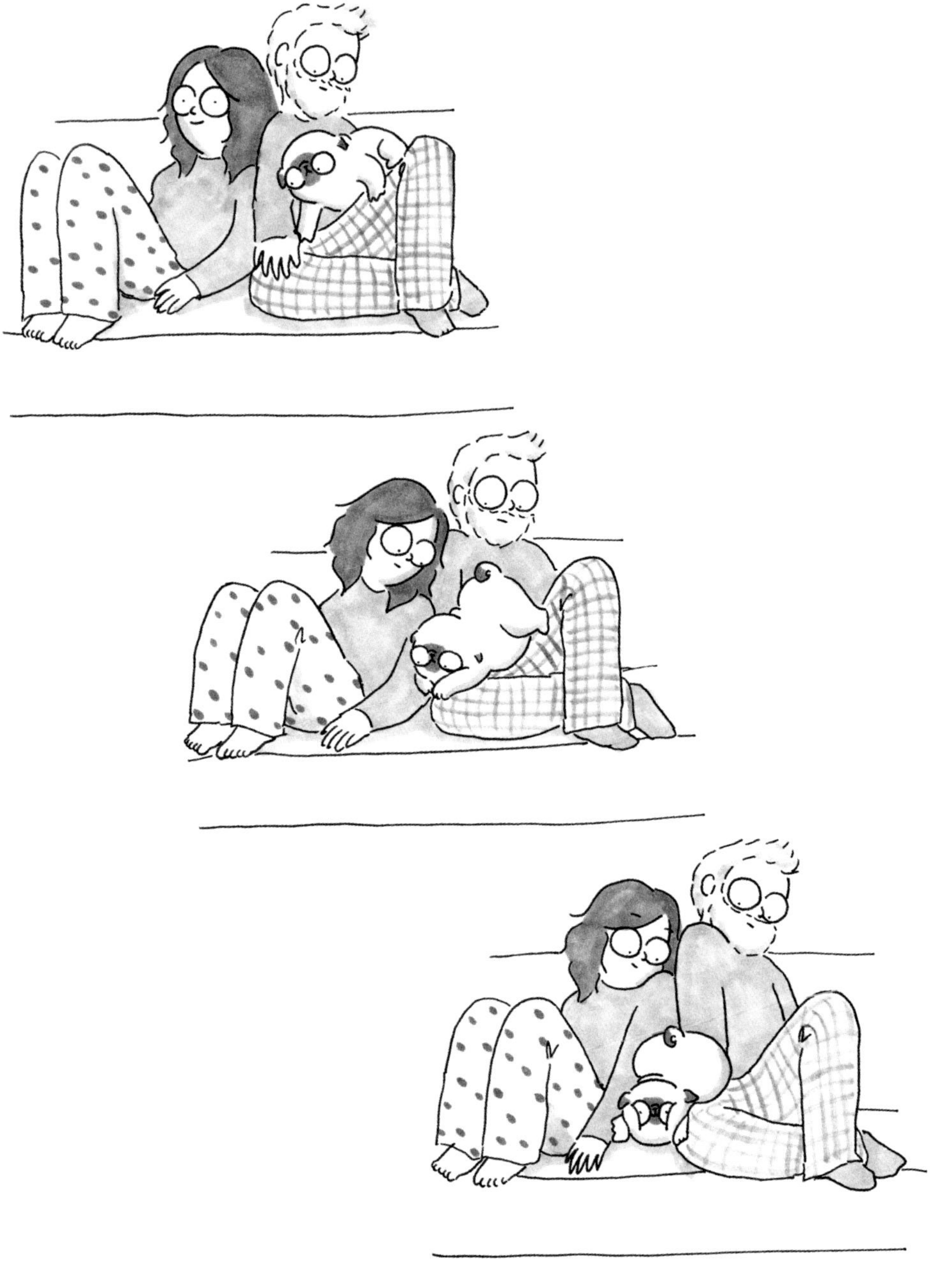

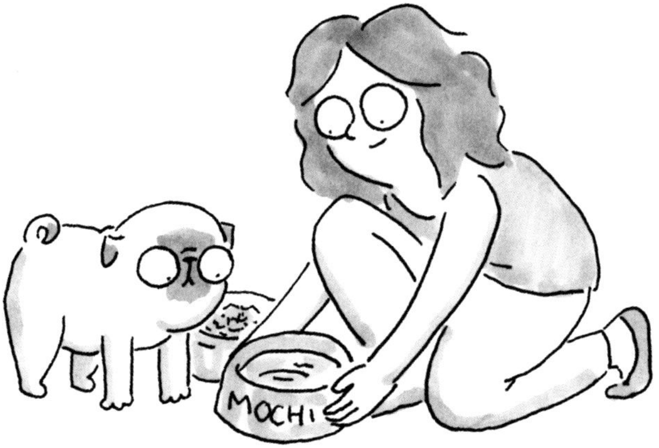
MOCHI

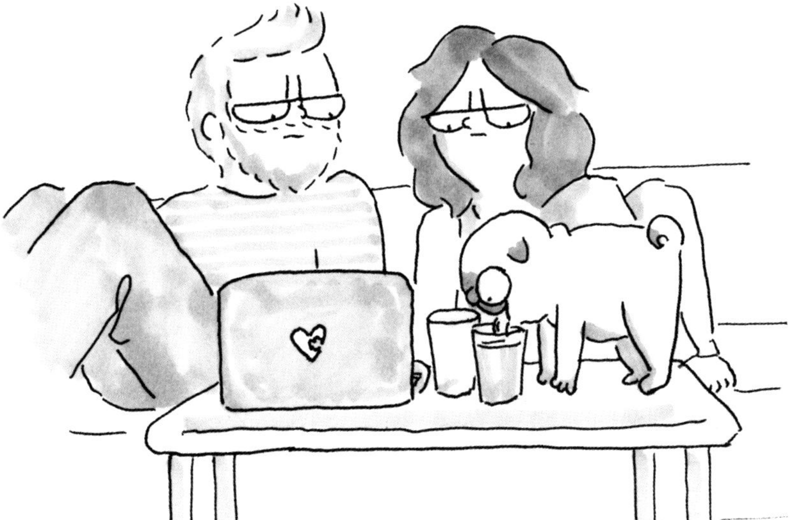

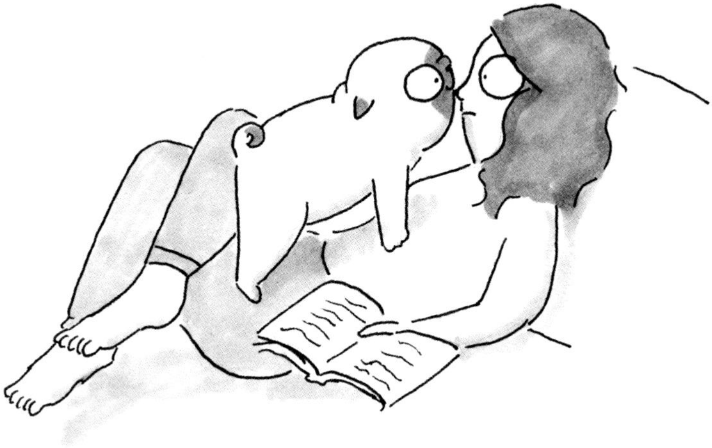

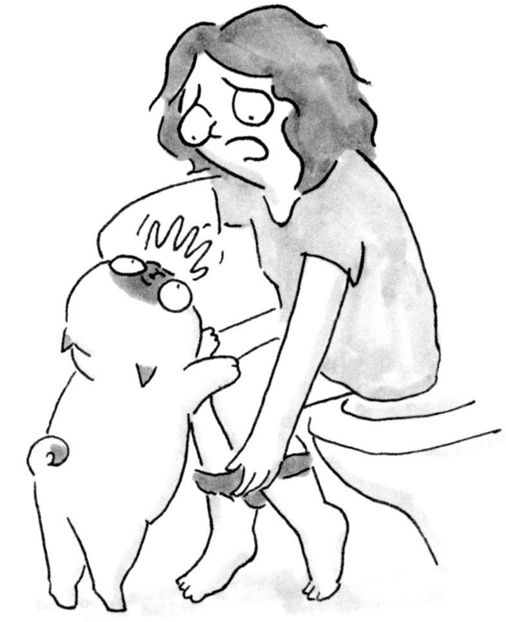

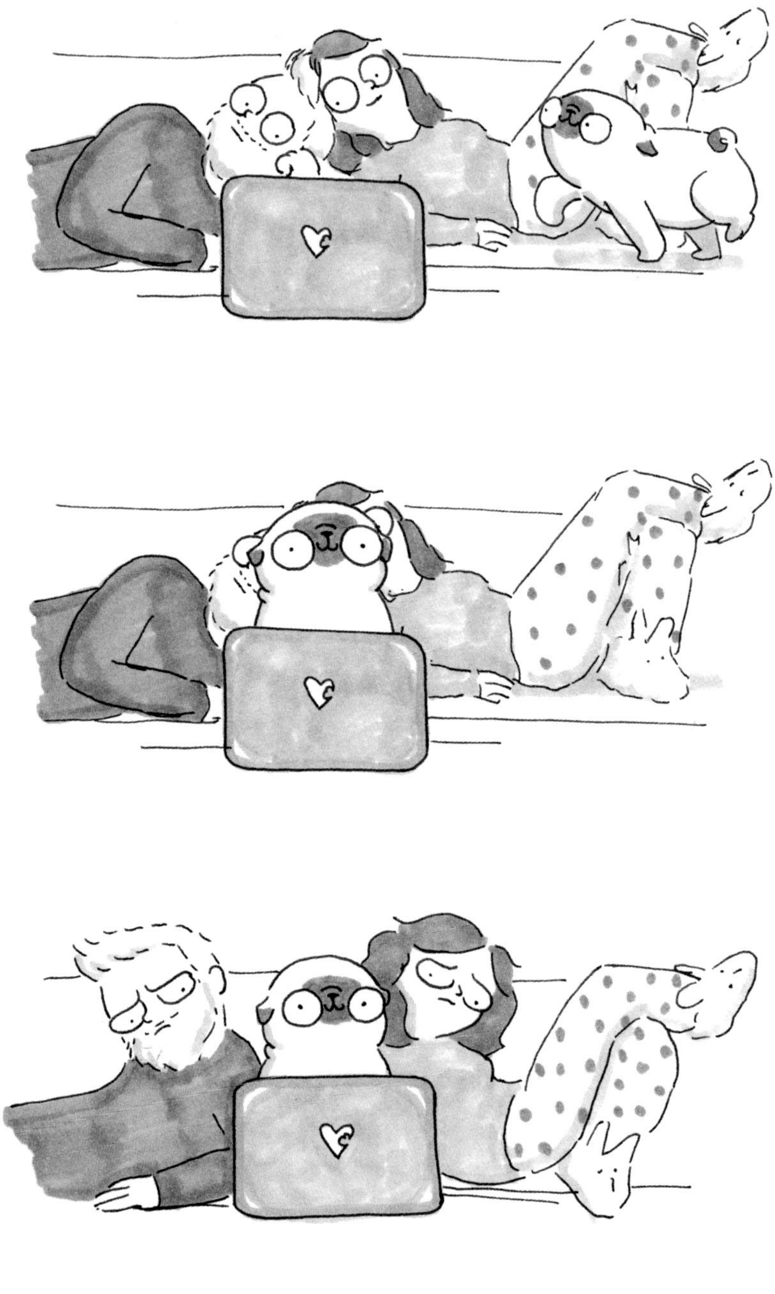

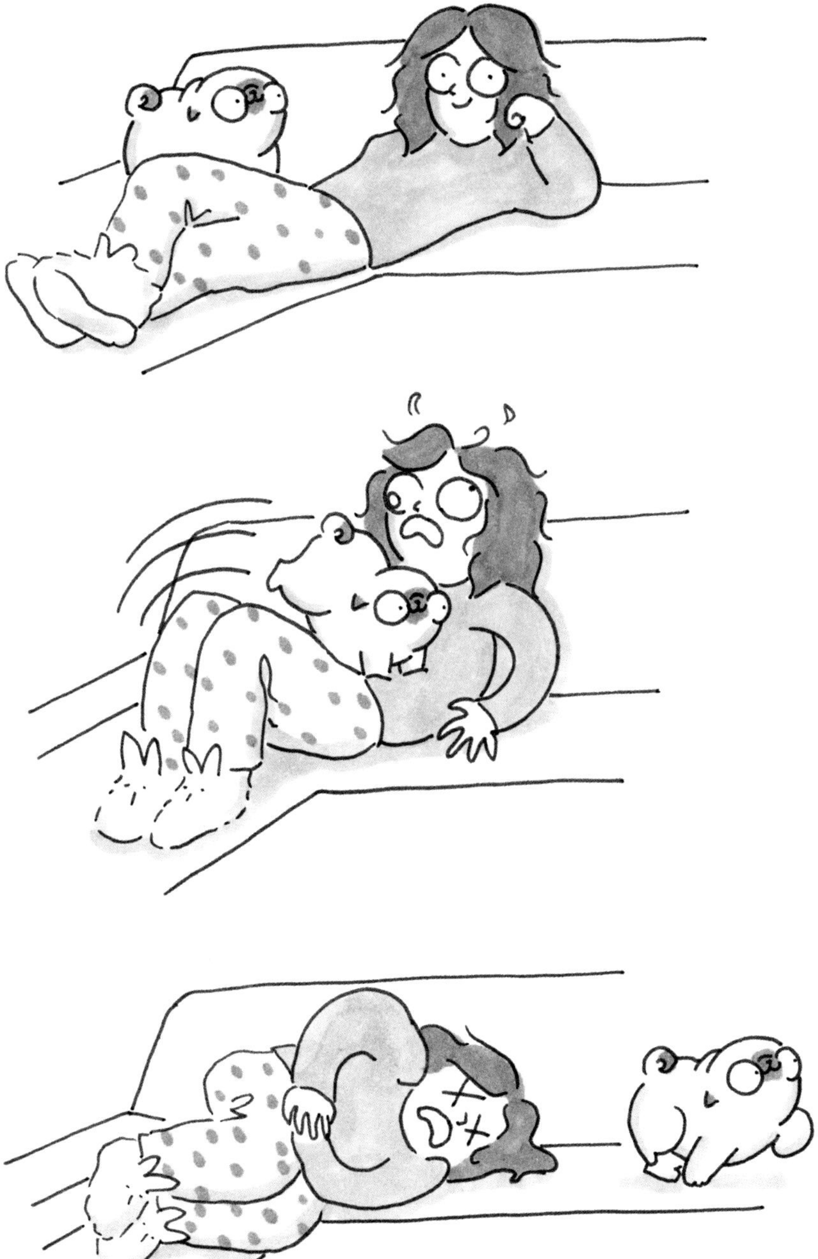

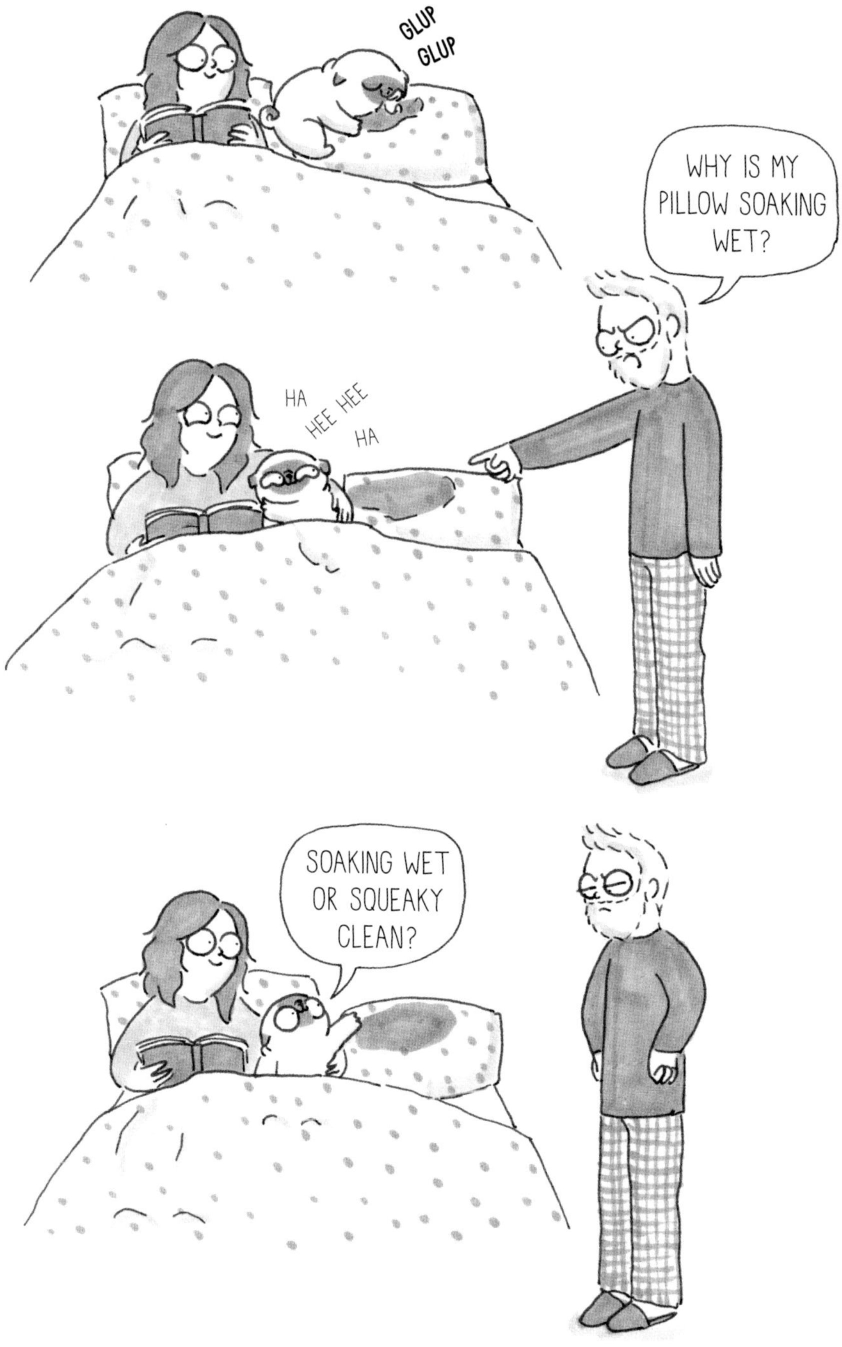
GLUP
GLUP
WHY IS MY PILLOW SOAKING WET?
HA
HEE HEE
HA
SOAKING WET OR SQUEAKY CLEAN?

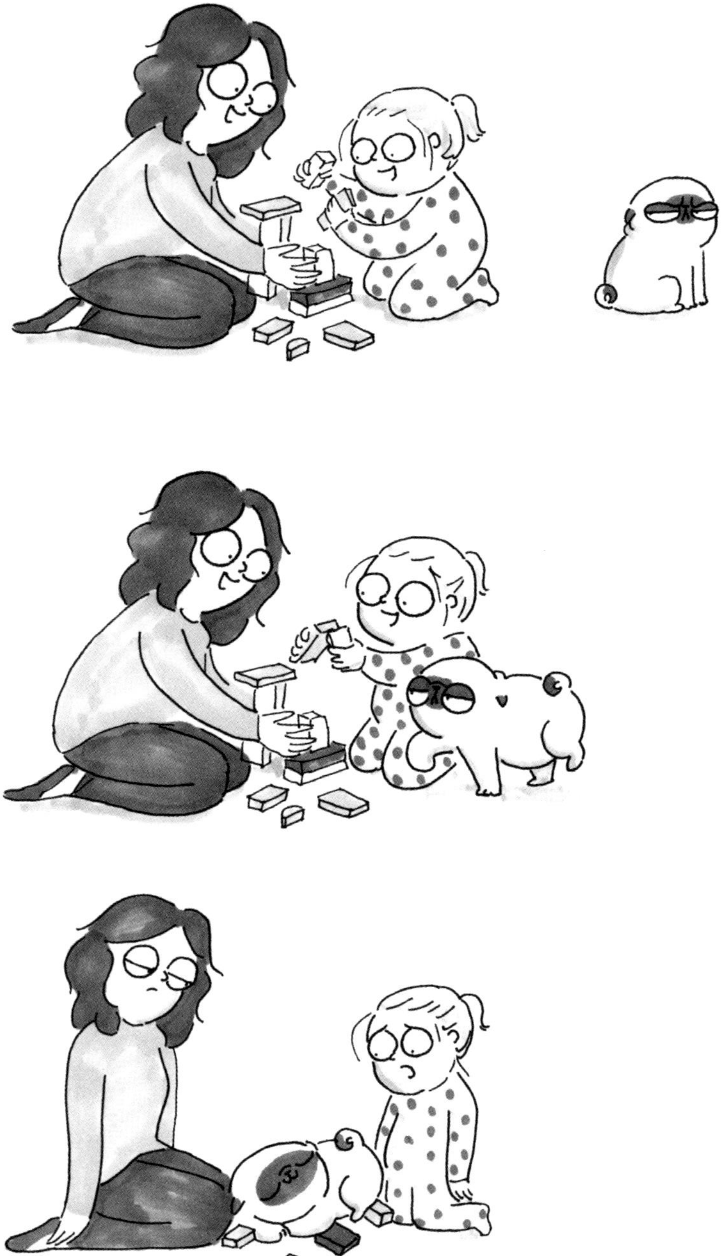

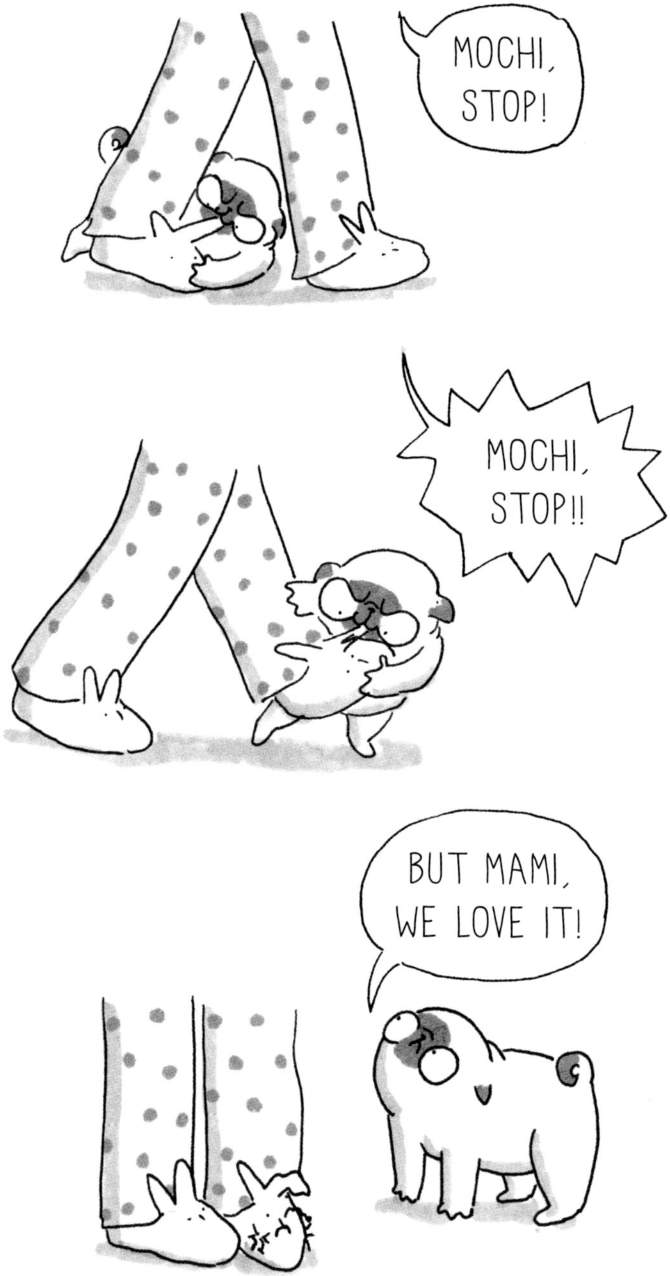
MOCHI, STOP!
MOCHI, STOP!!
BUT MAMI, WE LOVE IT!

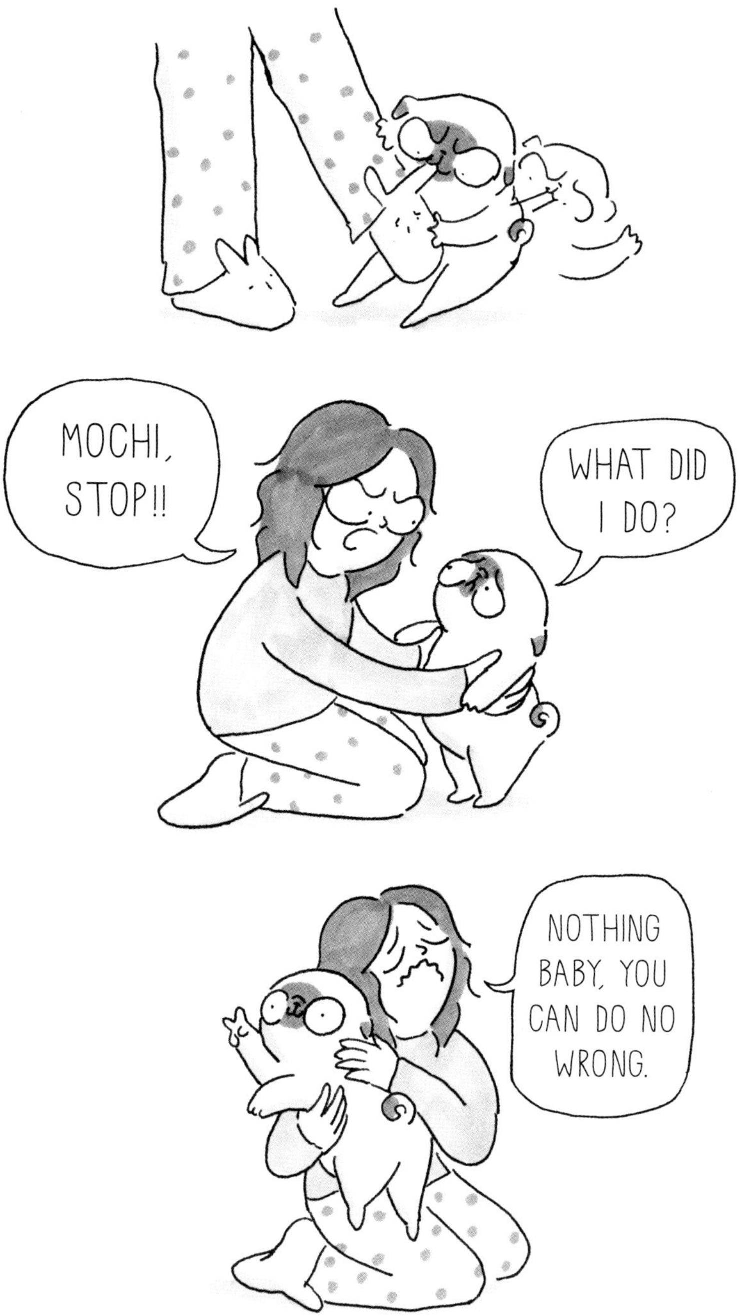
MOCHI, STOP!!
WHAT DID I DO?
NOTHING BABY, YOU CAN DO NO WRONG.

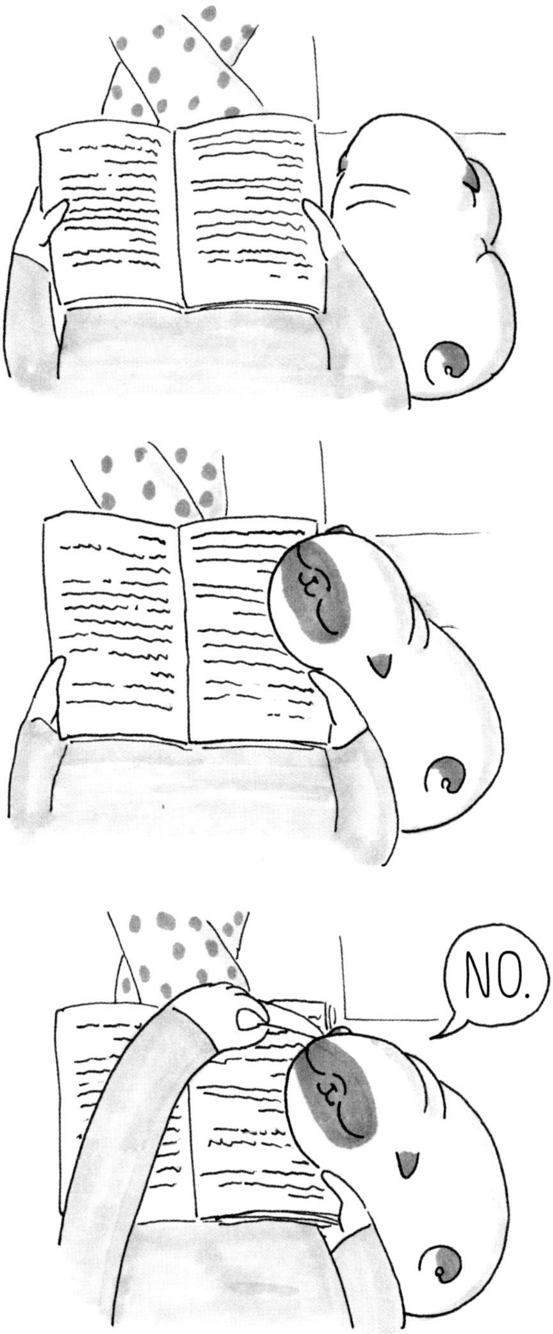
NO.

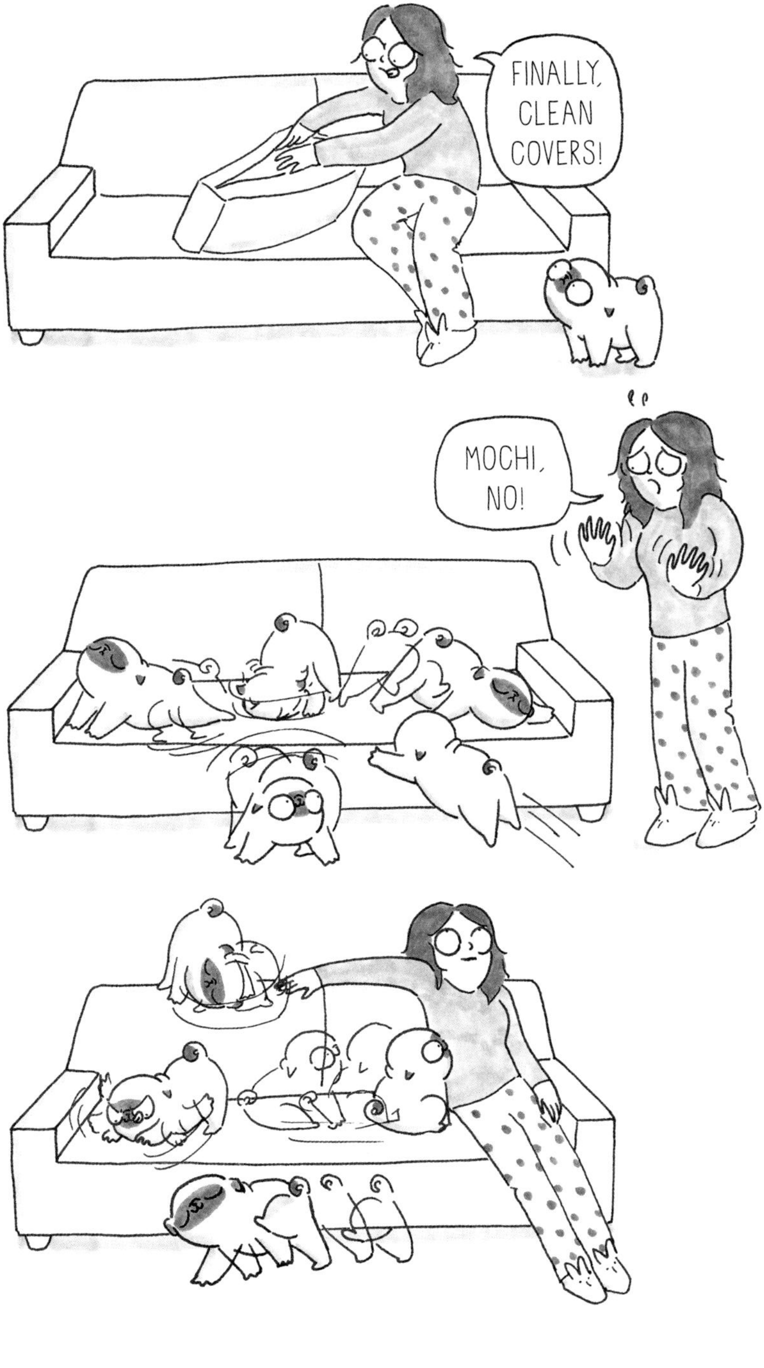
FINALLY, CLEAN COVERS!
MOCHI, NO!

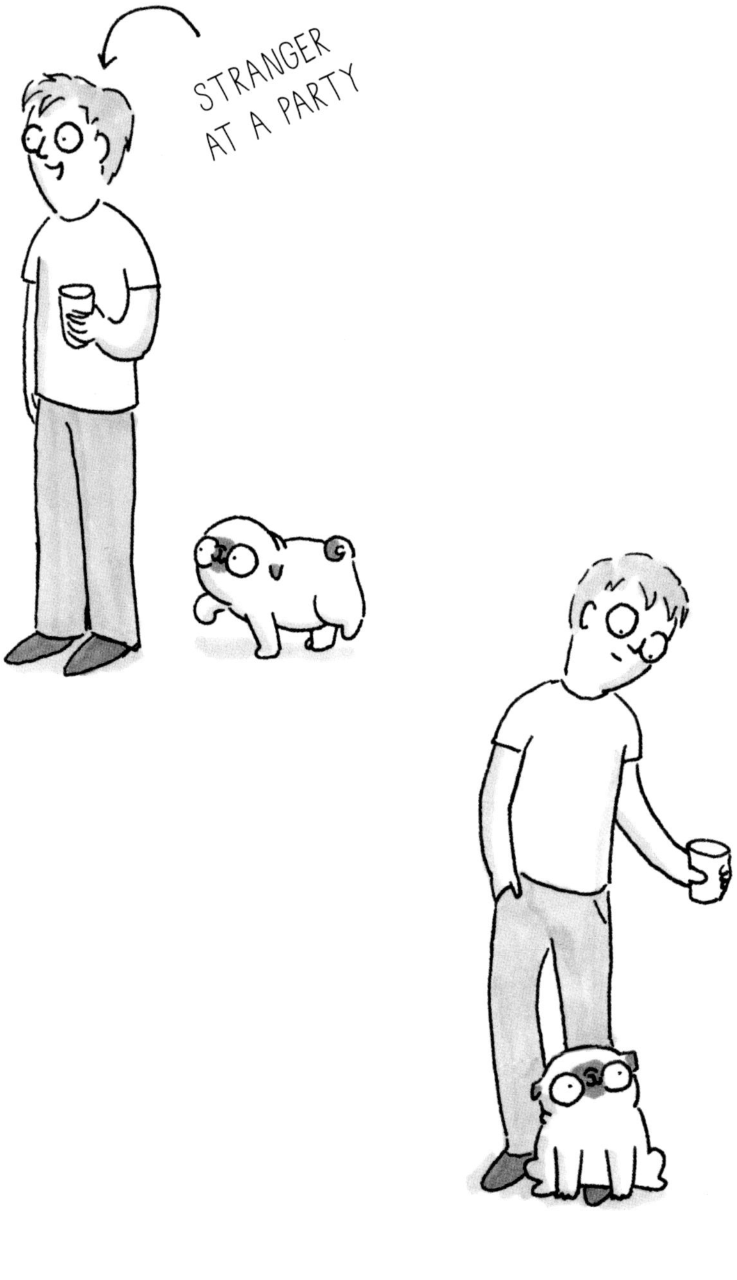
STRANGER
AT A PARTY

ACHOO!

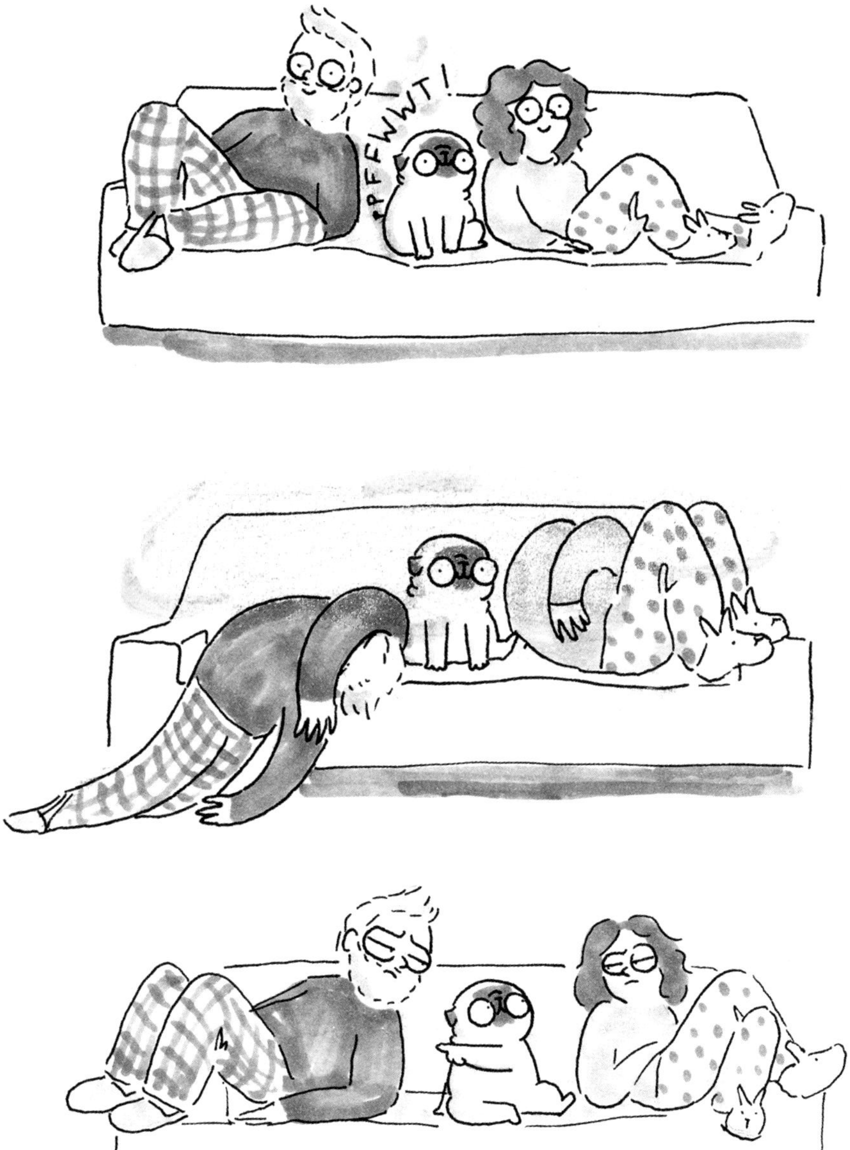
PFFFWWT!

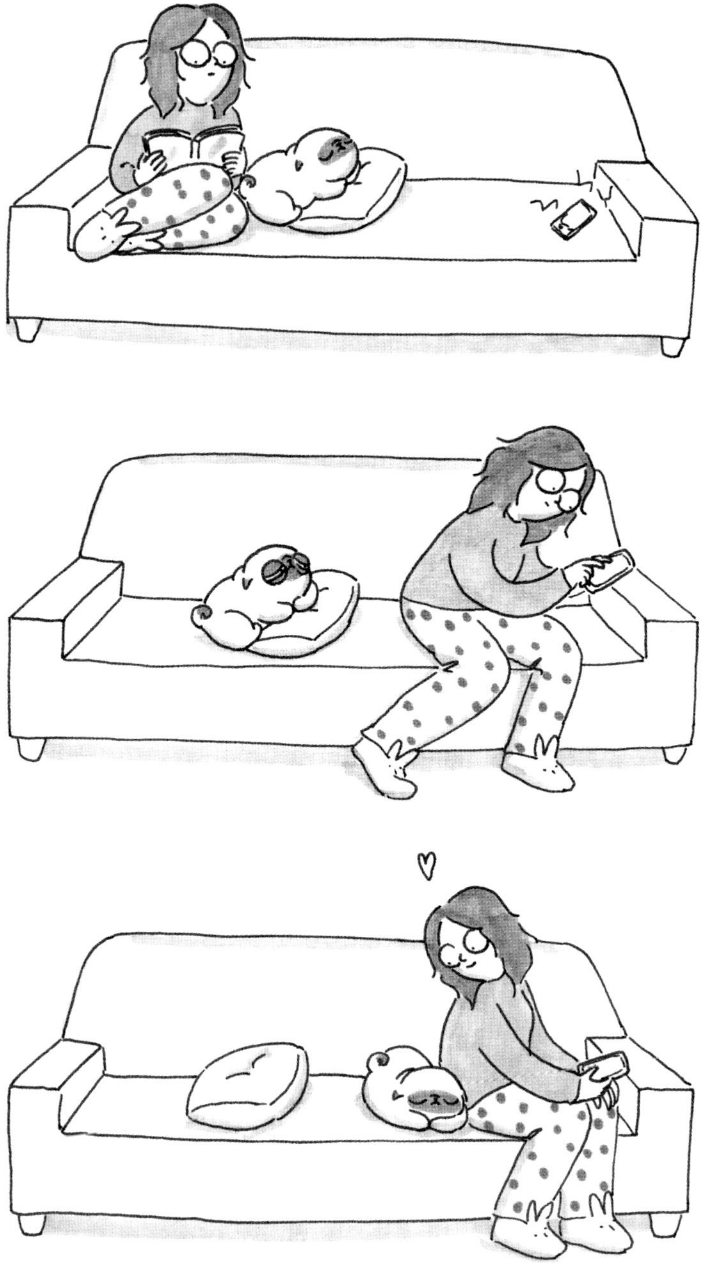

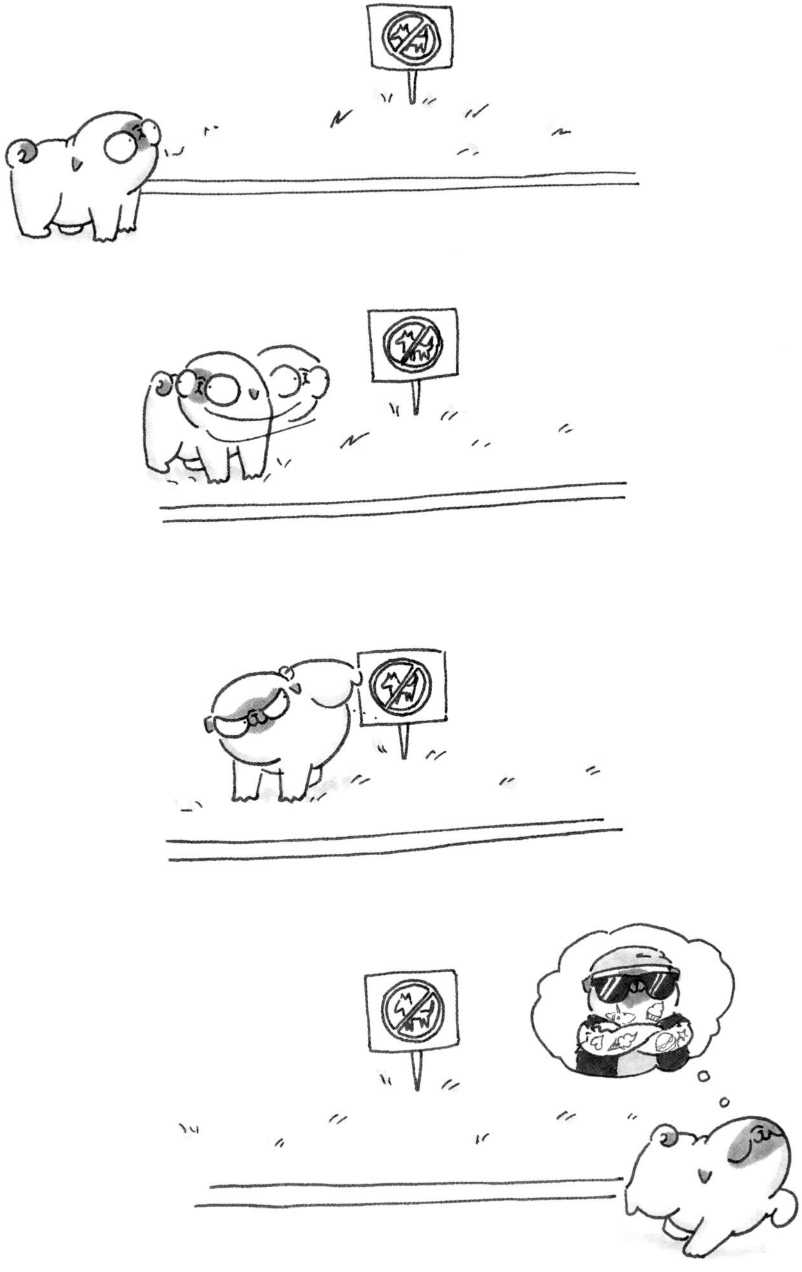

FRIENDSHIP

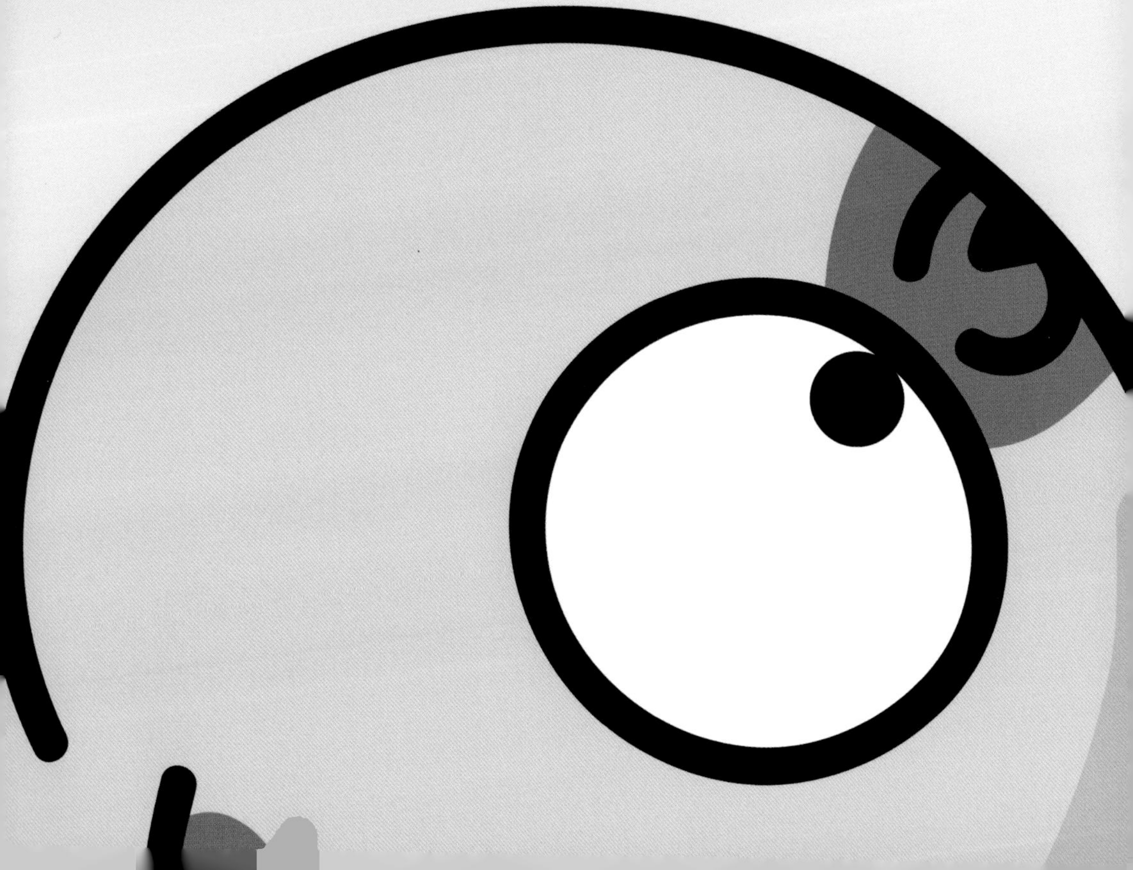

MOCHI HAS NEVER BEEN THAT INTO OTHER DOGS

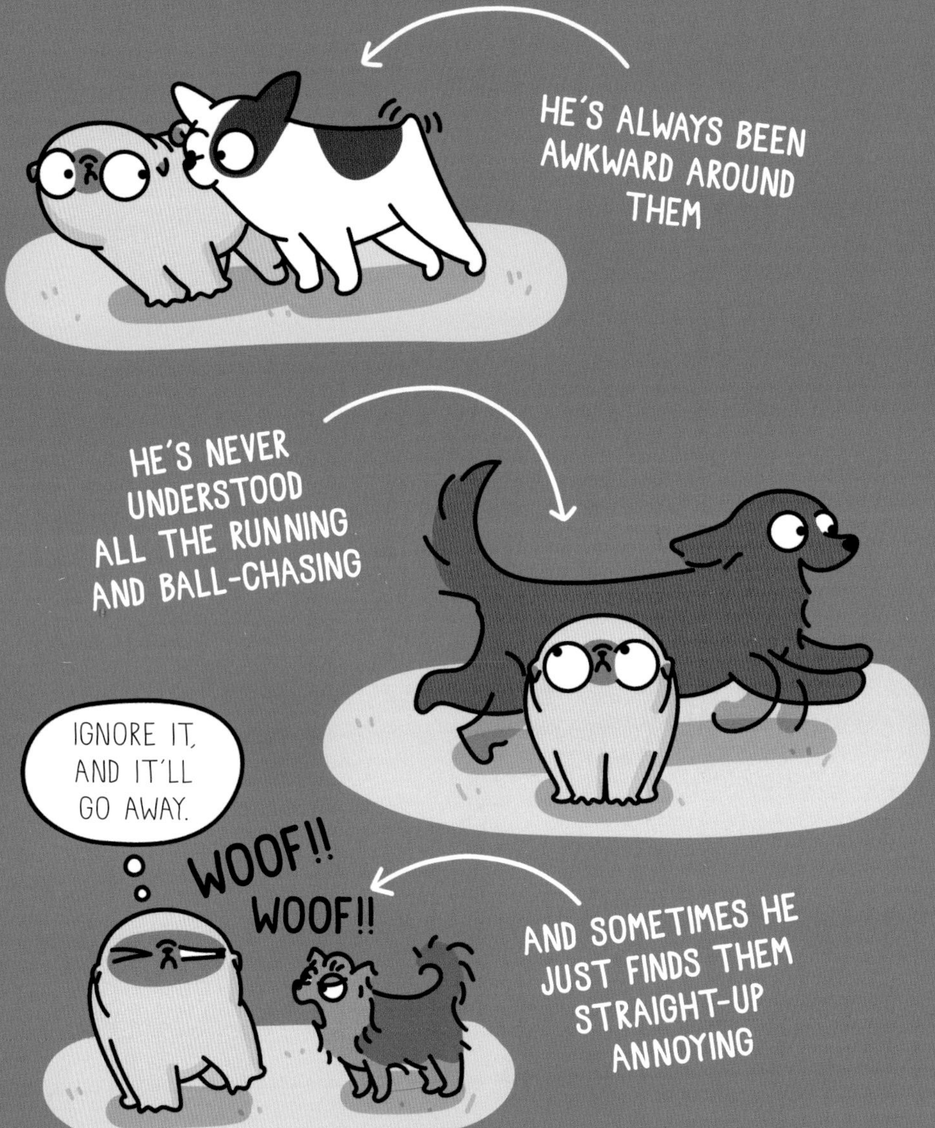
HE'S ALWAYS BEEN AWKWARD AROUND THEM
HE'S NEVER UNDERSTOOD ALL THE RUNNING AND BALL-CHASING
IGNORE IT, AND IT'LL GO AWAY.
WOOF!!
WOOF!!
AND SOMETIMES HE JUST FINDS THEM STRAIGHT-UP ANNOYING

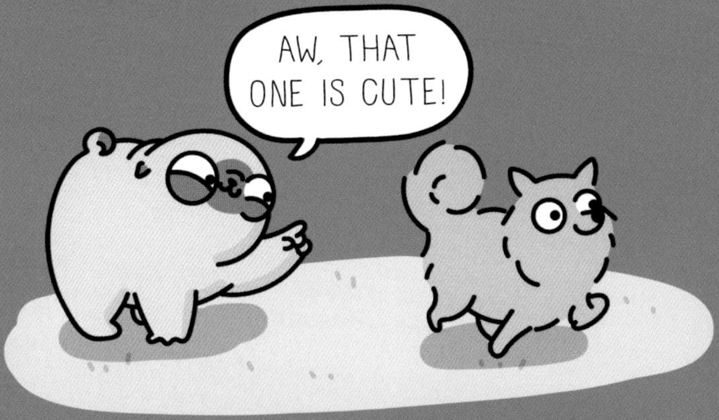
AW, THAT ONE IS CUTE!

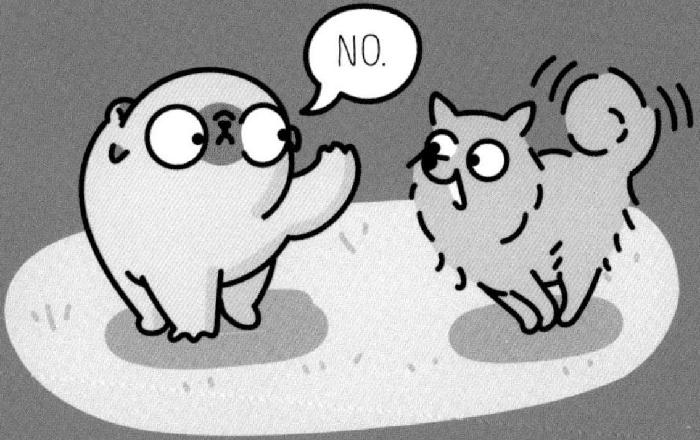
NO.

BUT ONE DAY, EVERYTHING CHANGED. THAT DAY IN THE PARK, MOCHI SAW SOMEONE WHO WAS FINALLY BEST FRIENDSHIP MATERIAL . . .

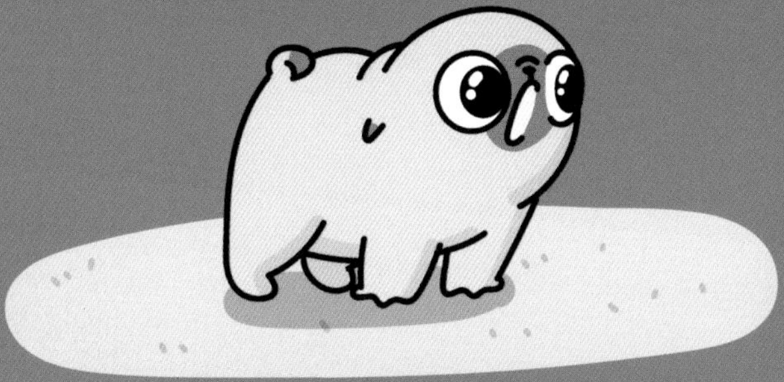

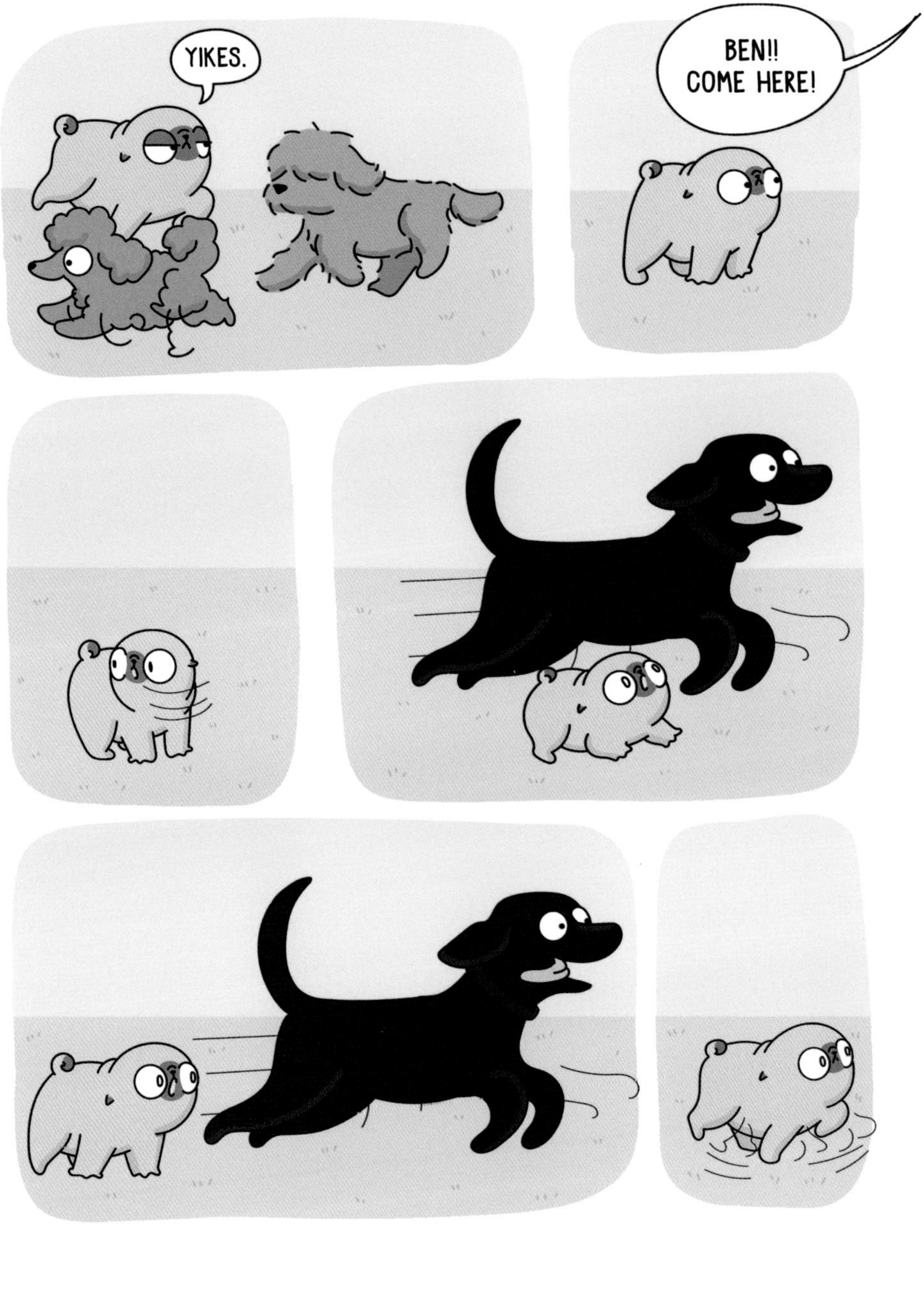
YIKES.
BEN!! COME HERE!

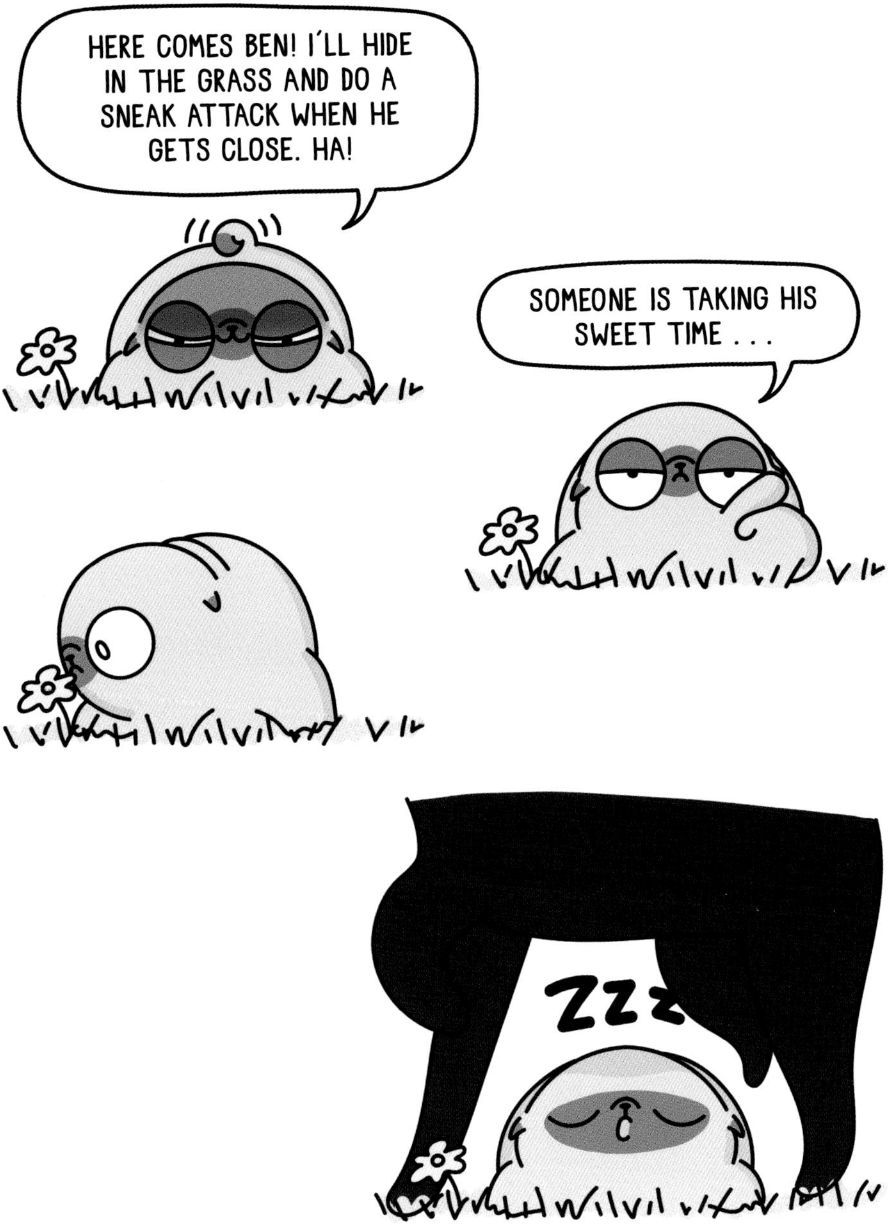
HERE COMES BEN! I'LL HIDE IN THE GRASS AND DO A SNEAK ATTACK WHEN HE GETS CLOSE. HA!
SOMEONE IS TAKING HIS SWEET TIME . . .
ZZZ

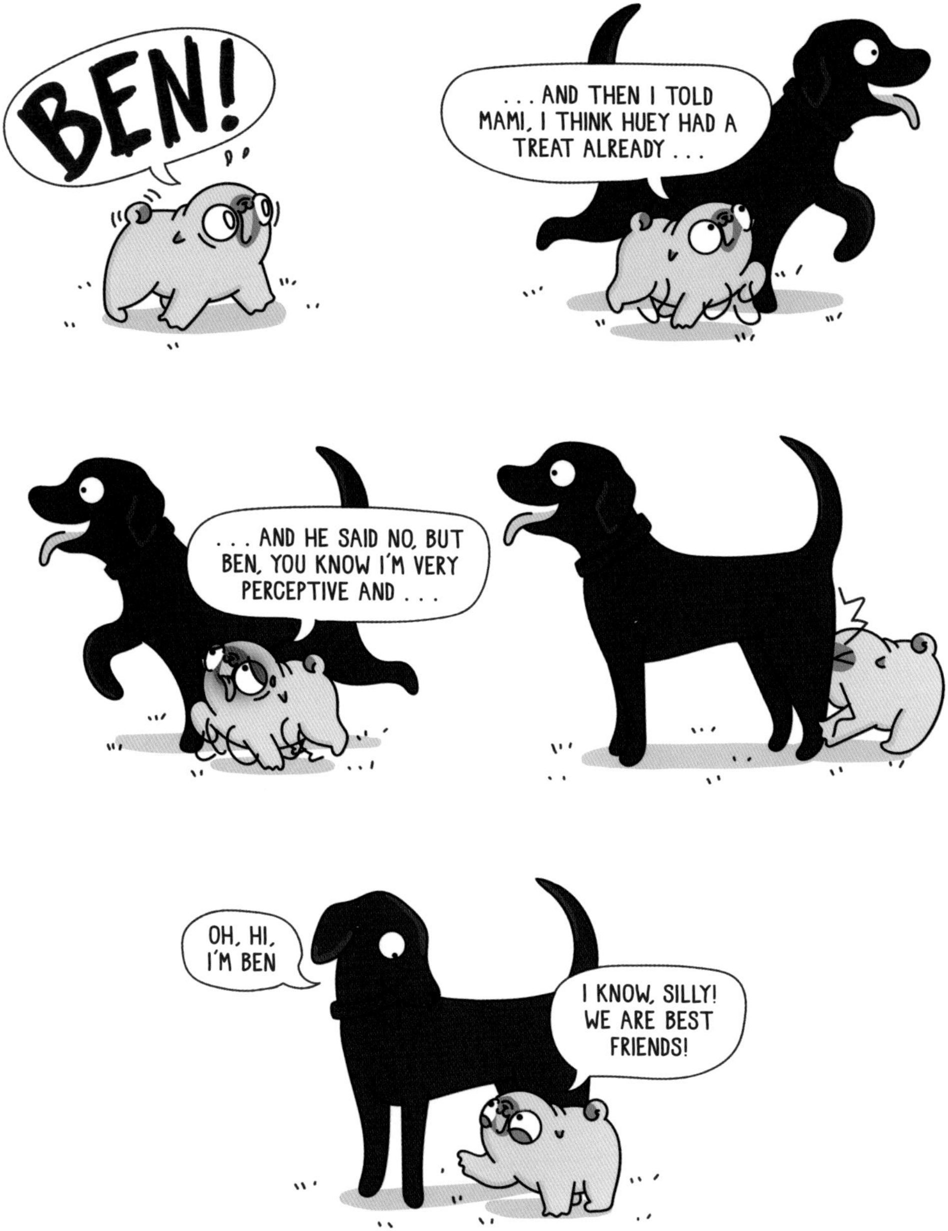
BEN!
. . . AND THEN I TOLD MAMI, I THINK HUEY HAD A TREAT ALREADY . . .
. . . AND HE SAID NO, BUT BEN, YOU KNOW I'M VERY PERCEPTIVE AND . . .
OH, HI, I'M BEN
I KNOW, SILLY! WE ARE BEST FRIENDS!

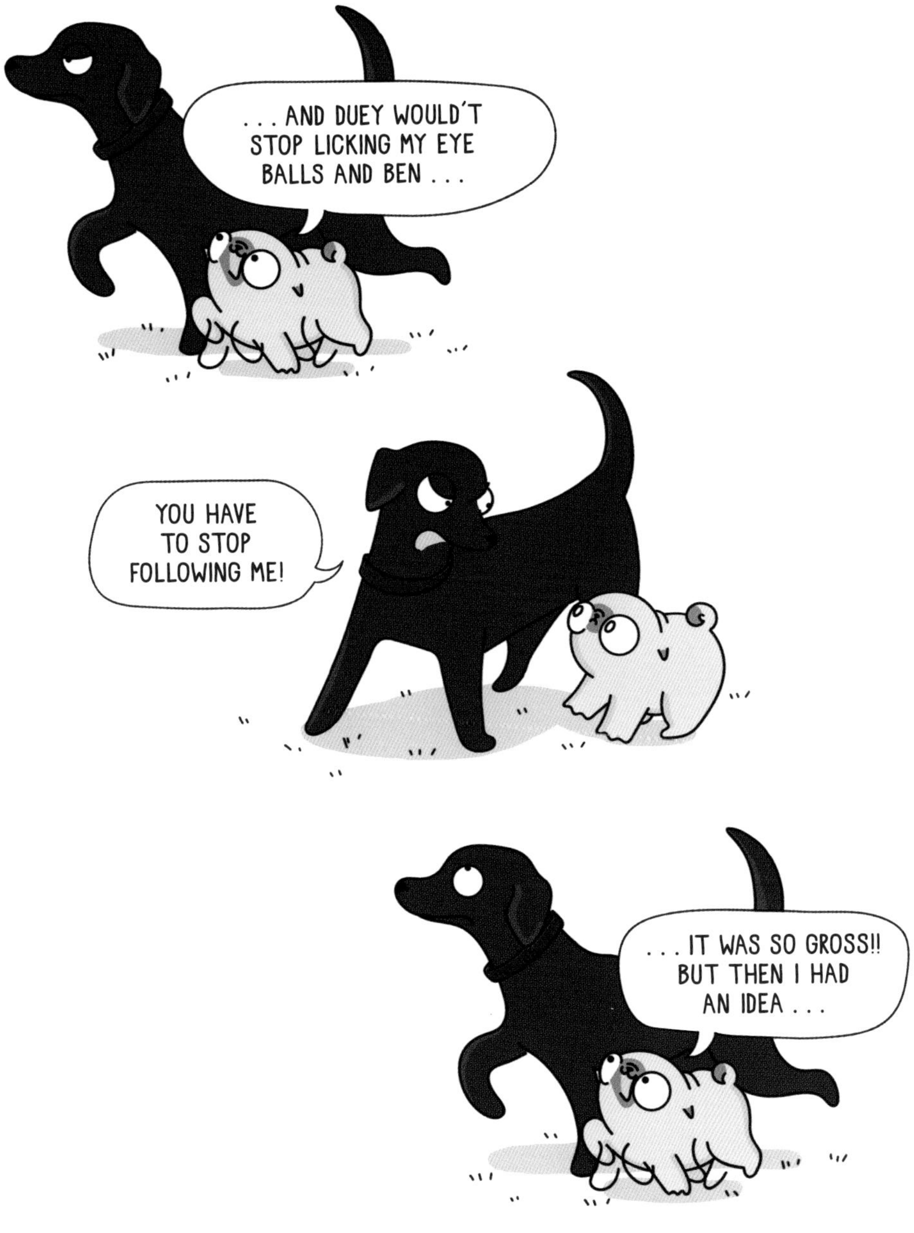
. . . AND DUEY WOULD'T STOP LICKING MY EYE BALLS AND BEN . . .
YOU HAVE TO STOP FOLLOWING ME!
. . . IT WAS SO GROSS!! BUT THEN I HAD AN IDEA . . .

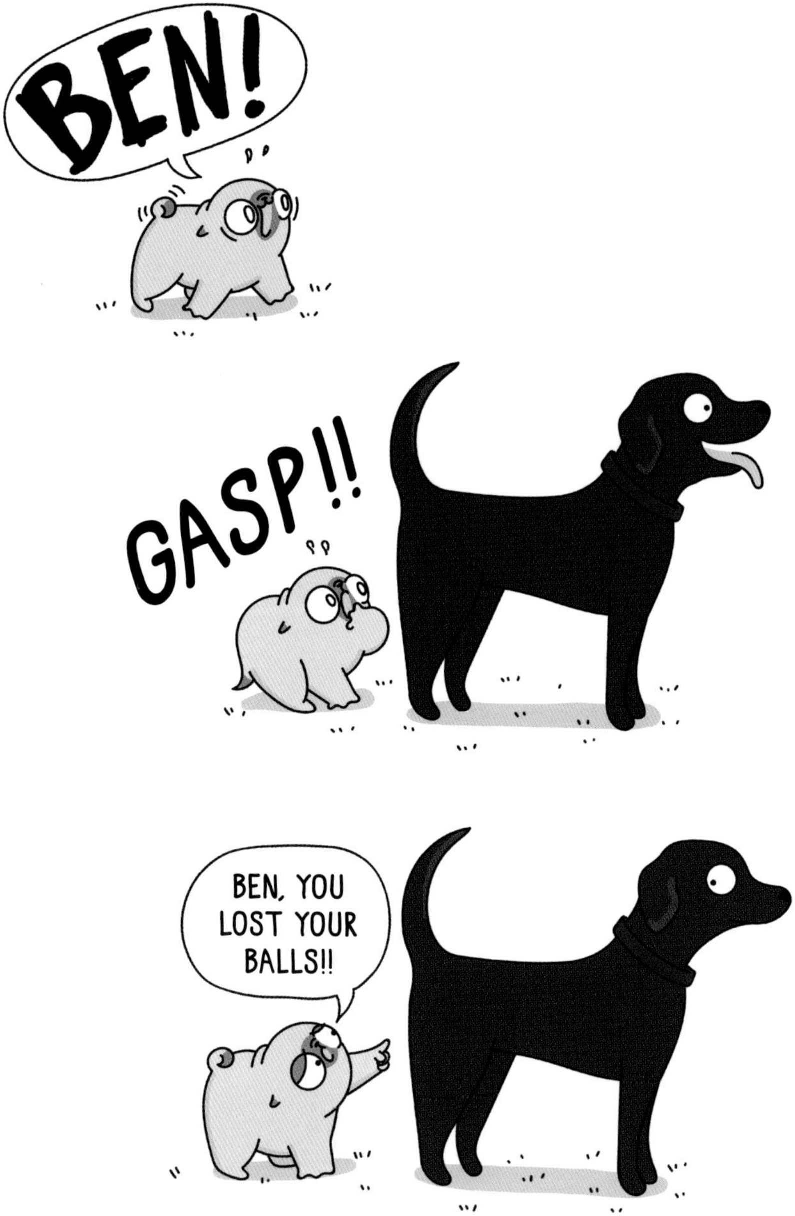

BEN!
GASP!!
BEN, YOU LOST YOUR BALLS!!

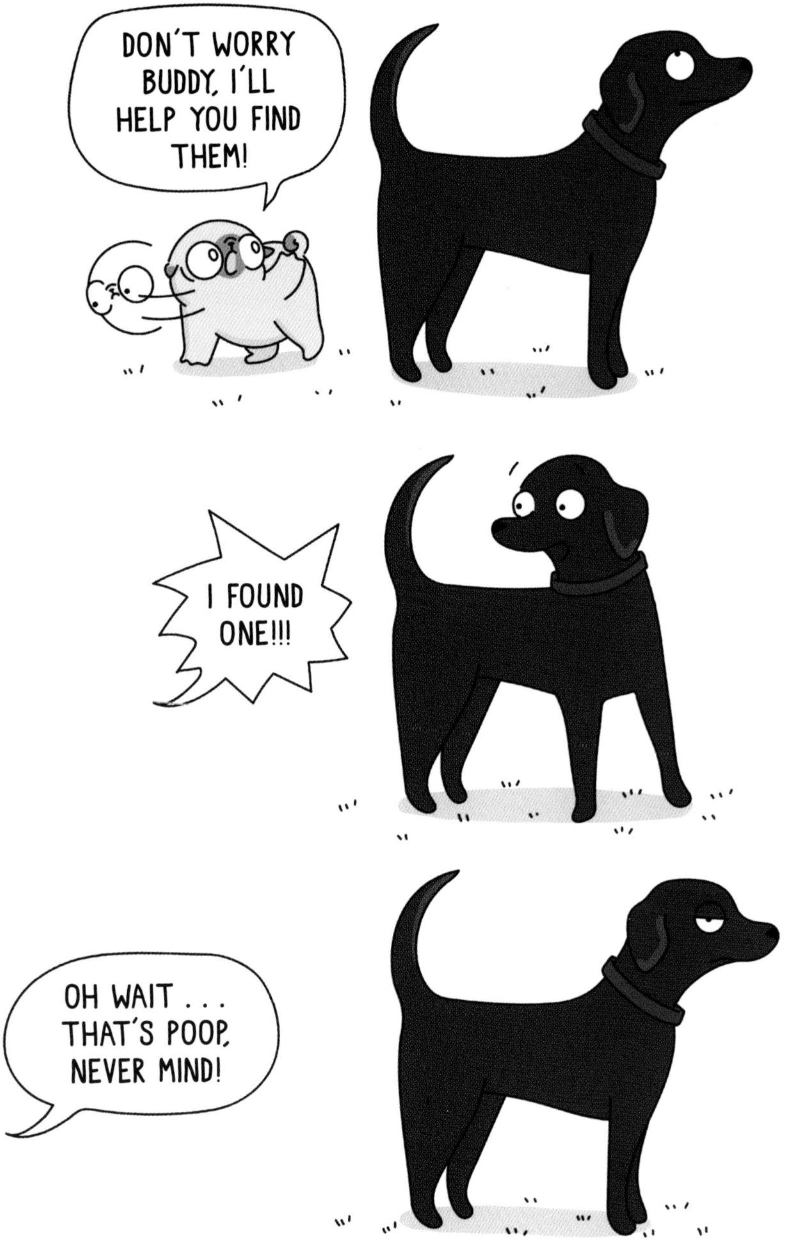
DON'T WORRY BUDDY, I'LL HELP YOU FIND THEM!
I FOUND ONE!!!
OH WAIT . . . THAT'S POOP, NEVER MIND!

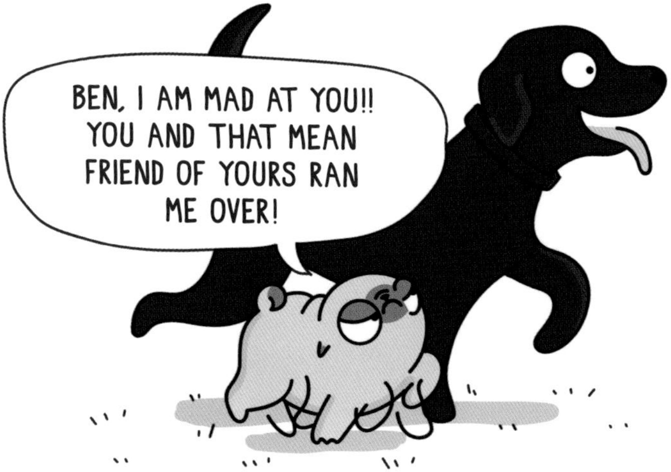
BEN, I AM MAD AT YOU!! YOU AND THAT MEAN FRIEND OF YOURS RAN ME OVER!

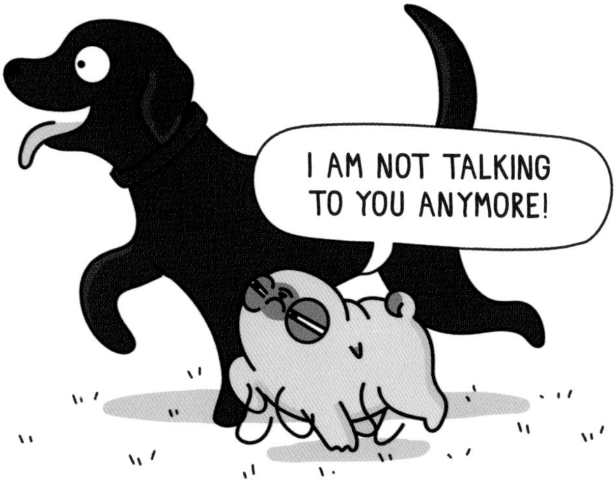
I AM NOT TALKING TO YOU ANYMORE!

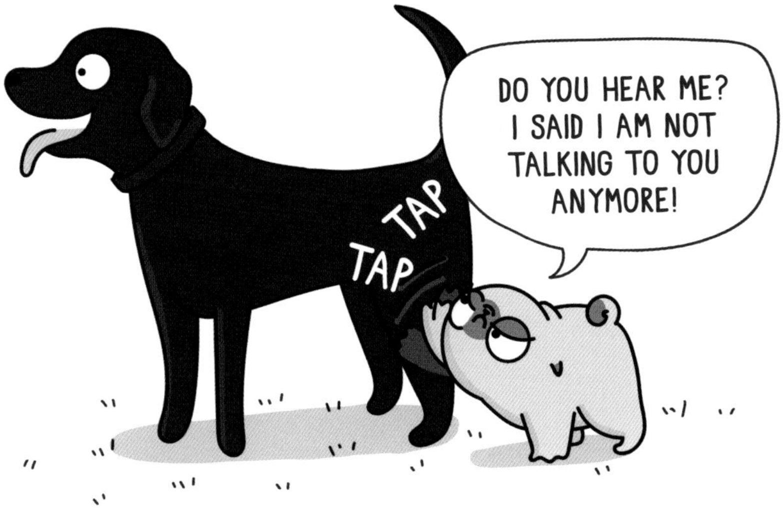
TAP
TAP
DO YOU HEAR ME? I SAID I AM NOT TALKING TO YOU ANYMORE!

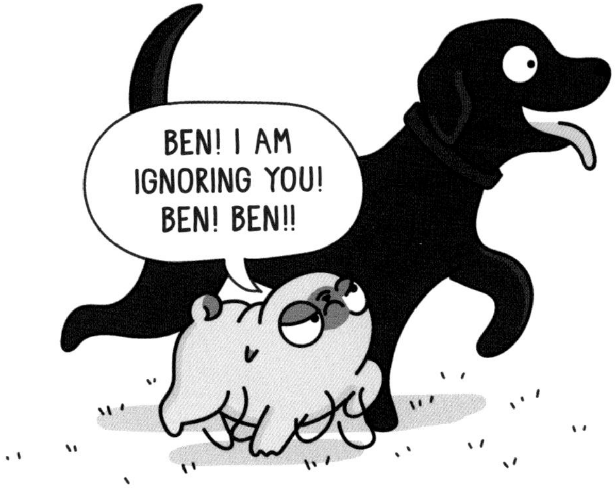
BEN! I AM IGNORING YOU! BEN! BEN!!

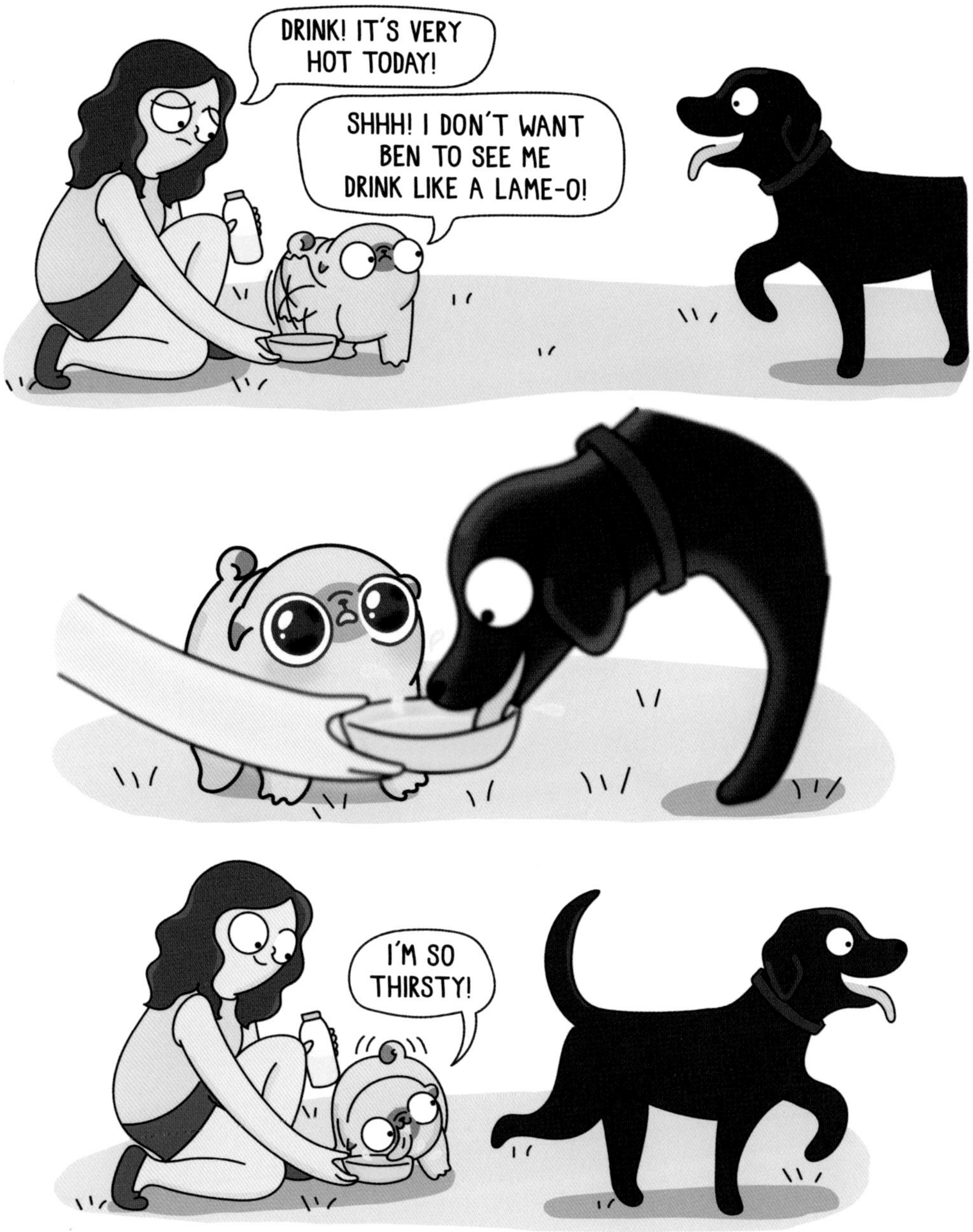
DRINK! IT'S VERY HOT TODAY!
SHHH! I DON'T WANT BEN TO SEE ME DRINK LIKE A LAME-O!
I'M SO THIRSTY!

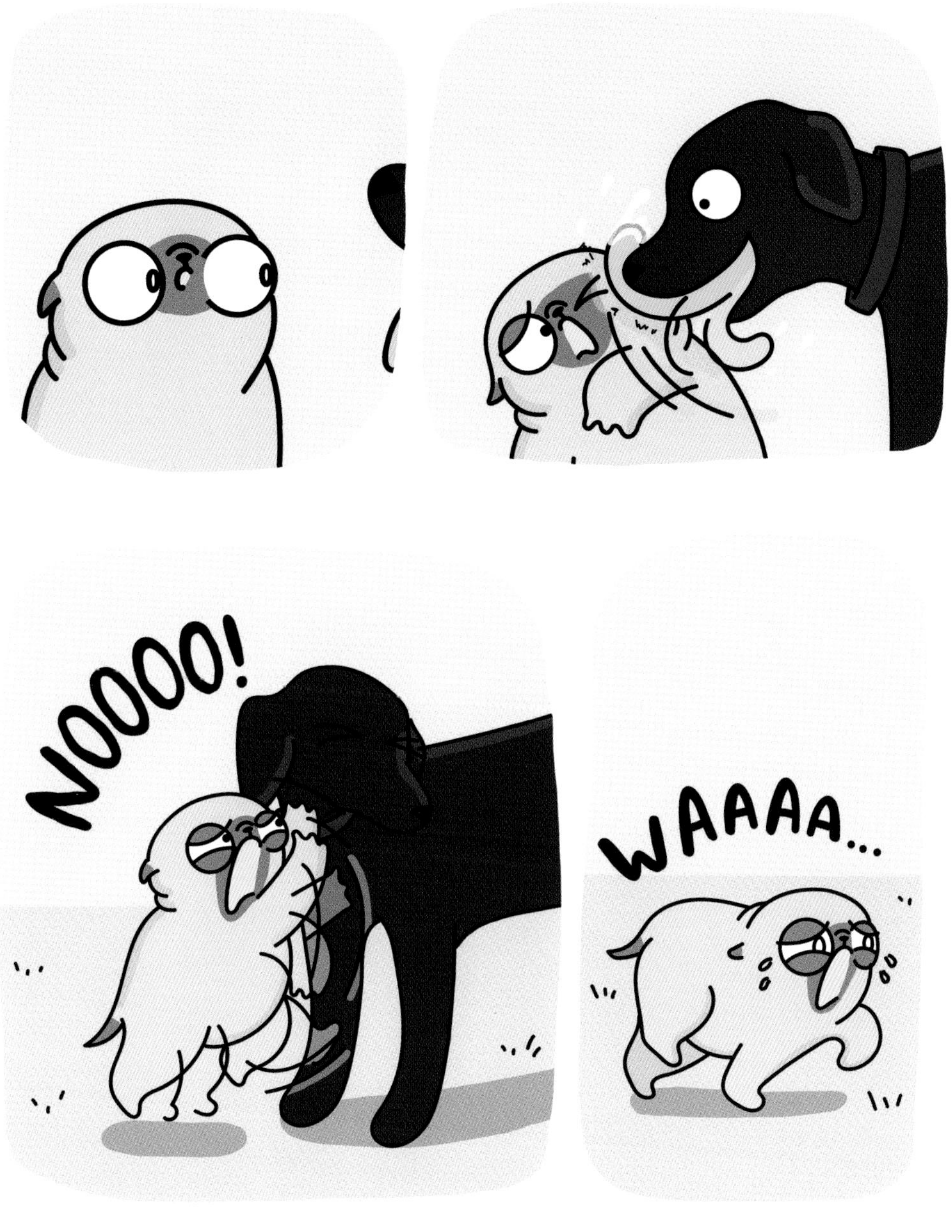
NOOOO!
WAAAA...

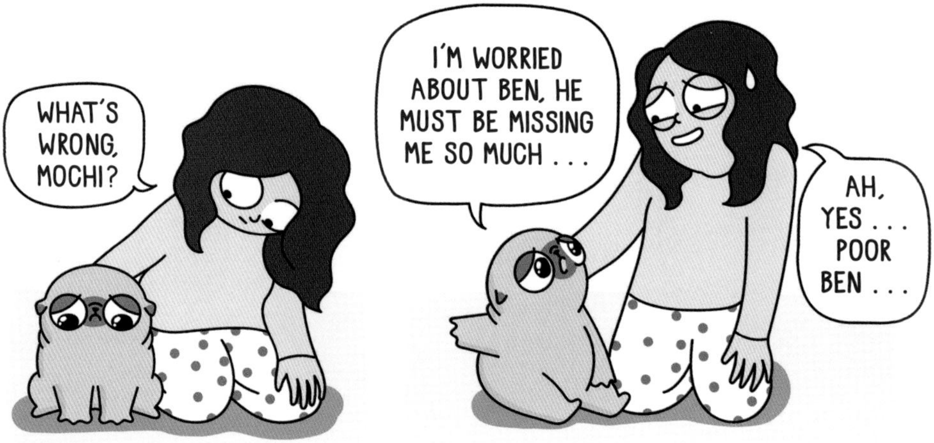
WHAT'S WRONG, MOCHI?
I'M WORRIED ABOUT BEN, HE MUST BE MISSING ME SO MUCH . . .
AH, YES . . . POOR BEN . . .

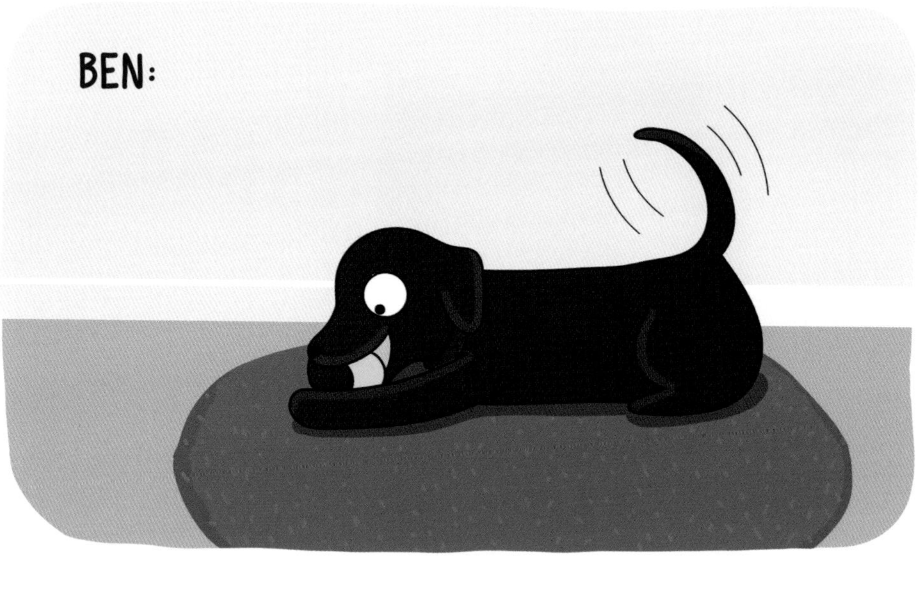
BEN:

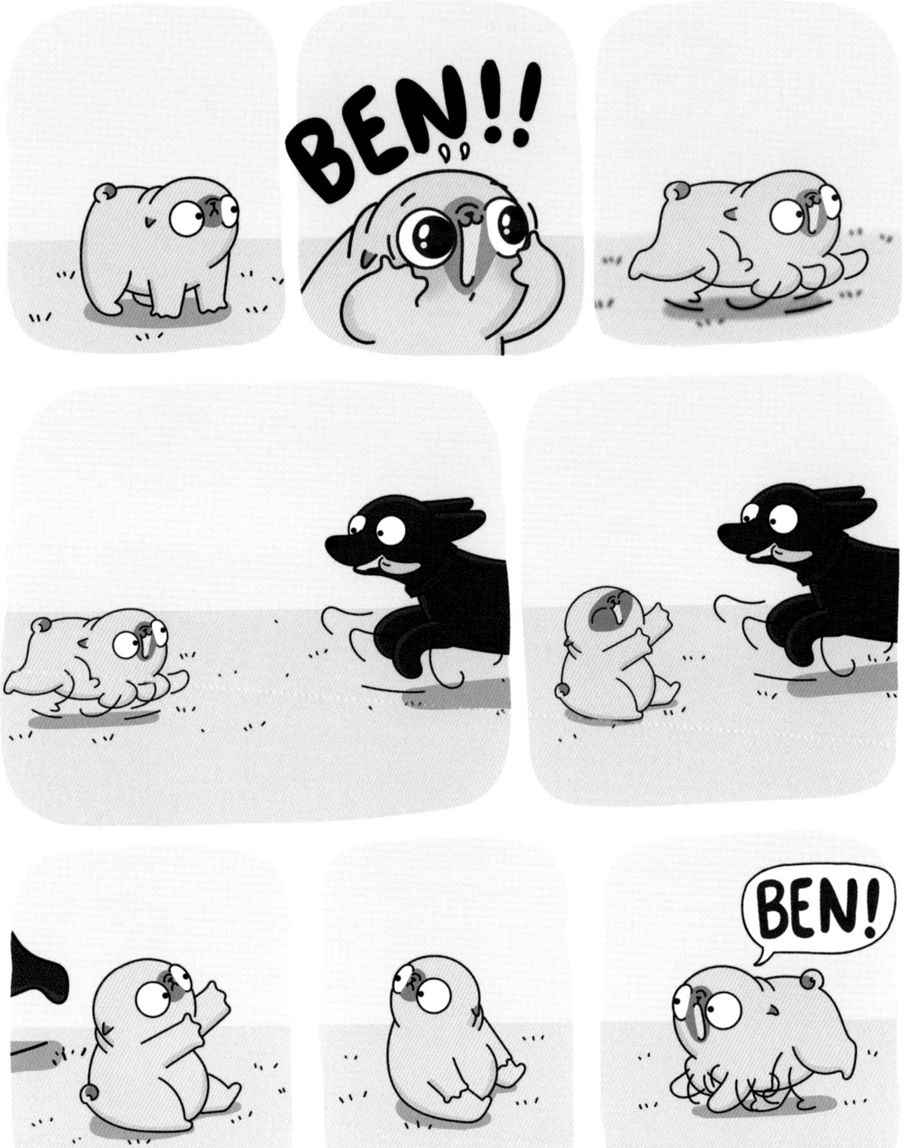
BEN!!
BEN!

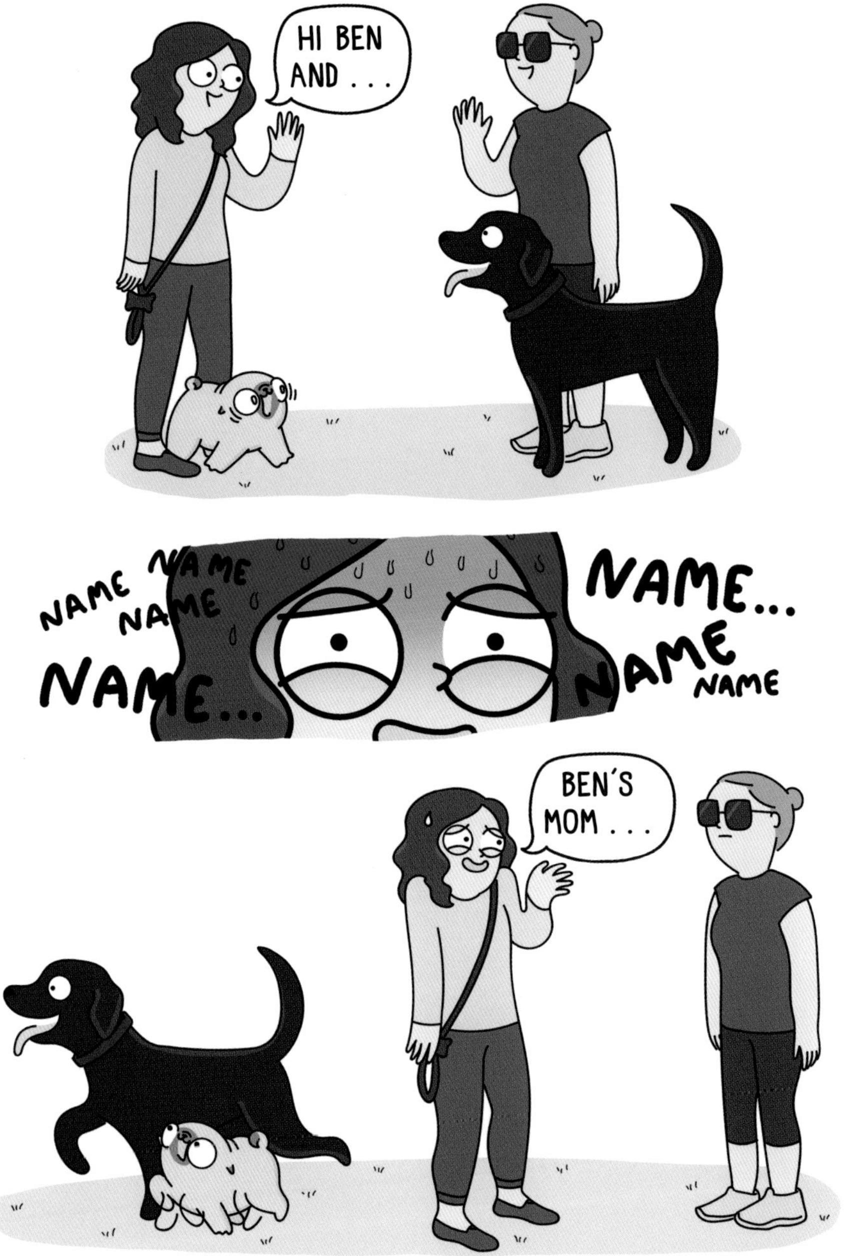
HI BEN AND . . .
NAME NAME NAME NAME
NAME...
NAME...
NAME NAME
BEN'S MOM . . .

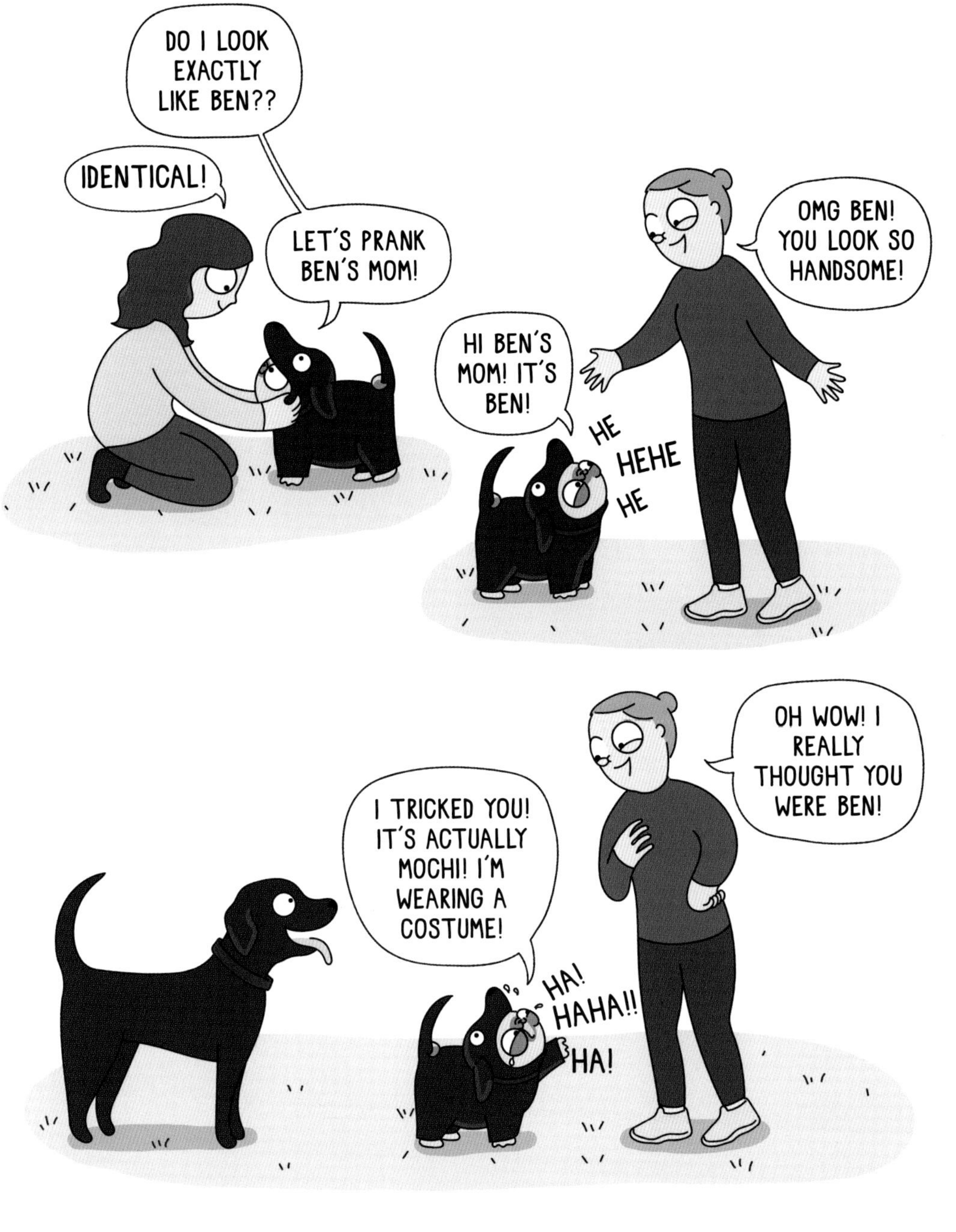
DO I LOOK EXACTLY LIKE BEN??
IDENTICAL!
LET'S PRANK BEN'S MOM!
OMG BEN! YOU LOOK SO HANDSOME!
HI BEN'S MOM! IT'S BEN!
HE HEHE HE
OH WOW! I REALLY THOUGHT YOU WERE BEN!
I TRICKED YOU! IT'S ACTUALLY MOCHI! I'M WEARING A COSTUME!
HA! HAHA!! HA!

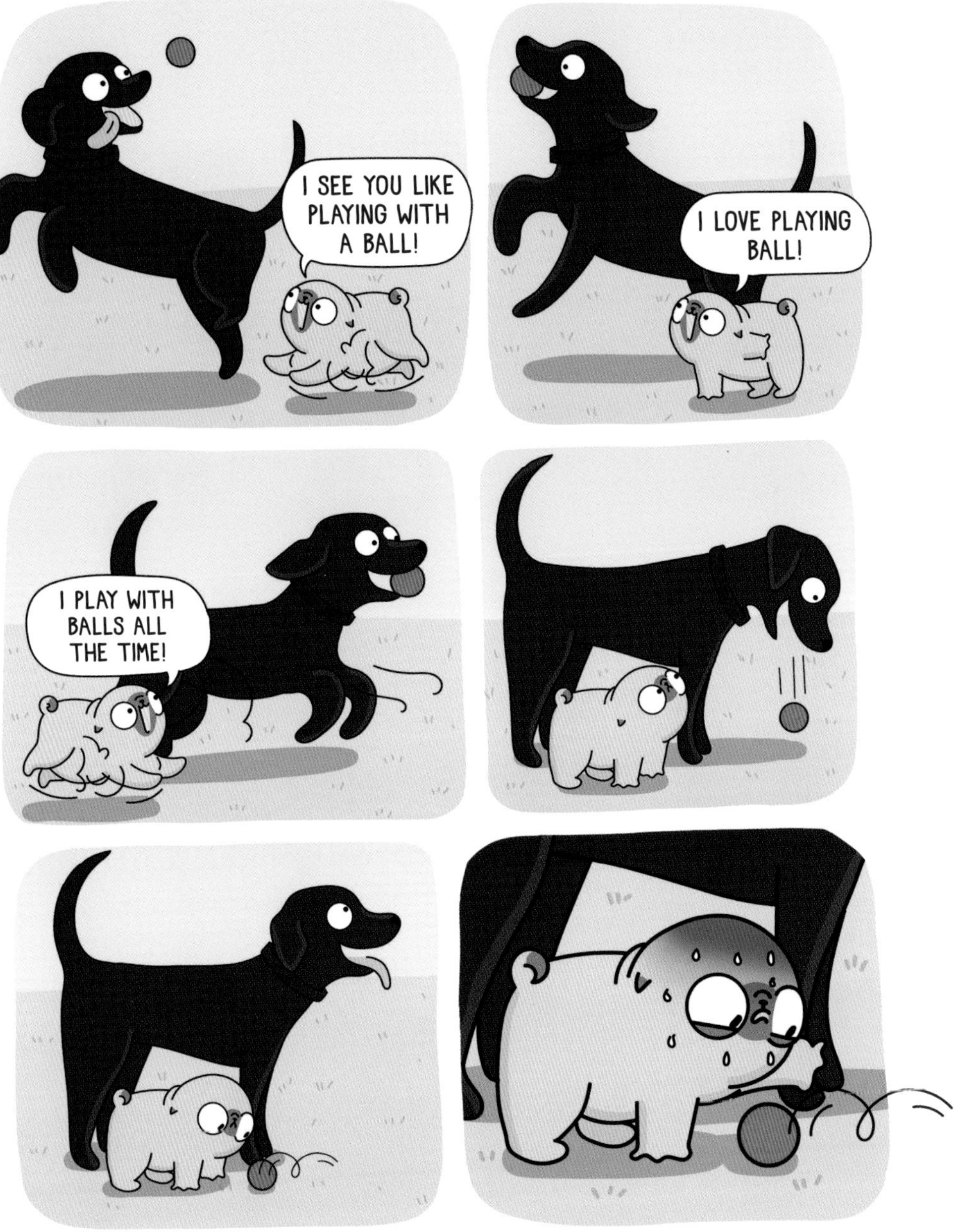
I SEE YOU LIKE PLAYING WITH A BALL!
I LOVE PLAYING BALL!
I PLAY WITH BALLS ALL THE TIME!

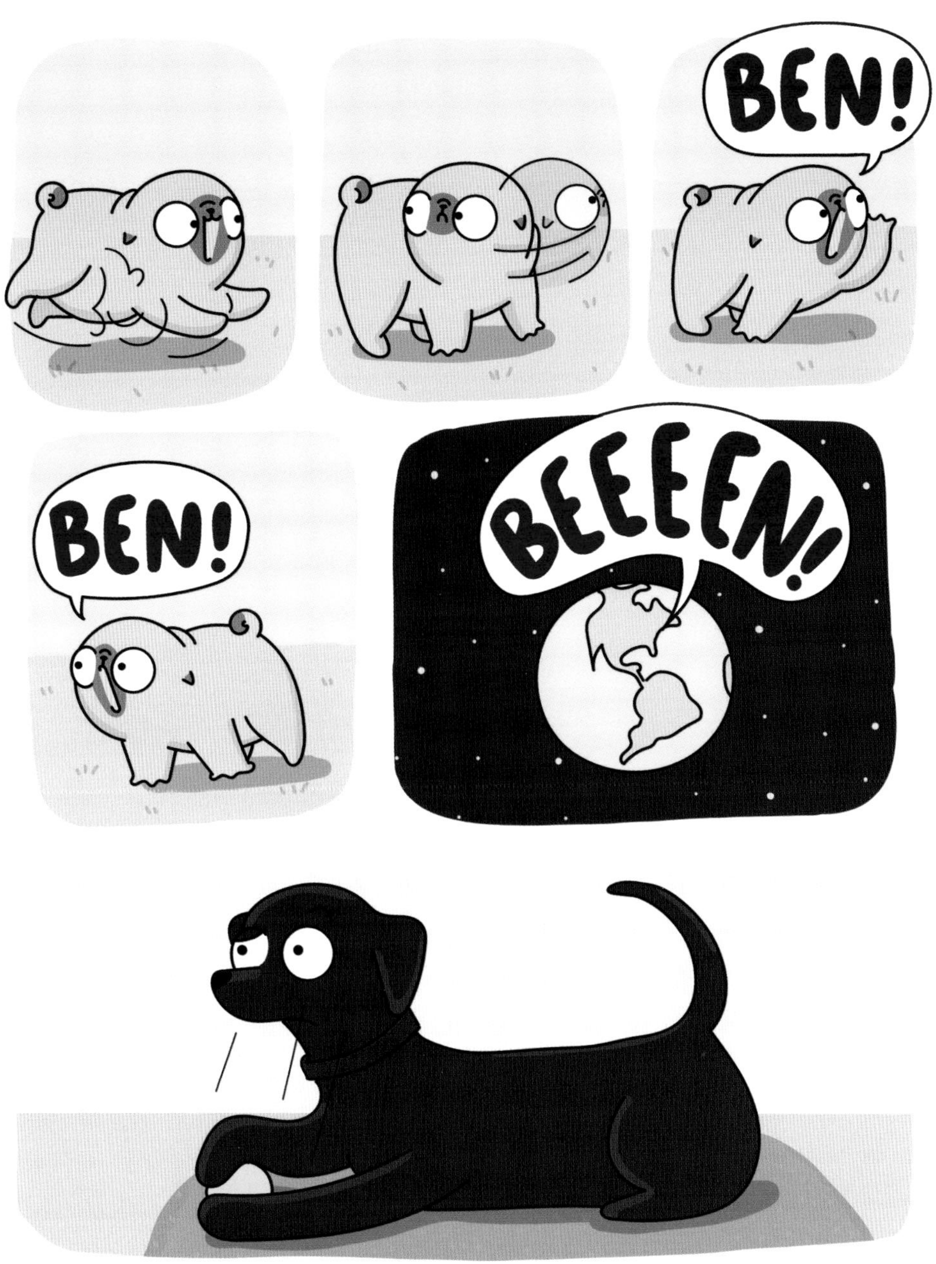
BEN!
BEN!
BEEEEN!

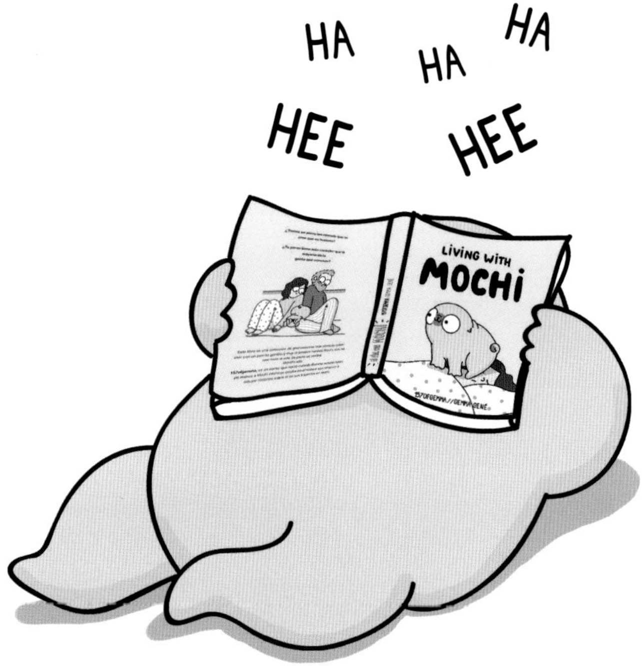
HA
HA
HA
HEE
HEE
LIVING WITH
MOCHI

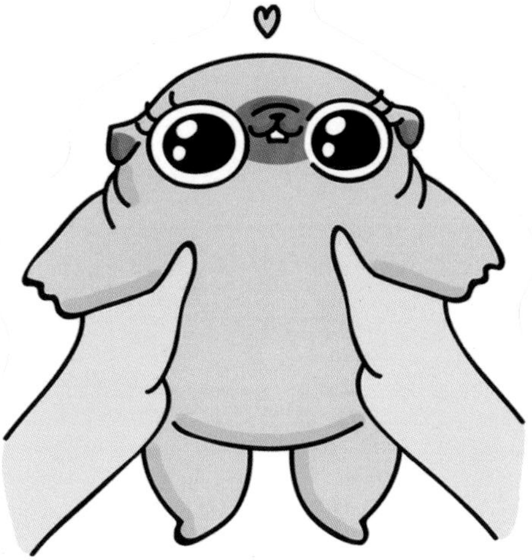

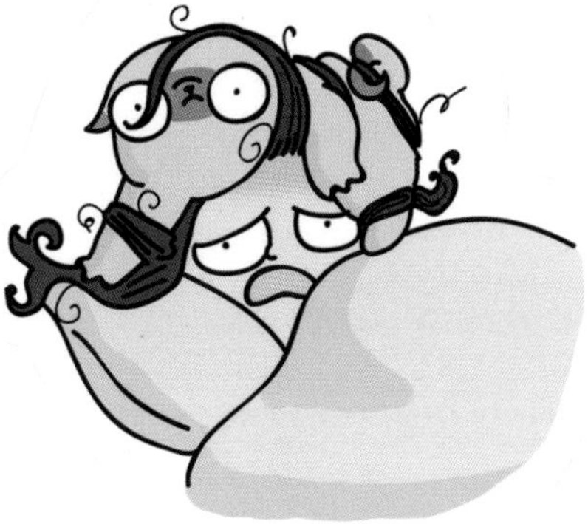

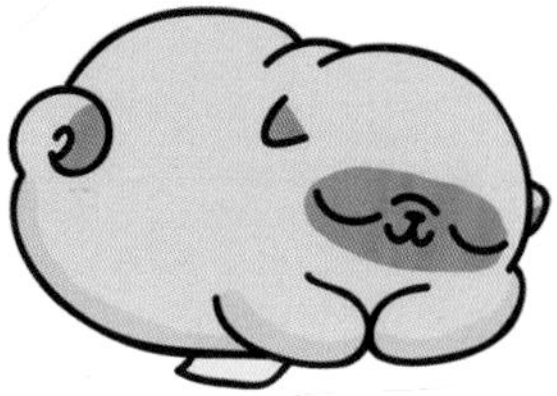

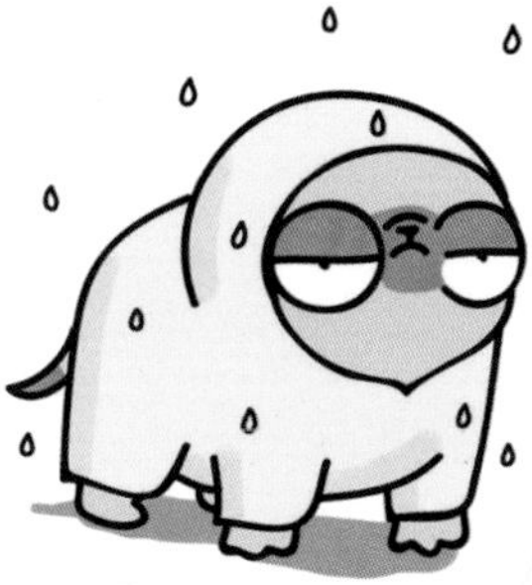

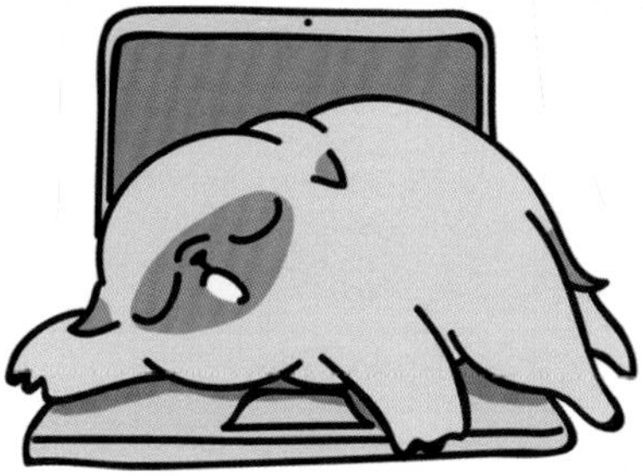

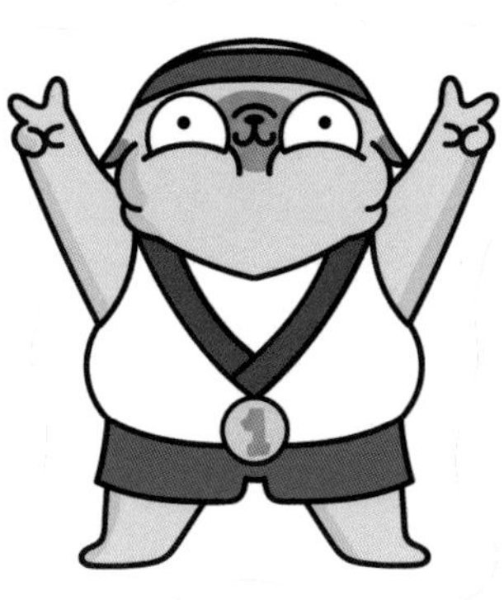

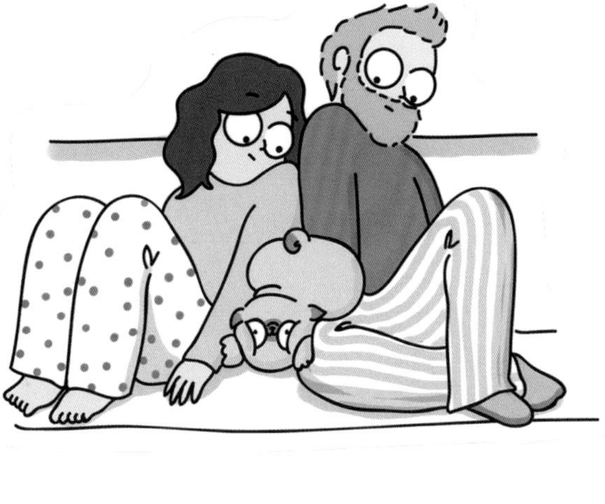

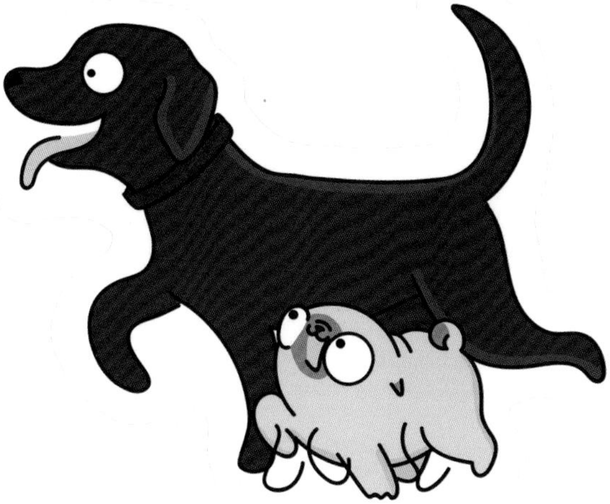

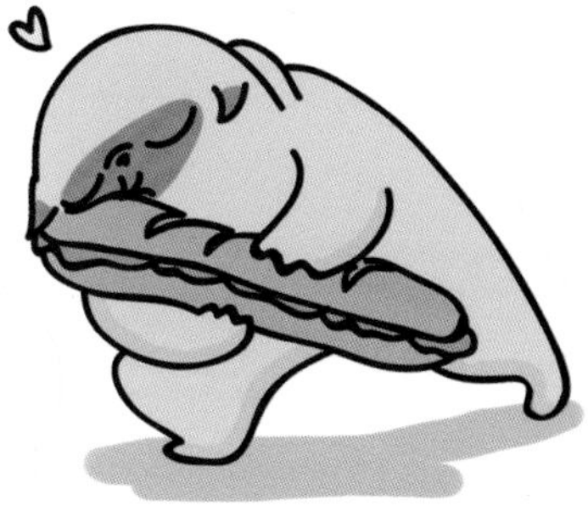

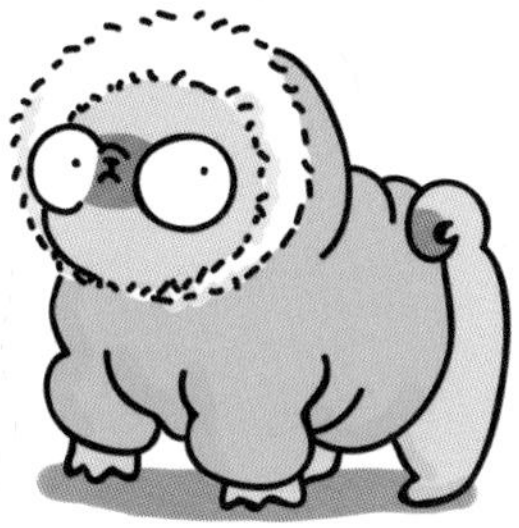

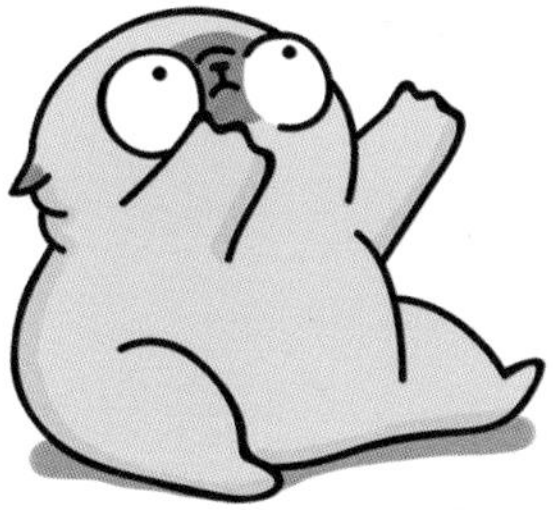

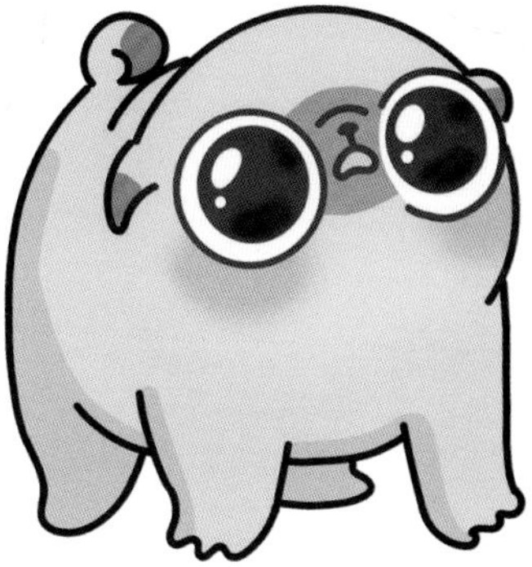

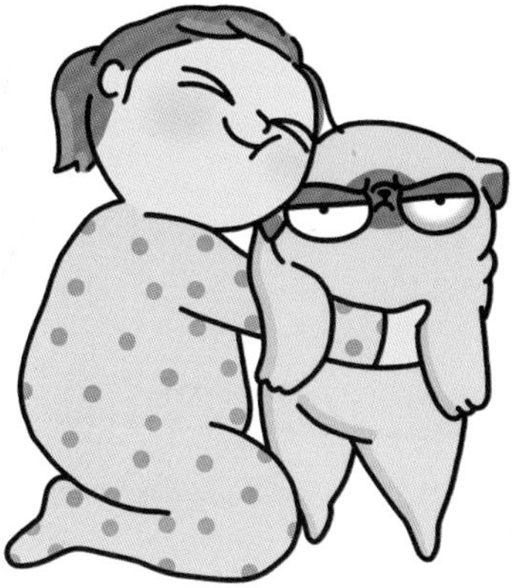

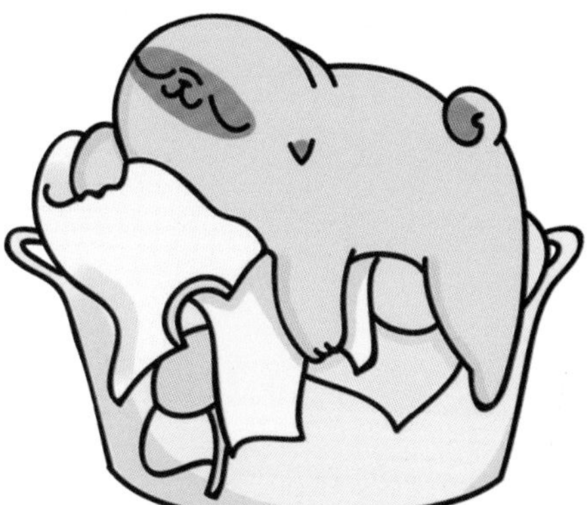